Demystifying AI for the Enterprise

Demystifying AI for the Enterprise

A Playbook for Business Value and Digital Transformation

Prashant Natarajan
Bob Rogers
Edward Dixon
Jonas Christensen
Kirk Borne
Leland Wilkinson
Shantha Mohan

Routledge
Taylor & Francis Group

A PRODUCTIVITY PRESS BOOK

First published 2022
by Routledge
605 Third Avenue, New York, NY 10158

and by Routledge
2 Park Square, Milton Park, Abingdon, Oxon, OX14 4RN

Routledge is an imprint of the Taylor & Francis Group, an informa business

ISBN: 978-1-138-49139-7 (hbk)
ISBN: 978-1-032-14520-4 (pbk)
ISBN: 978-1-351-03294-0 (ebk)

DOI: 10.4324/9781351032940

Typeset in Garamond
by SPi Technologies India Pvt Ltd (Straive)

Prashant Natarajan dedicates his work to his children, Shivani and Neel; his better half, Vishnu; and his parents, Saraswati and Dr. V. N. Iyer.

Bob Rogers gratefully dedicates this book to his sons, John, Graham, Jack, Austin, Bryce and Mason, and their families; to his kind and nurturing parents, Duke and Nancy; and especially to his supportive and wonderful wife, Teri, whose natural intelligence and wit inspire Bob's efforts in artificial intelligence and beyond.

Edward Dixon would like to dedicate this book to his best critics and most patient supporters - his family.

Jonas Christensen would like to dedicate this book to the loves of his life: his wife, Julia and his daughter, Viola.

Kirk Borne would like to dedicate this book to his wife and children - Colleen, Marie, and Karen.

Leland Wilkinson dedicates his chapter to Marilyn Vogel.

Shantha Mohan would like to dedicate this book to her grandchildren—Illy, Kavi, and Beck.

Contents

APPENDIX

Preface

The desire to put Artificial Intelligence (AI) and robots to work in order to improve the human experience, amplify human intelligence, and automate the mundane have been consistent and long-lasting human endeavors. Greek, Indian, and other ancient epics contain multiple references to human-created AI concepts with the hope that the resultant solutions would complement and supplement human needs and activities.

Recent advances in computing power and the availability of data—coupled with the needs of the modern enterprise—have now brought us to a place where AI is no longer the stuff of epics and legend. We are seeing AI becoming integral, increasing influences on customer experiences and human needs. AI is already around us in various shapes and forms, even if we don't recognize the innter workings at first glance. We interact with AI via machine learning (and learning algorithms) on a daily basis. Some examples include email spam filters, entertainment recommendations, mail sorting, online shopping recommendations, and the next generation of medicines and therapies. The applications of AI are increasingly at the core of many uses in consumer products, e-commerce, banking, insurance, life sciences and healthcare, manufacturing, energy and utilities, law, and education.

The design and uses of AI in the enterprise are no longer nice-to-have or experimental technologies. It is rapidly becoming the foundation of digital transformation for small, medium, and large businesses. However, there is still a digital divide between the AI "haves" and "have nots"—with innovative and data-first technology companies, financial services, and e-commerce being relatively ahead of the curve, compared to other verticals. Additionally, this digital divide is exacerbated by strategy maturity, regional/geographical locations, talent availability, and funding. The good news is, thanks to the cloud, modern data platforms, machine/deep learning, and easier connectivity to systems of record and systems of engagement—digital transformation driven by AI is more realizable than ever before.

While the technology is available, and continues to evolve rapidly, a substantial number of AI-led digital transformation efforts fail to deliver, or only partly deliver, on business outcomes, value generation, and Return on Investment (ROI). Our goal with this book is to change the current reality by increasing awareness and providing the knowledge you can use to drive your organization's success with AI. The intelligent enterprise of tomorrow will be one that leverages business endeavors, human intelligence, and AI to their utmost via symbiosis.

A global team of business leaders, technology executives, and data scientists, the authors of this book bring the best of their expertise and cross-functional professional experiences to the table. We go beyond data science, AI, cloud, and technology topics to focus on the following representative questions:

- What are the value drivers for the enterprise and specific business verticals?
- How can you ensure business outcomes and digital transformation successes?
- How will you measure the benefits to employees, collaborators, and consumers?
- What are the best practices in strategy, tactics, and scalability of AI-driven inventions and process innovations?
- What do you need to do in order to ensure repeatable ROI?
- How can you leverage AI to create happier employees and customers?

AI technologies are horizontal in capability, but the applications and uses of AI have to account for the specific needs of humans, processes, change management, and opportunities in each vertical. The uses of AI - through business applications, process optimization, and engagement models - must be broad (benefitting the greatest number of people), deep (delivering impactful domain-specific solutions), responsible, fair, and transparent.

To account for these multi-faceted needs, we have put together a comprehensive playbook that executives, managers, and practitioners can leverage to:

1. Determine the most appropriate strategic needs for your organization, users, and customers
2. Account for both opportunities and challenges via the IMPACT framework (Chapter 1)
3. Obtain an executive and conceptual review of AI and machine/deep learning
4. Understand how to identify, ideate, and implement use cases and solutions
5. Leverage best practices and case studies from thought leaders and leading organizations
6. Learn how AI can help with talent acquisition, learning and development, supply chain, and customer experience management
7. Extend and customize examples and lessons from the uses of AI in more mature verticals (financial services, retail, and e-commerce)
8. Address community needs, policy requirements, and develop corporate social responsibility programs
9. And, for more technical readers, a discussion of visualization, solution architectures, and our predictions on the evolution of AI

Using this book as a foundation, the authors will be conducting events, organizing workshops, conducting executive briefings, and engaging on podcasts and social media. Our goals are to keep the conversations up to date, refresh the body of knowledge, and expand professional fellowship.

We hope you can leverage the practical learnings and validated case studies from this book to inform strategies and tactics that are essential to success with data, analytics, and AI—and enable progressive and successful digital transformation. We look forward to engaging with you in your journey and celebrating your successes.

We enjoyed sharing our experiences and recommendations in this book and hope you enjoy reading it. We wish you the best in your journey and much success with AI, data science, and digital transformation.

Acknowledgements

Prashant Natarajan acknowledges the co-authors of this book, case study contributors, and Kristine Mednansky. He is grateful to his colleagues at H2O.ai – specifically, SriSatish Ambati. He thanks Mark Landry, Megan Maxwell, Greg Keys, and Venkatesh Yadav for their contributions to the Document AI case study. Prashant appreciates his colleagues, partners, and clients who have provided many opportunities for learning and sharing over the years.

Bob Rogers acknowledges the inputs and assistance from:

Chapter 3: Blake Williamson, Alyson Crafton, David Evans, Yulia Kushner, John Hart, Ed Dixon, Veeresha "VJ" Javli, Jeff Balentine, Lee Clewley, Theresa Hart, and Jon Spencer

Chapter 4: Genetha Gray, Alexis Fink, Alyson Crafton, Parnian Kaboli, Laetitia Vitaud, Helen Aldred, and Theresa Hart

Chapter 10: Emma Bluemke (who contributed the entire section on privacy-preserving computing), and Theresa Hart. Lisa Thee acknowledges Anthony Accetturo, Carolyn Peer, and Garrett Thee

UCSF-H2O.ai Case Study: Ramakrishna Yerramsetty, Lu Chen, Aaron Neinstein, Michael Blum, and Molly Hovorka

Ed Dixon acknowledges inputs from Alexei Bastidas, Catherine Guinan, Michael Karlin, Andrew Moeller, Tiffany Moeller, Robert Wiblin, RIchard Smith, Isaac Tamblyn, and Helen Toner.

Jonas Christensen acknowledges his draft reviewer and wife, Julia Nicholls. He is also thankful to his case study contributors: Felipe Flores, Henry Ma (WeBank), Gil Guan (WeBank), and Tyler Aveni (WeBank).

Kirk Borne thanks his colleagues across numerous organizations for enlightening discussions and their brilliant shared knowledge on a variety of AI and data-related topics, including topics discussed in this book and many more. He especially gives big thanks to his family for their support and encouragement always.

Shantha Mohan acknowledges her co-authors, Ed Dixon who reviewed an early draft and provided valuable feedback, and Kirk Borne, who did an extensive review; his suggestions for revisions made a great difference to the quality of this chapter. She also acknowledges case-study contributors: Shahmeer Ali Mirza of 7-Eleven, and Ranga Ramesh of Georgia-Pacific.

Author Bios

Prashant Natarajan is an executive who focuses on the intersection of business outcomes, technology strategy, and digital transformation programs. Based in the USA, he is Vice President of Strategy and Products at H2O.ai. He is passionate about customer happiness, digital transformation successes, and innovation at scale—with AI, advanced analytics, cloud computing, and data. He has conceptualized, created, and led business and technology transformation successes in insurance, banking, health sciences, and manufacturing. Prior to joining H2O.ai, Prashant served as a Principal at Deloitte Consulting (Australia), Portfolio Director of Product Management at Oracle, and Global Director for Data Science at Unum Group. He is a keynote speaker, popular panelist/moderator, and has been interviewed on many podcasts and in media over the years.

Prashant is an author/co-author of five books, all of which are practical, industry-focused titles that demystify digital transformation, data, machine learning/AI, and emerging technologies. He is an invited Co-faculty Instructor at Stanford University, a Distinguished Fellow at the Health Innovation Alliance, and Member of the Advisory Board at Pistoia Alliance AI Center of Excellence. Prashant has also been asked to contribute as an industry thought leader and expert advisor by members of the US Congress, the White House, and leading private sector organizations, and global governments. He has an undergraduate degree in chemical engineering, a graduate degree in technical communication and linguistics, and is a Stanford Certified Project Manager.

Bob Rogers, PhD, is Expert in Residence for AI at the University of California San Francisco's Center for Digital Health Innovation, where he applies his experience solving problems with advanced analytics and Artificial Intelligence to help build world-class medical AI technologies. He is also co-founder of Oii which uses novel technology to automate global supply chains. He is a member of the Board of Advisors to the Harvard Institute for Applied Computational Science. Prior to UCSF, Bob was Chief Data Scientist in the Data Center Group at Intel, and was also co-founder and Chief Scientist at Apixio, a healthcare AI company.

Bob began his career as an astrophysicist, developing computer models of physical processes near supermassive black holes. His research expanded to include artificial neural networks. He co-authored the book, *Artificial Neural Networks: Forecasting Time Series*, which led to a 12-year career as co-founder of a quantitative futures trading fund. In 2006, Bob transitioned into healthcare as a medical device product manager. He received his BA in physics at the University of California, Berkeley and his PhD in physics at Harvard.

Edward Dixon's interest in AI stems from a hope that, someday, a robot will iron his shirts. Edward is Principle at Rigr AI, a small consultancy focused on AI for sensitive data, with a special interest in the application of AI to Digital Forensics, stemming from his work with Intel's Safer Children program and the Interpol DevOps technical working group.

Jonas Christensen has spent his career leading data science functions across multiple industries. He is an international keynote speaker on data science and analytics leadership, a postgraduate educator and advisor in the field of data science and machine learning, and the host of the Leaders of Analytics podcast. He holds a Masters of International Finance and a Masters of Accounting from Deakin University, as well as a Bachelor of Economics and Business Administration from Copenhagen Business School.

Jonas is passionate about what data science and AI can do for the world of business and beyond. He believes data science and AI will be as revolutionary to the way we do business and interact with each other as IT and personal computing has been over the past 40 years.

Kirk Borne is a data scientist and astrophysicist, providing thought leadership, global speaking, content creation, mentoring, training, and consulting activities in data science, machine learning, and AI across multiple disciplines. He is the Chief Science Officer at DataPrime.ai where he applies his extensive experience and knowledge of the trends in these critical fields to developing data-intensive professions and mentoring data scientists of all experience levels. Previously, he was the Principal Data Scientist, Data Science Fellow, and an Executive Advisor at global technology and consulting firm Booz Allen Hamilton from 2015 to 2021. Before that, he was Professor of Astrophysics and Computational Science at George Mason for 12 years in the graduate and undergraduate data science programs. Prior to that, he spent nearly 20 years supporting data systems activities for NASA space science programs, including a role as NASA's Data Archive Project Scientist for the Hubble Space Telescope, and 10 years as a contract manager in NASA's Space Science Data Operations Office.

Dr. Borne has degrees in physics (B.S., LSU) and astronomy (Ph.D., Caltech). He is an elected Fellow of the International Astrostatistics Association for his contributions to big data research in astronomy. In 2020, he was elected a Fellow of the American Astronomical Society for lifelong contributions to the field of astronomy. As a global speaker, he has given hundreds of invited talks worldwide, including keynote presentations at dozens of data science, AI, and analytics conferences. He is an active contributor on social media, where he promotes data literacy for all, and has been named consistently among the top worldwide social influencers in data analytics, data science, machine learning, and AI since 2013.

Leland Wilkinson is Chief Scientist at H2O.ai and Adjunct Professor of Computer Science at the University of Illinois Chicago. He received an A.B. degree from Harvard in 1966, an S.T.B. degree from Harvard Divinity School in 1969, and a Ph.D. from Yale in 1975. Wilkinson wrote the SYSTAT statistical package and founded SYSTAT Inc. in 1984. After the company grew to 50 employees, he sold SYSTAT to SPSS in 1994, and worked there for ten years on research and development of visualization systems. Wilkinson subsequently worked at Skytree and Tableau, before joining H2O.ai.

Wilkinson is a Fellow of the American Statistical Association, an elected member of the International Statistical Institute, and a Fellow of the American Association for the Advancement of Science. He has won the best speaker award at the National Computer Graphics Association and the Youden prize for best expository paper in the statistics journal *Technometrics*. He has served on the Committee on Applied and Theoretical Statistics of the National Research Council, and is a member of the Boards of the National Institute of Statistical Sciences (NISS) and the Institute for Pure and Applied Mathematics (IPAM). In addition to authoring journal articles, the original SYSTAT computer program and manuals, and patents in visualization and distributed analytic computing, Wilkinson is the author (with Grant Blank and Chris Gruber) of *Desktop Data Analysis with SYSTAT*. He is also the author of *The Grammar of Graphics*, the foundation for several commercial and open-source visualization systems (IBMRAVE, Tableau, Rggplot2, and PythonBokeh).

Shantha Mohan is a mentor and project guide at Carnegie Mellon University Integrated Innovation Institute's iLab. She co-founded Retail Solutions Inc. (RSi), a leader in retail data analytics, and ran its global product development organization. Her prior experiences include technical and educational consulting, and running worldwide product development for Consilium, a Manufacturing Execution System (MES) company (acquired by Applied Materials). She graduated with a Ph.D. in Operations Management from the Tepper School of Management, Carnegie Mellon University. Her undergraduate degree is in Electronics and Communication is from the College of Engineering, Guindy (CEG), India; she is honored to be a Distinguished Alumnus.

Shantha is passionate about equality, diversity, and sustainability, and is a member of the Society of Women Engineers (SWE), where she is a volunteer and mentor. She is the author of *Roots and Wings: Inspiring Stories of Indian Women in Engineering*. She is a Distinguished Toastmaster (DTM) and is active in two clubs. She serves on the board of CEG alumni, North America (CEGAANA), and is instrumental in the creation of the Ask a CEGian student mentorship program and the CEG Betterment program.

Chapter 1

AI Strategy for the Executive

Prashant Natarajan
H2O.ai

Contents

DOI: 10.4324/9781351032940-1

1

Introduction

Human and organizational needs, business trends, evolving customer behaviors, and rapid data and technology innovations are some of the key drivers that are making Artificial Intelligence (AI) an essential foundation of the modern enterprise. In a business landscape that is increasingly informed by both global and local trends, the need to put data to work is more important and relevant than ever before. In the past, leaders and managers have relied on a combination of instincts, intuition, and Business Intelligence (BI) ("what happened in the past?") to make decisions around services/products, processes, and people.

While instincts, intuition, and BI can be right, at times, the demands on today's leaders, managers, and as importantly, the demands on and needs of staff/customers, require both decision-making and question framing to be done using a robust framework that privileges quantitative and qualitative data (that represents experience and behaviors). More importantly, digital transformation requires the modern enterprise to put these data to work by taking advantage of the latest developments in AI in all its forms, and thinking beyond automation in favor of augmentation and amplification.

An enterprise still has an option of ignoring AI, or keeping AI boxed to limited value generation; however, the consequences of doing so are severe for the following reasons:

- Competitive disadvantage—an enterprise that puts all its data to work via AI is better placed to create new advantages and positive differentiation w.r.t. the competition—existing and upcoming. In today's globalized landscape, the competition is not only known entities within a country but also foreign/transnational enterprises and startups/unicorns that are leveraging AI extensively
- Customer and employee experiences—using AI to understand a customer's or employee's personalization needs, and address it via micro-campaigns/products/experiences creates a better human experience and drives competitive advantage
- Suboptimal leverage of human resources—by focusing on mundane and robotic tasks in lieu of enabling employees/associates/professionals focus on what matters more
- Misalignment between business strategy and tactical solutions—technology is no longer a nice to have. The best business strategy can't be realized unless the enterprise can identify/design/develop appropriate data and technology solutions
- Top line and bottom line—by not using AI, an enterprise won't be in the best position to manage opportunity or risk, and maximize top- and bottom-line revenues, margins, and profitability
- Prepare for new conditions—measuring what's working or not and predicting known and unknown "unknowns." Managing appropriate/corrective measures are increasingly being recognized as being necessary to thrive, or at the very least, survive in turbulent times and when faced by "black swan" events such as pandemics, war, major recessions, and market conditions (the Kodak Effect being a well-studied example of not responding in a timely fashion to market and user preferences)

Applications of AI

The applications of AI span multiple industries/verticals, business units/departments, and users—as you will discover in the chapters in this book. While there is value in targeted applications of learning algorithms and visualization, the greatest impact of AI can be realized by treating it as a fundamental and foundational capability—and recognizing that AI can transform any part of your business or organization.

Many enterprises that are currently in this journey of deploying AI are doing it in B2B, B2C, and peer-to-peer customer contexts. Verticals as diverse as e-commerce, retail, banking, insurance, government, healthcare, manufacturing, smart cities, defense, and construction/real estate among many others are deploying AI on structured and unstructured data to optimize and create new value in

- Customer engagement and happiness
- Marketing and Sales
- Supply chain and operations
- Finance and accounting
- Regulations, compliance, and risk management
- Product development and pricing
- Talent acquisition and human resource management
- Operations
- More granular/specialized subdomains and processes

We are confident that the applications of AI will only continue to grow in commercial enterprises, governments, and nonprofits as expectations and talent availability grow, and AI becomes a commodity and democratized as we have seen with other scaled technology innovations in the past 150+ years.

Determining Practical Realization: Considerations

Technology doesn't exist in a vacuum and this fact must be recognized to ensure the successful applications of AI, or at the very least, reduce the challenges and frustration that will happen when AI is not deployed in the right context.

Success with AI requires company boards, executives, and change leaders to recognize that the readiness and maturity to incorporate the insights and new AI-driven workflows will vary—across cultural, technical, and process dimensions—in your organization. Getting buy-in across the department or an organization including among the workforce is essential as is the need to determine and prioritize use cases, cost–benefit analyses, and value generation.

If there is no precedent in your organization or if you're taking baby steps, it is critical to define your AI strategy before setting up teams, hiring costly talent, or investing in a machine learning (ML) or analytics product. We also recommend that you validate your strategy with market analyses and customer interviews (when possible) and be prepared for that strategy to change as you learn from tactical successes and operationalization of AI in business processes and workflow solutions.

The current state of AI technologies relies on and leverages data that are created or entered by humans or generated (for example, in the case of IoT or automation) by human-engineered systems. Data may be insufficient in some cases, may not have the appropriate data fidelity, or may require business process changes to get the required data in place for the AI application to generate the intended results. While techniques such as imputations, extrapolations, and trying your best with what's available are options—the relationship between data and AI follows the bedrock principle of GIGO (Garbage in, Garbage Out). We will discuss best practices around data and AI later in this chapter.

Separating AI from the rest of your legacy technologies is necessary at times—a new AI application can add value by itself (for example, in Natural Language Processing, Computer Vision, and Predictive Analytics) or in conjunction with a new application or digital transformation strategy. That being said, you will find that your ability to design/deploy the latest in AI and applying these to the lowest common technology denominator—spreadsheets, documents, and legacy systems—allows you to successfully meet users where they are and bring value to them—without necessarily requiring widespread revamp, large investments, or needless disruptions.

There may also be cases, especially with "black swans" or "never events," where an event of large magnitude has no/little precedent; and the available data are sparse, changing rapidly or is not a reliable indicator of future performance. As the business world is discovering with COVID-19, underlying challenges cannot be solely papered over with AI—though in many cases it can help. It is important for decision makers to understand when AI can't always predict the present or the future with a high degree of confidence or accuracy, understanding what's normal and what's an anomaly, and knowing when to supplement AI with human experience.

Similar to starting first with an enterprise strategy, creating the right business case and documenting business/functional requirements are important for executives and mid-level managers before they go down the path of staffing, solutioning, and spending. What works for another vertical, or even a competitor, may not be the best fit for you given your unique organizational needs, culture, and situation. Be enthusiastic about saying yes to high-impact AI solutions and keep an open mind to opportunities. Equally, be open to saying no to a specific use case or business solution where AI is not required—in favor of other more impactful ones. Don't give in to the temptation of having a vendor or a siloed internal technology team develop and deploy a solution for its own sake—as leaders, it is our responsibility to ensure long-term successes, which are typically not Big Bang but an accumulated journey of individual success stories.

Finally, the intended uses of AI must follow tried and tested best practices (discussed later in this chapter) and ethical considerations. Responsible AI and Explainable AI are increasingly becoming de-rigueur across enterprises of all sizes and types—not just for regulatory/compliance reasons—but also because it's the right thing to do for the various human stakeholders involved in the strategy, design, and use of AI. Some principles to consider on this topic are

- First, do no harm to your customers, employees, or business
- Build continual feedback loops to ensure and maintain a high degree of trust
- Historical data can be biased; pay attention to resulting algorithmic results and how these results are integrated into transaction systems or operational/business processes

- Set aside time and money to address ethical/responsible dimensions on each individual project
- Encourage collaboration—not just between data scientists and other technologists; but more importantly, between data scientists, data and analytics leaders, business stakeholders, and customers
- Interpretability (enabling a data scientist to understand how the algorithm came about its results from mathematical and data perspectives) and explainability (the ability for a nontechnical user of the solution to understand the process and results in plain language) are related but also serve different uses and audiences
- Understand that we will have to address tradeoffs between interpretability, explainability, time, and accuracy—and there is no single formula. Keep in mind that not every AI solution needs to be interpretable to the nth degree, depending on the use case it supports (some use cases will require more; others will need less)

Definitions

Our goal is to distill data down to refined and actionable Intelligence. The raw materials are different kinds of data, the tools are analytics and learning algorithms.

Let's define our terms more precisely.

Intelligence

- **Human intelligence**, is the "mental quality that consists of the abilities to learn from experience, adapt to new situations, understand and handle abstract concepts, and use knowledge to manipulate one's environment."[1]
- **Artificial Intelligence**, is "a branch of computer science dealing with the simulation of intelligent behavior in computers, or the capability of a machine to imitate intelligent human behavior."[2] In this context, AI as defined for the purposes of this book is the ability to decide on an action or make an inference given some data or information.

Data. Data are any kind of fact or piece of information that we can record, store, and subsequently retrieve for further processing. Data do not drive action in its own right but can be processed or interpreted within a specific context to make an inference or to drive an action. There are three classes of data that we deal with in analytics, data science, and AI:

- **Structured data**: These are data whose meaning is agreed upon ahead of time and is defined at an atomic level. For example, a table containing names and contact information for customers would typically be structured data. It can be arranged in rows and columns where each row pertains to a different customer, and each column is a different very specific piece of information. In fact, each column is the answer to a very specific question like, "what is the middle name of this customer," or "what is the area code of the phone number of this customer." Structured data, when properly cleaned, formed, and labeled (if needed) is ready to be used directly in supervised or unsupervised ML algorithms.

■ **Semi-structured data**: These are data that are structured in some way, but which are not defined at a granular enough level to be immediately defined as discrete rows and columns In a customer database, as described above, a semi-structured field might be a column called "notes" or "customer comments." These fields might contain a mix of data in text and/or numerical form which must be further refined into atomic components to be used in decision-making. For example, perhaps the subject of customer comments needs to be inferred, or the overall sentiment of the comment needs to be assessed before the data in this field can be used to define further action. Semi-structured data may be labeled with the answer to a vague or broad question ("what did the customer say?"), but the data in this field can answer many more questions ("Was it a positive comment? What product was the customer complaining about?) so it is not in its most atomic form.

■ **Unstructured data**: These are data in their most raw and natural form, such as audio or video files, images, or natural text. Often there is no structure on these kinds of data except the broadest definition or content like, "video from CCTV camera," "legal contract," "medical referral form," or "news article." There are many questions that such data can answer, and many different ways to break it down into atomic elements, depending upon what actions we are trying to drive. For example, a photograph of a rabbit presented to a child might come with the question, "what kind of animal is this?" but the same image presented to a naturalist might be, "what kind of rabbit is this?" In order to break unstructured data down to the right atomic elements, we need to determine what the domain of the data is and how might we process it further to answer increasingly granular questions. Recent advances in ML and algorithm advances in the fields of natural language processing (NLP) and computer vision (CV) are allowing us to process and obtain value from unstructured data with greater performance and efficiency than what was possible with rules-based systems in the past.

Analytics. Analytics is the mathematical and systematic process of converting raw data in all its forms – structured, semi-structured, and unstructured – into human-consumable assets, contextual insights, and business value. The process of creating analytics assets leverages one or more of the following methods and techniques:

■ Organizing, cleaning, or transforming data into more usable and derived forms
■ Discovering patterns in data
■ Hypotheses testing, for example using A/B tests
■ Logical reasoning, correlation, and causality analysis
■ Observational ethnography and anthropology, for example, in user experience labs
■ Applying other simple and advanced statistics and probability
■ Data journalism and storytelling

Analytics can be further categorized based on methods, techniques, and usage as

■ **Simple Analytics**: Simple analytics are generally used to describe, clean, or transform data using simple statistical methods to understand what happened in the past. For example, we might use a mean or median to describe the central tendency of a collection of values, or standard deviation to describe how much these values vary from an average value. Cleaning may be the application of a regular expression to identify dates in a database column that deviate from our preferred format, for example, Jan-01-2020 vs. 01/01/20. Sometimes simple analytics take the form of putting an address into a function to convert it into latitude and longitude, and then calculating the distance from that point to some other reference point. Many business intelligence (BI) functions, including dashboarding and basic visualization of data, would fall into the category of simple analytics.

■ **Advanced Analytics**: Advanced analytics uses methods that generally require more mathematical sophistication resulting in a focus on statistical inference, forecasting, modeling, simulation, text mining, and predictive modeling, which are typically beyond what's achievable or done in BI. The key difference between simple analytics (BI) and advanced analytics is further informed by the contexts of purpose and usage. Simple analytics is used to determine and understand the retrospective or current state of our business, market, or users. Advanced analytics, on the other hand, leverages and extends historical data and patterns to predict the future state of our business, markets, or users.

■ **Learning Algorithms**: we draw a distinction between learning algorithms (such as machine learning and deep learning) and advanced analytics. Learning algorithms are methods for making inferences or predictions from data that can automatically learn from new data to generalize and improve their performance over time. This does not require that learning algorithms must have automated feedback and training loops, only that the underlying algorithms lend themselves to such learning. While essentially a definition for machine learning, within this book for practical purposes, we make a further distinction between machine learning and deep learning (even though technically deep learning is a kind of machine learning):

■ **Machine learning (ML)**: Algorithms such as logistic and linear regression, random forests, support vector machines, clustering algorithms, and anomaly detection algorithms that take a feature vector as input and then output some new vector which may be a prediction of a future value, a new sequence, or a classification of the data into a category. In supervised learning, for example, these algorithms generally are exposed to examples of past input vectors and are often given the desired output for these examples. These ML algorithms then "learn" how to compute the correct output based on these training examples. Until the recent explosion in deep learning, these algorithms required input vectors that were carefully curated to contain distilled information that was highly relevant and specific to the decision-making computation, a process called feature engineering. When we refer to a ML algorithm in this book, we are generally talking about a learning approach that requires curated input via feature engineering.

■ **Deep Learning (DL)**: These are the algorithms, whose practical utility has only really emerged since 2006, that do not require upfront or extensive feature engineering. They are built from layers (often very many layers) of very simple computing elements called neurons, who pass their outputs to subsequent layers of neurons in various patterns. This architecture was originally inspired by how the brain computes with neurons, although there are many important differences between the brain and DL systems including the fact that the human brain is still one of the least understood biological systems. There are two significant characteristics of deep learning systems: The first key characteristic of DL is that they can generally take raw input, such as a passage of text or an image, without significant upfront feature engineering or manipulation (other than making sure the input data are fairly clean and consistent). This means that deep learning systems learn from examples that are closer to real-world unstructured data, making them highly flexible and robust. The second key characteristic of most DL systems is that a DL system developed for one application can be easily adapted to solve a new problem, a process called transfer learning. The ability to use transfer learning in computer vision has made sophisticated, highly targeted vision applications available at low cost and effort to almost every enterprise user. Convolutional neural networks (CNNs), Recurrent Neural Networks (RNNs), Transformers, and Deep Q Reinforcement Learning systems are just a few examples of the huge variety of deep learning systems that are available today.

Data Science: Data science is the multidisciplinary field of transforming data into value. This process combines some of the following capabilities:

- To work with business stakeholders, often applying their own subject matter expertise, to identify which questions need to be answered by AI systems to advance the state of the business
- To design experiments and define data collection methods that allow for drawing strong conclusions
- To collect, clean, transform, store, retrieve and analyze data in a variety of computing settings
- To build pipelines of simple analytics, advanced analytics, and learning algorithms to make valid inferences from data, often at high pace incoming data and at scale
- To make statistically valid inferences from data and communicate these results to enterprise stakeholders, including through the use of advanced visualizations.

IMPACT Framework for Enterprise AI

To summarize considerations for enterprise usage of AI, we have developed the IMPACT Framework that will provide a broad and structured set of guidelines for you to implement across your strategy, tactics, and business needs—and keep them relevant during all times, both normal and exceptional. (Table 1.1).

The IMPACT framework addresses opportunities, challenges, and provides a framework that can be used and repeated as a checklist to create business value and ensure the lasting success of digital transformation with data, analytics, and AI (Figure 1.1).

Table 1.1   IMPACT Framework for Enterprise AI

I	Imagination
M	Maturity
P	People
A	Augmentation, Amplification, and Automation
C	Culture
T	Transformation

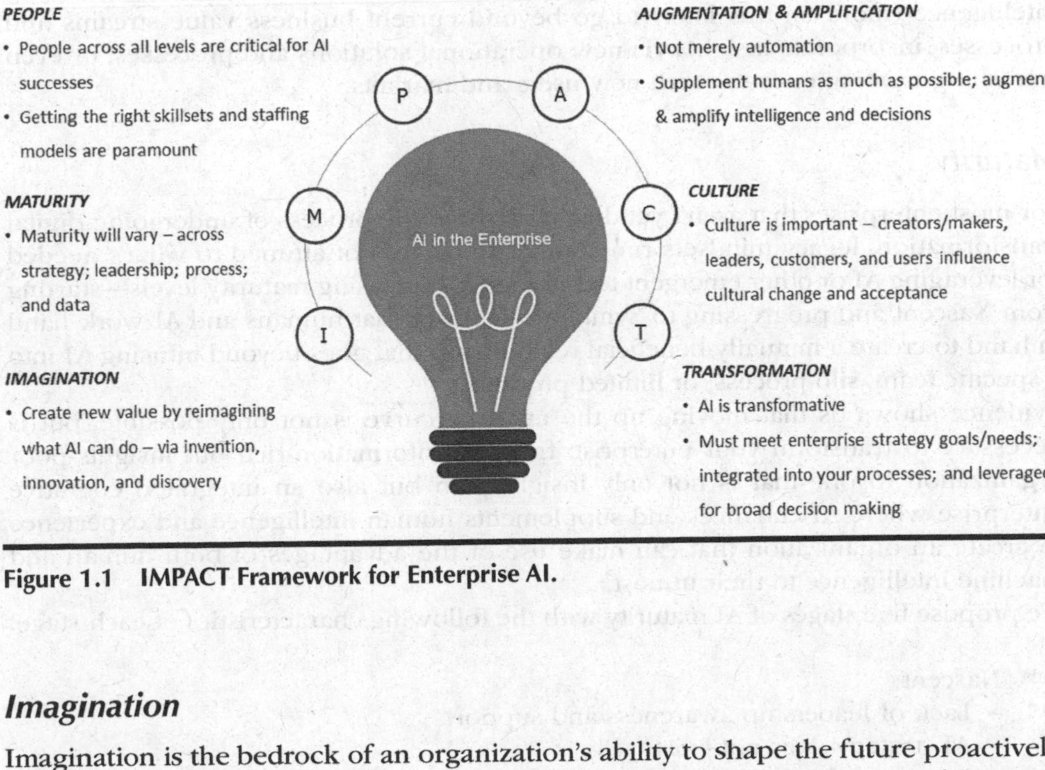

PEOPLE
- People across all levels are critical for AI successes
- Getting the right skillsets and staffing models are paramount

MATURITY
- Maturity will vary – across strategy; leadership; process; and data

IMAGINATION
- Create new value by reimagining what AI can do – via invention, innovation, and discovery

AUGMENTATION & AMPLIFICATION
- Not merely automation
- Supplement humans as much as possible; augment & amplify intelligence and decisions

CULTURE
- Culture is important – creators/makers, leaders, customers, and users influence cultural change and acceptance

TRANSFORMATION
- AI is transformative
- Must meet enterprise strategy goals/needs; integrated into your processes; and leveraged for broad decision making

AI in the Enterprise

P   A
M   C
I   T

Figure 1.1   IMPACT Framework for Enterprise AI.

Imagination

Imagination is the bedrock of an organization's ability to shape the future proactively by encouraging new technologies, changing organizational mindsets, and empowering new ways of creative thinking. The most successful organizations—be they enterprises like Amazon or Tesla or Apple, or several start-ups and unicorns—thrive on creating new markets, new users, or even new uses for existing products. They do so by going beyond adaptation to circumstances or fine-tuned operating expense management to go boldly forth where no humans have gone before. They thrive by shaping the future and leveraging collective internal and external knowledge and intelligence—and are increasingly using AI to drive

- **Invention:** the conceptualization and creation of a net-new product, process, or service
- **Discovery:** creation of new increments of institutional and market knowledge
- **Innovation:** a better way of doing things

Given the sheer amounts of multi-dimensional little and big data across the enterprise, putting that data to work through AI requires connecting 2 V's of big data usage (Value and Veracity) to 3 V's of data characteristics (Variety, Velocity, and Volume).[3] When faced with opportunities or challenges alike, the AI-driven enterprise of today is being able to go beyond renewal and adaptive strategies and classical planning-based strategies—to visionary and shaping strategies, which require imagination.[4] AI presents organizations with tried and tested methods to apply imagination by enabling leaders to leverage new data-driven insights and amplified/augmented intelligence (more on this later) to go beyond current business value streams and processes, incorporate insights via new operational solutions and processes, or even refreshing existing ones to reach new users and markets.

Maturity

For most enterprises that aren't yet digital or are in the process of undergoing digital transformation, legacy mindsets run counter to or are not attuned to what's needed for leveraging AI or other emergent technologies. Increasing maturity levels—starting from Nascent and progressing to Symbiotic—ensure that humans and AI work hand in hand to create a mutually-beneficial relationship that goes beyond infusing AI into a specific team, silo process, or limited products.

Evidence shows us that moving up the maturity curve is not only possible, but is necessary to transform your enterprise from an information-rich but insights-poor organization to one that is not only insights-rich but also an integrated cognitive enterprise where AI enhances and supplements human intelligence and experience to create an organization that can make use of the advantages of both human and machine intelligence to their utmost.

We propose five stages of AI maturity with the following characteristics of each stage.

- Nascent
  - Lack of leadership awareness and support
  - AI strategy does not exist
  - Data are siloed and are not reusable assets
  - Analytics is simple – spreadsheets, reports, and BI dashboards
- Basic
  - Leadership is aware of AI
  - AI strategy awareness is not developed fully for any business unit or department
  - Data is not managed as a repeatable asset
  - AI-related funding and projects are subject to leadership distractions
  - One or two AI projects or products in development

- Intermediate
  - Leadership supports the use of AI in principle
  - AI strategy is not unified across the enterprise
  - Structured data is well managed and governed
  - Three to five AI projects or products in development and production
  - Results of these AI efforts are not always connected to business outcomes or value is not measured consistently
- Advanced
  - Leadership vision and support are mature
  - Business strategy is finetuned based on AI results and learnings
  - Data in all their forms are well managed and governed
  - AI models, applications, and products are governed and managed proactively
  - Multiple AI projects in production and operationalized within workflows with mature change management in place
  - Human decision-making leverages AI
- Symbiosis
  - Humans (employees and users) and AI have a symbiotic relationship across strategy, operations, outcomes, and decision making
  - AI is fundamental to growth, operational efficiencies, and competitive advantage
  - All data is well managed, governed, and leveraged as a reusable asset for multiple AI use cases and solutions
  - AI is baked into all business processes, is finetuned for organizational culture, serves as a foundational asset for monetization, and generates both continuous and contextual value

Admittedly, there are a few frameworks from different consulting companies and vendors; however, many of them require buying into that specific vendor's approach, proprietary frameworks, and lengthy workshops. To make it easier for leaders and managers, we propose the following dimensions and self-determinants of AI maturity and a straightforward approach that you can use to determine your organization's maturity.

Dimensions of AI Maturity

According to a survey of senior executives by Deloitte on the maturity of data, analytics, and AI, very few organizations are consistently embedding data and AI-based insights into their decision-making process.[5] When contrasted with companies that have data and AI as a part of their digital DNA, the difference is striking. AI-mature organizations which started as digital-first are understandably higher up the maturity scale and are getting better by building upon early successes. While not an exhaustive list, examples of such organizations that use AI at the core of decision-making are Amazon, Google, Lemonade, Credit Karma, Apple, and Facebook in the USA and allied markets, with significant examples from China being iFlyTek, SenseTime, and Baidu among others.

In order to improve your competitive advantage and thrive in this new AI-first landscape, we propose that a fine-tuned understanding and management of AI maturity along the following dimensions: Strategy; Leadership; Process; and Data.

Managing these foundation elements—especially via a staged approach as opposed to doing them all at the same time—allows you to progress rapidly and move up the AI maturity scale and accomplish what you want for your business, employees, and customers.

Strategy

AI strategy for your enterprise must not be based on looking back from what works or not based on your AI implementations but rather looking forward from your business strategy to determine what you need from your AI strategy. As a result, your AI strategy is determined by your organization's goals, desired outcomes, imagination, and a frank evaluation of opportunities for improvement across other dimensions—leadership, process, and data. The strategy must also account for investments, financial outcomes, quantitative and qualitative measures/KPIs, enabling a culture of experimentation, change management, and a tolerance for fast and early failures or middling successes.

The questions you should be asking yourself are:

- What is your business strategy and what are the opportunities for AI to support your business goals—both as a catalyst and as a driver of organizational change and process optimization?
- How can AI help deliver on your strategic goals? How will you identify where AI <u>cannot</u> help?
- What are the opportunities you want to address or problems your enterprise wants to solve?
- Can your AI strategy go beyond simple automation—and deliver value by amplification and augmentation, in order to create a symbiotic relationship between humans and their AI solutions?
- How will you identify high-value use cases and enhance the ability to operationalize the insights across business information systems, processes, and people?
- Are there any opportunities to deliver early and impactful successes in an agile fashion and without breaking the bank?
- How will you use these early successes to inform and influence the landscape for future AI priorities—especially as you move up these maturity levels?

Leadership

Large-scale recent surveys of executives demonstrate that the opportunities of AI are mostly unrealized—only 8% of companies engage in core practices that enable widespread adoption of AI and advanced analytics. Most firms have only run ad-hoc pilots or are applying AI in business processes.[6] To change this reality and move up the maturity levels, the role of enterprise leadership (CEO, CIO, CFO, CDO/CAO "chief data or analytics officers," other CXOs, business leaders, and senior executives) is paramount, not just for AI strategy definition but also for inculcating supporting cultures by driving AI-enabled decision-making.

The questions you should be asking yourself as a leader are

- How are you incorporating the principle of thinking globally (learning from global AI-forward companies) while competing vertically (within your industry/domain)?

- With new insights and solutions on your radar, are you learning to unlearn and relearn?
- Are you encouraging the adoption of AI and driving the adoption of its results into processes, teams, and decision-making? What collaboration and reward programs will you be using to recognize teams that make the change?
- Are you working with cross-functional teams to determine effective communication strategies for investors, regulators, customers, employees, and senior/mid managers?
- Do you have the right leaders and team structures in place to identify high-value use cases that will deliver early successes?
- How will you focus on repeatable and scalable successes—across your enterprise—in order to realize financial outcomes and address qualitative feedback (for example, employee and customer satisfaction)?
- Are your leaders and their teams thinking about how to account for governing and leveraging data in all its forms, unstructured, structured, and semi-structured?
- How will we reward the people in our organization that adopts AI in their business strategy and processes?

Process

The greatest impact of the discoveries and learnings of AI requires integrating them and enhancing or re-imagining your current business, technology, and change management processes. Converting these AI insights and results requires system integrations to operationalize these insights into the user/customer workflow, and also make them readily consumable by humans without additional cognitive overload.

Appropriate socialization of results and training to allay understandable, but overblown, fears of "The Singularity" and job losses must be managed proactively as part of any process redesign.

The questions you should be asking around your processes are

- Will your processes account for agility and a willingness to experiment?
- Will your change management support the willingness to change existing processes or openness to defining new ones?
- Are you considering how to marry AI success to processes—even within legacy systems and data—without requiring huge new investments?
- How will your processes support an increasing maturity of decision-making and the ability to consume new insights and efficiencies?
- What metrics will you use, or develop, to measure and correct changes to processes?

Data

Data are the fuel for the AI and analytics engine and the quality of AI's results are only as good as the data used by learning algorithms. Increasingly, managers in enterprises require insights and decisions based on AI's pattern recognition and sense-making that only a deliberate data strategy and approach can yield.[7] Yet, many organizations are still working through the information, processes, and tools to make informed, responsive enterprise decisions with AI. To best manage the data (big, little, and everything in between), we recommend examining data strategy and corresponding usage in AI according to the 5 V's described below—while recognizing that each use case (or the domain you are in) will dictate which of these are the first among equals and matter more than others: Volume, Variety, Velocity, Veracity, and Value.

The questions you should be asking around your data, as it relates to AI, are

- Are you taking advantage of all the data that exist in your enterprise?
- Do you have a coherent and comprehensive data strategy that has been communicated across your organization?
- Have you set up a Chief Data Officer or Chief Analytics Officer role in your organization, and are they empowered to take both proactive and hard decisions around your data and its uses?
- Are you using a data governance strategy that goes beyond privacy and regulatory compliance needs?
- Are you taking advantage of diverse approaches to maintain and manage your data via the use of data warehouses, data lakes, data virtualization, and business/use case-specific data marts and cubes?
- Are you accounting for data fidelity over data quality especially as it relates to AI? (More on this topic later in this chapter)
- Are you putting your unstructured data to work in addition to your structured and semi-structured data?
- How are you integrating or separating your data strategy and tactics to support your AI strategy and solutions?

Assessing and Increasing AI Maturity in Your Organization

As a sage said, a 1000-mile journey begins with a single step. We recognize that all organizations are not alike and may be in different stages of an AI journey. However, in the spirit of building an enterprise where human and AI work together in integrated ways, we offer the following assessment framework that you can use to both assess and improve how you design for and leverage AI in order to become an enterprise where humans and AI benefit each other in a symbiotic environment (Figure 1.2). In a symbiotic organization, humans and AI complement each other in the following ways to drive the quality of discovery, decision-making, and return on human and capital investments.

People

The most advanced organizations that are digital at heart exhibit a fine-tuned reliance on people—in leadership, across cross-functional teams, within data, data science, and analytics teams. In order to define the most-appropriate AI strategy and to deliver on it, enterprises that recognize the natural symbiosis between human and AI display a few striking qualities.

When investing in AI, think of people first, not technology first. Technology is important, but people will create value, drive adoption, and ensure human–AI symbiosis for your business. Invest in your employees so that building AI knowledge

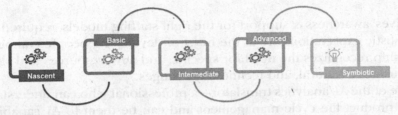

Nascent
- No AI strategy and lack of leadership awareness
- Data is siloed – not a reusable asset; limited to reporting and spreadsheets
- Limited to no processes or governance

Intermediate
- Some AI strategy exists; not unified across the enterprise
- Structured data is well managed
- 3-5 AI production projects; results not connected to business strategy

Symbiotic
- Humans & AI enjoy a symbiotic relationship: strategy, outcomes & shared decision making
- AI is the basis of competitive advantage
- All data is governed & leveraged for AI
- AI is baked into process, culture and monetization

Basic
- AI strategy-aware
- Data not managed as a repeatable asset for AI
- AI-related processes and projects/funding are at whims of leadership distractions
- 1-2 AI applications in development

Advanced
- Enterprise strategy is managed & finetuned based on AI results & learnings
- AI success is measured based on business outcomes
- Un-/structured data are well governed and managed
- Multiple AI projects in production & operationalized
- Human decision making leverages AI

Figure 1.2   Assessing and Increasing AI Maturity Levels.

Digital Transformation: Connecting AI Strategy to Solutions

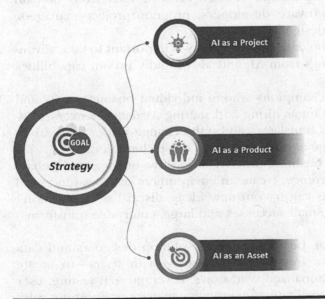

Value Generation: Represents the AI/analytics workstreams/projects that bring business value to a specific department or business unit - via application deployment and operationalization. The focus is on OpEx, C-SAT, and E-SAT.

Value Generation: Uses AI/analytics to identify and create products that can be monetized via Sales for both internal and external audiences. The focus is net new revenue generation via deploying and maintaining products at scale.

Value Generation: Represents the AI/analytics assets that drive transformation across the enterprise and bring business value to multiple business teams. The focus is on repeatable digital transformation value.

Figure 1.3   Leveraging AI for Digital Transformation.

and learning to incorporate it into their roles becomes a long-term strategy that can unlock institutional knowledge, untapped expertise, and drive new value with your existing workforce & new hires.[8]

In AI-driven organizations, the considerations listed below are practiced consistently and frequently.

■ Executives' awareness & support for the right staffing models, required funding, and realistic expectations are at the heart of developing people competencies.

■ Leadership recognizes the need for specific, and new, resources and skillsets to drive business, cultural, and technology changes.

■ The role of the AI/analytics translator—a professional who can understand business & product life cycle management and can tie them to AI capabilities—is increasingly seen as a mandatory and core skill. While this role is as difficult to find as a unicorn, professionals who have prior experience in playing these multiple roles or who have a keen interest in bridging business, processes, and systems can fill this role successfully.

■ A good AI/analytics translator has the ability to translate business requirements into AI solutions—while also having the important ability to explain the results of AI to a business/operations/lay audience (someone who is not a data scientist or machine-learning engineer) and also craft and deliver a compelling story/narrative.

■ AI capabilities are centralized when it comes to evangelism, digital transformation, and in some cases, design/development/deployment. In certain other organization models, the design and development are federated with leadership responsibilities and accountability being centralized for greatest efficiencies.

■ AI and data science efforts are a team sport—in order to drive successes, the development of narrow AI capabilities require contributions from domain experts, technologists and software developers, program/project managers, business system analysts, UX designers, and users.

■ Upskilling your existing team on data and AI literacy is important to take advantage of the insights and findings from AI, and also rapidly groom capabilities across your company.

■ Recognizing and building AI champions among individual business units and functional teams are as important as hiring and staffing AI/data science/analytics teams, and the AI/analytics translator can be the change leader who drives the dissemination of knowledge and results across these champions.

■ Once you have identified the business process, workflow, or impacted behaviors where AI can make a difference, create an environment of cross-functional experimentation—where teams can try out new ideas, discard ones that don't work, and productionize both small successes and large, enterprise transformation assets.

■ Have the AI/analytics translator, business experts, solution designers and data scientists/engineers collaborate frequently and early—with users—to create both visual impact and operationalized workflows. Leverage A/B testing, user interviews and feedback, and qualitative/quantitative metrics to fine-tune solution creation and future updates/maintenance.

Considerations on the Data Scientist Role

"The data scientist must have analytics ability, strong mathematics/statistics background, the ability to present/communicate their ideas, and most importantly, lead teams and delegate tasks. These individuals are in great demand and command substantial salaries. For many organizations, finding a suitable employee requires time, and once one is hired, the challenge becomes using the resource effectively. Being a highly skilled, independent agent with proficiency across multiple disciplines, these individuals can handle a variety of different data-focused tasks and analytics/AI deliverables. They can assess data fidelity and quality, merge datasets, write SQL queries, perform statistical analysis, create code in Python and R, and so on. Leading organizations are realizing that in order to obtain the greatest value from this talent, it is important to surround these people with a team.

Constructing a team to support a data scientist is driven by the tasks and the skills required for that specific AI and analytics use case, in addition to the considerations above. Sometimes, organizations hire data scientists because that's what their peers are doing without thinking about the required leadership and support models. Such an approach is suboptimal and typically leads to underwhelming results. Commonly, supporting team members include the AI/analytics translator-leader, data engineer, modeler, project manager, and business analyst. For smaller teams, these can be part-time roles, and in larger organizations, these are usually served through a pool of resources. Obviously, depending on the problem at hand, other skills exist that would be useful and would be pulled into the team as necessary.

Adding a data scientist role into an existing organization can be disruptive, as it changes the structure and reporting relationships. Many individuals do not grasp the role that these employees play and what value they can bring to the team. Given the novelty of the position, oftentimes, a data scientist is similarly confused and requires guidance and structure. This is a management challenge. Clarity of the role as understood within the organization is critical for their and your shared success. In some ways, these challenges exist more as a scaling problem. Having an experienced AI and analytics translator on your team ameliorates these risks and increases both the value and productivity of your data scientists.

From a personnel standpoint, many organizations' data and analytics resources are distributed across the enterprise. This is usually a remnant from the best-of-breed silos or a department-based organizational focus. Within these teams exist deep resources with understanding of the specific transactional systems and local analytics needs. Effectively engaging these groups in an enterprise effort is difficult. The local resource owners are worried about loss of talent to a centralized project, and the IS team is concerned about lack of agreement with methodologies and data standards, resulting in project disruption. In order to succeed, each team must learn from the other.

Building federated teams is one successful approach. With this methodology, the central IT/IS organization is responsible for creating the tools and artifacts for ingestion, curation, governance, and analytics constructs. This would include master data elements that are core to the business. These are foundational to the platform and embody strategic decisions made within the institution. In creating these constructs prior to the engagement, the project team is able to teach each federated group how the project works and the standards for participating. The distributed teams bring deep understanding of the subject matter, business needs, and processes. Each group contributes dedicated members to the effort with the understanding that this is a long-term commitment. The IS team would provide overall project management. Skill composition for a federated delivery team would include a data modeler, a data integration developer, a business analyst, and a data scientist or AI/analytics developer matched one for one by individuals from the distributed team.

As the combined teams work together, diffusion of knowledge occurs, and an ongoing commitment to training is necessary to help fill skills gaps identified in the distributed team. Rapid delivery of analytics insight is critical. Early in the project plan, analytics use cases must be clearly identified. These must serve the business need and bring early value to the customer. Working backward, data targets are identified for ingestion to support the analytics.

Using an agile method for AI delivery, multiple deliverable iterations are built over time. With this approach, the business realizes value quickly from the effort, and the teams are naturally directed toward high-value data first. As the federated groups collaborate in this effort, they continue to grow in the understanding of the data, supporting structures, and methodologies. For the customer, they have the opportunity to size the teams dedicated to this effort as they see results. If the business finds value, augmenting the team with additional resources to proceed more quickly is the next step. If there is little value shown, or if other more compelling business opportunities arise, the contribution shrinks. Using this approach, the limited resources of the central IT/IS team are concentrated in domains in which the data owners have high interest and need. Whatever the outcome, the central IT/IS organization continues to understand the customer data and to ingest, steward, and govern for the enterprise.

For organizations without distributed teams or limited resources, collaboration becomes even more critical. Building an inclusive structure to leverage individuals who have deep knowledge within these customer areas is the first step. Attempting to expropriate data or exclude local experts slows down any effort and results in political consequences. Focus on rapid analytics deliverables with many small additive iterations is important so that the customer can learn and understand what these products contain and begin to leverage them as soon as possible within the course of business. As the products become well understood, the customer is in a much more informed position to direct the next cycle of development and to bring business value. This walk of analytics maturity between the development team and the customer helps to build trust and understanding of the process between the partners."[9]

Automation, Amplification, and Augmentation

The rapid development and the hype cycle of automation in an enterprise context have sometimes tended to focus on Robotic Process Automation (RPA). Despite the claims of some vendors, RPA is not (and cannot be) AI given the fundamental differences in definition, learning, and usage. The reasons why RPA is not AI are straightforward when we understand these fundamental differences in how these systems work and what they do.

- RPA is task and process automation by software agents (AKA RPA robots) – there is no data-driven learning involved in the creation or use of an RPA robot

- Every repetitive task that is automated by RPA must be explicitly defined and programmed by a human in advance
- Once defined explicitly, the RPA robot mimics what to do and how to perform the pre-defined task – process inefficiencies, errors, and other warts/blemishes included.

AI – unlike RPA – uses data and learning algorithms to learn, recognize unseen patterns, generalize when presented with unseen/new data, and become better over time. This significant difference means that AI doesn't require pre-defined rules or pre-recorded task/process definitions and guardrails to complete their tasks.

An inordinate focus on RPA-based software and does a disservice to buyers, leaders, professionals, and users. RPA-based automation vastly underperforms AI even on basic tasks such as document processing as is incapable of performing natural language processing, computer vision, or intelligent character recognition. An enterprise that focuses on RPA as the only method for automation risks ignoring the many opportunities for leveraging data, building a learning ecosystem, and ignoring significant cost reduction and revenue opportunities.

Most importantly, an RPA-only automation strategy underplays the true value of AI in creating new strategy, operational, and human value. AI is fundamental and integral to business and technology strategy and optimization as it has a broader applicability and value creation using one or more of the following:

- Automation
- Amplification
- Augmentation

Automation, using AI, is removing the robot out of the human and allowing the latter to focus on higher value efforts and value creation rather than mundane tasks. Automation enables us to be more human and focus on things that matter more to our sense of professional satisfaction, happiness, values, and sense of purpose while also improving operational efficiencies. AI automation provides ways to eliminate needless repetitive tasks, increase the quality of work products, and reduce the challenges presented by large quantities of data that are being collected and processed more frequently than before.

Amplification—using AI—is doing something new that hasn't been done before in a reliable and repeatable way to supplement human knowledge and capabilities. AI-based amplification allows symbiosis by enabling new tasks and activities things that humans can't do as efficiently by themselves.

Examples of amplification include real-time anomaly detection (by monitoring at scale and identifying outliers quicker and more reliably than humans can on their own), computer vision (picking out a "face in a crowd" or a difficult to find tumor), discovering hidden patterns, identifying computational biomarkers, and the like.

Augmentation—using AI—is complementing humans by creating new knowledge, helping users discover new questions, testing hypotheses, and finding new insights. Augmentation requires humans and AI to work together and to addresses the limitations the "other" has—for example, in the case of humans, fatigue, cognitive biases, and the desire to focus on the sublime instead of the mundane.

Similarly, the augmentation of AI by humans allows for true symbiosis by teaching the algorithm the ethics, the differences between right & wrong, correcting data-driven biases, and providing continuous feedback and improvement on

- Algorithms
- Business process re-imagination
- Outcomes

As you will read later in this book, amplification & augmentation are essential to create new successes while also avoiding problem areas such as gender, ethnic and racial biases (Amazon),[10] invasion of privacy (Target), or chat bots going off the rails (Microsoft Tay).[11]

The new opportunities presented by AI-driven amplification & augmentation will create new opportunities in healthcare & life sciences (vaccines, new uses for existing drug molecules, etc.), retail (customer engagement and happiness), supply chain (inventory and fulfillment optimization by forecasting the need for masks and PPE), insurance (predicting health/job threats and income protection), and corporate social responsibilities.

Culture

One of the biggest challenges is ensuring widespread adoption of AI in any organization is building, inculcating, and maintaining the cultural foundations of openness and change across business, people, and technology. "AI initiatives face formidable cultural and organizational barriers. But we've also seen that leaders who at the outset take steps to break down those barriers can effectively capture AI's opportunities. [...] While cutting-edge technology and talent are certainly needed, it's equally important to align a company's culture, structure, and ways of working to support broad AI adoption."[12]

To address the challenges associated with cultural shifts and accelerate the pace of change, we recommend the following considerations.

- AI and the resulting symbiosis will result not only in optimization but also bring about new perspectives, data, and results. In order to take advantage of the latter, leaders and mid-managers must demonstrate the willingness to change existing business processes and an openness to defining new ones.
- Experimentation, the "right to fail," and being open to progressive Return on Investments (RoI) are key to building the cultural foundations needed by an imaginative enterprise.
- When faced with success—the desire to maintain the status quo and accompanying resistance are, at times, the initial reactions. Storytelling allows you to ameliorate these concerns in addition to explaining the benefits of making the changes and the costs to the business of not doing so.
- Deploy AI-driven solutions without always requiring huge new investments or Big Bang systematic changes success. Being able to deploy within legacy processes, existing systems, and all available data allows you to manage the costs better—while also proving an apples-to-apples comparison on benefits.

- Cultural maturity also means that AI being incorporated into normal decision-making processes—and not exceptional ones—in every relevant business context
- Removing the fear of AI from people in the trenches and how it affects their jobs is important
- Understanding that AI is not always superior to humans, and in all cases, requires humans to provide validation and feedback is key. Additionally, leveraging the satisfaction, pride, and motivations that individuals get out of their roles in order to explain how AI can "remove the robot out of the human" will help address both the hype and fears around a dystopian work future.
- Empowering employees in asking questions, enabling symbiotic decision-making, and encouraging informed skepticism will contribute to bringing about the needed cultural change across your enterprise.

Transformation

At the turn of the last century, organizations had a dedicated role to incorporate then-new technology—electricity—into their businesses, the Chief Electricity Officer (CEO). "We needed them for about 20 years while we figured out what this electricity stuff was about."[13] While the role was important given the context, as businesses transformed into using electricity and making it core to their daily business, both the role of the then-CEO and dedicated programs and funding around electricity disappeared.

In a similar fashion, as today's enterprise transforms from being AI-First to one where AI is intrinsically baked into roles, processes, and symbiotic decision-making, roles such as Chief Data Officer, Chief Analytics Officer, or Chief AI Officer—and dedicated transformation programs—will evolve and may become transitionary.

As the realities and both opportunities/constraints of AI become clearer, overblown fears of general AI (AKA "The Singularity.") the general public's fear (and contributing media hype), will give way to understanding and appreciating the role that AI plays in transforming organizations, their people, and their customers. For the enterprise, singularity is of minimal practical relevance and impact. What matters more to the enterprise are applications of AI within a specific domain, business process, or system workflow based on the availability of high-fidelity data or addressing data deserts (where data are unavailable, incomplete, or of insufficient fidelity).

As a result, transformation efforts must focus on

- Imagination, as defined earlier in this chapter
- Creating new AI-enabled products & services—physical products, digital services, and human experiences
- Learning how to staff teams, filling the AI/analytics translator role, and deploying hybrid AI development and implementation approaches including
  - Coding from scratch using accelerators and open source
  - Using native applications features (Salesforce Einstein, Oracle Cloud Applications, etc.) and/or cloud ML/AI services (Amazon Web Services, Google Cloud Platform, Azure, etc.)

- Leveraging AI platforms (H2O.ai Hybrid Cloud, Data Robot, etc.)
- Purpose-built, domain-specific and off-the-shelf packaged AI applications
■ Addressing the influence of lore and legend when they become impediments, or preferably, building upon them and learning from past experiences
■ Democratizing AI within the enterprise—by demystifying technology, usage, and progressively making it unseen/part of the background
■ AI becomes ubiquitous and human–AI interaction becomes a mindset—not a goal or a tool.
■ The transformative power of AI is woven into enterprise fabric, digital DNA, and legacy/new workflows and systems.
■ AI is no longer its own thing but is leveraged by leaders and people in the trenches alike
■ Connect and revise strategy based on tactics and results and vice versa

Best Practices for the Use of Data in AI

Collecting, managing, and storing data is a costly exercise if we can't convert such data into high-value, actionable insights or influence workflows in a timely fashion. Generating knowledge from data requires the use of machine learning for various reasons—cognitive, organizational, technical, and operational. Any discussion on using data must include a corresponding discussion on machine learning and AI; frankly, they can seldom be separated anymore.

Data are the fuel for the AI engine in your enterprise, and your success with AI begins with sourcing, managing, and using data in all its forms—structured, semi-structured, and unstructured. The relatively low rates of AI usage and adoption are not reflective of the realities or capabilities of relevant vendors or technologies—but are reflective of the current challenges with data literacy, learning curve, organizational inertia, resourcing challenges, and the challenges of managing both legacy and new data sources.

The promise of AI is real, and in order to drive its increased adoption, large majorities of businesses and leaders recognize the management of big and little data as critically important. Best practices are propagated through a vertical or industry after success has been demonstrated. This is apparent in the case of best practices in data management as well.[14]

To use data for AI, readers may find it helpful to understand both the characteristics of data and its usage.

Characteristics of data are defined in terms of

■ Volume
■ Variety
■ Velocity

Determinants of data usage in AI are examined via the lenses of

■ Veracity
■ Value

Volume

Volume remains a key characteristic of data as it applies to AI—not just for the determination of how to manage these volumes through appropriate strategy and technologies—but also as a key influencer of appropriateness, training, and test data for the use cases in question. Organizations generate, manage, and use large amounts of digital data for customer acquisition, engagement, business operations (supply chain, finance, etc.), record keeping/compliance/regulatory requirements, production/manufacturing, and the amount of data—big or little is only increasing.

While the trends within a department or organization may be well understood, there is a new world that exists beyond any organization's four walls and new customer (or even employee) behaviors that are increasingly contributing data that may be complementary—or even contradictory—to the existing body of knowledge that exists within current transactional source systems and institutional knowledge. The widespread adoption of smartphones, personal monitors, network-enabled devices, and social networks are creating new opportunities and a world of truly big data for AI to leverage. In addition to these new data sources, any organization has access to, and is simultaneously creating huge volumes of unstructured data (text, videos, images, and audio) that have mostly been mined insufficiently for insights, and present opportunities for AI.[15]

Choosing the most appropriate storage and computing technologies must include an examination of the following factors on data volumes:

■ **"Be specific" approach**. Data storage and management requirements are scoped for analytics/other AI use cases. This approach is preferred for pilot projects/proof of concepts.
■ **"Bring it all in" approach**. Expansive approach in which scoping is driven by the need to manage most/all data using big data technologies. This approach is used when there is a desire to do large data-set analysis, when taking sources offline, or when it is cheaper to use distributed storage for archiving purposes.
■ **Types of data and metadata to be managed**. Un-/semi-/structured sources including large text, images, dark data, streams, etc.
■ **Versioning**. Historical data, updates, and corrections, change rate, slowly changing data.
■ **Deployment model**. Cloud, on-premise, and hybrid.
■ **Operations**. Data loading, migration, archiving, backup/restore requirements.
■ **Future needs**. Planning for more sources and more use cases must be an early consideration, especially when your pilot is successful.

Variety

Variety in big data refers to the diversity of data sources, data types, and use cases. Given its antecedents as a solution for large volume, semi-structured web analytics questions, and volume has been the most discussed of the 3V's. However, this emphasis on volume has been biased by the industry in which it was applied—e-commerce (specifically web advertising)— and the use cases it was used to enable. As a result, many people think of large volumes of data as a synonym for big data. It is not the ability to process and manage large data volumes that are driving successful AI outcomes. Rather, it is the ability to integrate *more* sources of data to create more features that is more relevant in the AI context.

Variety in data includes "traditional" data sources such as transactional source systems, spreadsheets, EDWs/data marts/cubes, as well as newer sources that include semi- and unstructured data. In addition to sources, understanding variety requires analysis and profiling of:

- **Form/data types**. Numbers, text, graphs, video, audio, composite
- **Function**. User requirements, economic, and emotional drivers that drove data creation and use
- **Data fidelity**. Data quality *in the context of its usage and user*. Focuses on whether data as a whole is "fit for purpose," as opposed to merely profiling/fixing data quality (which is usually measured at the entity/attribute/relationship levels).

Velocity

Any solution must account for velocity in big data by addressing Data in Motion, where data are processed and analyzed instantaneously and with subsequent physical storage; and Data at Rest, where data are physically stored for different types of analytics or for regulatory purposes. Techniques for dealing with Data at Rest are well described elsewhere and are beyond the scope of this book. However, real-time analytics or real-time analytics feedback into workflows are relatively new, and hence, a short description here of the process may be useful for readers. In most scenarios, high-velocity data can have large implications on computing or storage requirements. From legal and regulatory perspectives, traceable data lineage must be available when raw data are used for real-time, decision support. Almost every use case requires signals to be separated from noise, and they must be validated by an appropriate human user prior to being used in workflows.

When don't you need high-velocity data management?

- When the application doesn't need it
- When there are easier ways of getting to data, for example, queued data (near real time), hourly batch, change data capture, etc.
- When cost of processing/analytics outweighs user benefits

For time-sensitive secondary uses, value is directly proportional to velocity and indirectly proportional to latency. Creating quicker time-to-value for patients and providers will require us to expand the use of streaming analytics, real-time decision support, and using secondary (annotated, derived, or extracted) data to enable analytics-driven workflows. For time-sensitive uses, stale data are poor-quality data.

Value and Veracity

It's useful to examine Value and Veracity, as they specifically influence the use of data in decisions that go beyond solution implications—i.e., good business practices, customer happiness, legal, compliance, health, life, or death.

Focusing on "what data needs to be" or "what data needs to do"—in addition to its essential defining characteristics—is foundational to understanding the role of data in AI applications, timely identification of solutions and architectures, determining appropriate governance models, achieving RoiI, and ensuring informed employees and users.

Value

Most often, data are inconsequential and minimally useful unless put to work. The value of data lies not in its existence or storage, but in how that data are put to use to improve business processes, workflows, and human/system behaviors. Therefore, value is defined as the usefulness of data for business or personal purposes. The value of data must be measured via appropriate quantitative and qualitative metrics, and secondary uses of AI, such as data sharing, collaboration, monetization, and data-driven workflows, must also be measured as we determine the immediate and incremental value of data and AI efforts.

While organizations keep value in mind for their primary and secondary data uses today, the coming existence of external data from beyond the organization's four walls will require us to measure achievable value on an ongoing basis. A framework for calculating the lifetime value of data must be broad enough to address the benefits to users, employees, financial performance, and customer engagement. Such a metric (or more likely, a KPI composed of constituent metrics) could also address value as determined by:

- Impact via measurable human and process outcomes
- Behavioral analysis and modification
- Impact on business processes and workflows (time saved, steps reduced, etc.)
- Number of users served "on demand" with relevant information
- Individual and organization progress in treating analytics as an asset, including improved data governance, quality, and fidelity
- Monetization (financial value of de-identified data, new product development, and value of integrating institutional and consumer data)

Veracity

The influence of data quality is an enduring one in the enterprise as the quality of insights and pattern recognition via AI is only as good as the data that are used as fuel. Hence, it is important to examine the role of veracity. Veracity in data is more than data quality, and practical considerations dictate that we examine the role of data fidelity.

Reasons for poor data quality can include:

- **Data entry**. Did the user enter the information correctly at the originating source? Are there any system errors?
- **Squatting**. Are two objects identified correctly to be the same or different based on semantics and structure? Does this same field in the source or target contain different types of data?

- **Data management**. Was the integrity of the information maintained during write/retrieval/movement through the system?
- **Integration quality**. Is all the known information about a data element referenced to appropriate master and dependent data, de-duplicated, and integrated with other data sources?
- **Staleness**. Have the data aged enough that their validity is no longer relevant or trusted? Are data past their best-by and use-by dates for business or personal use?
- **Usage**. Is the information aggregated, transformed, and interpreted correctly at presentation? Are the data used as expected to achieve known business goals?

Data quality in warehousing and BI is typically defined in terms of the 4 C's—are the data clean, correct, consistent, and complete? However, to err is human. Perfect data quality in human-created/managed data is very difficult or very costly to achieve in reality. Human data creation is context sensitive. What's appropriate for data entry and specific business processes may not be consistent or accurate enough for AI and analytics use cases.

Data Fidelity over Data Quality

Data fidelity is defined as data quality and validity in the context and appropriateness of its intended uses. Where appropriate, veracity of big data must be informed by data fidelity and not just "one-size-fits-all" data quality (measuring/ensuring adherence of source data to the 4 C's—cleanliness, correctness, consistency, completeness—and independent of <u>intended uses which can change per application and over time</u>). For example, certain secondary use cases (data discovery and some types of machine learning) don't require perfect data quality for every data attribute that exists in your data stores but only for the ones that are relevant to feature engineering.

Unlike traditional data quality management, data fidelity allows you to better-accepting data "as-is" and manage corrections to be based on the use case and user context than an upfront exercise that takes months/years across, especially across the span of an existing data warehouse or data lake. Learning algorithms improve as the amount of data increases, with little or no additional spend in human resources. As more data are fed into a machine-learning system, the more it can learn from the data and human feedback loops in order to identify appropriate patterns, self-correct, and refine insights.

You should invest in ensuring that data are of the highest fidelity using the best of human resources (use-case definition, data stewardship, governance/oversight, and approval), processes, and evolving options in machine learning (e.g., more accurate training models, labeled datasets, unsupervised machine learning, and human feedback loops). When forced to work with less than ideal data quality, strive for a state in which data fidelity improves continually as a result of analytics-driven workflows, learned user behaviors, and learning algorithms.

While it's beyond the scope of this book to examine data architectures in detail, it's useful to understand some definitions.

- Schema on Write. Data in a warehouse are loaded based on semantics and structure and is validated based on pre-defined logical and physical data models.

- Schema on Read. In a data lake, we load the raw data, as is—warts, blemishes, and all. When the data are ready to be used, we apply a data model or interface/API on it to provide semantics and structure.

In our world of AI usage, there will always be a need for both schema types. Existing source systems and analytics will stay and thrive—just as new data sources will come into existence requiring new BI, advanced analytics, and AI-ML. The data warehouse and the data lake will need to coexist, as newer technologies such as data virtualization will allow you to create federated data strategies and architectures.

In summary:

- Data lakes/data mesh/data fabrics are flexible and useful. However, they are only one component of a data management solution.
- Data lakes are not in situ replacements of your existing data warehouse (DW) or data marts. Use the lake to supplement your DW—establish bidirectional relationships between these stores—and combine little and big data.
- The DW provides important context via little data, historical and versioned data, and serves as a lodestone that establishes semantics and governance beyond any single source/department silo.
- The cure for the difficulties in managing a data warehouse is not a data swamp. In reality, for data in a lake to be usable for AI, it needs to be organized, governed, curated, and well understood and trusted by users and domain experts alike.

Conclusions

The key to success with AI is to treat it as a fundamental capability in business strategy and operations. Digital-first organizations succeed by making AI strategic and symbiotic. In other words, AI is an integral part of our normal business processes, operations, growth, and revenue. It is embedded into our workflows, culture, employee development and personalized understanding of our customers, The path to success lies in treating AI as a core competence that drives amplification and augmentation.

AI is not a widget, a software tool, an infrastructure deployment, or a application-specific black box. In order to get the most out of AI and to drive business outcomes and digital transformation at scale, enterprises must involve their business users and leaders into opportunity identification, product and solution development, outcomes, and insights Merely treating AI as a technology that is driven by data science, analytics, data, or IT teams is the surest way to underwhelming success and failure.

Executives and business/technology leaders must recognize that the applications and uses of AI in the modern enterprise are — and will remain—human endeavors. Upskilling teams and individuals to understand AI, use it in normal decision making, and learning how to make AI deliverables usable, sticky, and successful are essential to success across the entire enterprise.

The IMPACT framework recognizes these different drivers and provides validated and clear signposts to drive excellence with AI in your enterprise. Imagination;

assessing and increasing maturity; people and staffing models; augmentation, amplification, and automation; culture; and transformation are key to lasting success with AI.

In the following chapters, we will examine specific examples and use cases from horizontal enterprise functions such as retail, financial services, insurance, customer experience, supply chain management, and human resources/talent management. We also look at successful case studies from diverse vertical industries to further demystify AI from business, leadership, and nontechnical lenses. Our hope is that this book will provide you with the knowledge, validated best practices, and lessons from our experience so that you can be armed with the knowledge and best practices to out the IMPACT framework into practice.

Notes

1 Sternberg, R. J. 2020. "Human intelligence." Encyclopedia Britannica. December 10, 2020. Available at https://www.britannica.com/science/human-intelligence-psychology.

2 Merriam-Webster.com Dictionary. n.d. "Artificial Intelligence." Updated September 29, 2021. Available at https://www.merriam-webster.com/dictionary/artificial%20intelligence.

3 Prashant Natarajan, Smaltz, Detlev H., and John C. Frenzel. 2017. *Demystifying Big Data and Machine Learning for Healthcare*. 1st ed. Boca Raton, FL: CRC Press.

4 Reeves, Martin and Jack Fuller. 2020. "We Need Imagination Now More Than Ever." Harvard Business Review. April 10, 2020. Available at https://hbr.org/2020/04/we-need-imagination-now-more-than-ever.

5 Tom Davenport et al. 2019. "Analytics and AI-Driven Enterprises Thrive in the Age of With." Deloitte Insights. July 25, 2019. Available at https://www2.deloitte.com/us/en/insights/topics/analytics/insight-driven-organization.html.

6 Fountaine, Tim, Brian McCarthy, and Tamim Saleh. 2020. "Building the AI-Powered Organization." Harvard Business Review. June 1, 2020. Available at https://hbr.org/2019/07/building-the-ai-powered-organization.

7 Prashant Natarajan, Smaltz, Detlev H., and John C. Frenzel. 2017. *Demystifying Big Data and Machine Learning for Healthcare*. 1st ed. Boca Raton, FL: CRC Press.

8 Wilson, H. James, and Paul R. Daugherty. 2019. "Creating the Symbiotic AI Workforce of the Future." MIT Sloan Management Review. October 21, 2019. Available at https://sloanreview.mit.edu/article/creating-the-symbiotic-ai-workforce-of-the-future/.

9 Prashant Natarajan, Smaltz, Detlev H., and John C. Frenzel. 2017. *Demystifying Big Data and Machine Learning for Healthcare*. 1st ed. Boca Raton, FL: CRC Press.

10 Dastin, Jeffrey. 2018. "Amazon Scraps Secret AI Recruiting Tool That Showed Bias Against Women." ed. Jonathan Weber and Marla Dickerson. Reuters. October 10, 2018. Available at https://www.reuters.com/article/us-amazon-com-jobs-automation-insight-idUSKCN1MK08G.

11 Prashant Natarajan. 2016. "A Tale of 2 T's: When Analytics and Artificial Intelligence Go Bad: Healthcare It Today." Healthcare IT Today|Fresh, Daily, Practical Healthcare IT Insights. July 13, 2016. Available at https://www.healthcareittoday.com/2016/07/13/a-tale-of-2-ts-when-analytics-and-artificial-intelligence-go-bad/.

12 Fountaine, Tim, Brian McCarthy, and Tamim Saleh. 2019. "Building the AI-Powered Organization." Harvard Business Review. Updated June 1, 2020. Available at https://hbr.org/2019/07/building-the-ai-powered-organization.

13 Thibodeau, Patrick. "Chief Data Officer May Go the Way of Chief Electricity Officer." Computerworld. August 25, 2014. Available at https://www.computerworld.com/article/2598530/chief-data-officer-may-go-the-way-of-chief-electricity-officer.html.

14 Prashant Natarajan, Smaltz, Detlev H., and John C. Frenzel. 2017. *Demystifying Big Data and Machine Learning for Healthcare*. 1st ed. Boca Raton, FL: CRC Press.

15 Prashant Natarajan, Smaltz, Detlev H., and John C. Frenzel. 2017. *Demystifying Big Data and Machine Learning for Healthcare*. 1st ed. Boca Raton, FL: CRC Press.

Chapter 2

Learning Algorithms, Machine/Deep Learning, and Applied AI: A Conceptual Framework

Prashant Natarajan
H2O.ai

Bob Rogers
UCSF Center for Digital Health Innovation
Oii Incorporated
Harvard University IACS

Contents

DOI: 10.4324/9781351032940-2

Introduction

Collecting, managing, and storing data (big or little; structured or unstructured) is a costly exercise if we can't convert such data into high-value, actionable insights or influence workflows in a timely fashion. Generating knowledge from data increasingly requires the use of machine learning for various reasons—cognitive, organizational, technical, and operational. Any discussion on data must include a corresponding discussion on machine learning (ML); frankly, they cannot be separated anymore.

In order to obtain the most value of out of large, diverse, and fast data, we need to consider options beyond rules-based deductive reasoning, "traditional" systems engineering, and descriptive analytics. Artificial intelligence, specifically the subfields of machine and deep learning, provides optimal and cost-effective options to expand the universe of knowledge and solutions for the enterprise. Machine learning enables new use cases by:

■ Ameliorating the effects of certain human limitations—cognitive (repetitive accuracy, human limitations, and information overload), physical (fatigue), and emotional (mood, human biases, etc.)

■ Enabling new knowledge creation or data reduction via learning and prediction

■ Finding hidden patterns/insights that are not visible

■ Processing repetitive data management tasks more efficiently, consistently, and with greater performance

■ Serving as the foundation for workflows and secondary uses of data via analytics, intelligent search, speech and text Natural Language Processing (NLP), and computer vision

Chapter Overview

While there are a plethora of books, videos, websites, and other resources on machine learning, most content is either too generic or, on the other end of the spectrum, requires an advanced understanding of linear algebra, probability, statistics, and/or computer science. In addition, there appears to be a paucity of resources on applied machine learning—in which learning algorithms, data sets, and best practices are optimized for and applied in a specific domain/industry/vertical or across horizontal uses. As with any emerging technology, ensuring the successful design/deployment and "production" use of machine learning requires knowledge that enables you to connect theory to practice and convert general principles into domain-specific applications.

If you are interested in learning more about this exciting field, or just want a better understanding of the truth behind the hype of "how <<Brand X>> <<machine/deep learning>> can cure <<problem 1>>," then this chapter is for you.

A Brief History of AI-ML

AI and machine learning (abbreviated henceforth as, AI-ML) are not new topics. They have been researched, argued over, and used by computer scientists, applied linguists, engineers, etc. for more than 70 years. The mathematical foundations of ML are rooted in algebra, statistics, and probability developed over the last 2000 years. However, modern development of AI and ML in the 1950s and '60s began with the works of Alan Turing, John McCarthy, Arthur Samuels, Alan Newell, and Frank Rosenblatt, among others.

Samuel's self-learning and optimizing Checkers program is recognized as the first working instance of an ML system. Rosenblatt was instrumental in creating the Perceptron, a learning algorithm inspired by biological neurons that became the basis for the field of artificial neural networks, which we will touch upon later in this chapter. "Feigenbaum and others advocated the case for building expert systems— knowledge repositories tailored for specialized domains such as chemistry and medical diagnosis."

In the 1990s, research on ML moved from knowledge-engineering-based expert systems to statistical and data-driven approaches. The subsequent time period saw the refinement of backpropagation ("the workhorse algorithm of learning in neural networks") as also the development of the precursors of what we call "Deep Learning" today by Hinton and others. A more in-depth history of ML is beyond the scope of this chapter. However, interested readers will find the rest of this book to be chockful of practical business vertical and horizontal applications of AI-ML.

What's Different about AI-ML Today?

After many fits and starts over the past decades, ML has come out of the hibernation that happened during the "AI winter" that followed the last hype cycle in the 1980s and '90s. ML is also no longer a knowledge-engineering effort as it once was. It's been redefined and optimized to be data intensive instead, hence its appropriateness to handle all types of data. Today, ML (and for that matter, deep learning) is maturing to a point where targeted applications are practical and real. There is increasing business and user demand, and AI-ML is here to stay.

AI-ML is ready for prime time for the following reasons:

■ Moore's Law. Continuing advances in computing and storage are allowing us to store and process very large data sets in a cost-effective and scalable manner.
■ Availability of more data. ML is primarily a data-driven endeavor. As a result, the creation/availability of large data sets coupled with the ability to share/

transport such data are allowing us to get further than ever before in predicting or determining new knowledge.

■ New sources in native unstructured data formats. Several big-data sources are unstructured. ML is ideally suited and is rapidly evolving to better support the generation of insights and analytics directly off native formats such as videos, images, voice, and large un- or semi-structured text (Table 2.1).

We interact with AI-ML on a daily basis; examples include self-driving cars, email spam filters, Netflix movie suggestions, Amazon shopping recommendations, social media, and postal-code–based mail sorting using handwriting recognition. ML applications are rapidly being deployed and used in the commercial space across diverse verticals—retail and e-commerce, government, finance, healthcare, insurance, transportation, agriculture, space exploration, and manufacturing, among many horizontals (HR/talent management, supply chain, and finance).

Table 2.1 Typical Sources for Data

Data	Examples	Key Characteristics
Images	Geospatial images Medical imaging Pictures of people, biological organisms, and things	Increasing use of digital imaging resulting in rapid evolution from terabytes to petabytes of data. Storage size requirements are high and directly proportional to number of images. Still expensive to share/manage/use, including with distributed computing. Use cases that emphasize pattern recognition, automated attribute extraction, and "just in time" data mining/analytics/integration can alleviate active storage requirements.
Un-/semi-structured text	Voice Large Text (Narratives, Contracts, Reports, other documents in varying formats) Spreadsheets Transcripts	Contributes to large volumes in any enterprise, even with the increased adoption of structured transactional systems. Storage requirements are lower than images - higher than structured-only data. Value not volume: raw text may require curation and integration with structured data based on the use case. Use cases that emphasize data exploration and discovery, pattern recognition, relationship analysis, and NLP can justify actively storing and managing large volumes of such data.

(Continued)

Table 2.1 (Continued)

Data	Examples	Key Characteristics
Streaming	IoT/IIoT Remote monitors Medical devices and implants Fitness bands and smartwatches Smartphones	Volumes may be low in terms of storage size; however, frequency of receipt/use could be very high. Data/metadata are usually highly structured Managing large volumes of streaming data must address filtering noise, redundant versions, and elimination of false positives. Becoming more pervasive, including in the developing world, as data capture, transmission, and storage costs are rapidly reducing. Use cases that emphasize observational data capture and analytics justify the costs of managing this big data.
Social Media	Facebook/Twitter/Instagram TikTok Web forums	Volumes of data can be large and in real time. Storage requirements will be large for enterprise deployments if use cases are not well defined. Data/metadata are usually unstructured text or images.
Structured Data	Transactional systems ■ Workflow systems ■ Finance ■ HR and Talent Management ■ Customer Relationship Management ■ Supply Chain Management	Volumes of data can be large based on historical data or number of sources. Storage requirements and data governance are intensive for mid-large for enterprise deployments. Represents little data that provides all-important context to big data. Data/metadata are usually structured—squatting, quality, and master data management remain challenges.
Dark Data	Business process data Server logs Application error logs Account information Emails Documents	Constitutes data sources of rich metadata that are already being stored in your environments. Volumes of data to be processed could vary from small to large depending on the type of data. Data is usually in a structured form but may not always be human friendly and may require a computer to pre-process first.

Note: Dark data is operational data that is collected by hardware and software systems during the course of normal business activity but finds limited use for business purposes.

What Is Machine Learning?

Arthur Samuel is credited with defining ML as the field of study that gives computers the ability to learn without being explicitly programmed. "Machine Learning is a paradigm that enables systems to automatically improve their performance at a task by observing relevant data."[1]

One useful perspective on machine learning is that it involves searching a very large space of possible hypotheses to determine one that best fits the observed data and any prior knowledge held by the learner.[2]

Indeed, ML has been the key contributor to the AI surge in the past few decades, ranging from search and product recommendation engines, to systems for speech recognition, fraud detection, image understanding, and countless other tasks that once relied on human skill and judgment.

As we will review in the next section, ML is different from traditional software programming due to its emphasis on:

- Learning algorithms versus "traditional" algorithms
- Reasoning that is primarily Induction and Abduction, with a selective use of Deduction
- Dealing with uncertainty and variability via the use of mathematical models that are driven by probability and statistics as compared to deterministic rules
- Prediction: using data you have to extrapolate data you don't have in order to infer probability of outcomes

How Do Machines Reason and Learn: A Crash Course in Learning Algorithms

A learning algorithm is an algorithm that is able to use all types of data and metadata to learn continuously and progressively. ML is different from traditional programming (see Figure 2.1). In ML, "we provide the input (data), the desired result, and out comes the [learning] algorithm."[3] Learning algorithms—also known as learners—are algorithms that create new knowledge or demonstrate new skills by learning from old (training data) and new (generalized) data. A learning algorithm uses data and experience to self-learn and to perform better over time. During the process, a learner also optimizes itself to progressively come up with better predictions (Figure 2.2).

Learners are the foundation of any ML system, and they help us achieve generalization via induction or abduction.

Generalization is making predictions (using the data you have to create data you don't have) and creating new knowledge and insights.

We will introduce two basic concepts here:

- Training Dataset (the data you have that is used as input to the learner to train the model), and
- Test Dataset (dataset that MUST NOT be the same as training data and that's used by the learner for validation and optimization).

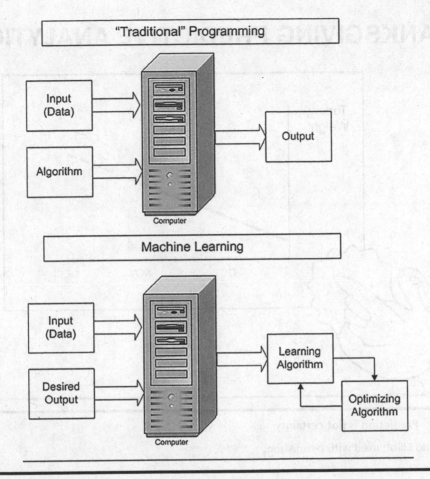

Figure 2.1   Traditional programming and machine learning: a comparison.

An ML system consists of the following basic components:

■ Learning and optimizing algorithms
■ Training and test datasets
■ Training model
■ Cost function

In summary, "a well-defined learning problem requires a well-specified task, T; performance metric, P; and source of training experience, E."[4] A formal (and personal favorite) definition of learning states, "A computer program is said to learn from experience E with respect to some class of tasks T and performance measure P if its performance at tasks in T, as measured by P, improves with experience E." (Table 2.2)[5]

THANKSGIVING PREDICTIVE ANALYTICS

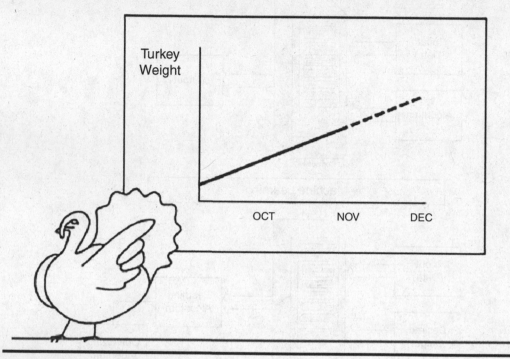

Figure 2.2   Prediction is not certainty.

Source: Timo Elliot; used with permission.

Table 2.2   Some Example Learning Problems

Example Learning Problem	Task T	Performance Measure P	Training Experience E
Learning Checkers	Playing checkers	% of games won against opponents	Learner playing practice games against itself
Handwriting recognition	Recognizing and classifying handwritten words within images	% of words correctly classified	Training dataset of handwritten words with given classifications
Self-driving car	Driving from Cupertino to Livermore on public roads	Average distance traveled before an error (as judged by a human overseer)	Sequence of videos, still images, and steering commands recorded while observing a human driver

Mastering the Basics of Machine Learning

Now that we've reviewed Mitchell's definition of ML, we can examine Tasks, Performance, and Experience in more detail.

Task, T

A *Task* is something that we want the ML system to do: "the process of learning itself is not the task. Learning is our means of attaining the ability to perform the task."[6] To illustrate further, a task for a self-driven car would be to make the journey autonomously from Peoria, Illinois, to Livermore, California. The learning algorithms and the rest of the ML system that the car uses to learn and recognize street signs, sidewalks, other vehicles, people, etc. constitute the means by which this task is completed successfully.

Examples of tasks that can be done by an ML system are classification, classification with missing inputs, regression, transcription, machine translation, structured output, anomaly detection, synthesis, density estimation, denoising, imputation of missing values, named entity recognition, etc.

In ML, a *Feature* is the combination of an attribute and its value. For instance, "Color is blue" is a feature, where color is the attribute and blue is the value. Another example: "The features of an image are usually the values of the pixels in the image."[7] Note that some authors prefer to use the terms Feature and Example as synonyms. An *Example* is defined as a collection of features that have been quantitatively measured from some object or event that we want the system to process." A *Task* is defined in terms of how the learning system should process an *Example*, and a *Dataset* is a collection of Examples.

In ML, we are very interested in understanding and addressing *Dimensionality*, which is defined as the number of features that contain most of the useful or actionable information, as well as *Parameters*, which are attribute values (of high-value features) that control the behavior of the learning system. Parameters are important, as they can be modified by the learning algorithm to determine better performance (accuracy) or contextualization of prediction. So, for example, the predicted sale price of a house may be impacted more by parameters such as nearness to school or number of bedrooms, rather than the type of roof shingles or color of exterior paint.

With data, it has become easier to collect/store/manage data than to obsess over or minimize what is collected.

> We are in the era of massive automatic data collection, systematically obtaining many measurements, not knowing which ones will be relevant to the phenomenon of interest. Our task is to find a needle in a haystack, teasing the relevant information out of a vast pile of glut. This is a big break from the past, when it was assumed that one was dealing with a few well-chosen variables—for example, using scientific knowledge to measure just the right variables in advance.[8]

Understanding dimensions allows us to discuss *Dimensional Reduction*, which is reducing the number of features required in an example. Dimensional reduction refers to the algorithmic processes by which a dataset having high dimensions is converted into a dataset with fewer dimensions so that as much information as possible about the original data is preserved. This is done in ML to address what is known as Bellman's Curse of Dimensionality, in which

> many learning algorithms that work fine when the dimensions are low become intractable when the input is high-dimensional. But in ML [the curse] refers to much more. Generalizing correctly becomes exponentially harder as the dimensionality (number of features) of the examples grows.[9]
>
> Dimension reduction can be accomplished via *Feature Extraction* and *Feature Selection*. Feature extraction creates new features resulting from the combination of the original features; and feature selection produces a subset of the original features. Both attempt to reduce the dimensionality of a dataset in order to facilitate efficient data processing tasks.[10]
>
> Weights determine how each feature affects the prediction. If a feature receives a positive weight, then increasing the value of that feature increases the value of our prediction. If a feature receives a negative weight, increasing the value of that feature reduces the value of our prediction. If the weight is 0, there is no effect on prediction.[11]

One of the primary purposes of ML is for the system to perform on "unknown unknowns," or new, previously unseen data—not just the training dataset with which the model was trained. A good ML system generalizes well from the training dataset to any data from the problem domain. This allows the system to extrapolate and predict on "never seen before" data. Wilson explains further:

> Learning in backprop seems to operate by first of all getting a rough set of weights which fit the training patterns in a general sort of way, and then working progressively toward a set of weights that fit the training patterns exactly. If learning goes too far down this path, one may reach a set of weights that fits the idiosyncrasies of the particular set of patterns very well, but does not interpolate (i.e., generalize) well.[12]

"Generalization is the ability to perform well on previously unobserved inputs. Generalization Error (also called Test Error) is defined as the expected value of the error on a new input."[13]

Overfitting has significant impacts on the performance of the ML system. Overfitting happens when a learner mimics random fluctuations, anomalies, and noise in the training dataset, thus adversely impacting the performance of the system on new data." [W]ith large complex sets of training patterns, it is likely that some errors may occur, either in the inputs or in the outputs. In that case, it is likely that [the learner] will be contorting the weights so as to fit precisely around training patterns that are actually erroneous."[14]

Performance, P

In order to evaluate the abilities of an ML algorithm, we must design a quantitative measure of its *Performance, P*. Performance is usually measured on the task being carried out by the ML system and is typically measured in terms of *Accuracy*, which is the proportion of examples for which the model produces the correct output, or *Error Rate*, which is the proportion of examples for which the model produces the incorrect output.

We conclude our brief discussion on performance by reviewing *Noise*, which in ML refers to

> errors in the training data for ML algorithms. If a problem is difficult enough and complicated enough to be worth doing with ML techniques, then any reasonable training set is going to be large enough that there are likely to be errors in it. This will of course cause problems for the learning algorithm.[15]

Experience, E

Experience in ML is primarily determined by the amount of supervision (during the learning process) and the availability of labeled data in the dataset.

In *Supervised Learning*, algorithms are designed to learn using labeled training datasets. Supervised learning is

> a kind of ML where the learning algorithm is provided with a set of inputs for the algorithm along with the corresponding correct outputs, and learning involves the algorithm comparing its current actual output with the correct or target outputs, so that it knows what its error is, and modify [sic] things accordingly.[16]

Input data is labeled based on existing knowledge (for example, is the email in the training dataset 'spam' or 'not-spam?') The model continues to train until it achieves a desired level of performance on the training dataset, and the training model is then fed new and unknown data, as described earlier.

In Unsupervised Learning, input data is not labeled, and furthermore,

> the system is not told the 'right answer'—for example, it is not trained on pairs consisting of an input and the desired output. Instead, the system is given the input patterns and is left to find interesting patterns, regularities, or clusterings among them.[17]

30

In Semi-Supervised Learning, as the experience suggests, input data may be only partially labeled, and the expected results may or may not be known. The ML system will include both supervised and unsupervised learners.

Active Learning is a semi-supervised learning experience in which "the model chooses by itself what unlabeled data would be most informative for it, and asks an external 'oracle' (for example, a human annotator) for a label for the new data points."[18] The learner aims to "achieve high accuracy using as few labeled instances as possible, thereby minimizing the cost of obtaining labeled data."[19]

Deep Learning is a type of ML experience that uses learning algorithms called artificial neural networks that attempt to simulate or replicate the functioning of the human brain. Think of deep neural networks as "ANNs with lotsa depth."[20] Before we review deep learning, let's take a quick look at artificial neural networks and understand why they serve as a basis for understanding what deep learning does.

Artificial Neural Networks: An Overview

■ Biological neuron.

From the artificial neural network point of view, a biological neuron operates as follows: electrical pulses from other neurons cause the transfer of substances called neurotransmitters (of which there are several varieties) from the synaptic terminals of a neuron's axon (think "output") across a structure called a synapse to the dendrites of other neurons (call them downstream neurons). The arrival of the neurotransmitter in the dendrite of the downstream neuron increases the tendency of the downstream neuron to send an electrical pulse itself ("fire"). If enough dendrites of a neuron receive neurotransmitters in a short enough period of time, the neuron will fire.[21]

■ Artificial neuron.

A simple model of a biological neuron used in neural networks to perform a small part of some overall computational problem. It has inputs from other neurons, with each of which is associated a weight—that is, a number which indicates the degree of importance which this neuron attaches to that input.[22]

■ Artificial neural network.

An artificial neural network is a collection of simple artificial neurons connected by directed weighted connections. When the system is set running, the activation levels of the input units is clamped to desired values. After this the activation is propagated, at each time step, along the directed weighted connections to other units. The activations of non-input neurons are computed using each neuron's activation function. The system might either settle into a stable state after a number of time steps, or in the case of a feed-forward network, the activation might flow through to output units. Learning might or might not occur, depending on the type of neural network and the mode of operation of the network.[23]

Deep Learning

Deep learning is a specific kind of ML. In order to understand deep learning, one must begin with a solid understanding of the basic principles of ML. Deep learning is a "kind of learning where the representations you form have several levels of abstraction, rather than a direct input to output."[24] Think of "deep" in deep learning as having many more layers (or Depth) than were possible with ANNs and as the ability to deal with very large datasets due to Moore's law and data availability. The principle driving deep learning is "guiding the training of intermediate levels of representation using unsupervised learning, which can be performed locally at each level."[25]

Deep learning particularly does well on sequential, unstructured, or analog data such as images, audio, and video and is becoming very popular today due to its high performance.

> Deep Learning discovers intricate structure in large data sets by using the backpropagation algorithm to indicate how a machine should change its internal parameters that are used to compute the representation in each layer from the representation in the previous layer.[26]

Deep learning currently excels at supervised learning. However, we see as much or greater potential for using deep learning in unsupervised learning, primarily because large datasets contain greater amounts of unlabeled data that require labeling, which is time-, effort-, and cost-intensive and prone to human labeler inconsistencies and errors.

Let's discuss some types of deep neural nets, including *Feed Forward Neural Networks*; *Recurrent Neural Networks*; *Convolutional Neural Networks*; and *Reinforcement Neural Networks*.

- **Feed Forward Neural Networks**.

> A kind of neural network in which the nodes can be numbered, in such a way that each node has weighted connections only to nodes with higher numbers. [...] In practice, the nodes of most feedforward nets are partitioned into layers—that is, sets of nodes, and the layers may be numbered in such a way that the nodes in each layer are connected only to nodes in the next layer. The first layer has no input connections and is termed the input layer. The last layer has no output connections and is termed the output layer. The layers in between the input and output layers are termed hidden layers, and consist of hidden units.[27]

- **Recurrent Neural Network**. Sequence-based neural networks that play a key role in natural language processing, machine translation, video processing, and many other tasks.

> The idea behind RNNs is to make use of sequential information. In a traditional neural network, we assume that all inputs (and outputs) are independent of each other. But for many tasks that's a very bad idea. If you want to predict the next word in a sentence you better know which words came before it. RNNs are called recurrent because they perform the same task for every element of a sequence, with the output being depende[nt] on the previous computations. RNNs [...] have a 'memory' which captures information about what has been calculated so far.[28]

- **Convolutional Neural Networks**. A "type of feed-forward artificial neural network in which the connectivity pattern between its neurons is inspired by the organization of the animal visual cortex."[44] CNNs excel at dealing with sequential, analog, or unstructured data and are showing great promise in healthcare—particularly in image/audio/video recognition, recommender systems, and natural language processing. The model is made of a "recursive application of convolution and pooling layers, followed by simple NNs. A convolution layer is a linear transformation that preserves spatial information in the input image. Pooling layers simply take the output of a convolution layer and reduce its dimensionality."[29] An excellent example of how deep learning and CNNs are being used in healthcare is the work being done by Pratik Mukherjee MD and his team at UCSF.

- **Reinforcement Neural Networks**. Neural networks in which the learner learns and performs tasks via trial and error, much like a child learning to ride her bicycle. "In a sense, RNNs are the deepest of all neural networks [...] that can create and process memories of arbitrary sequences of input patterns."[30]

A Guided Tour of Learning Algorithms

Every ML algorithm is good at answering a specific kind of question. Let's take a look at some of the most important algorithms and the questions they are being used to answer.

Don't be intimidated by the sheer number of ML algorithms that are out there. While there are countless ML algorithm implementations out there, all of them are really variations on a few major themes.

The list of algorithms described below is not exhaustive. Our goal has been to give examples of the most commonly used methods to answer different types of question in the enterprise. In addition to the type of question being answered, there is another useful way to characterize ML algorithms: Whether or not they need input data that is labeled with known answers to create them. Methods that require input data with known labels are called "supervised training" algorithms, and those that do not require any prior knowledge of what answers are expected are called "unsupervised." The majority of the algorithms below are supervised learning algorithms. We indicate the unsupervised learning algorithms with an asterisk (*).

Classifier: Does data belong to class A?
Example: Is this a legitimate transaction?

- **Logistic regression**: Logistic regression is the workhorse of classifiers. It is a linear classifier, which means it uses a single, straight cut to divide the world of possible features into two groups. If a patient's characteristics fall on one side of this cut, they are in class A (e.g., they are judged to have heart failure), otherwise they are *not* in class A. In problems with many features (some problems can require millions of features), logistic regression is the preferred method because it works well and is straightforward to compute.
- **Support Vector Machine (SVM)**: SVM is a linear classifier with a twist: The world of possible features is split by a single line as in logistic regression, but this line can be curved. This additional flexibility makes SVM highly adaptable, but because of the way the curvature is introduced (though something called a "kernel") they are still simple to compute and to interpret.

- **Decision tree, random forest, boosted trees**: Trees and forests are an entire family of algorithms, all based on the idea of creating a tree of decisions about features that lead to a specific classification. For example, to identify heart failure, the algorithm may start with ejection fraction. Is ejection fraction above or below 50? For each of these paths, a new question would be considered, such as, "Does the echocardiogram show Left Ventricle Hypertrophy?" At the end of each series of questions, the patient either falls into a "heart failure" or "not heart failure" bucket. Random forests improve upon decision trees by dividing the input data into many different subsets and creating a different decision tree for each of these subsets. All of the different resulting decision trees then vote to determine the final classification of the input. This process reduces the risk of making the final buckets too small and subsequently being fooled by random variations in the original labeled training data. Boosting is a trick for creating decision trees and random forests that can significantly improve their ability to generalize from example data. We call them out specifically here because boosted tree classifiers tend to be among the best-performing algorithms in public classification competitions such as Kaggle (www.kaggle.com).
- **Deep Learning**: Deep learning, and indeed neural networks in general, can take raw data as input and produce a class (or a vector of probabilities for many classes) as output. All neural network models consist of multiple layers of "neurons": Each neuron in a layer receives the outputs of neurons in previous layers, combines these inputs and uses a threshold to determine whether to output a value closer to 0 or closer to 1 for processing by the next layer. Deep learning algorithms are unique in their ability to automatically generate features of interest in input data, as long as they are provided with sufficiently many training examples (usually in the millions).
  - Deep learning in the form of Convolutional Neural Networks (CNNs) is already extensively used in image and video understanding in all domains, and it is commonplace to use one of the many CNNs available on the Internet for classifying images and answering classification questions about their contents.
  - Encoder-Decoder Semantic Segmentation algorithms, also members of the Deep Learning family, are used extensively in segmentation, in which each pixel of an image is identified as being part of a number of different types of object. The result is that different objects in the image are labeled with accurate borders, rather than just a bounding box. The UNET is an oft-used example of a Deep Learning segmentation algorithm.
  - Instance Segmentation takes semantic segmentation one step further to identify each specific instance of an object in an image. For example, instead of just identifying where five people in a photo are, these algorithms can label each individual and track them in a video. Mask R-CNN is an example of an instance segmentation algorithm.

Common uses: Classifiers are the most commonly used ML algorithms in all analytics applications. Classifiers are used to:

- Identify products on store shelves or in customer carts
- Identify fraudulent or suspicious transactions

- Determine which candidates for a role are qualified
- Identify the action taking place in a video
- Recognize defective manufactured parts
- Organize customers into groups to better serve or reach them
- Many, many more

Memory-based Learning*: How does this new piece of data compare to past data? Example: Who are the customers most like this customer?

- **Associative memory**: An associative memory system compares incoming data with past data to identify what the new data most like. The comparison can be based on any subset of the attributes of the data, so no assumptions need to be made about what is "important" in the data, and very large numbers of features can be included. This makes these algorithms especially useful in marketing applications, since the number of attributes and measurements that *could be* applicable to a customer is very large.

  Common uses: Memory-based learning can be used to

- Create cohorts of customers to compare a specific patient with. This is the "customers like me" question that plays a role in product suggestions, communication, and many other marketing activities
- Identify insurance fraud

Topic Modeling: What is this document about? Example: What topics are being discussed in these emails?

- **Latent Dirichlet Allocation (LDA)**: LDA assumes that content is made up of a combination of underlying topics. A single document may be 80% about an upcoming deal and 20% about a competitor challenge. LDA can identify the combinations of terms and phrases that make up the underlying topics. LDA can be applied to many different sources of information, from single documents to groups of documents.
- **Probabilistic Latent Semantic Analysis (pLSA), Latent Semantic Analysis (LSA)**: These algorithms are similar to LDA but make stricter simplifying assumptions about how topics are distributed in documents and how words are distributed in topics. With modern computing and large datasets available for analysis, these assumptions are no longer necessary, so LDA is the dominant methodology.

Common uses:

- Reliably identify the topics covered in documents for:
  - Legal discovery
  - Customer care
  - Regulatory review
  - Assimilation and indexing of research documents

Forecasting: How much will this time series change in the next time period? Example: How likely are sales to be 10% above forecast?

- **Linear regression***: Draws a straight line through the time series of past data, assuming that the current linear trend will continue. This approach requires that the predicted output is a continuous variable.
- **Neural networks***: A neural network, which can be as simple as a Multi-layer Perceptron (MLP) or as complex as a recurrent deep learning model (e.g., LSTM), takes past values as inputs and produces the predicted next value as output. All neural network models consist of multiple layers of "neurons": Each neuron in a layer receives the outputs of neurons in previous layers, and combines these inputs and uses a threshold to determine whether to output a value closer to 0 or closer to 1 for processing by the next layer.
- **Exponential smoothing***: This is a simple, but surprisingly useful, method for predicting the next value in a time series based on a weighted average of the most recent past values. It gives the most weight to the most recent measured value, then reduces the weight by multiplying by a number between 0 and 1 for each subsequent previous value, resulting in an exponential decrease in the impacts of older previous time series values.
- **Auto-regressive Integrated Moving Average (ARIMA) modeling***: This is a general group of forecasting methods (of which exponential smoothing is actually a member) that uses weighted averages of past time series values, past differences between time series values, past differences between rates of change of past values, and so on, to calculate future values of the time series.
- **Gaussian Processes/Bayes Methods***: These methods find a family of curves that might represent different ways a time series can play out and then condition them on the observed data, resulting in a forecast that gives an expected value in the future, and importantly, also a range of other possible outcomes and their probabilities. Such probability information is very valuable in assessing future risk.

Common uses: The expected next value of a time series is often used as part of a larger predictive modeling application. For example,

- Sales forecasts are time series predictions
- Lifetime value of a customer is a prediction of future transactions
- Almost all trading activities have forecasting at their core

Probability Estimation: What is the most likely interpretation of the data? Example: What is the most *likely* failure rate of a part, given a series of observations?

- **Probabilistic Graph Model (PGM)**: PGM algorithms, such as Bayes networks, identify key observations, measurements, and outcomes and link them together to identify causal relationships. Each of these factors would be represented as a node in a graph, with connections between nodes indicating causal relationships. These graphs can be learned directly from data or constructed by human experts. The PGM algorithm then uses actual data to determine the amount of influence each combination of variables (nodes) has on the others.

■ **Logistic regression**: Logistic regression models assume that the log of the odds of an event occurring (or an interpretation being applicable) can be calculated from a simple weighted average of a set of observations. In practice, this means that they can be used to predict the likelihoods of categorical values such as outcomes or class assignments.

Common uses: Fraud detection, statistical quality control, root cause inference

■ Root cause inference: For example, a model for identifying the sources of stock-outs in a supply chain might include historical information such as past delivery performance and inventories, current conditions such as weather, temperature, and news (for example a workers' strike), along with complexity in the network and connections to other supply chains (for example for products that depend on similar raw materials). Each of these factors would be represented as a node in the graph, with connections between nodes indicating a causal relationship. The presence or absence of a combination of these factors will influence the probability that a particular factor is primarily responsible for the stockout.

■ Risk forecasting: The likelihood that an individual or partner will be creditworthy in the future is a typical application.

Image and video understanding: What is in this image? What is happening in this video?

Example: Is there a defect in this x-ray of a part?

■ **Deep learning**: Deep learning systems, especially convolutional neural networks (CNNs), are very powerful methods to recognizing objects or patterns in complex images. The power of deep learning algorithms is that, given enough data, they can learn what is important for understanding an image without being explicitly told. In practice, to recognize a cat in a photo, a nodule in a chest x-ray, or a defect in an image of a part, a deep learning system may need to be shown millions of images, each labeled with the desired answer for that image. This training process can be very computationally intensive, and require long times to complete (hours, days, and even weeks), but once the algorithm is trained, then it can be easily used to quickly recognize the objects it has been taught, a process called "inference" or "scoring." Note that recent advances in techniques to automatically create labeled training data have really decreased the dependency of Deep Learning methods on human-labeled data.

A few of the many applications of computer vision: This area is exploding right now. At the time of writing, there are compelling deep learning results being developed for:

■ Automated identification of almost anything in an image or video.
■ Tracking of objects in video, which is highly relevant to applications like robotics, autonomous vehicles, and security.
■ Recognition of document types and contents.

- Literally any application that can benefit from information in images or video can be developed easily now, using pretrained deep learning models which can be downloaded from the Internet, making much of computer and machine vision a commodity.

Speech to text: What is the transcribed text for this audio stream?
  Example: What did the customer ask for?

- **Hidden Markov Models (HMM)**: HMMs assume that there are underlying processes that we can't see, but which are nonetheless consistent and predictable, that create outputs that we can see. For example, in a sentence, if the word "mellitus" is detected, the previous word is far more likely to be "diabetes" than it is to be "disabilities." This is very valuable in speech-to-text processing, since it is not possible to clearly hear or identify each word in an audio stream. The HMM can help choose the right interpretation of the sounds to result in the correct overall transcription. HMM has been used historically in a number of commercial dictation transcription systems.
- **Long Short-Term Memory (LSTM)**: LSTM models are members of the Deep Learning family, like the Convolutional Neural Networks described above, and as such can automatically learn what attributes of an audio stream are important for predicting what words it represents. Given sufficient data, which is readily available to online service providers such as Google and Baidu, it is possible to train LSTM models to very accurately convert spoken language into text, in almost any language.
- **Attention-based Deep Learning Models**: A new class of deep learning method based on the concept of attention has become very important in speech-to-text and other natural language understanding problems. These methods have the ability to "remember" the context of a word or sentence for much more than just a few words back, enabling them to assign higher impact to words of higher importance. This technology has become the state of the art for spoken language understanding applications and will likely play an increasing role in clinical transcription applications.

Common uses:

- Dictation systems
- Conversational systems for many applications, including customer care
- Machine translation for near-real-time translation of speech from one language to another
- Voice controls for computer systems and machinery
- Call center resources and agent coaching to help call center operators provide appropriate information and resources to customers

Recommender Systems: What was the behavior of other people like you?
  Example: What product is this customer most likely to buy next?

- **Collaborative filtering**: Collaborative filtering includes several different methods for predicting a user's rating for a specific item given the user's history of ratings for other items, combined with the history of all users' ratings for all items. Intuitively, if a user rates an item highly, then they are likely to give a high rating to a very similar item. For marketing, users could be customers, items could be products and ratings could be likelihood of a purchase.

- **Memory-based learning**: Memory-based learning systems, such as Saffron, compute the difference between a new data point and previously seen data, for a number of different contexts. When the new data is near previous data, it is possible to predict the outcome based on what happened in the past. These systems tend to learn continuously on an ongoing basis as they are exposed to more data, and they can be used to reason on very complex data.
- **Association rules**: Association rules are a data mining method in which algorithms use historical data to identify items or events that commonly occur together.

Common uses:

- Matching customers with products and services
- Detecting fraudulent insurance claims
- Call center optimization and customer experience

Clustering: Can the data be grouped into natural categories or buckets?
  Example: Are there natural groupings that can help me understand my customers?

- **Unsupervised Clustering***: Unsupervised clustering algorithms, such as K-Means, can automatically identify naturally occurring groups of similar items. Typically, the algorithm is given a set of attributes for each item (for example, diagnoses and lab measurements for each patient) and a number of clusters to create. The algorithm will then work out which combinations of attributes most accurately divide the items into that number of groups. The resulting "clusters" can usually be interpreted by humans by looking at which attributes are most important in the cluster.
- **Hierarchical clustering***: This family of methods creates a tree or dendogram of clustering scenarios for data, creating a single cluster containing all the items, which then splits into two clusters, each of which further splits into two clusters, and so on until each "cluster" contains only a single item. Based on the problem under consideration, this process can be stopped at any point to create meaningful clusters.

Common uses:

- Customers like me: To sell effectively to customers, it is valuable to understand how different communications have worked with customers in similar situations, but this information is only useful if the past customers are similar enough to the current customer to have predictive value. Clustering can be very useful to identify the most similar customers.
- Clustering algorithms can be used to track groups of objects in complex computer vision applications.

■ In Human Resources, it is often valuable to organize employees into groups of similar characteristics in order to better prioritize and deliver programs such as training.

Text understanding: What does this text mean?

Example: Is this a properly documented diagnosis of diabetes with peripheral neuropathy?

■ **Natural Language Processing (NLP)**: Natural language processing includes an extensive toolkit of different text processing tools and steps, combined with the goal of understanding the meaning or practical implications of a piece of text. In clinical text analysis, text understanding depends on being able to recognize distinctions between diagnoses attributed to a patient, those mentioned in a differential diagnosis, family history and negations ("patient does not have diabetes mellitus"). There are a number of open-source tools for general NLP and for clinical NLP that can be incorporated into application development. Full NLP analysis of text can be computationally expensive, both in terms of CPU cycles and memory required.

■ **Text mining**: Text mining is the application of extensive dictionaries of terms to identify occurrences of key terms in text such as clinical notes, consult letters, and discharge summaries. Text mining has the advantage of being able to recognize vast variations in terminology, including abbreviations, misspellings, regional variations in usage, and transcription errors from scanned documents (often using optical character recognition, or OCR). Text mining methods are often augmented with specific NLP tools to help understand the context of the terms that are identified in the text. For example, negation detection can be combined with search for diagnoses to help understand the difference between a positive statement of a diagnosis and a negative statement that a diagnosis does not apply.

■ **Deep learning**: As described above, deep learning has the ability to learn key features of data without explicit programming. In the case of text understanding, deep learning has begun to show value for identifying complex ideas in text and interpreting the implications of their context.

– **Transformer Models**: *There has been a revolution in Natural Language understanding with Deep Learning since about 2018.* Transformer Algorithms are changing the game for text analytics, and indeed many other areas of AI in which sequences are processed. These methods have several key attributes. First, they use attention mechanisms to identify which words in the input are most relevant to the processing of each other word in the input, and to each word in the output. Furthermore, the most successful transformers in text processing utilize multiple attention "heads," allowing them to pay attention based on a variety of factors. For example, one attention head might pay more attention to nearby words, and another to words further from the current word, or they may focus more on key terms. Think of how you might summarize a paragraph to different listeners (child, adult, expert, et cetera): Each attention head can be thought of as creating such a summary. The second key feature of transformers is that they take all of their input at once, rather than word by word. This allows them to do a lot of their processing in parallel, leading to the ability to accelerate training and inference using GPU computing accelerators. The significance is that powerful models trained on enormous corpora are now available, and these models can be modified for use in many applications beyond what they were originally trained for. This ability to apply transfer learning to text problems is completely new and revolutionary. (See BERT and related models.) The biggest challenge with transformers is that they can require a lot of computer memory when their input sequences are long. The quest to address this challenge has led to recent, more memory-friendly transformers such as Reformers and Longformers.

Common uses: Humans generate speech and text continually, so the ability for computers to "understand" the written word is transformational.

Examples of applications include:

- Computer translation
- Extraction of key facts from documents. This capability applies to almost every activity in the enterprise.
- Automated topic assignment and indexing of documents, from manuals, to emails, to research papers to social media articles.
- Voice control of computers, systems, and machinery
- Integration and interpretation of documents on the Internet, everything from tracking social media trends to supporting the prediction of supplier disruptions in supply chain management

Anomaly Detection: Have I seen this pattern before?

Example: Is there something wrong with this input data?

- **Clustering-based Anomaly Detection***: The definition of a "new" pattern is really a statement about how similar an observation is to past observations. The clustering algorithms described above (K-means, etc.) can be used to identify groups of similar patterns. When a pattern is not close to previously seen clusters, it can be flagged as an anomaly.
- **"OF" algorithms***: Overlapping with clustering-based anomaly detection algorithms are the Outlier Factor methods. These are generally based on comparing how densely data points are distributed around a new data point, compared with all the other data points. If a new observation is in a significantly less dense area than others, it is likely to be an outlier or anomaly.
- **Isolation Forest**: The idea with these algorithms is that they identify how hard it is to isolate a point from most of the other points, on a feature-by-feature basis.
- **One-class classifier***: In this method, a classifier (typically a Support Vector Machine) is trained on inliers only (that is normal points that are not considered outliers or anomalies). The algorithm creates a boundary around the normal points, and is penalized for including more space around the points than is needed. When testing a new point, if it is outside this boundary, it is considered an outlier.

- **Principal Components Analysis (PCA)***: PCA analysis identifies the minimum number of variables that are needed to describe data. Once these variables are computed, then each data point can be constructed from them with minimal error between the input data point and the PCA version of the data point. Anomalies do not fit the pattern of the PCA analysis and therefore have larger errors in their PCA versions, allowing us to automate the identification of anomalies.
- **Autoencoder***: Deep learning systems called autoencoders can be trained to reconstruct data they have seen from incomplete or noisy inputs. When they try to reconstruct data they haven't seen before, a noisy output is created that is generally quite different from the input. The error, which is the quantitative measure of this difference, will be high for patterns that haven't been seen before, providing us with an anomaly detection algorithm.

Common uses:

- Fraud detection. When a transaction or activity doesn't fit the normal pattern of activity, there is likely to be something wrong.
- Identification of data errors. Data flows into the enterprise through many paths and systems. When something goes wrong, it is critical for anomaly detection algorithms to be in place to flag these errors before they propagate too far into the system.
- Manufacturing flaws: Since it is not usually possible to define all the ways a part can fail during manufacturing, anomaly detection is critically important in manufacturing quality assurance.

Reinforcement Learning: What action should I take next?

Example: Can I defeat a human at the game Go?

Reinforcement Learning (RL) assumes that we want to construct an agent that takes actions in an environment to achieve a goal. For example, we want to defeat our competitor in the game of Go. The agent receives rewards or penalties as the result of each action, and over many trials the agent learns what the best action is for each situation. This learned strategy is known as the policy, and the core principle of RL is that it is possible to construct a mapping from states in the system to actions carried out by the agent in that system that optimizes the overall reward.

This is a powerful paradigm, because a policy can be very sophisticated, and can contain a tremendous amount of knowledge about how things might play out in the future, leading to very complex series of actions. Autonomous robotic systems that can carry out amazing series of detailed movements to complete a task are examples of such behavior.

There are many ways to construct a policy. Here, we will just highlight one, based on recent advances in deep learning:

- **Deep Q-Learning***: In Deep Q-Learning, a deep learning model is used to process the inputs from the system to recognize the state, and to encode the policy. For example, an early success in deep Q-Learning was the demonstration of a system that could win Atari video games. A convolutional neural network was used to view the screen and interpret what was being seen to determine the state of the environment (the video game itself), and then further neural network layers learned a policy to determine and output which action to take (right, left, jump, shoot, etc.) at any point in the game. By playing the game over and over, the neural system is able to build up a vast array of "strategies" for winning the game.

Common uses:

- Autonomous robotic systems
- Traffic light control systems
- Elevator control systems
- Network and computing resource optimization
- Complex process control, for example, optimizing chemical reactor outcomes
- Many more, including future applications in healthcare

Best Practices for Successful Machine Learning and AI Applications in Your Enterprise

Ask a Specific Question

Your ML algorithm should answer a very specific question that tells you something you need to know and that can be answered appropriately by the data you have access to. The best first question is something you already know the answer to, so that you have a reference and some intuition to compare your results with. Remember: you are solving a business problem, not a math problem. Ask yourself, "What valuable action will be taken as the result of my analytics?"

Analytics and artificial intelligence systems come in two flavors: (1) knowledge management systems that interpret questions and provide information to answer these questions, and (2) very targeted quantitative systems designed to provide information for a specific use case. Don't try to build both types of system in a single effort.

Start Simple

This is true for model selection and the data you consider using for your analysis. You want your results to be robust, so less model complexity and fewer parameters are always beneficial. Regarding data, don't start by building a huge data lake with every kind of data you could possibly get your hands on. Instead, start with the minimal set of data that could get you to a good result.

Try Many Algorithms

Most ML toolkits support multiple algorithms. Try a few to see how they work. This approach allows you to find the best tool for the job. Also, if one classifier works incredibly well and another doesn't seem to work well at all, be cautious. You may have an overfitting situation, which means you won't really have much predictive power. You may also want to combine methods: use deep learning to extract features from unstructured data and then use these features, along with others, in a classical ML algorithm to get interesting results.

Remember that data is more important than the exact algorithm you use. More training data is always desirable. In addition, for classical ML applications, the better your features, the better your performance will be.

Treat Your Data with Suspicion

Look at your data, dig into its details, look for correlations, suspicious gaps, systematic biases, errors, and flaws. Use statistics and visualizations here. Text has transcription errors, misspellings, and abbreviations. These challenges often exist for structured data as well: you will find that data is recorded inconsistently both across your data set and even within a single field.

Normalize Your Inputs

ML algorithms can perform poorly if there are large differences in scale between different features.

Validate Your Model

Separate your data into training, test, and validation sets, or if you are using K-fold cross-validation, at least hold out a validation set. You need to keep some powder dry for most applications. Also, be aware of biases in your split. Remember: there is no such thing as a random set of data, only a random process to generate data. If you randomly flip six coins and they all come up heads, that's not going to be a very good validation set.

Ensure the Quality of Your Training Data

For supervised learning algorithms, you will want to look closely at your training data. Does it cover all the use cases? Is it biased in some way? For example, did multiple humans create it? Can you see biases or differences among different folks?

This is particularly challenging when unstructured data is critical and source data comes from multiple silos. Extra effort in developing a high-quality training set will pay major dividends. Because of the variation in how information is represented in different enterprise settings, the more diverse the sources of data you use in your training set, the more transferable your results will be.

Set Up a Feedback Loop

Think through how you will use the output errors of your ML system to improve it. Downstream users can provide feedback on when your algorithm got it wrong. How are you capturing this feedback so you can bring it back into training? Note: This is great for false positives, but can miss false negatives, so you will want to pay special attention to false negatives as you train and use this experience to help you find missed results in production data review so you can include them in your next round of training.

Don't Trust Black Boxes

Some ML methods are more transparent than others. Clustering, topic modeling, and recommender systems tend to be easy for humans to interpret, because they create groupings of concepts that humans can associate with known influences. Linear regression can tell you how important each feature is to the final output. This is true to a lesser extent with linear classifiers. Random forests are difficult to interpret. Deep learning is mostly a black box, with very little transparency to how internal mechanisms work or what is important in the decision-making process.

Note that there is a lot of research and development in this area of ML, so better products for helping us understand the decision process exist and more advanced product features are on their way. In fact, the prevailing trend now, due to business and regulatory reasons, is toward *Interpretability* and *Explainability*. As ML systems become ubiquitous, there has been a surge of interest in interpretable ML: systems that provide an explanation for their outputs.[31] The deployment of ML systems in complex applications has led to a surge of interest in systems optimized not only for performance but also other important criteria such as ethics, fairness, regulatory mandates, safety, avoiding technical debt, providing the right to explanation, or simply, human curiosity.

Interpretability refers to methods and models that make the internal mechanisms, behaviors, and predictions of an ML system understandable to data scientists, ML engineers, and technical users.

Explainability is related to interpretability—and is defined as the "what," "why," and "so what" descriptions of underlying data, algorithms/models, or typically, the results of ML. While many articles and books on the topic conflate or tie interpretability and explainability at the hip, we'd like to differentiate the two based on the

Type: technical reasons/details vs. every day narratives or general philosophical questions

Intended audience: technical user/data scientist vs. non-technical/business user/executive/regulator

Artifacts used: model decomposition and algorithmic surrogates vs. plain language narratives

Reason: Mathematical and scientific vs. Social

Correlation Is Not Causation

It's easy convince yourself that two factors that move together imply that one causes the other. Just remember that in many cases there is a hidden factor that could be causing both factors to move together.

Monitor Ongoing Performance

How will you monitor the performance of your algorithm on an ongoing basis? Data drifts and systems evolve. You can do this monitoring manually by spot checking your results against the incoming data, and you can monitor data and algorithm statistics with a dashboard. Simple moving averages can tell you a lot.

Keep Track Of Your Model Changes

Always track the revision of your model and report it with your results. As you improve different parts of your data analytics pipeline, you will want to go back and re-analyze data. Recording which model was used at which time helps you understand what to recalculate.

Don't be Fooled by "Accuracy"

If you're looking for a rare event that only happens 1% of the time, and you never actually find it, you can report your accuracy as 99%. Obviously, that's meaningless. Instead, figure out before you start your project what precision and recall or other sensible metric your application requires to be useful. Build your application to these metrics.

Acknowledgments

We'd like to acknowledge permissions granted by authors Goodfellow et al. to quote definitions from their book, *Deep Learning*. We'd also like to acknowledge the permissions granted by William H. (Bill) Wilson to quote from his online resource, *The Machine Learning Dictionary*. For those interested in going deeper into the basics, Mitchell's *Machine Learning* remains a reliable resource. An in-depth read on deep learning architectures is available in Bengio's paper, "Learning Deep Architectures for AI." To learn more about ML interpretability, please refer to Christoph Molnar's "Interpretable machine learning. A Guide for Making Black Box Models Explainable."[32]

Notes

1 Stanford (2016). "One Hundred Year Study on Artificial Intelligence, Appendix I, A Short History of AI." Available at https://ai100.stanford.edu/2016-report/appendix-i-short-history-ai
2 Mitchell, T.M. (1997). Machine Learning. McGraw Hill. p. 27
3 Domingos, P. (2015). The Master Algorithm: How the Quest for the Ultimate Learning Machine will Remake our World. Basic Books. p. 5.
4 Mitchell, T.M. op. cit.
5 Mitchell, T.M. (1997). Machine Learning. McGraw Hill. Page 2
6 Goodfellow, I. et al. (2016). Deep Learning. Book in preparation for MIT Press. Information available at http://www.deeplearningbook.org. p. 99
7 Goodfellow, I. et al. (2016). Deep Learning. Book in preparation for MIT Press. Information available at http://www.deeplearningbook.org. p. 99

8 Donoho, D.L. (2000). "High-Dimensional Data Analysis: The Curses and Blessings of Dimensionality." Stanford University. Retrieved from http://statweb.stanford.edu/~donoho/Lectures/CBMS/Curses.pdf. p. 17.

9 Domingos, P. (2012, October). "A Few Useful Things to Know about Machine Learning." Communications of the ACM. Volume 55, Number 10, p. 81.

10 Dash, M. and Liu, H. (n.d.). "Dimensional Reduction." Retrieved from: http://www.public.asu.edu/~huanliu/papers/dm07.pdf

11 Goodfellow, I. et al. op. cit. pp. 107–108.

12 Wilson, B. op. cit. http://www.cse.unsw.edu.au/~billw/mldict.html#generalizebp

13 Goodfellow, I. et al. op. cit. pp. 110

14 Wilson, B. op. cit.

15 Wilson, B. op. cit. http://www.cse.unsw.edu.au/~billw/mldict.html#fi%20rstN

16 Wilson, B. op. cit. http://www.cse.unsw.edu.au/~billw/mldict.html#fi%20rstS

17 Ibid.

18 Gal, Y. (2016). Uncertainty in Deep Learning, Phd Thesis, University of Cambridge. Retrieved from http://mlg.eng.cam.ac.uk/yarin/blog_2248.html. p. 11.

19 Settles, B. (updated 2010, January 6). "Active Learning Literature Survey." Computer Sciences Technical Report 1648, University of Wisconsin–Madison. Retrieved from http://burrsettles.com/pub/settles.activelearning.pdf

20 @natarpr (author) on Twitter. (2016, December 8).

21 Wilson, B. op. cit. http://www.cse.unsw.edu.au/~billw/mldict.html#bioneuron

22 Wilson, B. op. cit. http://www.cse.unsw.edu.au/~billw/mldict.html#neuron

23 Ibid.

24 Norvig, P. (2016, March 18). "Deep Learning and Understandability versus Software Engineering and Verification." available at http://youtu.be/X769cyzBNVw

25 Bengio, Y. (2009). "Learning Deep Architectures for AI." Foundations and Trends® in Machine Learning, Vol. 2, No. 1, p. 7. Information available at http://dx.doi.org/10.1561/2200000006

26 Deep Learning, LeCun, Y., Bengio, Y., and Hinton, G. (2015 May 28). Nature, Vol. 521, pp. 436–444. Retrieved from http://www.nature.com/nature/journal/v521/n7553/abs/nature14539.html

27 Wilson. op. cit. http://www.cse.unsw.edu.au/~billw/mldict.html#firstF

28 "Recurrent Neural Networks Tutorial, Part 1: Introduction to RNNs." (2015, September 7). Retrieved from http://www.wildml.com/2015/09/recurrent-neural-networks-tutorial-part-1-introduction-to-rnns/

29 Yarin, G. (2016). op. cit. p 5.

30 Schmidhuber, Jurgen. (2014, October 8). "Deep Learning in Neural Networks." Technical Report IDSIA-03-14 / arXiv:1404.7828 v4 [cs.NE]. p. 4.

31 Doshi-Velez and Kim, https://arxiv.org/pdf/1702.08608.pdf

32 https://christophm.github.io/interpretable-ml-book/

Chapter 3

AI for Supply Chain Management

Bob Rogers
UCSF Center for Digital Health Innovation
Oii Incorporated
Harvard University IACS

Contents

DOI: 10.4324/9781351032940-3

Introduction

This chapter will begin with a broad overview of the key AI capabilities that can be leveraged in Supply Chain Management (SCM) and then narrow to a more granular review of the different applications of AI in SCM. Specifically, we will begin with an overview of the principle challenges of SCM, and then move to a discussion of the four key things AI systems can do to create value in SCM: Understand, Automate, Predict, and Optimize. We will look at where AI is impacting the activities of the key supply chain roles and what kinds of tools are available to facilitate these activities. AI is also harmonizing or optimizing across supply chain roles so we will look at opportunities to integrate AI functionality across the supply chain. This leads to a brief discussion of the impact of AI on supply chain staffing, including building analytics teams. A more detailed discussion of the impacts of AI and automation on the workforce will be presented in Chapter 10 on Corporate Social Responsibility. Finally, in our Case Study on Orchestrated Intelligence ("Oii"), we will look at the requirements for capturing the relevant data needed to optimize the supply chain with AI and the integration of analytical supply chain tools with existing supply chain software.

We don't need to tell you that the Supply Chain is the machinery that keeps every company alive and moving forward, bringing in raw materials, transforming these raw materials into products and then orchestrating the steps required to get these products to consumers. It will also not be news to you that the Supply Chains of most companies are incredibly complex, with multiple inputs, a variety of interconnected internal processes, and outputs that must be distributed to many consumers, all subject to constraints of time, regulation, resources, and profitability. Ironically, this description of the Supply Chain could also be used to describe the process that is used to create Artificial Intelligence systems themselves: One starts with a variety of input data, cleans, organizes, and transforms that data, then applies a variety of optimization methods to turn those data into a decision-making process which can output any number of results or recommendations to multiple consumers within the company. So there is a "meta" going on when we talk about AI in SCM: AI can play a role in supporting, accelerating, and simplifying individual activities within the Supply Chain, but it can also be used to optimize the Supply Chain as a whole, harmonizing the activities of different parts of the company in the service of the specific strategy of the enterprise (Figure 3.1).

Let's be more specific about that. A key goal of SCM is to negotiate between the need to provide a high level of customer service, for example providing near-real-time fulfillment of customer orders with high Service Level, and the need to control manufacturing, transportation, and inventory holding costs. This is a constrained optimization problem. How do we configure our planning, manufacturing, fulfillment, and warehousing to match the customer satisfaction strategy of the company, while generating maximum profitability? Just as we use mathematical techniques to optimize the behavior of AI systems, we can use these same optimization techniques to manage our Supply Chain to achieve the organization's stated goals. In both cases, the first requirement is to quantify every *relevant* aspect of the Supply Chain process so that it can be measured and tuned. We will see that this ability to measure, or "Understand," is a critical role for AI in the Supply Chain of nearly every enterprise. Next, because we can't instantaneously create product in response to demand, we need to be able to

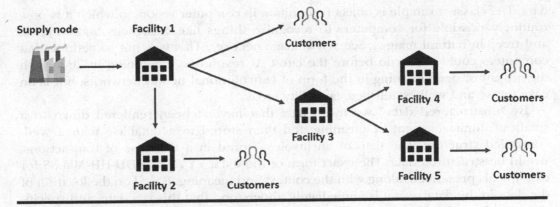

Figure 3.1 Supply Chain Network Diagram.

Source: Anshul Agarwal; used with permission.

"Predict" future demand as accurately as possible over the longest time horizon that applies to our procurement, manufacturing, and delivery processes. Again AI, this time in the form of predictive analytics, becomes a critical capability at the center of the SCM puzzle. In order to work efficiently at high velocity, and with as much agility as is needed to adapt to changing market conditions and product requirements, much of the work done within the functional areas of the Supply Chain must be "Automated." AI-driven automation technologies, ranging from robots and autonomous vehicles to automated software workflows and customer interactions, are becoming mandatory in today's enterprise. Finally, it will not be shocking to you that the world does not always smoothly conform to our plans and processes, so there is a constant need to adjust to change and reconfigure the components of our Supply Chain to "Optimize" for the overall objectives of the company. Optimization in the enterprise typically incorporates the three goals of maximum profitability, maximum customer satisfaction, and minimum risk, and is an area of SCM that is ripe for AI-centric innovation.

In what follows, we will look at how each role in SCM is impacted by AI, and how emerging AI capabilities are being incorporated into the work of each person in the Supply Chain to help them be more efficient and agile in the pursuit of optimal business outcomes. First, let's learn more about how AI systems Understand, Automate, Predict, and Optimize so that we can put the detailed impacts of AI into context for each SCM role.

Understand

Understanding is a central concept in our working definition of AI as computer software that is able to perform tasks that could only be done by humans in the past. Futurists will immediately jump to the conception of AI understanding as the abilities to sense, reason, and act under fairly general conditions and to apply these capabilities to many different application areas, but this is actually more ambitious than the definition of AI understanding that we will employ here. By understanding, we mean that AI systems can recognize a well-defined concept in a chunk of unstructured data. The classic example is object recognition in computer vision, in which it is now routinely possible for computers to recognize things like cats, dogs, motorcycles, and trees in natural images. See www.image-net.org/. This was not something that computers could easily do before the latest AI revolution, beginning in 2006 with the advent of deep learning in the form of convolutional neural networks, but is an easy-to-use and well-established capability today.

By "unstructured data," we mean data that haven't been rendered down to a smallest atomic element of meaning and then stored in a database with a well-controlled structure. The date of an invoice, stored in a database of transactions, would be structured data: The exact form of the data, YYYY-MM-DD-HH-MM-SS for example, is prescribed, along with the context and meaning. Based on the location of the data in the database, it is immediately understood that this is a date, and specifically the date of a certain kind of invoice, as recorded by a known department in the company for one exact purpose. Unstructured data, on the other hand, most often comes in the form of free text, audio, video, or images. A document that contains the sentence, "The invoice should be processed tomorrow," contains a date ("tomorrow") and a reference to an invoice, but without further context it is not possible to definitively identify what type of invoice that date refers to. Nevertheless, the information contained in this sentence could be critical to the ability of the company to satisfy its obligations to a customer. The good news is that AI can be used to extract very specific meaning from text to solve this problem. Images and video are similar: The manufacturing of a part can have many outcomes from a quality perspective, including visual flaws, mechanical problems, and even the orientation of the part on a manufacturing line as it hits the next piece of tooling in the process. The ability to use software, rather than humans, to identify quality issues in manufactured parts is now a commonplace application of AI in the Supply Chain (Figure 3.2).

Data scientists refer to the "understand" activity of AI systems as "inference." For the manufactured parts QA problem described in the previous section, we infer the answer to a very specific question such as "Will this part live up to our quality

Figure 3.2 Cracks in solid surfaces are automatically detected and mapped using commonly available deep-learning-based computer vision tools.

Source: Arthur Flôr; used with permission.

standards?" With AI, this question can be asked of unstructured data such as an image or video. Every AI tool can be viewed as the answer to a similar kind of question. Beware of statements about "getting insights from data." This is the sign of an underspecified expectation from an AI system, which is guaranteed to lead to disappointing performance. Every application of AI should be tied to a razor sharp and specific question. As another example, consider a computer vision application for quality assurance in a manufacturing process. If you pass an image of a part as it moves between process steps to your application, you expect the application to be very specific in its functionality. It could answer any of the following specific questions: "Is the part defect-free? Is the part oriented correctly in the tooling? What kind of deviation is exhibited by the part? Does some attribute of the part (reflectivity, surface texture, color, etc.) indicate that an upstream process should be adjusted? Every one of these questions is likely to be addressed by a different algorithm that has been developed specifically for that purpose.

As we saw in Chapter 1, "Understand" is one of the most common and fundamental AI capabilities in SCM, because it is the first step in quantifying complex processes in order to understand and control them. We use AI understanding to answer a broad range of questions about our supply chain, from what is written on an order form, to where the flaw in a part is, to what the customer's written feedback is about, and even how risky a supplier is based on what's being written about them on the Internet.

Automate

Automation is the process of reducing or removing human steps in a process. Automation is one of the most powerful aspects of the development of AI in the Supply Chain because it increases the speed and agility of processes while simultaneously reducing the variability that typically accompanies work that is done by humans. We are not promoting the replacement of humans by AI-powered automation, but there is no question that it is possible to automate many tasks with AI today that could not be automated in the past. Concerns about the impact of AI on jobs and society are an important topic that we will discuss at length in Chapter 10 on AI and Corporate Social Responsibility. For now, the key takeaway should be that automation typically reduces the amount of time that humans need to spend on repetitive or rote tasks, but does not take humans out of the process. In addition to accelerating the speed at which tasks can be done, AI automation often makes the results far more consistent and repeatable, which is a valuable benefit throughout the Supply Chain. Regarding automation, we prefer to think of AI as *Augmented* Intelligence rather than Artificial Intelligence.

Predict

Predictive Analytics is a term that we hear often in reference to the data-driven enterprise, and indeed, prediction is the ultimate goal of many AI algorithms. What people don't often appreciate is that there are actually two different meanings of the word prediction convolved into the term *predictive analytics*. The first meaning is the most obvious: Prediction of what will happen in the future, as in time series forecasting and predictive maintenance. The second is more subtle, but covers many of the most important use cases in the enterprise. It is the inference of a state that we can't directly measure, such as whether a mobile phone user is running an online search because he/she is hungry for lunch, or whether a series of transactions is suspicious. In fraud detection, we are not predicting that fraud will happen in the future, we are making an inference about the motivations or financial implications of a series of actions that have already happened or are happening right now. In both cases, we can't directly measure the intent of the target party, so these are predictive algorithms in the sense that they "predict" what you would measure if such a direct measurement were possible. As we will see, both types of prediction are highly impactful to the effective operation of a supply chain.

Forecasting the Future

> It is far better to foresee even without certainty than not to foresee at all.
> —Henri Poincare in *The Foundations of Science*

Forecasting the future is an activity that is suspended in the tension between two diametrically opposed propositions. Proposition 1: Knowing the future with certainty leads to maximum profits with no risk. Proposition 2: It is impossible to know the future with certainty. Prognosticators live in the no-man's land between these truths through the application of probability. Specifically, to make forecasting useful we combine every predicted outcome with the probability that we think that outcome will actually happen, allowing us to set up risk management guardrails that include good outcomes, better outcomes, and poor outcomes, all with their concomitant likelihoods. A sales forecast of one million units is really a statement that there is an 80% likelihood that sales will be between 800 units and 1.1 million units. Once we have this map of future states and their probabilities of actually materializing for our business, we can take actions to optimize our outcomes. It is critically important to include probabilities with forecasts, because we have observed that the consumers of predictive analytics often gloss over this part of the prediction, with some very negative consequences.

In the world of SCM, the most obvious and important predictive task is demand forecasting. To restate the process of forecasting for the demand forecasting use case: If we know how many widgets customers will buy at any given time, then we can orchestrate our processes to ensure that we build the right number of products and have them in the right place at the right time. This allows us to minimize our production and warehousing costs while providing ultimate customer service. Furthermore, knowledge of future demand allows us to adjust pricing and promotions to hit the optimal part of the price elasticity curve (Figure 3.3).

But how do we actually forecast demand? The fundamental idea at the heart of nearly all time series prediction methodologies is that past behavior is the best predictor of future behavior. From a mathematical point of view, this means that forecasting is phenomenological and not prescriptive, or in other words, we do not build first-principles models of the demand for a particular product in a particular place. A first-principles model is like a mathematical description of how something works, the way a physicist or engineer would study the behavior of a system by building a

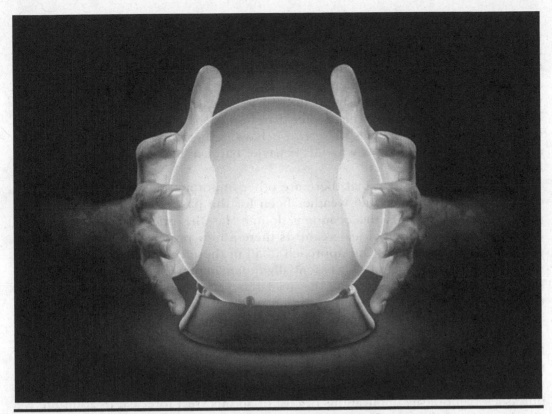

Figure 3.3   Predicting the future is one aspect of the role of AI to Predict.

mathematical replica of the system and then simulating how the system would evolve over time. It would be great if we could do this, but for complex systems like market behavior, we have several factors working against us. First, we don't know what all the fundamental building blocks of underlying behavior are, and in any market they are so numerous we are not likely to have great information about what is happening with each of them. For example, how does a change in temperature impact the amount of ice cream a Londoner will eat, and further, how does this pattern vary by day of the week? The second challenge is that some of the important factors for future buying behavior that we would include in a model are themselves time series we would need to forecast. The weather in the ice cream example is one such factor, and while there may be a great number of good forecasts being generated by the national weather services, they are still only reliable within modest ranges and over short time frames. Finally, and perhaps the most discouraging of all, much of what happens in the future is the result of nonlinear processes, which can be *literally* impossible to predict as a result of their underlying mathematics. In popular culture, the butterfly effect is cited as an example of nonlinear behavior making prediction impossible. A visually compelling and "understandable" example of the challenges of prediction in nonlinear systems is the motion of the double-rod pendulum. See the Wikipedia article on the Double Pendulum.

We've established that we don't usually build predictions in analytics from first principles, so now let's look at the approach we typically *do* take. The core idea is that the previous behavior of the time series itself is the best guide to predicting future behavior. If the sales of a product are increasing 10% each year, then in the absence of any other information, we might predict that they will go up 10% next year. If they also simultaneously go through seasonal cycles (ice cream sales may be slower on average during the winter than during the summer), we can come up with a formula that combines these two behaviors to predict the monthly sales in the next year. We don't know why this behavior happens, we just know that's what's happened in the past.

Intuitively, we imagine that there are other important factors that will impact our prediction. What has the weather been for the past week? What is the temperature today? How is the economy doing? Has the price of milk increased, thus impacting the price of ice cream? Is there a new product on the market that competes with ice cream? Our approach to all of these challenges in the world of machine learning (ML) and AI is essentially quite simple. For each time in the past for which we have data we input the available data, often restricted to a specific time window, into an algorithm and then use the next measured demand value as the "answer" that we want to train our algorithm on. An interesting twist in demand forecasting that is not present in many other forecasting problems is the fact that we sometimes have time-boxed commitments from our customers or distributors to purchase certain amounts of product. This known information about the future has a material impact on both our methodology for forecasting and also our assessment of the implications or cost of an incorrect forecast. In addition, we also have the ability to influence the future by timing our promotional activities to achieve specific corporate goals.

In general, the art in the forecasting process is deciding what information to include in the inputs, and what type of algorithm to train with our data. This is a methodology that has been used for decades to forecast time series, so where does the AI come in? What has changed is that new deep learning algorithms, including neural networks that contain feedback loops (for example, Long-Short-Term Memory or "LSTM" models), have shown themselves to be very powerful for forecasting many time series (for example[1]). Given enough data, these methods have proven to be very general in their applicability and they have the added, very important, benefit that they don't require the input data to be manipulated or transformed in any way. They can actually work out from the data itself what attributes of the time series are most important to their prediction problem. The critical caveat is that they need a lot of data, a topic we'll cover more at the end of the chapter.

Predictive Analytics as Inference: What's Behind Curtain Number Three?

Predictive Analytics is a vast area of analytical work in the enterprise whose primary goal is to predict something that we would like to measure directly, but for some reason cannot directly measure. There are many reasons that we might not be able to measure something that is relevant to our business. The most obvious reason that something can't be measured is because it hasn't happened yet. Generally, if we are interested in predicting a future value of a series that we are measuring, such as the price of a commodity, that would be considered time-series forecasting, as described in the previous section. The use case for predictive analytics is that we want to analyze existing data to predict the likelihood of an event or outcome in the future, such as using past payment history, credit scores, and current market trends to calculate the likelihood that a customer will default on future payments (Figure 3.4).

But the future is not the only veil that shields our eyes from information that we would like to know. There are many characteristics that influence supply chains that are not directly measurable, even if they happened in the past or are happening now. One of the most well-established applications of predictive analytics is fraud detection, for example in the authorization process for credit card transactions. The problem setup is that we have a history of transactions and perhaps other information about a credit card user (e.g., the fact that they are on a business trip to Europe) and a new transaction is being requested. The question is: How likely is it that this is a fraudulent transaction? From one point of view, this is a classification problem, which would be appropriately characterized as part of the AI ability to Understand. Another way to look at it is that we are trying to understand the intent of the party requesting the transaction. We can't measure intent directly, but we can infer the likelihood that the intent is unlawful or fraudulent, so this activity is really predictive analytics. When we infer something that we can't directly measure, we are working in the realm of Prediction.

We've now seen that predictive analytics can help us reveal useful information about the likelihood of future events and it can help us infer the nature of an event that is happening now. How do we develop predictive algorithms?

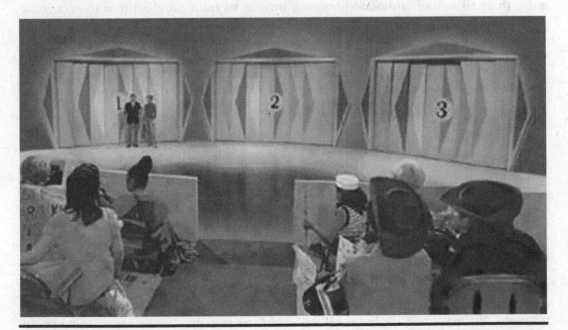

Figure 3.4 Another way AI can Predict is to "predict" or infer what would be measured now if a measurement were possible. We ask the algorithm, "What is behind curtain number three?"

From a ML or AI perspective, the predictive analytics process is simple in principle. Collect as many examples of fraudulent transactions as possible and create a data set that includes all of the historical data that might be relevant. This might include details of all of the customer's past transactions, past transactions for the vendor with other customers, contextual information about the customer (where they live, what their credit score is, whether they have indicated that they will be in Europe for business, et cetera). Then add data for approximately the same number of transactions that are known to **not** be fraudulent. This is the training data, also known as "gold standard," "annotated" or "labeled" data, that will be used to train the algorithm to "predict" whether or not a transaction is fraudulent.

In the world of traditional ML, it is usually valuable to perform a process called feature engineering on the input data before feeding it to the algorithm. For example, it may only be necessary to input the most recent transactions for each party, or to compute the average number of transactions and average dollar amounts of transactions during one or more specific periods. The idea is that traditional ML is best at identifying patterns in data that have been distilled down to its most important characteristics.

Modern AI-based predictive analytics algorithms change the game for two main reasons: First, if they are given plenty of data, they can come up with the features on their own, so they eliminate the need to try out many different variations of features to get to good results. Second, in many cases, it is possible to start with an AI algorithm that has been trained on lots of data for one problem and then tweak it with a modest amount of new data to make it work for a new problem. This second process is called Transfer Learning, and it is a critical part of the AI toolkit. Because the data requirements to create a robust AI system are so stringent, for example, it takes more than 10 million annotated training images to train an algorithm to recognize objects in photographs, transfer learning is a fundamental part of most real-world AI applications because it allows us to customize existing AI solutions using the modest amounts of data we are likely to have at our disposal.

The bottom line is that both traditional ML and AI are having huge impacts on our ability to do predictive analytics, and we will see below that there are many applications of the capability to Predict in SCM.

Optimize

The MacMillan Dictionary defines the word optimize as, "To make something such as a method or process as good or as effective as possible." To apply this directly to the challenges of SCM, let's recast this definition in terms of SCM goals for a couple of different corporate strategies. Imagine an organization that has defined its annual goal in terms of maximum profitability, with minimal priority on customer service. Then our definition of optimize will be to make Supply Chain decisions "to make the enterprise as *profitable* as possible." Alternatively, if the organizational strategy is to emphasize Service Level within some range of acceptable profitability, our definition becomes, "to make Service Level values as high as possible, while maintaining profit margins above some level." In realistic SCM scenarios, we may need to optimize some product portfolios under strategy one and others under strategy two!

Each of these paths to optimize the Supply Chain is valid, yet they are very different and lead to different decisions in different functional areas of the enterprise. In the first case, we might minimize the number of manufacturing line changeovers to keep costs down, despite the risk that some products may go out of stock temporarily while they wait for their turn on the line. Note that the critical difference between these two examples is that they are seeking a maximum value for a specific mathematical quantity; in the first case the quantity is profits (or revenue-costs), while in the second example we seek maximum customer satisfaction usually measured as Service Level, as long as we do not simultaneously allow profits to dip below a fixed level or allow inventory carrying costs to get too high.

The crux of Supply Chain Optimization in a data-driven, AI-centric world, is to frame the strategy of the enterprise in terms of a mathematical formula. This is known as the "objective function" in ML parlance. Then we instrument the different choices and activities across the Supply Chain so that they can be controlled, and their influence on the objective function measured. We then devise strategies to control each process point to achieve the maximum value of the objective function. These steps are typically done manually by planners in supply chains today, but one of the most exciting areas of AI in SCM is the implementation of automated optimization techniques to harmonize activities across the supply chain to make them more effective in achieving corporate goals. The opportunity for AI is to connect the different activities within the entire Supply Chain to increase the flexibility, control, and transparency of the overall Supply Chain, ultimately improving the likelihood that the organization will hit its stated objectives with minimal variability and risk. (See Oii Case Study)

Let's see how optimization as a mathematical process works. First, imagine a product, the Wonder Widget, whose sales increase proportionately to the number of dollars spent on promotions. This optimization is easy: Spend the most advertising dollars possible for maximum sales. You don't need any fancy AI for this. Algorithmic approaches get interesting when there are feedbacks and constraints that work together to influence the outcome. In our Wonder Widget example, we can make the story more realistic by assuming that once we have spent $1 million on promotion, then the incremental increase in sales per advertising dollar spent begins to drop. There is a point at which it no longer makes sense to spend additional money on advertising because it just doesn't pay off enough. Somewhere between this point of diminishing returns and only spending a tiny amount there is a sweet spot. We can write a formula for profit as a function of advertising spend, run any math tool to optimize this situation and come up with the advertising spend that optimizes profit. Obviously, this is just Econ 101, but you have probably noticed that the world of SCM is much more complex than anything we ran across in Econ 101. There are different kinds of promotion. There are potentially quality issues with our product as we push the manufacturing line to maximum production. Some of our products cannibalize others. How do we allocate spending among them to get the most overall value? This is where AI comes in: If we instrument our Supply Chain adequately, AI algorithms can recommend strategies for optimizing profit, customer service ratings, time to delivery, or any other objective function that is implied by the strategy of the enterprise as a whole.

To see how AI algorithms can help us find the optimal decisions for running our supply chain as things get progressively complicated, let's look at our Wonder

Widget example, but let's increase the number of factors we need to take into consideration. We've already seen that, everything else being equal, there is a sweet spot for our advertising spend, as depicted in the diagram below. We want the algorithm to tell us what value of marketing spend gives us the best profitability. An algorithm essentially moves along the spend curve, reading off the profitability until it finds the spend value with the highest profitability. That is our optimum (Figure 3.5).

Now let's add a new variable. Imagine that we can configure our manufacturing process to run in batches of different sizes, which we will call "Batch Size," and which can run anywhere from 100 units per batch to 10,000 units per batch. We need to select the best combination of Batch Size and Marketing Spend to get the best profitability. The process is the same as for the previous case in which only Marketing Spend was available to adjust: We humans can see from the graph where the highest peaks are and decide what would be the best combination of Batch Size and Marketing Spend. An algorithm can do this for us as well by automatically trying different combinations of Marketing Spend and Batch Size until it finds the highest peak. So far, we're just seeing that the algorithm can automatically do what a human can do (Figure 3.6).

The reality, though, is that there can be many more than two variables in play in a real-world SCM problem, and we start to see the value of the AI algorithm as we add our third variable: Product Mix. There are two different sizes of Wonder Widget and we need to set the percentage of Wonder Widgets that are the large size, so it is a value from 0 to 100. To optimize profitability now we need to read off the

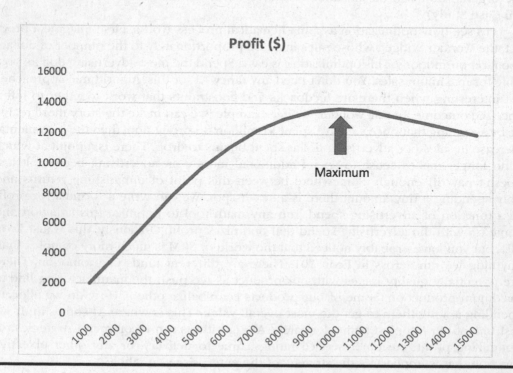

Figure 3.5 An example of optimization in one dimension. In this plot of profit vs volume, the optimal choice of volume can be determined by inspection.

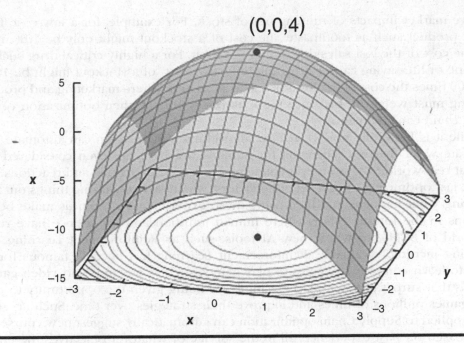

Figure 3.6 Optimization in two dimensions. Humans can identify the "peak" on this plot and read off the optimal values of x and y. But what happens if we have 1000 variables rather than two? That's where algorithmic methods come in.

profitability in a three-dimensional space comprised of Batch Size, Marketing Spend, and Product Mix. For each choice of these three variables, there is a profitability, and as humans we could painstakingly navigate our way through different combinations to find the best combination, but it is certainly not easy to visualize, and the work is downright tedious. The algorithm, on the other hand, doesn't care how many variables we include. It will merrily navigate through all the combinations to quickly come up with the best result.

This is just the tip of the iceberg in terms of how AI algorithms can help us optimize our Supply Chain. We did not look at risk or quality variability at all. For each possible choice of Batch Size, Marketing Spend, and Product Mix, there is both a Profitability number and also a measure of the risk or variability of the process. To take these factors into account, by imposing a maximum allowed quality variability for example, dramatically increases the difficulty of the task for a human analyst, but is a simple additional factor for the AI algorithm to include as it automatically determines the best choices for us to make.

Often the crux of Supply Chain optimization is inventory management and replenishment strategy. AI can be used to optimize these parameters across an entire supply chain using an objective function that is often cast in terms of monetary units (dollars, Pounds Sterling, Euros, etc.). Some elements of the objective function are easy to define this way: cost of lost sales due to stockouts, cost of transportation, factory changeover costs, et cetera, which can literally be added together. It is not as simple to take the reputational costs of different Service Levels into account, but it is often sensible to apply a multiplier to the cost of lost sales to take into account the negative market impacts of running out of stock. For example, for a low-cost, low-impact product such as toothpaste, the cost of a stockout might only be 10% more than the cost of the lost sales due to that stockout. For a highly critical drug such as a vaccine or life-saving cancer drug, the "effective cost" of a stockout might be 10 or even 100 times the cost of the lost sales. This is an area where marketing and product planning must weigh in, but once the multipliers are set, then optimization of the supply chain can commence.

While it is hopefully now clear how algorithmic optimization can automate and accelerate work that is challenging for humans, we have not even considered the fact that real-world SCM is an ever-changing landscape of actions and reactions. We are not just optimizing a static set of behaviors, we are actually trying things out and observing what happens and then using these experiments to help us make better decisions in the future. This is where human intuition and experience have ruled the world of SCM, but where new AI tools, such as Reinforcement Learning, are becoming incredibly valuable. Reinforcement Learning has become famous for its ability to learn complex strategies to play games such as Go and Atari video games at levels that surpass human players, simply by being given the opportunity to play these games millions of times and improve their strategies over time. Such an algorithm applied to Supply Chain optimization can automatically suggest new courses of action based on past experience, all in the service of whatever objectives the enterprise wants to optimize.

Now that we have examined the ways AI can act in general to help us Understand unstructured data, Predict what we can't directly measure, Automate processes that are challenging for humans, and Optimize our overall decision making to achieve corporate strategic objectives, we are ready to look at the panoply of AI tools that impact SCM. For each functional role in the Supply Chain (Plan, Buy, Make, Sell, Deliver) we will look at how AI is already impacting that work, or where the impact of AI is heading.

In what follows, we view the overall process of SCM to comprise five main functional roles: Plan, Buy, Make, Sell, Deliver. Of course, this is not the only way to define a supply chain, and in fact, within this description, there are many cases in which functions overlap, or in which the critical activity is actually coordination or optimization between different functional areas. Our main goal here is to provide a framework for exposing the different ways that AI can impact SCM in a way that is indexed roughly by who is the likely consumer or beneficiary of the AI. Within each SCM functional area, we further organize the specific tools and AI capabilities based on what kind of AI behavior they depend on.

Plan: How AI Can Improve the Life of a Planner

Our first functional SCM area to examine in detail is overall supply chain planning. Of course, planning is a key activity in many of the functional areas of the Supply Chain. For example, it is not possible to run a manufacturing process without carefully planning for the availability of materials, resources, and equipment needed to actually build a product, but we are including this detailed level of planning for manufacturing in the Make functional area below (Figure 3.7).

Figure 3.7   Planning is a global optimization problem, ripe for AI to improve efficiency, reduce costs and increase transparency for decision making.

Here, we are more focused on the enterprise-level planning for the front end of the supply chain: product production, intermediate warehousing, transportation, inventory management, and product replenishment strategy, balancing the tension between projected demand, actual demand, and customer service level.

Understand. For SCM planners, for AI to Understand means you are able to ingest data from multiple sources into the planning process, especially unstructured data such as text on the internet or in reports, and images of documents coming in through forms and faxes. Here are some examples:

▪ As a planner, you are already using a demand forecast as part of your planning process. Depending on your experience and your organization's history, that demand forecast could be a highly sophisticated time series forecasting model (see Predict below) or it could be an intuitive forecast based on your experience (a "lick your finger and stick it in the air to see which way the wind is blowing forecast"), but in either case you are most likely using primarily structured data about sales, replenishment, and stock-on-hand. It is critical that the data you use for planning be reliable, accurate, and complete, but because each reported value for each product is aggregated from many incremental pieces of information, usually coming from multiple sources, AI tools that monitor your incoming data and look for data quality anomalies are important, even when most of your data is coming from your system of record. In fact, it is important to insist that your ERP system or other enterprise system of record include advanced data monitoring tools to automate the detection of data problems.

■ Data monitoring has value far beyond simply detecting problems with data sources: A number of AI tools now exist to monitor operational data to automatically detect unusual patterns that may indicate important market events. These tools are usually referred to as "anomaly detection" algorithms, but they can also include detection of important patterns that you need to track as they emerge. For example, an unusual drop in sales of a product in a particular region could indicate a localization bug in a new software version (such as a translation error or failure to update a local security password). Recognizing such an event quickly will help prevent downstream impacts on the supply chain. In some cases, the signal may be an unexpected increase in demand, which may require adjustments to inventory planning. In either case, monitoring of data streams is a core source of value for AI in SCM.

■ As your organization moves toward more sophisticated forecasting tools, it will become imperative to incorporate new factors into your demand forecasting that go beyond structured data and are based on unstructured data. Specifically, you will want to use text analysis AI to process data from the Internet and other sources of documents to understand what external factors have influenced demand. For pharmaceuticals, for example, changes in payment policy, regulatory approvals, safety concerns, or public declarations by key opinion leaders, will meaningfully impact demand. Text mining and traditional Natural Language Processing (NLP) can be powerful tools to identify important information online, and we are seeing rapid advances in the utility of Recurrent Neural Networks and hierarchical attention models to extract useful meaning from complex documents. Access to such information from unstructured sources can allow your analytics team to tune demand forecast models to achieve significantly greater accuracy.

Automate, Augment, and Amplify. Supply Chain planning is the hub of a tremendous number of activities. SCM planning requires execution of many tasks, with many stakeholders, including ingesting significant amounts of data and negotiating with stakeholders based on large volumes of diverse, and often problematic data. For planners, automation of tasks reduces time to value, reduces the risk of human errors in processes, and ensures that supply chain parameters (safety stock, reorder frequency, etc.) for all products in the portfolio are set to optimal values. For example:

■ Supply chain inventory management parameter optimization. Each product in a portfolio must have the right safety stock and reorder frequency parameters set to ensure the desired service level is achieved with optimal held inventory. These parameters must reflect the unique sales pattern and delivery profile of the product, which can vary over time. The ability to automatically monitor these parameters over time and flag significant changes is a huge opportunity in supply chain inventory management. (See Oii Case Study)

■ Automation of most processes in the Supply Chain planning process is coming, but the trend is for higher frequency, shorter term activities to be automated first. These are activities such as data aggregation and anomaly monitoring, short-term demand forecasting by SKU, and reporting. Advanced techniques in time series forecasting such as Gaussian Process Regression have made it much easier to generate automatic short-term forecasts that can be quite reliable, when a reliable forecast is possible. When a reliable forecast is not possible, these methods provide quantitative ranges of predictions by confidence level, so that the probabilities of different ranges of future values can be understood. There are a number of excellent tools for anomaly detection to identify unexpected conditions in data from a wide range of sources from financial systems, IoT sensors in the factory, to failure rates in web services. Automated monitoring of data stream quality can recognize major failures early so that planning tools can be used with confidence.

Predict. Prediction is at the heart of SCM planning. Planning is, by definition, oriented around what's going to happen in the future, and of course we can't measure the future now, so we must predict it. More specifically, the more accurately we can predict actual demand for our products and anticipate variations in supply, demand, and our ability to deliver on our promises to our customers, the better we can plan. Consequently, to be able to Predict is the single most valuable AI tool in the planner's toolkit. Here's how AI prediction is impacting the life of the SCM planner:

■ Predictive models are a key ML capability and nowhere in the enterprise is the value proposition for prediction more compelling than in demand forecasting. Demand forecasting in the form of time series forecasting has been around for years, but there are recent developments driven by AI research that are showing significant new value in demand forecasting. Gaussian processes and Bayes Gaussian Processes are being used to create flexible time series forecasts that can incorporate location, product, and time into robust, often very accurate demand forecasts. A highly valuable feature of these methods is that they do not just predict a most likely future value, but also the range of values that can be expected for a specific level of confidence. The good news is that many ERP systems are now incorporating demand forecasting automation into their product offerings, so the sophistication of tools planners are already comfortable with will continue to grow.

There has recently been significant expansion of our ability to simultaneously predict demand for multiple products in different geographies simultaneously. The benefit of this approach is better accuracy with the same data, primarily because of our ability to use transfer learning across related product types, squeezing higher-confidence predictions out of the same data (see[2], for example).

Optimize. This is the frontier of AI in SCM. Even when all of the functional areas of SCM have exploited each of the five AI capabilities, they will still be operating in silos. The opportunity to coordinate across Supply Chain functional areas to optimize the overall Supply Chain will likely have huge impacts on how the modern enterprise is run. To be more specific, consider how interconnected demand forecasting and marketing are: To operate optimally, we want to drive demand through promotion and pricing when it is most likely to have the biggest impact, but assuming that we can manufacture to this demand in a timely and cost-effective way. This relationship is the central focus of S&OP processes that are being discussed and developed fervently in nearly every enterprise. All of our SCM activities are engaged in a complex interplay, which is just where AI optimization shines. Very few organizations are well-enough instrumented to really use algorithms to optimize planning across the entire Supply Chain, but this is exactly where they want to go, to create proactive SCM processes rather than the reactive patterns that are most common in Supply Chain Planning today.

■ Supply chain inventory management parameter optimization. Each product in a portfolio must have the right safety stock and reorder frequency parameters set to ensure the desired service level is achieved with optimal held inventory. These parameters must reflect the unique sales pattern and delivery profile of the product, which can vary over time. The ability to automatically monitor these parameters over time and flag significant changes is a huge opportunity in supply chain inventory management. (See Oii Case Study)
■ Multi-tiered Supply Chain network optimization: It is now possible to use AI tools to optimize inventory levels and replenishment strategy across all nodes in a Supply Chain network. In the past, it has been nearly impossible for multiple planners to coordinate their work to optimize the entire network at a system level, but algorithmic optimization is making this a reality. The benefits often include simultaneously reducing overall inventory and complexity while increasing service level and visibility to what factors most impact service level performance.

Buy: How Buyers Can Leverage AI for Better Pricing and Availability

The Buy function, or Procurement, in the Supply Chain is responsible for acquiring the raw materials needed to manufacture products and do the work of the enterprise. Of course, this means that the Buy function is responsible for far more than simply buying goods and services. Incoming goods come from a complex ecosystem of suppliers and sources, each with differing pricing, availability, reliability, and quality characteristics. Buyers must continually monitor the supplier ecosystem to detect risks and predict pricing trends. Furthermore, buying is transactional, so there is a tremendous amount of interaction between the enterprise and its suppliers which generates a large amount of data, with myriad opportunities for cost and risk management. Buyers are also responsible for setting quality and ethics standards for the supply ecosystem of the enterprise (Figure 3.8).

Understand. The world of the Buyer is filled with data from diverse sources, all of which must be ingested and understood in order to ensure that the right inputs to

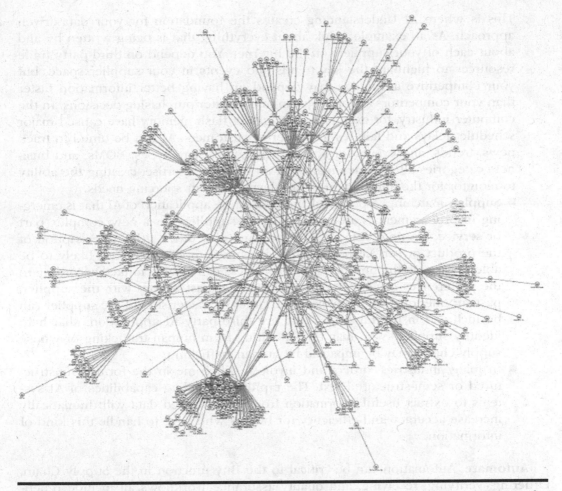

Figure 3.8 Sourcing is a complex network problem with numerous variable suppliers and a complex value function, ideal for algorithmic optimization.

the company are being acquired at the right price and at the right time. While much of the transactional data in the supply chains of many industries is now standardized, a lot of important information continues to flow into the enterprise via unstructured data. There is still plenty of order entry and invoice data that can most efficiently be ingested with AI. Furthermore, in order to understand and monitor what is happening in the supplier ecosystem, it's critical to be able to understand online documents, social media, news, and other vast, unstructured data sources. Monitoring of purchased product quality and adherence to standards often requires the analysis of product QA image data at scale. Here are some specific examples:

■ Supplier monitoring: The goal of AI in many sourcing activities is to automate the selection of suppliers and to incorporate as much good information as possible into the decision-making process. In order to support the automation that we will describe below for automating sourcing decisions, it is critical to have the right information captured in a computer-usable format in a timely manner.

This is where AI Understanding creates the foundation for your data-driven approach. As an example, think about everything that is being written by and about each of your suppliers on the Internet. You depend on third-party trade resources to highlight the key trends and events in your supplier space, but your competitive advantage may depend on having better information faster than your competitors so that you can make better purchasing decisions. In the computer industry, for example, shortages of flash memory have caused major schedule delays and failures to deliver to customers. AI can be tuned to track news, trends, and events for specific companies, part types, BOMs, and business categories all with minimal work and no AI expertise, creating the ability to monitor for the information most relevant to your sourcing needs.

■ Supplier matching: A powerful and interesting application of AI that is emerging in procurement is around identifying suppliers for a new, complex part or service. Starting with a request for quote or other written description of the product or service required, AI can find suppliers who are likely to be able to provide the product. These suppliers can also be ranked according to the preferences of your organization, so that past history with the supplier, past supplier quality or timeliness, or other characteristics of the supplier can be included in the ranking. There are third-party AI applications that help identify suppliers who may be benefitting from human trafficking or whose supply chains may be impacted by human trafficking.

■ In many industries, orders and invoices still come in the form of unstructured or semi-structured text. The rapidly expanding capabilities of AI systems to extract useful information from unstructured data will dramatically increase accuracy and efficiency for buyers who have to handle this kind of information.

Automate. Automation can be critical to the Buy function in the Supply Chain. Ordering, verifying, receiving, and quality assurance workflows all include repetitive steps that can be automated to increase speed and flexibility, and to reduce error rates. Automation helps leverage the information that AI provides buyers in the Understand mode. Automation of data collection and analysis of the supplier ecosystem is a high-value application of automation.

While there are a number of ways that purchasing and transactional workflows are being automated, robotic process automation or "RPA" being the most common, the area of growth that is most interesting is at the nexus of new AI-driven computer vision capabilities and AI-based natural language understanding. Specifically, we are talking about the very recently minted ability of AI systems to process document images and understand what is in them. By understand, we mean that the system is able to make good inferences about what information is contained in forms and other transactional documents, inferences that make sense in the context of each document.

To do this requires the ability to identify different parts of a document, perform optical character recognition (OCR) to "read" the words and characters on the document, and then to infer the values of the desired pieces of information. Without a good understanding of context it is hard to do this accurately because document images often contain enough noise to make them difficult to OCR. For example, a "B" and an "8" often look the same in a document, but if we are reading a field that should never have an 8 in it, then we have a better chance of inferring that the observed character is a B.

One may wonder whether this ability is going to become less and less valuable as supply chain systems become more and more standardized around e-requisitions and data interchange formats. We think the answer is no, because even when the financial parts of a transaction have been formatted for electronic transaction, there are many other activities in the purchaser-supplier interaction that still require communicating information back and forth in documents (for example, requirements, specifications, clarifications, responses to customer inquiries or variances when a product is not provided as expected). We are a long way from "electronifying" all of those document-based activities.

Predict. For buyers, prediction has several key value areas. First, it is critical to monitor the health of the supplier ecosystem. Having AI and analytics tools that can flag potential problems with suppliers, and indeed to predict when supply challenges are emerging, is highly valuable to buyers. Furthermore, considering the large supplier ecosystems that many enterprises have, the more these predictions can be automated to scan and alert for supply challenges, the better. Second, as a buyer, you are critically sensitive to the future price and availability of any raw material that your enterprise requires. Predictive models for pricing and availability are crucial tools in your arsenal.

■ Best pricing for inputs: Time series forecasting has been around for years, and there are many well-known methods to forecast time series, so what has changed in the era of AI? There are two major areas of advance to keep abreast of: First, new types of models are being used for forecasting such as gaussian processes and Bayesian Gaussian processes. In fact, a major benefit of these new techniques is that they emphasize the likelihood of variations around the predicted future value. Often, in market forecasting, small differences between reality and the forecast are not all that important, but a large swing in either direction can have major consequences. Models that quantify the likelihoods of large swings can be very valuable. We believe we are also on the brink of seeing some interesting deep learning methods for time series forecasting. The second advance is that AI allows us to retrieve valuable information from unstructured sources of data, for example, market information from the Internet, that can be used as part of the input data to models. When properly incorporated, these inputs can have a large impact of the accuracy and resiliency of our forecasts.

Optimize. For the Supply Chain buyer, optimization is about putting AI-generated results in the hands of engineers, designers, and other people who create value for the enterprise so that optimal buying decisions can be made automatically. For example, if lot-size pricing, historical vendor reliability, and historical part performance are included directly in engineering design tools, then engineers are able to make optimal part selections in their designs without requiring separate input from buyers. This drives overall cost of manufacturing down and gives buyers a powerful way to influence design for optimal part cost and overall system performance.

Make: AI Helps Manufacturing Make More, Better, Faster, and Cheaper

Understand: For manufacturing, AI Understanding has a huge number of applications. In order to effectively operate and improve manufacturing processes, their tools, parts, and people must be monitored via sensors, which can include anything from video to metrology to plain old analog meters and measuring devices to human notes and observations written in logs and reports. All of these data types must be rendered into a computable form to be used to improve and control manufacturing. As a simple example, any part being made in a manufacturing process can be inspected automatically through very inexpensive video, powered by modern AI machine vision tools that allow for a highly flexible and agile quality monitoring process with little development overhead.

In many cases, the result of AI Understanding may be a critical input to an AI Predict function. Consider predictive maintenance of aircraft as an example. In order to understand how a mechanical failure relates to past failures, one must be able to process mechanics' logs and reports to extract key findings from these documents and then input these findings into predictive models to connect the related failures.

- Classify part failure: Manufacturing processes are complex, so when a product fails quality testing, we seek to understand the cause of the failure quickly. Usually, the first step in this process is to determine what kind of failure we are seeing, and to ask whether we've seen it before. Computer Vision (CV) is an important input to this process: Modern CV systems can be easily trained to detect important features of bad parts in images. These features can be used on their own to classify the problem, or they may be used in conjunction with other information like machine and sensor logs and operator notes. Algorithms include Boosted Trees, CNNs.
- Logs: There are a number of products, with ever-increasing analytical sophistication, to analyze text log outputs from systems. Logs are generated by software systems, of course, but are also routinely generated by manufacturing machinery and sensors in the manufacturing line. The ability to monitor the information in unstructured and semi-structured logs is crucial for quickly diagnosing equipment failures and quality issues. Furthermore, technology to combine this kind of data with video and audio is becoming a powerful tool for predictive maintenance. Given the enormous cost of unplanned mechanical failures in enterprises from light manufacturing through aircraft fleet management, this is an important area of development in AI for the Supply Chain.

Automate. Automation in manufacturing is not new and it could easily be the subject of an entire book. Obviously, robots and automated mechanical systems are already critical parts of nearly all manufacturing systems. Where things are changing most rapidly is in the transition from bespoke robotic tools made for very specific purposes to more programmable, agile systems that can be easily repurposed. Much of the progress in this space is at the junction of machine vision and deep reinforcement learning.

To illuminate what is just possible now and where things might be headed, we will look more closely at one example: The use of Virtual Reality to drive reinforcement learning (Figure 3.9).

First, recall that reinforcement learning is an approach to training AI systems in which one or more agents (algorithms responsible for making narrow decisions at a specific point in the context of a larger task) are given rewards and punishments to help them develop the ability to make good decisions and ultimately carry out a specific task. Perhaps the most famous example of this is the ability of deep reinforcement learning algorithms to learn how to play video games at a level far beyond the abilities of human players. The goal of the task is to win the game, so there is a big reward for winning and a big penalty for losing. Furthermore, intermediate rewards and punishments, for example, finding a useful resource in the game or losing a life, can be applied. The algorithm starts with a basic strategy and then "plays" the game over and over, each time improving the strategy of the agent, until the strategy is good enough to win consistently. It is easy to see that an agent that has learned from millions or even billions of games played could become better than a human.

So what does this have to do with manufacturing? Much of manufacturing can be seen as a reinforcement learning problem. The goal is to build an object of component parts through a number of transformational processes (assemble, form, cut, stamp, etc.). Poorly formed results are penalized, as are clumsy, slow efforts. A part that passes QA generates a reward. Even within a single step of a manufacturing

Figure 3.9   Robotic automation in manufacturing is ubiquitous.

process, for example picking up a part, rotating it, and attaching another part, one can apply this process. But how do we train the algorithm through many "trials?" It would be prohibitively expensive to fail at building a part over and over in the real world, but in the digital world we have a secret weapon: simulation. If we can create a realistic computer simulation of the assembly process, then we can have the algorithm attempt to perform the desired task over and over until it masters it. There is no cost of damaged parts or QA failures, just accrued computing time, which tends to be quite inexpensive in the context of manufacturing automation.

Ok, so we can use simulation to train a reinforcement learning algorithm to perform a task in our manufacturing process. That's powerful, but where does Virtual Reality (VR) come in? Virtual Reality is a simulation environment that includes the ability to take in human actions and react to them. The power of combining VR with reinforcement learning in manufacturing automation is that we can actually have a human provide a few examples of how to perform a task, completely within a VR environment (with a VR glove that detects hand and finger movements) and then use that to simulate a variety of related simulations that can be used to train the automation AI. This is a powerful paradigm in which humans can teach AI directly to perform tasks in the physical world. We expect to see a lot more of this approach in manufacturing in the near future.

Predict. Prediction is critical to manufacturing efficiency. Predictive maintenance for manufacturing equipment continues to be one of the most critical areas of AI application in the Supply Chain. Accurate prediction of what will fail, when it will fail and why, is critical to managing the powerful tension between planned maintenance and unscheduled failures. When equipment goes down unexpectedly, the costs can be enormous, but if we are overly conservative with our predictive maintenance planning, we replace expensive parts prematurely and also reduce the potential productivity of our manufacturing lines. The better our prediction of when a part will fail, the better we can plan for it.

Interestingly, predictive algorithms are not only critical for predicting the future of equipment failure, but also for identifying what are the root causes of complex failures in the first place. There are many situations in which root cause analysis can help us not only anticipate failures, but design systems and processes to reduce the frequencies and impacts of these failures.

Optimize. Optimization is a critical part of any manufacturing operation. What's the best way to stage the different manufacturing steps? How do we synchronize manufacturing activities to minimize downtime for expensive tooling and people? How do we size our manufacturing inputs to get the best bulk pricing for raw materials while preserving optimal agility in what we manufacture, when? Until recently, most of these questions were answered by humans, mostly acting on their own or with some algorithmic optimization tools to help compute tradeoff costs. AI has a huge role to play in decreasing the time to solution for these problems and in many cases arriving at better solutions than those proposed by humans.

This is another area in which simulation can play a key role. In the arena of manufacturing, this is usually referred to as a "digital twin" methodology in which a complex manufacturing environment is rendered into a simulation and the impacts of a variety of modifications and improvements can be computed. While these methods are fundamentally algorithmic in nature, next-level AI allows us to scour and interpret vast amounts of data generated by digital twin systems in order to identify optimal strategies. This can include a reinforcement learning approach or it can be a strategy in which we train deep learning systems to predict outcomes of different changes and then apply transfer learning to quickly adapt past training to new situations.

Two of the challenges with this digital twin approach are that it takes a lot of knowhow to set up simulations that are good enough to meaningfully model real-world systems, and once these systems are set up, they can be extremely computationally expensive. It is intriguing to note that AI is beginning to help with this part of the problem too: Deep learning systems have been developed to predict the physical behavior of complex systems and to then short-circuit the computational demands of some parts of the modeling process. This has been done in computational chemistry[3] and in complex weather modeling[4] and we expect this approach to continue to grow in importance across many manufacturing domains.

Sell: How AI Can Improve Marketing, Promotion, and Operations Planning in the Supply Chain

Understand. The opportunities for extracting understanding from unstructured data in marketing are enormous. Many of them are already well-incorporated into the enterprise, and are in fact discussed elsewhere in this book. However, it's worth looking at the interplay between marketing and demand, and how these impact the supply chain. Job number one in marketing is to understand customers: what motivates them, what do they need, how are their needs and activities changing, what are they actually buying, consuming or seeking out? The interesting thing about customers is that they primarily generate unstructured data in the form of text, audio, and video, all of which are in the bullseye of AI technology. While machine vision has been a key application area of AI for the past several years, at the time of writing there are dramatic, exciting changes happening in the way we can understand written and spoken language, enabling us to harness the data created by our customers in increasingly powerful ways.

For AI to understand human speech, a set of technologies that are advancing rapidly but are not yet up to a human standard, is the holy grail for marketers and salespeople who need scalable ways to interact with customers and respond quickly to their product needs. This is an area where the capabilities of text- and voice-based systems have been overhyped, leading to disillusionment about the gap between AI promise and reality, but this is primarily the result of overzealous selling and storytelling. Technologies that are applied appropriately to well-defined use cases are in good use today, and we have no doubt that this is an area that will continue to improve as the underlying AI models evolve.

- Computer vision has become a valuable tool in complex technical selling environment in which incoming customer requirements need to be matched to a specific solution. For example, new computer vision tools to interpret blueprints are being used to speed the time to generate a quote.
- The ability to identify fraudulent purchase transactions continues to be a huge area of investment for the enterprise. This topic is discussed at length in our chapters on retail and on banking.

■ Shrinkage: Theft of products is a major tax on every physical business, so of course a lot of effort has been put into reducing theft loss, or shrinkage. While video monitoring systems have been in place in retail locations for many years, the utilization of this data has been minimal. Typically the only use of in-store video is to provide court evidence in the rare instances that a perpetrator has been arrested and is being tried. The real goal of retail is to prevent the theft in the first place, which really requires constant ongoing monitoring of video in many locations, which is not economically viable without technology to automate it. This is an area of rapid growth in AI. AI systems can now identify objects, people and actions in video, and suspicious behavior can be flagged automatically to allow action by store personnel. It also turns out that it is possible to detect patterns of movement of items in stores that can indicate an increased risk of theft. Both of these analytics advances rely on high-quality sensing equipment to be effective. Most of the in-store video that is deployed today does not provide high enough resolution data to be effectively analyzed by AI models. Similarly for product location tracking, commonly deployed RFID technology generates a very blurry location signal with many artifacts due to reflection and noise from overlapping signals. Another consideration in this arena is bias, which we will discuss at length in Chapter 10 AI and Corporate Social Responsibility. It is vital to have a healthy relationship between AI technology and the laws that will be developed to regulate it. Poorly conceived AI tools that act unfairly based on biased data could cause unnecessary challenges in our ability to deploy technology to reduce shrinkage.

Automate. The actual selling of products is transactional, and generally involves verification, fulfillment, and customer service workflows which have traditionally been based on human activities. These workflows are being increasingly automated with the help of AI technologies.

There are many areas in which AI is driving the automation of sales processes. Some of these include:

■ Order entry automation
■ Robotic process automation for repetitive sales and marketing activities
■ Chatbots and automated speech systems that can facilitate communication with our customers and enhance our ability to infer important information about them

There is a very compelling discussion of the ways that AI is impacting selling activities in the enterprise in our Chapter 7 on Retail.

Predict. The use of AI to predict in sales and marketing is fundamental, and some kind of prediction has been in place in the enterprise for decades. Predicting demand, which we discussed in the context of Supply Chain planning is an example, but even more elementary are the traditional functions of predicting future business growth and setting sales goals. These are increasingly handled by advanced ML, and the opportunities to expand in this area are great. In the context of optimizing across the entire Supply Chain, a key opportunity for AI is to more accurately predict the response of a market to promotions and changes in price, and to more directly

Figure 3.10 **AI and ML have played a crucial role in reaching customers since the advent of the Internet.**

couple these predictions to the rest of the Supply Chain. This is the goal of S&OP processes that are driving investment into development in many industries (Figure 3.10).

In addition to finding better ways to understand and interact with its customers, the enterprise must also protect itself and its customers by understanding the behavior of individuals and organizations with more nefarious intentions. Fraud detection and prevention of "shrinkage" are critical applications of AI Prediction, in which the output of AI to understand video, audio, transactions, and/or text are used in predictive models to compute the likelihood that an observed activity or transaction is fraudulent.

Optimize. What do we optimize in marketing? For a given amount of money to spend on promotions, what actions can we take to generate the most revenue, profit, unit sales, or whichever metric is most relevant to the strategic objectives of the enterprise? Taken in the context of the Supply Chain as a whole, one of the biggest opportunities in AI for SCM is the use of algorithms to harmonize activities across multiple functional areas of the Supply Chain. For marketing, one of the biggest areas of development effort right now is in developing models to determine the timing and scope of different marketing promotions to get the most end-to-end value for the organization. Specifically, enterprises are working toward automating multiple parts of the Supply Chain so that they work optimally: Demand generated by promotion in sync with actions by planners to set up procurement, manufacturing, and delivery so that profits are maximized, and waste and inefficiency are minimized.

Deliver: AI Automates and Streamlines Logistics

Understand. In logistics, an example of AI understanding is the interpretation of an image of a product that is damaged upon delivery or the inference from video that a specific transfer process can be made more efficient or safer for the product. In the world of delivering web-based experiences, the analysis of video, audio, text, and clickstreams is critical to understanding whether customers are having a positive experience, and indeed whether they are successful in using the product.

The analysis of video is a key tool in the fight against shrinkage in retail, which is a huge cost driver. This topic is covered in Chapter 7 Retail (Figure 3.11).

Automate. Automation in delivery and logistics is exploding right now due to the growth of autonomous vehicles and robotic systems, which depend almost entirely on AI to work properly. Like automation in the factory, these could be the subject of an entire book. We will focus below on how Supply Chain Control Towers are enhancing our ability to automate responses to logistics events.

Predict. In order to ensure that the right resources are where they need to be to deliver products in a cost-effective and timely way, every aspect of the logistics

Figure 3.11   The efficient movement of products globally depends on multiple layers of analytics and AI.

ecosystem must be predicted. As a result, predictive algorithms continue to be critical for forecasting how much demand there will be, by time and location, and what the demand will require in terms of resources. What are the transportation modes to be employed, what are the minimum shipment sizes, is there enough safety stock to manage unexpected demand or supply disruptions? Such questions apply to almost every enterprise, whether is it a pure manufacturer, provider of services, or even a nonprofit that is intent on reducing food waste and increasing the availability of surplus food to those who experience food uncertainty. Analysts and data scientists have been using analytical tools to forecast the future for many decades, but advances in AI continue to strengthen our capabilities. In particular, we are getting better and better at building AI models from smaller, sparser data sets which can benefit from learning with larger data sets in other domains. Improvements in the underlying computing infrastructure provided by the cloud also allow highly granular forecasting to be applied in near real time based on activities happening all over the globe and measured by multiple local sensors.

In the world of logistics, we would be remiss not to mention that there is a rapidly growing number of AI tools for predictive maintenance that make our transportation systems more reliable as well.

Optimize: Logistics are increasingly being optimized in the context of Supply Chain Control Towers. Below we will talk about how the Control Tower concept is being used to integrate visibility, automation, and optimization across multiple Supply Chain functional areas both inside and outside of enterprise borders.

Supply Chain Control Towers

The Control Tower concept is being used as a framework to discuss integration of visibility and automation across multiple Supply Chain functional areas both inside and outside of enterprise borders. There has been a lot written recently on the successes and failures of Supply Chain Control Towers to create visibility to data across different parts of the Supply Chain and we recommend that the reader refers to some of these sources to learn more about the challenges that enterprises face in implementing a Control Tower strategy.

For the purposes of this chapter, we will describe some of the basic Control Tower types, and assuming that they have been implemented successfully, we will articulate how automation, prediction, and automation can naturally fit into these systems. The core principle here is that visibility of data through a Control Tower implies that the underlying data is being retrieved in a timely way for integration and presentation within the Control Tower, and that in order for this data to be meaningful, it has also been cleaned and harmonized. Cleaning implies that gaps in data are identified, flawed or erroneous data is corrected and there is some minimum accuracy and reliability standard reflected in the incoming data. It is amazing how much incorrect data can find its way into enterprise systems! Harmonization ensures that data that are correct can also be combined and understood by a computer system. For example, one could enter a valid date as "January 19, 2020," "20200119," or "1579463689" (the Unix epoch, for all you fellow nerds out there). The challenge is that different enterprise data systems may spew out all three of these formats, so your Control Tower will have to ensure that there is a way to interpret all three formats correctly. Once this is done, your data is harmonized.

Our point here is that timely, clean, reliable, and harmonized data is a good starting point not only for visualizations and dashboards, but for analytics and AI. If you have a Control Tower, you can have analytics! Let's look at some of the prediction, automation, and optimization applications that can leverage the data in a Control Tower.

Control Towers for logistics

Some of the first Control Tower systems were developed to allow visibility to logistics networks and subsequently to provide an interface for reacting to logistics events. A dashboard that identifies a shipping problem must provide a way to re-route the shipment or to reconfigure logistics options for future orders. Such functionality is frequently implemented in successful Control Tower systems. It is only a small logical leap to expect these systems to automate some of these responses, or to at least automate the presentation of potential responses. Furthermore, once the data is flowing properly, the capability to predict where problems are about to occur is the next step in our AI for logistics progression. Finally, it is rare that overall logistics are optimized across multiple product lines or that any level of coordination exists in the delivery network. This is normal, since much of Supply Chain inventory management is reactive, but there is no question that AI systems will be increasingly available in Control Tower systems to optimize logistics and other Supply Chain activities, resulting in lower shipping and inventory costs for the same service levels.

Control Towers for Visibility Across the Enterprise Supply Chain

Another variant of the Control Tower paradigm is the Supply Chain Visibility Control Tower. The basic version of this is a system that provides visibility to inventory location and shipment status, a marriage between traditional ERP data systems and the logistics Control Tower we described above. Clearly, when these data are accessible to analytics systems there are opportunities to do more than just monitor status with a dashboard. Indeed, analytics solutions are being developed that allow end-to-end optimization of the Supply Chain network. As further information becomes available to the Control Tower, real-time information on delivery problems, and more concrete information on lead times in general, the opportunities to automatically predict significant impacts and take action to mitigate their effects will continue to increase. As with logistics Control Towers, the ability of the enterprise to simultaneously improve service levels and decrease inventory and logistics costs will have a significant impact on which organizations can compete effectively at a global scale.

Control Towers Transcending Organizational Boundaries

This is an interesting new trend in Supply Chain Control Towers in which the sourcing side of the Supply Chain equation is being taken into account by incorporating data about the attributes and performance of sources of raw materials. What's interesting about this is that it is not sufficient for any enterprise to simply track the delivery and quality experience that it has had with a supplier because this information is scant compared to the total number of interactions the supplier has with other customers, and because this information is not all that likely to help predict when an unexpected vendor problem will arise.

The conclusion is that third-party data aggregators can actually create a network of suppliers and customers, moving beyond the simple hub and spoke model that would be sufficient to represent a single enterprise and all of its suppliers, and providing timely insights that can help all consumers in the network improve their decision making. Once this aggregation model is in place, then a world of interesting algorithm development opportunities takes shape, much like in finance, where anti-fraud and anti-money-laundering algorithms are far more powerful when they can incorporate transaction and credit data from many sources.

This brings up the very interesting topic of privacy-preserving computing, in which novel encryption schemes such as homomorphic encryption and zero-trust computing models (secure computing enclaves, for example) make it possible to train and test models on data without actually exposing the data to the algorithm developer. We believe that the topic of privacy-preserving computing is highly relevant to how the next generation of AI will be developed and validated, but a general discussion is beyond the scope of this book. We do include an extended description of privacy-preserving computing technology in Chapter 10 AI and Corporate Social Responsibility, since it can be a key tool for enterprises to ensure that they are not leaking private information into the public domain (Figure 3.12).

As cross-enterprise data becomes available in the form of expanded Supply Chain Control Towers, we expect to see a variety of new prediction, automation, and optimization algorithms come to light.

Figure 3.12 Privacy-preserving computing, in which data is computed on in a secure environment without being shared, and without compromising the intellectual property in the algorithm, will play a major role in the development of AI in supply chain and beyond.

Supply Chain Staffing in an AI-Enhanced Enterprise

How do we build our Supply Chain organization to make use of this information? What software tools provide the capabilities we need? Do we have to build it all from scratch?

First, you don't have to build it all from scratch! In our research for this chapter, one message came through loud and clear from our experts: Let your SCM and ERP vendors do most of the heavy lifting for you. While many of the AI capabilities that we have described in this chapter are not available yet, or are not quite ready for primetime, they *are* coming. And they are coming in a form that is already consistent with your systems of record and inventory management tools.

The Oii Case Study provides an example of what data can be extracted from ERP and SCM systems to support AI optimization of Supply Chain inventory management parameters. It examines other types of information that can be used to maximize the benefits of the optimization process. It also discusses how the optimized parameters can be imported back into existing SCM software.

Does this mean that everything we've read about in this chapter is already commodity? We will assert that the answer is "No. Not everything is or will be commodity." The best advice we can give you is to look at your business and think about where your core competitive advantage lies. Many parts of the supply chain in manufacturing look like supply chain in retail, which in turn look like supply chain in services. Think of these as commodity, and just make sure you are using the tools provided by your SCM systems vendor as effectively as possible.

Then think about where your specific competitive advantage is and figure out what you can build for your enterprise that leverages AI as described above, and how you can begin to create unique value around it. In manufacturing, a key area of value is inventory and waste. In a specific example we know of, all of the bespoke efforts of a large enterprise went into building optimizations around inventory efficiency and waste reduction, resulting in huge cost savings to the organization.

From a staffing perspective, how does the emergence of new AI capabilities in SCM impact who we hire? To answer this, let's take a look at the three categories of skill sets that will be required to leverage AI benefits:

> **Asking the right questions of analytical tools**: In every functional role in SCM from buyers to logistics managers and everyone in between, you must be able to define your strategy in terms of the real capabilities of advanced analytics and AI, and to understand the strengths and limitations of data and algorithms. The good news is that this book will provide you with the foundation you need to ask good questions of both your analytics vendors and internal development teams.

There are many software vendors out there right now selling AI hype rather than robust, deployable solutions to your problems. Watch out for AI that "automates everything" or "solves all of your supply chain challenges." Often, the best question to ask of a vendor is "Give me an example of a specific problem that I have that your solution solves for me. How do you get the data you need, and how is your product connected to my existing systems?" If there is any lack of clarity in how they describe your problem, they are probably selling technology they've developed without any understanding of the detailed realities of the enterprise Supply Chain. Another great question to ask AI software vendors is: Exactly how are you using AI and how does AI improve your solution relative to other analytical approaches? The usefulness of this question is that it often exposes products that are using traditional analytical techniques that have now been rebranded as "AI" purely for marketing purposes. Sometimes the underlying "traditional" solution is still effective, but since it is being sold as AI, the vendor is being disingenuous. Our recommendation is to be very wary of committing to any vendor that is not honest about what its product is and is not.

Building and monitoring useful AI systems: You will very likely need access to technical analytics and AI expertise as you simultaneously incorporate AI solutions from third-party vendors and investigate areas in which you might invest in your own AI development projects. While there are many consultants around who can help map out an AI strategy and even define AI solutions for some of your internal problems, ultimately you will need at least one person with hard technical skills to be responsible for the care and feeding of your AI systems.

Elsewhere in this book you can read about some of the potential pitfalls of using an algorithmic approach to business problems. For example, it's important to understand the biases and limitations inherent in the data you are using, and to be able to very clearly define the question that each algorithm or AI solution answers. A good technical expert will have developed a "spidey sense" for when there are dangers lurking inside data sets.

The flipside is that a good in-house technical expert can also help you design for the future and get the most out of your ongoing AI efforts. One of the powerful advantages of ML solutions is that they can continue to improve over time as they are exposed to more information. Remember, it's called machine learn*ing*, not machine learn*ed*. Part of the role of your analytics and AI experts will be to design feedback systems that can capture input from users about the accuracy and usefulness of the output of your algorithms. This feedback allows your algorithms to learn incredibly quickly. Think about how we learn a task such as riding a bicycle: You start with some basic instructions which are not sufficient to actually ride a bike. As you gain experience, you learn which actions help stabilize you and which do the opposite. This feedback is the critical bridge between knowing about something and actually being able to do it. This is a good analogy for AI systems that start out with a rudimentary ability to perform a task and which can then become very skilled with a small amount of ongoing input and feedback.

In manufacturing, there is no question that you will need technical experts to help you develop AI-driven quality assurance tools. Computer vision is now so easy to implement and customize, that you can get a lot of value from a small number of computer vision experts who can optimize both your product quality monitoring and the control systems that can create a higher-reliability manufactured output.

Collecting and curating AI-worthy data: While your technical experts in analytics and AI can help you define what you can do with the data you have access to, and what data you might want to collect, there is almost always a need to have data engineering expertise in the IT department as well. Data engineers are the people who can both get the data that is needed by analytics systems and who can ensure that AI systems are deployed properly into production. It's no secret that 80% of data scientist time is spent cleaning and transforming data to make it useful for algorithms, so there is always a need to have individuals who understand algorithmic methods involved in the extraction and curation of data for use by AI. Additionally, having staff with the wherewithal to build and deploy automated data quality monitoring and anomaly detection tools in the data pipeline will pay huge dividends as your enterprise becomes increasingly dependent on the data streams generated during the course of doing business.

On the deployment side, these same data engineers can ensure that algorithms developed internally or provided by third parties are actually deployed properly. It's important to remember that broken algorithms can output numbers that on the surface appear indistinguishable from the outputs of good algorithms. How can an algorithm be broken? you ask. Here are a few examples of how good algorithms go bad in deployment:

- The wrong stream of numbers is connected to the algorithm. For example, last month's sales numbers are coming in rather than this month's numbers. They look the same, but the answers are wrong!
- The wrong version of an algorithm is deployed. Often, there are multiple versions of an algorithm created during the training and development process, with the earlier versions usually providing less accuracy. They all look the same from an inputs–outputs point of view, so it's critical to ensure that the right version of each algorithm is being used in production.
- The algorithm is "mis-translated" from one language to another. Algorithms are often developed in the Python programming language, but many production systems actually require code to be written in Java, C, or some other language, so someone must accurately translate the algorithm to the new language. That means not only paying attention to getting the different translated parts to

work together properly, but also ensuring that numerical differences in rounding numbers and calculating complicated functions don't have a material influence on the final answers coming out of the system.

Increasing use of advanced analytics and AI will necessitate more robust data storage and maintenance strategies. This is likely an area that your enterprise is already thinking about a lot, and in fact you may have already added a Chief Data Officer to your executive team. We have been surprised at how many enterprises have access to current values of operational data, such as inventory and supply chain configuration parameters, but that they are not recording this information anywhere for future analysis. Remember, analytics and AI require data, and the more history you have, the better. You will find that you will need someone to be responsible for architecting and driving your data strategy so that you do not end up with bespoke pockets of curated data living separate and precarious lives in different parts of your IT infrastructure. This leads to a variety of risks including poor storage and backup strategies (often at higher cost than a more integrated approach) and potential variations in data quality caused by changes in upstream systems. If your ERP updates a database schema, will your downstream AI systems all break? Your CDO or other responsible party can ensure that you have a plan in place to keep all of your systems working reliably as different components change.

Conclusions

The key takeaway from this chapter is simple: AI can Understand, Automate, Predict and Optimize in almost every area of the Supply Chain, and these capabilities are becoming easier to implement and benefit from every day. Much of this functionality will become part of our ERP and SCM software systems as these companies acquire the innovative third-party startups that are driving growth in this area.

Furthermore, whether in the form of external privacy-preserving aggregation systems, or internal platforms for improved data transparency and utility, we have seen that the Supply Chain Control Tower is an important concept in the development of AI in the Supply Chain. Whether future solutions are actually Control Towers, per se, we are not sure, but the ability to integrate and make use of data across the enterprise, and indeed, beyond the enterprise, will quickly become table stakes in the AI-driven Supply Chain.

Notes

1 Beaufays, Françoise, "The neural networks behind Google Voice transcription" (Research Blog, August 11, 2015), retrieved June 27, 2017.
2 "Forecasting at Uber: An Introduction," Uber Engineering, accessed September 2021, https://eng.uber.com/forecasting-introduction/.
3 Garrett B. Goh, Nathan O. Hodas, and Abhinav Vishnu, "Deep Learning for Computational Chemistry," arxiv.org, https://arxiv.org/pdf/1701.04503.pdf.
4 A. G. Salman, B. Kanigoro and Y. Heryadi, "Weather forecasting using deep learning techniques," 2015 International Conference on Advanced Computer Science and Information Systems (ICACSIS), Depok, 2015, pp. 281–285, doi: 10.1109/ICACSIS.2015.7415154.

Chapter 4

HR and Talent Management

Bob Rogers

UCSF Center for Digital Health Innovation

Oii Incorporated

Harvard University IACS

Contents

DOI: 10.4324/9781351032940-4

91

Introduction

Human Resources. Is it a contradiction to talk about Human Resources in a book about Artificial Intelligence? Or to apply AI to Human Resources? Our thesis in this chapter is a resounding, "No!," but with the caution that there is a powerful tension between the risks of AI and the benefits of AI when we apply it to human resources. In fact, the way AI plays out in HR in the Enterprise may well provide advance signals of how AI's relationship to humans will evolve in general. We are not talking about SkyNet or the Singularity, but rather the mundane but profound implications of applying powerful technology to important problems. AI indeed can be wielded as a powerful agent that is inherently neutral and widely tunable, but as a powerful tool it can be misused, either intentionally or through clumsy application by the uninitiated, resulting in less than desirable results. The outcome is entirely in the hands of the human users of AI.

We should be more specific about this in reference to HR, because it's a very important point. It has been proven by many studies (for example,[1] and references therein) that humans express very powerful biases when they make hiring decisions. For example, people tend to hire others who "look like" themselves. This can be about age, ethnicity, gender, or almost any other factor. We have read many articles that tout AI as an almost magical cure for this kind of bias, owing to the fact that algorithms are not autonomous organisms. Ironically, we have also read many articles excoriating the use of AI in many applications, including HR, because people assume that algorithms are intrinsically unbiased when they actually reflect the bias in the data that is used to train them.

A naive response would be to argue that we should remove the bias from the data, but this misses the point. Because they do not have internal motivations and past experiences beyond the data we have shared with them, AI algorithms are able to make predictions about the world as it actually is. Our challenge as practitioners or users of these models is to understand how to ensure that our data is not improperly biased, and to condition our interpretations of what algorithms tell us with our overall goals in using the algorithms in the first place.

Let's look at an example. Following[2] imagine we are in the credit card business and we want to predict the probability that a person has an income $50,000 per year. We can use the presumably reliable data in the database to predict income level holding out all explicit data about sex or race. We train a simple classifier to predict income > or < $50k, and we find we can get an AUC of 0.91. In other words, we can predict income pretty well with this model. But what does it say about male vs female income? It turns out the model predicts women have a lower probability of being in the higher income group than men. We have seen this called out as a statement that the model is unfair, but that is not actually true. The model is actually only unfair if it somehow systematically underestimates the actual incomes of women relative to men. The problem is that we have framed the bias problem incorrectly. The model is asked to predict income, which it does accurately based on the data it has.

It is true that we would like the incomes of women and men to be equal, all other factors being equal, but we would argue that it is not productive to expect algorithms to fix inequities in our society. On the other hand, we may have a fairness problem if we apply this result incorrectly.

To understand the difference, we must ask ourselves, "Why are we predicting income?" If it is being used as a proxy for the likelihood of defaulting on credit card debt, then we are going to give relatively fewer credit cards to women, and that may well be unfair. What went wrong? To be fair, we need to predict the probability of defaulting on credit card debt, not simply annual income. Another situation we may encounter is that we have a policy that requires we offer credit cards with equal frequency to male and female applicants. In that case, if we must use the predicted income level to make our determination, then we should set a different threshold for men and women. For example, in this data set the thresholds to get equal probability are $50k for men and $45k for women. This is a tricky policy to apply in practice though, because next we will need to look at our practices for offering cards to different ethnicities. In this data set, nonwhites are predicted to be less likely to have incomes above $50,000 than whites. So now we need to set new thresholds for black/male, black/female, white/male, white/female. But what about other ethnicities? Other sensitive factors? (Figure 4.1)

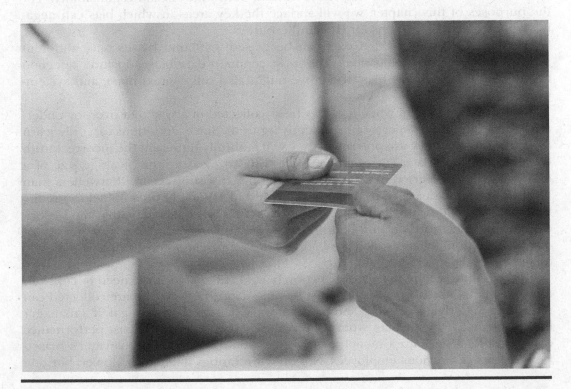

Figure 4.1   Who is creditworthy enough to receive a credit card?

Ultimately, nearly every situation is different, but the most important takeaway is that, when using algorithms to make decisions about human outcomes, it is very important to predict a measure that is as close as possible to the actual outcome you are controlling for. Do not confuse a predicted proxy with the actual association you need to understand.

To highlight further why it is usually not desirable to "tweak" the predictions of an algorithm to remove bias, imagine substituting heart attack risk for the income prediction in our credit card scenario. We are now predicting risk of a heart attack based on multiple factors, presumably so that we can take sensible life-saving actions such as prescribing a statin or blood pressure-lowering drug. It is clearly NOT a good idea to modify the algorithm to remove differences in predictions for men and women or for different ethnic groups. This would result in some groups being denied life-saving treatment—certainly not the outcome we are looking for in the name of fairness.

We have argued that it does not generally make sense to modify algorithms simply for the sake of removing bias, but we have been making the assumption that the algorithms are based on data that is an accurate reflection of an underlying statistical reality. There is another situation we need to worry about: What if the data itself is biased, either because it has been improperly collected or has been collected as the result of a process that is already biased? This is a very important topic to consider in the face of applying AI to decisions about the careers and lives of humans. Since biased data is not rare and because it impacts all algorithmic and AI solutions, we will take a close look at it in Chapter 10 "AI and Corporate Social Responsibility." For the purposes of this chapter, we will surface the key areas in which bias can negatively impact AI applications for Human Resources.

There are many ways that data can be biased. Different biases have different impacts and potential mitigations. The most common data biases include selection or sample bias, prejudice bias (which we might also call context bias), and system-perpetuated bias.

Selection bias occurs when data has been collected in a way that over- or under-represents important aspects of the underlying truth. Since algorithms can only learn from the data that they are presented, they will faithfully represent the incorrect truth contained in their data. For example, if we want to measure the "average size of a dog," we would expect very different results if our test subjects are Rottweilers than if they are Chihuahuas! An example in the world of HR might be a model to predict how likely a candidate will be successful in a role. The challenge is that the historical data we have to train our algorithm may be constrained to the past history of our organization, which is likely to badly under-represent some groups of perfectly qualified candidates (Figure 4.2).

To help mitigate the impact of selection bias in HR analytics, we need to consider more insidious sources of bias than just missing data. The way data are collected can reflect the underlying opinions and biases of those who are collecting it. If a manager believes men are better than women in a particular role, then the past performance data that would go into a model for this role would include that manager's biased assessments of previous employees. Not only are ratings likely to be lower, but due

Figure 4.2   What is the average size of a dog? It depends on which dogs are in your study.

to negative behavior on the part of the manager, other metrics like longevity in a role are likely to be biased as well. Even though an algorithm trained on such data might not be given gender as an input, there are many ways that the bias in the data could still play out in the form of an algorithm that is biased against female candidates. The onus of identifying this kind of false logic in the application of algorithms is squarely on the data scientist since it is unlikely that decision-makers who are less experienced in analytics will appreciate these risks (unless of course they have read this book!).

The second major type of bias we must understand is prejudice bias, or what we prefer to refer to as "context bias." This occurs when an algorithm learns a pattern or makes a conclusion that is incorrect or misleading and which could lead to incorrect conclusions that run counter to our broader policies or beliefs. For example, algorithms have been developed to identify what sport is depicted in an image. There have been some examples, shared widely on the Internet, in which an image of an Asian who is not playing any discernible sport will be labeled as "table tennis." Obviously, it is not desirable for an algorithm making decisions in a Human Resources context to make assumptions that would be considered racist if they were made by a human.

How do we detect that our models are being fooled by bias in our data? How do we guard against using models that are propagating, and possibly reinforcing, an incorrect statistical view of the world? How do we build models that do not make incorrect assumptions in the face of biased data and data that is missing representation of key factors? Much of the responsibility lies in the hands of the data scientists we have entrusted to build or apply our algorithms. Well trained and/or experienced data scientists have a highly tuned sense for when there is something suspicious lurking in the data, a capability we refer to as data scientist "spidey sense." It is not just best practice, but required from an ethical perspective, to look critically at the data that is being used to build models to look for under- and over-representation of different groups or underlying factors, like ethnicity, gender, or undergraduate degree. Beyond distortions in the sampling of data, it's important to also look for ways human assumptions might be able to percolate into the data collection process. Finally, it's crucially important to scrutinize the output of models under various scenarios to look for unexpected patterns. In the case of prejudice bias, we can often recognize false inferences if we look at the output of the algorithm when we give it ambiguous data. In the case of the sports recognition algorithm, images of people doing ambiguous activities tend to expose unusual or unexpected results.

There is an additional point that we must make here. Every inference by an algorithm should have a confidence level associated with it that represents how confident the algorithm is that it got the right answer. It is never advisable to use AI systems that don't provide confidence levels along with inferences. To understand the importance of this, recall our sports detection algorithm. A photograph of an Asian male depicting no discernible sport is labeled as table tennis. This is concerning until we note that the confidence level reported by the algorithm is only 20%, so we would not be wise to use this inference in the first place.

We conclude that no AI technology should ever be used if it does not provide confidence levels along with results. Another important practice is to include ongoing feedback on specific AI outputs or inferences during the day-to-day use of the technology. This can be in the form of collecting feedback from users or customers: "We think this is table tennis: Did we get it right?" or it can be a behind-the-scenes QC process that is carried out by nondata scientists who can assess the accuracy of an inference or prediction. This is a powerful model that not only allows for the detection of undesirable results, but when the data is collected properly, it can be used to improve the accuracy of models.

One final word on the topic of bias in AI for Human Resources, and indeed for AI in the enterprise, is training: not algorithm training, but *people* training. We have stressed in this discussion that data scientists bear a lion's share of the burden in identifying sources of bias and undesirable algorithmic consequences. The more experienced a data scientist is, the better his or her "spidey sense" will be, but even a seasoned data scientist can be fooled. It is critically important that anyone who uses the results of AI in HR be trained in Ethics for AI so that they can be on the lookout for unintended consequences. This is a core principle that we promote in the education of data scientists and other professionals who are tasked with deploying algorithms in the enterprise. A strong understanding of the statistical sources of bias, of the ways processes and humans can influence the data available to algorithms, and the dangers of mis-applying or misinterpreting algorithmic results will only increase in importance as the enterprise becomes more and more reliant on AI.

Because of the additional risks to HR in applying AI and algorithmic approaches in general, we have seen some authors claim that algorithms must be able to somehow explain their decision-making processes explicitly in order to be used in HR. We would argue that this is not generally a proper conclusion. In fact, human decision-making is almost always far less transparent than algorithmic decision-making, and we wouldn't conclude from this that humans should be barred from HR. Rather, we need to be sensitive to the implications of our decisions and follow policies that allow us to measure and monitor the impacts of decisions and the quality of the information that goes into them. For more information on ways that algorithms can be made more transparent, see Chapter 10 on AI and Corporate Social Responsibility.

Now that you have been properly chastened about the risks of using AI in Human Resources, we return to our core thesis that, while not a panacea, AI is an incredibly powerful tool to improve the state of the art in Human Resources. In fact, despite the fact that algorithms are not inherently bias-free, we would argue that it is much easier to remove the bias from an algorithm that it is to remove the bias from a human!

With this in mind, let's begin to explore where AI is most impactful in HR. For the purposes of this discussion, we will organize the functional areas of Human Resources in terms of the following questions:

- Hiring: Who will you hire?
- Compensation: How will you compensate them?
- Training: How can you help them succeed in the enterprise? (compliance training, onboarding, customer)
- Retention: How can you retain them?
- Risk Management: How can you minimize risks to them and to the enterprise?
- KPIs: How will you measure the performance of your Human Resources efforts?

To put these activities in context with AI, we will look at examples from a complete career lifecycle. Meet Jane, a mid-career Supply Chain manager as we follow her through a normal workday at mid-size manufacturing company Manufacture-X to see where AI impacts her daily activities. Let's look at Jane's Human Resources experience at Manufacture-X, picking up the story before she was hired and following her through to her decision to move to a new role within the company.

Workforce Planning and Hiring

The story begins with the decision to hire a new planner to direct the overall supply chain process for the new XWidget, the latest product line from Manufacture-X. This decision to hire a new planner, as opposed to adding the new product line to the purview of an existing planner, was the direct result of a workforce planning activity in which overall trends in the industry and patterns within Manufacture-X were analyzed. The resulting algorithm suggested that additional planner capacity would be needed in the future, and furthermore, that new skillsets for planners would be needed to allow Manufacture-X to benefit from new AI planning and automation capabilities. So the decision to hire a new planner with an expanded skill set was taken.

The next steps in the process were to define the role and requirements and then to source the best pool of candidates who could fulfill these requirements. The HR manager responsible for filling the position works with the hiring manager and the results of the workforce planning analysis to identify what skills should be added or removed from a previous job posting. This posting is then analyzed with an NLP AI product to identify how it can be improved to increase its attractiveness to strong candidates and to ensure that it does not contain language that biases it away from any particular candidate demographic. Yes, this *is* an example of AI actually *reducing* the bias in HR! Furthermore, given the ability to generate text with current AI systems, it seems likely that the creation of job postings could be fully automated, based on a few inputs from a human, in the very near future.

Sourcing

Now Manufacture-X needs to assemble the best pool of strong candidates that it can find. The goal is not necessarily to find a huge list of potentially mediocre candidates, it is to create a strongly ranked list that will result in the best placement possible, without requiring a huge amount of human effort. Note also that ranking can be optimized for a variety of factors: most experience, strongest background, most likely to be a good fit in the organization, most likely to accept an offer, or any combination (Figure 4.3).

Can AI help with that? Of course! There are a number of platforms and tools that can aid in the sourcing of strong candidates. The core objective of sourcing technology is to reduce the time required to source candidates, while simultaneously

Figure 4.3 Algorithmic approaches can play a major role in improving the reach, effectiveness, and fairness of talent sourcing. It's crucial to avoid bias in assumptions and data.

increasing the average quality and fit of those candidates. AI algorithms accomplish this in two ways. First, they use text analytics and language understanding to process information about millions of potential candidates from many online and private sources. Blogs, LinkedIn articles, stack exchange posts, resumes, social networking, and many other Internet sources can be scoured to create lists of candidates who may be a good fit for a role. Second, these systems use predictive models to identify who are likely to be the best candidates for the role so that a large set of candidates can be prioritized. Many of these systems also integrate communication with candidates and pipeline tracking into their interfaces, creating the opportunity to use feedback to improve predictive models over time. In fact, we would argue that any AI technology that is not tracking user feedback, and in many cases, the longer-term performance of the candidate, will quickly lose ground to other products over time, even if they begin with a strong offering. In machine learning (ML), feedback to allow continuous improvement and refinement of results is critical to long-term success.

So Manufacture-X found Jane online, placed her near the top of the candidate list based on the attributes of her background (broad industry experience in manufacturing, having worked in organizations with known strong supply chain disciplines, a training course in AI methods for supply chain planning, etc.) and even reached out to her to encourage her to apply for the role.

Candidate Assessment

At this stage, our human hiring manager came into the picture to review top candidate applications and to interview them, including Jane. But Jane's interview was not AI free. Her first screening interview was carried out via video conferencing, and with her permission it was recorded. The recording was analyzed by an AI system to observe her behavior when asked challenging questions and to analyze her language and micro-expressions for clues to her truthfulness and her fit for the company. Algorithms now exist to extract information from clues as subtle as tiny changes in expression, and body surface temperature changes and pulse rate that can signal comfort level during an interview. This kind of analysis can be controversial and is not done by all enterprises, but as long-term performance data for employees becomes better organized in AI-driven HR organizations, this kind of analysis is likely to become more prevalent because it will likely become more predictive of candidate fit and future performance (Figure 4.4).

Background Checks

The great news for Jane was that she came through her interviews with flying colors and the hiring manager determined to offer her the role. But first, the HR department needed to do a background check. Why? Because there are increasingly many cases of individuals creating fraudulent online personas and building them up over time via a variety of online platforms. We have seen some stunning cases of individuals successfully (at least temporarily) living out fraudulent personas, even in the health-care space! The challenge is that background checks are time-consuming and costly, making them a terrific target for AI-based automation. There are many automated, online background check services available today, utilizing a variety of data sources

Figure 4.4 Candidate assessment is being aided by AI, from analysis of micro-expressions to crafting of less biased written and verbal tests.

and technologies. What is evolving rapidly as a result of AI is the ability to make more connections in a broader variety of data. Traditional algorithms tend to look for specific types of information to verify what has been stated in a resume or job application. AI systems can of course do this, and with additional contextual awareness which requires less human review and error checking, but they can also make inferences that can identify red flags. For example, what was left off of a candidate's history? What can be inferred about a past fact based on connections with other pieces of information? This is the realm of AI, and we expect AI-driven background checks to rapidly improve over the coming years. In fact, given our own experience, we would anticipate that all job candidates will be subject to sophisticated, automated background checks in the near future. Of course, being a conscientious and experienced professional, Jane's stated history matched the results of her background check easily.

Compensation

As a result, the hiring manager was ready to make Jane an offer. But how should the company compensate her? Again, an analytics-driven approach has become the standard in the enterprise, with statistics being the go-to tool in the toolkit. Typically,

Figure 4.5 Compensation is critical to employee retention, but it's not all about salary. Analytical assessment of the value of benefits to employees improves company offerings.

HR will arm the hiring manager with industry-standard averages and variances for different levels of experience within Jane's general job description. Coupled with the hiring manager's recent experience in hiring for this type of role, assuming that there have been recent hires, a good starting range may be easy to come up with. But there are a lot of caveats to that nice, tidy story. For example, Jane is being hired because she is not only a seasoned Supply Chain Planner in the industry, but she has special training in AI-based Supply Chain management. This is new, and it's not clear how to value it. Furthermore, there are some changes happening in the overall job market which may impact the likelihood of Jane accepting a specific offer. Perhaps there is a recent trend to provide more bonus and stock compensation and less salary in this industry. All of this underlying uncertainty increases the value of AI-based predictive analytics to help the hiring manager understand what level and type of compensation might be most meaningful to Jane. An additional benefit of a model-driven approach is that the hiring manager can understand the relative values of different compensation tradeoffs, such as more time working from home, or a slightly different title, or a higher fraction of nonsalary compensation, making it easier and more fluid to negotiate with Jane (Figure 4.5).

Helping Employees Succeed In the Workplace

Jane and the hiring manager negotiated successfully, and Jane began her new role as Supply Chain Planner for the XWidget product line at Manufacture-X a month later. Despite the fact that Jane is an experienced Supply Chain Manager, there is a lot for Jane to learn when she joins the company and it is the responsibility of HR to bring her up to speed on what she needs to know to be successful at Manufacture-X. This means that HR is taking a lead role in both Jane's onboarding process and her ongoing training.

Onboarding

In most enterprises, there are a number of employee onboarding activities such as payroll setup, insurance, bonus plans, employee cultural training, ethics training, etc., that every employee will need. For this first tier of onboarding activities, AI is therefore not needed to decide what content to provide to Jane: She will receive all of the information and training. Immediately following this, as Jane actually attempts to set up all of her employee systems, AI comes to the rescue repeatedly. For example, Jane is unsure about what insurance to sign up for. Her insurance will be primary for her family, she has two teenage children and she has a complicated medical history. She needs information on the details of each plan, and even some information on which of her current providers are covered by each plan. She asks a number of questions of an automated AI chatbot. Some of the information is useful and some isn't. The ability of the chatbot to understand and respond appropriately is clearly not perfect, but she is at least able to find some resources that will help her get to the answers she needs. While there are many text-based chatbot systems in use today to provide a first level of information for new hires, this is an area that will be evolving rapidly. Speech-based systems, with realistic call flows are becoming increasingly available for development of this kind of application. Perhaps even more interestingly for the purposes of this discussion, there is currently an explosion of new AI technologies that allow for real transfer learning in natural language understanding tasks, in multiple languages and with very impressive ability to be refined for specific knowledge domains. This is an exciting area in which new products will significantly reduce the time and human effort needed to onboard new employees.

In fact, it seems likely that AI systems will ultimately be able to suggest coverage options at onboarding time based on analysis of employee medical history. Of course, this requires some discretion around patient privacy and the visibility of patient health information to employers, but there are already technical and procedural solutions to such challenges.

Behind the scenes, there are ample opportunities for AI to identify when a new employee is struggling with a setup task and to proactively identify when further action needs to be taken. One new employee we spoke with logged into the HR information platform 15 times trying to figure out how to upload credit card expenses into the expensing system. Even in the absence of an automated solution to this problem, automated anomaly detection could have alerted HR that someone needed to reach out to help, potentially avoiding employee frustration and accounting issues down the road.

Training

We've seen that there is a basic level of onboarding and training that all new employees will receive, but there is also additional training that may benefit an employee based on their role, experience, and interests. In Jane's case, for her role as a Supply Chain Planner, several specific training courses on the supply chain tools and methods employed by Manufacture-X might have been appropriate, but given her extensive background in supply chain, including the additional knowledge about AI in Supply Chain Management that helped her get the job in the first place, some of this material would have been redundant or of low value. To address this, the training technology that Manufacture-X uses actually interviewed Jane to learn more about her knowledge and to match it with the training material. As a result, the training that Jane actually received was half as long as the basic training program and covered more of the relevant material in depth. The system also uncovered Jane's interest in managing a team in the future and was able to offer an additional training for operations managers at the company. This additional training not only increased Jane's engagement in the process, but began creating a path forward for her in the company. This is an area of potentially huge impact for AI in Human Resources that we will discuss more (Figure 4.6).

A moderately revolutionary idea about the future of AI-driven training holds that the creation of training programs and content will be increasingly driven by AI, synthesizing training material from a variety of sources including Internet video sites such as YouTube. Currently, since there is such a significant regulatory compliance component to training, this AI-centric future appears to be many years off. On the other hand, for technical training of programmers, data scientists, and infrastructure architects, online content is already a critical source of information, so it is easy to imagine more proactive AI-directed training content in these areas.

Another training concept that is beginning to take hold in HR circles is "just-in-time training," The idea is that as situations arise in the workplace, AI agents can detect that additional training might be appropriate. At the time of writing, #metoo is a significant cultural factor in the workplace. AI systems to detect tension in interactions early, with the opportunity to provide all parties with appropriate training materials could be a model for just-in-time training for a broad variety of topics. Another example might simply be the suggestion of Intellectual Property protection training arising from a new exposure of an employee to highly sensitive technical or business material. The opportunities are endless, and it is easy to imagine moderate levels of workplace monitoring yielding valuable and timely opportunities for additional training.

Figure 4.6 AI is being used to improve the quality of training for employees, matching the right content to the right person, for example, so that employees aren't trained on what they already know.

Coaching

Coaching of employees, especially managers and leaders, is rapidly becoming a core AI-driven activity for Human Resources in the enterprise. There are a number of reasons for this transition from human-managed coaching efforts to an AI-centric approach. For one thing, there is a significant training component to coaching, but the content for coaching tends to be more broadly applicable to managers across many functional areas and in different industries. This means that automated content curation can be a very effective way to both reduce the amount of human effort required to create coaching programs and to focus the content on the areas where coaching is most needed by each employee. Another major reason that coaching lends itself to AI optimization is that coaching can be tuned to address feedback from employees, and it is becoming increasingly simple to instrument feedback systems through AI interfaces. Specifically, the timing and contents of surveys that are presented to employees to get feedback can be managed algorithmically, and in fact if small amounts of information are gathered at any time, an approach known as micro-surveys, it is far easier to aggregate and track results with algorithms than through human efforts. Furthermore, the information gathered in the workplace to identify areas where coaching would be useful can be summarized with AI to provide high-level scores about employee satisfaction, areas of concern, and the effectiveness of coaching itself. The process is to measure, predict what would be impactful, execute on the recommendation and then measure the impact of the coaching. This virtuous AI development cycle appears to work very well in the enterprise, so we would expect such systems to continue to be embraced by companies looking to improve the effectiveness of their employees.

One word of caution in this area of AI-centric HR application: There is a vast number of "AI-powered employee engagement" products out there. They reach out to employees just like the AI-driven coaching applications described above, and they may even adapt their survey content, timing, and the size of the survey algorithmically, using ML. The big difference is that they are not tied to recommendations for coaching and the curation of coaching content for managers. This is a critical difference. To interact with employees and measure their attitudes, satisfaction and concerns is nice, and may even yield some dividends by making employees feel that the enterprise is listening to them, but at the end of the day, if these measurements don't drive specific action, they are missing out on 99% of the opportunity. Our advice is to avoid employee engagement or other HR products that can't directly influence decisions, or that can't help your HR organization decide which actions to take and then measure the impacts of these actions (Figure 4.7).

This is actually good advice for any AI-centric product. The virtuous cycle of measure, predict, act, measure, and repeat is the magic that will drive the value of AI far beyond the current generation of products that are looking to apply analytics to the various challenges that the enterprise HR organization faces.

Optimizing the Workplace

An interesting AI-driven change happened at Manufacture-X after Jane had worked there for six months. Effective Supply Chain Management in an organization depends

Figure 4.7 Algorithmic approaches are increasingly being used to identify coaching opportunities for employees, and to help managers improve how they coach their teams.

upon coordination and communication between diverse groups in the enterprise. As we saw in our chapter on AI in Supply Chain Management, predictive analytics, AI-based optimization, and process automation can have a significant impact on the operational efficiency of a supply chain. However, even in a moderately AI-centric organization like Manufacture-X, there are many humans in the loop, and communication between them can be crucial. In the case of Manufacture-X, management realized that there were gaps in communication between planning and manufacturing, so the company employed an AI-based optimization product to shuffle times of work breaks to create additional opportunities for people from different parts of the enterprise to interact, and hopefully communicate more effectively.

Did this effort work? This question is central to the puzzle of HR metrics and human centered measurement, which we will take up at the end of this chapter.

Retention: Keeping Employees

The marketplace is replete with products and technologies touting their impacts on employee retention. Why is this such an important area for HR to manage with technology? Because turnover rates are high in nearly every role in every industry, and the cost of replacing an employee can be astronomical. To be specific, the total separation rate for highly trained employees and career professionals in tech companies ranges from 12% to 25%. Turnover rates for all employees are typically double those for highly trained employees alone.[3] The cost to replace an employee is never small, but typically runs from 33% of annual compensation to 200% of annual compensation for the most difficult-to-fill roles.[4] 50% of the annual compensation times[5] 20% of the workforce is an enormous annual cost. The solution to this colossal challenge? Retaining employees.

But how? In the world of AI technology, the approach is to detect, predict, act, and automate.

To understand how we can apply AI to detect turnover risks, predict where turnover is likely and what is likely to cause turnover, act on the signals that our AI detects, and automate our detection, prediction, and action activities, we will need to first look at the main causes of employee turnover. We have observed five broad categories of factors that influence employee turnover.

Category 1: Employees Who Are Already Thinking of Leaving

How can AI help us with employees who already have one foot out the door? First, we need to know who they are. AI is currently being used to predict who is thinking of leaving based upon changes in workplace behavior, online activity, and contents of emails and other communications. Of course, knowing who is thinking of leaving, does not solve the problem, and in fact can lead to additional problems. It is not a desirable outcome for managers to begin to write off employees who have been predicted to be at high risk for leaving. In fact, given the fact that manager behavior is often connected to the desire of an employee to leave, the opposite behavior is likely to be desirable. Beyond this, the opportunity for AI to reduce the likelihood that an employee will leave is to detect patterns in which employees are intending to leave, and why. Emerging patterns of employee dissatisfaction can often be an early warning for a broader pattern in an organization.

Category 2: Bad Bosses

The old adage that "people don't leave jobs, they leave bosses" has been substantiated in many analyses of employee turnover. What are the key features of bad bosses that drive employees out? The most common factors are:

- Fairness: The perception that a manager or boss is not treating them, or others on a team, fairly.
- Blame: Managers who blame employees for organizational failures are highly likely to reduce the loyalty and engagement of employees.
- Negative Environment: Bosses who create negative work environments, in general, tend to drive turnover up.

AI-based tools are becoming critical to detect when these behaviors are happening so that corrective action may be taken. For example, it is possible to detect changes in communication patterns in meetings, email, and other interactions to identify situations that increase turnover risk. These technologies can detect employee behavior in response to negative environments and they can also detect the actual behavior of managers that may lead to losing good employees. Of course, many of these behaviors not only drive employees out, but they also negatively impact productivity in general. In fact, a personality pattern called "The Dark Triad," consisting of narcissism, Machiavellianism, and psychopathy, has been identified as a powerful negative factor in the workplace. The good news is that

Figure 4.8 The Dark Triad, a toxic mix of personality traits, is proportionally more common among enterprise leaders. Employee turnover is high for Dark Triad bosses. AI can help detect patterns of behavior related to the Dark Triad.

the prevalence of Dark Triad personalities is low in the general population (less than 1% of the population). The bad news is that it is believed that the prevalence of Dark Triad personalities within senior executives is 10 times higher than the general population, so it is relevant to identify the presence of these traits in the context of retention. It has been suggested in the psychology literature that Dark Triad-type leaders also have a high likelihood of derailing themselves, so ironically these bad bosses carry their own individual turnover risk! Fortunately, a number of AI-based tools, including linguistic analyses and gamified measurements have been developed to detect how employees score in this arena. In general, once negative patterns are detected in the workplace, then AI for coaching and training, as discussed above, becomes highly valuable (Figure 4.8).

Category 3: Corporate Culture and the Importance of the Work (Clarity, Meaning, Influence, and Feedback)

Research has found that there are some key attributes of the employee experience that live at the nexus of corporate culture and the importance of the employee's role, and which significantly impact turnover rates. Specifically, it is important for employees to have clarity in their responsibilities and in the definitions of the tasks they are expected to do. An emerging area of AI in this space is the application of algorithms and human interaction systems (e.g., chatbots, et cetera) in project management and Agile task management systems. In order to measure whether tasks are being performed efficiently and completely, they need to be specified in clear ways, which is leading to new products that help guide the writing of well-crafted task descriptions. Of course, tasks in a project management system are only a small sliver of the work that needs to be clearly defined to support employee satisfaction, but this work will likely be foundational to broader applications of AI in this arena. In our own experience, a broader lack of clarity in roles, responsibilities, and task expectations is usually accompanied by an overall lack of clarity in communication within a group. Specifically, when different members of a team communicate in vague terms, or with poor focus on shared definitions, expectations and boundaries between roles, this is both a symptom of low clarity in a work environment, and a cause of further propagation of low-fidelity definitions of work to be done. Both are deleterious to the retention of employees. We see an opportunity to use AI-based linguistic analysis to identify low-precision communication in presentations, emails, reports, project definitions, and even spoken communication in meetings, in order to flag communication that lacks clarity and coach teams to be more precise in their interactions.

We conclude that the definition of the work needs to be clear to minimize turnover. When this clearly defined work is perceived as meaningful or having significant value in the world, then satisfaction is higher and turnover is lower, in general. We are not aware of AI that specifically helps measure the meaningfulness of work… obviously this is a very human assessment, but there is an area of AI that is being used by Human Resources departments to measure employee satisfaction: engagement. Engagement is a huge topic in AI for HR circles, but the application of engagement in the enterprise has had mixed utility.

Engagement became a hot topic in HR after Gallup did a poll that measured "engagement" and which showed that only 13% of employees are engaged, and that companies with highly engaged workforces outperform their peers by 147% in earnings per share. This result has really gotten the attention of management and HR, and has led to a proliferation of AI-based tools to engage employees and to measure engagement. There have been two significant challenges with this line of effort. First, "engaging" employees is not always the same as increasing actual employee engagement. Often, AI for engagement automates alerts to managers to praise or reward employees to keep their engagement scores high. These efforts are nice, but don't address the corporate culture and meaningfulness of work questions that really matter. Second, many of these products don't provide any actions at all. They simply interact with employees, through microsurveys or chatbots, and measure an engagement score. Measurement without action is essentially useless. To be fair, we can't develop AI to improve engagement unless we are actually measuring it, and there are increasingly tools that correlate actions with changes in engagement scores to improve overall corporate outcomes. Our recommendation is to ensure that any AI-based employee engagement product you consider purchasing has clear actions and outcomes associated with them.

A final key factor in employee satisfaction and turnover is feedback and influence. Employees need to feel their input is being taken and that is has some influence on the decisions the company is making. This is an area where measuring employee engagement may actually improve things naturally by giving employees a sense that their engagement matters. But this is just one piece of a much larger puzzle that AI can help with. We are seeing an explosion in the number of technologies that can interact with employees, via text-based chatbots and speech-based dialog systems, allowing more opportunities for employees to provide in-depth input and feedback on managers, corporate culture, and even product direction. There is an opportunity in the future to use AI to summarize unstructured input from many employees and make this information more actionable. Interestingly, this is an AI generalization of statistical tools like the employee Net Promoter Score which is primarily survey based.

Category 4: Compensation, but not Just Salary

In a book chapter written for HR professionals, we don't need to explain why compensation is an important topic, and we've discussed previously how AI can be used in the recruiting and hiring phases to optimize compensation packages. In the context of retention, most research shows that benefits are more impactful than salary, so the relevant question for this discourse is "How can AI help make benefits more beneficial?" Our core assertion is that benefits that are difficult to use, or that employees are not aware of, are unlikely to increase retention. AI is being used to help with this.

On the utilization side, the core AI technologies that are relevant are human interaction and signal detection. Specifically, HR service desks are inundated with user questions about benefits: what they are, how to use them, what are the limitations, etc. There has been tremendous growth in tools to automate various aspects of service desk activities. Many enterprises already employ moderately intelligent chatbots to answer basic HR and benefits questions. Many of these are really intended as a filter to reduce call volume by catching the most frequent, simplest questions. In most cases, this is an 80/20 rule strategy, leaving at least 20% of people who spend time interacting with the chatbot having little to show for it except (hopefully) a service desk phone number to call. At the time of writing, natural language understanding tools are exploding, as Language Model-based AI systems are becoming powerful and have become viable for transfer learning. Simultaneously, spoken language understanding, speech-based dialog systems, and speech-to-text capabilities are growing rapidly, so there is every reason to believe that the sophistication of such systems will level up by a factor of ten in the near future. Our conclusion is that it should soon be a requirement of any HR information platform to support powerful speech-based automation to help employees use their benefits more effectively.

The other big opportunity to improve the positive impact of benefits using AI is the ability to suggest a relevant benefit at an appropriate time. After health, dental and vision insurance, which are the most influential nonsalary benefits, benefits relating to flexibility and work-life balance are most important. Flexible hours and the ability to work from home have been found to have a big impact. It is likely that employees don't always know what their options are in this area. Student loan assistance, tuition assistance, and paid maternity leave also impact employee retention so suggesting that these benefits are available at a time that is relevant to the employee is an important opportunity to create the maximum benefit. An algorithm that flags tuition assistance programs when an employee changes a child's insurance coverage after college enrollment is a simple example of AI in this situation. The challenge is that much of the employee data that would be relevant to the development and deployment of such AI systems is potentially private and although there can be a significant benefit to the employee to track such data, there are also major ethical concerns and risks to the organization. We will talk more about privacy and ethics, but the bottom line is that there are a lot of great things we could do with AI that we shouldn't do with AI, and a mature legal and ethical framework with regard to AI is critical for making decisions on what to implement and what not to implement.

An additional, and much more compelling and low-risk application of AI to keep employees around longer and more productively, is the augmentation of internal recruiting programs. The inability to advance in one's career within an organization is one of the most-cited reasons for leaving a company and in fact has been cited as "the primary driver of employee attrition."[5] On the flipside, there are a number of studies that indicate (for example,[6]) that promotion from within is less expensive in terms of salary and more successful in terms of corporate culture fit and employee productivity. So how can AI amplify promotion from within? A majority of HR professionals believe that AI can help match needs with skills of existing employees, improve access to relevant training through AI-driven training suggestions and by making employees aware of opportunities. We would expect to see recommender systems suggesting new career opportunities and training programs as if they were new products or movie choices. "You have these skills and took this training recently, you might want to try this new role…" From a privacy and ethics perspective this is a low-risk strategy and is completely within the current analytical purview of AI (Figure 4.9).

Figure 4.9 The number of options for employees to grow their careers within an organization is a major determinant of retention and employee satisfaction.

Category 5: Employees in Highly Competitive Roles such as Data Science

Roles that are difficult to fill because they are in high demand are likely to have high turnover. Data scientists, for example, have been notoriously difficult to find and hire, and they often move to new jobs quickly. How can AI help HR retain employees in these critical, but highly competitive roles? We believe that an ounce of prevention is worth a pound of cure. As we will see below, there are ways to improve retention with AI through engagement, better internal advancement, better sensitivity to working conditions, and well-crafted benefits, but these do not specifically address the significantly higher risk of turnover for high-demand roles. The best solution is to use AI preemptively in the recruiting phase to help identify the candidates that are most likely to stick around, despite being in high-demand roles.

Minimizing Risk

Managing regulatory, legal, and ethical risk is a major mandate of the Human Resources organization of any enterprise. Given that most risk is somehow related to the decisions or actions of humans, it is natural to imagine that AI will have a role in mitigating risk in the enterprise. We have seen that AI-based automation can reduce the variability in many processes. When these processes directly impact employee or consumer safety, it's an obvious win to reduce variability and hence, risk.

There are many other types of risk to employees and to the enterprise that HR is responsible for. A major category of risk to the enterprise is theft and fraud. Unfortunately, it is estimated that "shrinkage" accounts for more than $50 billion per year in costs to U.S. businesses alone.[7] In 2017, it was estimated that 30% of the total shrinkage was due to employee theft.[8] As a result, there is tremendous interest in detecting patterns of fraud and theft within the enterprise, and it's easy to see why AI technologies such as machine vision, natural language understanding, and predictive analytics would be central to these efforts. Video monitoring of warehousing and logistics environments is already widespread, but just as in the retail environment, it is impossible to utilize this data without automation from AI.

Risks to trade secrets can be detected via natural language understanding. Often, risks to Intellectual Property and trade secrets are the result of inadvertent exposure by employees rather than intentional disclosure for nefarious reasons. We have seen document and email monitoring systems that can flag situations in which sensitive material may be at risk for inappropriate distribution. The state of the art in this area is primitive, but given the explosive growth of natural language understanding capabilities, we would not expect this to be the case in the near future.

AI is already deeply embedded in network security technologies, making it possible to detect unusual patterns of network activity or data flow. While most of this technology is deployed and managed by IT, the role of HR in determining policies for monitoring internally-driven network activity is growing rapidly, and we expect that policies for monitoring will soon be jointly determined by HR and IT. In fact, we are seeing dramatic growth in the number of HR departments that have their own data science teams, working on efforts as varied as network activity anomaly detection and optimization of tools to detect negative behavior in the workplace.

This brings us to a source of risk to both employee and enterprise: Inappropriate behavior in the workplace. One could write an entire book on this topic. It is serious, damaging, and shockingly common in the workplace, increasing employee turnover, reducing workplace productivity, minimizing opportunities for synergies in mixed teams and creating significant potential liability for the enterprise. Much of the speech and physical behavior that constitutes inappropriate behavior can now be easily detected by AI algorithms, and there is significant interest by enterprises to monitor the workplace for these signals. There are two major challenges: First, while AI can detect negative speech and behavior, a lot of harassment in the workplace is based on nuance and implication, which are difficult to detect, for now. Second, and far more tricky, are privacy concerns, since it is not generally acceptable to monitor all employee speech and movement via video and audio. Again, there is much to consider in this domain as technology becomes capable of confidently detecting negative behavior in the workplace.

One capability that has seen some meaningful development in the area of workplace harassment is AI-assisted reporting of incidents. The U.S. Equal Employment Opportunity Commission recently reported that more than 70% of workplace harassment incidents go unreported[9], so reporting is an important gap that can be assisted via AI. A variety of technologies designed to interact with victims in a way that helps them feel comfortable relating difficult situations and providing an additional sense of anonymity have been developed. Other technologies provide information to employees about legal protections and guidelines on how to proceed in difficult reporting situations.

Finally, in many physically demanding work environments, AI is being used to directly improve employee safety. A number of wearable devices have been developed to detect dangerous situations for employees that cannot be recognized by a simple environmental detector. Prevention of back injuries in roles with repeated lifting requirements is a major target of these AI-based systems, which in some cases provide coaching through a speech interface to help employees perform tasks more safely. Slip and fall risks for employees and customers are also mitigated with video and sensor monitoring, backed by algorithms that detect dangerous or anomalous situations.

Given the importance of risk mitigation in Human Resources, it is not surprising that there are many applications of AI to help detect risk, identify behavior that could be dangerous to the organization and its employees and to reduce the impacts of theft and fraud. This is an area that we would expect to be covered extensively by new third-party product offerings and which are likely to be incorporated into HR information platforms quickly as well.

Measurement in HR: Statistics, Metrics, and Analytics

There is a famous saying in management, attributed to Peter Drucker, that "If you can't measure it, you can't improve it." To be 100% accurate, you might be able to improve something that you haven't measured, *but how would you know?* And how would you refine your methods as you make decisions and observe how the world plays out after your decision? Without measurement, there is no data. Without data, there is no data science. Without data science, there is no AI. So we need to measure, but we can't measure everything (a topic that we'll take on in our section on Privacy and Ethics), so what do you measure?

Human Resources has a long history of measurement, during which the availability of data and analytical techniques has constantly evolved. Analytics in HR can be broken into three categories: Organizational descriptive statistics, HR metrics which are operational measures of how "efficient, effective, and impactful an organization's HR practices are[10], and Talent Analytics which are more focused on identifying and defining decisions to be made and on guiding HR investment strategies. Our colleague Alexis Fink and her co-author Michael C. Sturman have written an excellent chapter on "HR Metrics and Talent Analytics" in the Oxford Handbook of Talent Analytics[11] that discusses in detail the evolution of measurement in HR. We encourage the reader to refer to this book for more details on how descriptive statistics, HR Metrics, and Talent Analytics fit together in the modern HR organization.

Talent Analytics, which is also known as workforce analytics and HR analytics, is the topic most germane to a discussion of AI in Human Resources. Much of what we have described above about recognizing patterns of behavior in the workplace, in identifying through analytics improved opportunities for advancement within the organization, and AI to help surface the most valuable benefits to employees, could all be categorized as Talent Analytics.

There is a critical implication for the management of HR teams themselves in this shift from HR Metrics to Talent Analytics. Traditionally, HR measurement and analytics in the enterprise has been an ongoing process of measuring and tracking specific well-defined values or KPIs. This means that staffing for utilization of HR metrics is much more about generating and reviewing reports and then communicating to management if something changes. The work is part of the broader workloads of a number of analysts or HR professionals and is mostly smoothly distributed over time, making it look a lot like ongoing financial reporting. Talent Analytics, on the other hand, is oriented around specific decisions or goals and is much more project oriented. In fact, to staff a series of ongoing talent analytics projects may require infrastructure support including IT, software development, and User Experience (UX) design working with HR subject matter experts and data scientists to define what the goal of the project is, what are the requirements for the outcome of the project and then to manage the development and deployment of the solution. This is work that looks like product creation, or at a minimum like project management with external technology integration.

This means that in order to support the HR measurement and talent analytics paradigm of the future, HR will either need to develop its own internal data science competency, or will need to have the ability to interface constructively with data science resources elsewhere in the enterprise. We have seen both models deployed with success, but our recommendation for larger enterprises that can afford to staff their own analytics and data science teams is to do just that. The reason is not that the analytics and AI technologies are different from other domain areas, but that the data environment in HR is significantly more sensitive to ethical, privacy, regulatory and legal concerns, so it is worthwhile to build a team that is better trained in these topics and is socialized to make them a priority. The truth is that we data scientists love data, and we love to do analytics, so we need to be trained thoroughly in the limitations of the data we can collect and frequently reminded about the guidelines and limitations on how we can use it. Some bespoke data science representation within the HR organization helps promote a more inclusive, ethical analytics program that will present less risk to the organization. Given that the biggest expense in most enterprises is human labor, this effort can be well worth it.

To be successful with Measurement and Talent Analytics, it is critical to be clear about the goal of each project or solution. It seems to be a safe assumption that the goal of a project would be paramount to its execution, but we have seen this assumption fail consistently. We are reminded of our children coming home from school, feeling dejected about a lower-than-expected grade on an exam. The conversation goes like this: "I thought you studied?" "I did study, and I understood everything, but I misread this one problem and got no points," to which we reply "You can't answer the question if you don't know what the question is!" In our careers in analytics leadership, we have had to remind project teams over and over the exact same thing. "You can't answer the question if you don't know what the question is!"

We would take this analogy further and characterize any AI-driven Talent Analytics project as the answer to a very specific question, nested within a number of goals and assumptions. First, we need to identify which major area of HR we want to impact. The goal may be to reduce turnover, increase productivity in a particular part of the organization, or perhaps to reduce the risk to employees in a particular function. Let's pick reducing turnover as our high-level objective. Next, we will need to have a working hypothesis. Perhaps we have some evidence or hunch that a critical predictor of employee attrition is the greeting that the employee receives at the reception desk each morning. We need to formulate a core question to answer in order to determine what action to take in this regard. We could ask "Is there an association between the greeting each employee receives and their 12-month probability of departure?" If we have historical information on the greetings received and the employment history of each employee, then we could compute this correlation. But would we be able to take action? Not necessarily. If the model tells us that no greeting is bad and any greeting is good, then we can create an "always greet" policy, but the situation is rarely that simple, and there is nowhere else to go. Another way to frame the problem would be to model the impact of each greeting or type of greeting (perhaps clustered into groups based on other text analytics such as sentiment score) on the departure probability of our employees. Such a model would then point us in the direction of better greetings as opposed to simply greeting or no greeting.

Privacy and Ethics

The Privacy and Ethics implications of AI are enormous, so we have dedicated the better part of our Chapter 10 on AI and Corporate Social Responsibility to them. In this chapter, we will look at the factors that make privacy and ethics even more sensitive when applied in the HR department, and we will examine some ways to ensure proper handling of data and analytics in HR (Figure 4.10).

Privacy is a huge concern for employees, and therefore for HR departments. Privacy laws are complex, far-reaching, and vary widely from location to location. Not only are there huge differences in privacy law between the European Union and the United States, but there are actually major differences in law between the states. Because the regulatory landscape is so complex, it is critical to have clear corporate policies in place about how different data collection and analytics projects may be carried out, and well-publicized and consistent procedures to obtain approval for studies. This process can be seen as an analog to the Institutional Review Board process that is followed for medical studies (both clinical and analytical), and HR leaders looking to guide governance will benefit from reviewing the history of the IRB process and learning where an "IRB lite" might be appropriate. To support AI projects in the HR department, it is important to have a good relationship with corporate counsel so that clear bi-directional communication can take place to identify areas of risk and mitigate these risks early in data collection and analytics efforts.

As we described above, it is beneficial for HR departments to have at least one in-house data scientist to work on AI development and deployment. A key reason for this is that the HR-centric data scientist will develop a more finely-tuned understanding of what is likely to be sensitive or legally impossible. Since the creation of

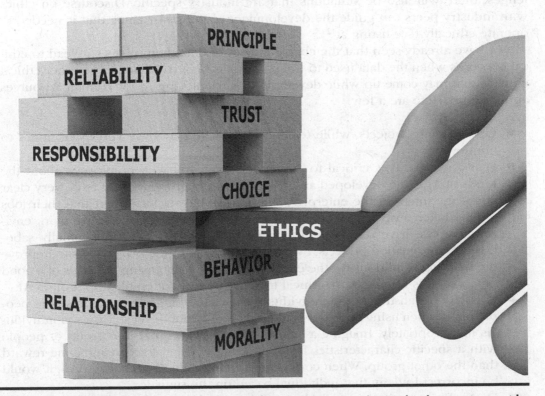

Figure 4.10 To build ethical AI systems, algorithm developers and AI technology users must be well trained in ethics. Good understanding of privacy, bias, and the unintended consequences of HR algorithms must all be second nature.

AI solutions is an iterative process, this heightened understanding of at least one member of the technical team provides a way to shorten project timelines, as fewer untenable ideas will be developed before they are exposed as counter to organizational privacy policy. Obviously, in addition to shortening timelines for projects, this approach reduces the overall risk that the company embarks on an ill-advised analytics program and finds itself in legal hot water.

Our conclusion is that privacy requires policies, processes, and some local HR expertise to stay on top of the rapidly changing regulatory landscape. Ethics is a bit different, because the exact definition of what is, or is not, ethical is more dependent upon the corporate culture, or upon cultural norms in general. These tend to change more slowly over time than regulations do. Also, since ethics are not in general required by law, the onus for creating an ethically robust AI program in HR is really on the HR organization itself, and often left to individual HR professionals and data scientists.

The implication of this observation is that HR departments will benefit from seeking guidance from other enterprises and from organizational consortia that are concentrating efforts to surface ethical challenges in AI for HR and that are sensitive to the specific challenges that arise in each industry. There is no doubt that healthcare, retail, banking, and manufacturing have very different ethical challenges, and while the HR departments in these industry verticals will see many similar ethical challenges, there will also be situations that are industry specific. Discourse on ethics with industry peers can guide the development of the governance that is needed to operate ethically (see listing at[12]).

We have already seen that the characteristics of data themselves can lead to ethical concerns when the data used to train models is biased. What are the other ethical gotchas that may come up while developing and deploying AI for Human Resources applications? Here are a few:

- Optics: Many projects, while technically ethical, may have very poor optics to employees.
- Fear about AI: It is critical to communicate clearly with employees about the kinds of AI being developed and used by HR departments, and to be very clear about the intent of the enterprise. Employees have a lot of fear that their jobs will be taken away by robots or AI, and this fear creates a negative work environment. We have seen several situations in which employees actually sabotaged AI automation projects, even when the goal of the project was to improve the working conditions for the employee. Besides increasing the odds of a good outcome, it is usually more ethical to allay the fears of employees around AI.
- Population statistics vs the individual: One of the biggest ethical mistakes people make when using analytics is to apply population-level statistics to individuals inappropriately. Imagine a statistic that indicates that one group of people with a specific characteristics has had a higher rate of receiving some reward than the other group. When considering an individual for that reward, it would be incorrect to deny that individual based on the statistic.
- Do No Harm: As in the medical case, it is critical that AI does no harm. Recently a social media company was found to have been attempting to alter the moods of users to determine the impact on behavior. Such a program run by an HR department could easily result in real harm to one or more employees: Imagine

a deeply depressed individual being pushed closer to self-harm by an AI "experiment." Definitely not ethical.

■ **Aggregated Data About a Single Person:** It's easy to make a major blunder with aggregated data that ends up exposing information about a single employee. It's a best practice to aggregate data to improve the statistical quality of the inferences and to mask individual data, but it is incumbent upon the data scientist to ensure that no view or restriction of the data can be easily inferred to be about a single person.

■ **Evil Data Scientists:** Not that data scientists are evil in general, but it is important to have some oversight on biases in algorithms that are intentionally promoted by individuals with negative agendas. Recently an internationally known professor of physics used spurious statistics to "prove" that women are inferior to men as scientists. We can only assume that this was driven by some personal agenda of this individual. Just remember that AI is trained with examples, and that the training is driven by objectives that have been defined by the data scientist.

■ **Bad Data:** Sometimes data is biased, but sometimes it is just low fidelity. It can easily become unethical to create algorithms or draw inferences from low-quality data. A version of this trap that we see all the time is the publication of an algorithmic result without a concomitant confidence measure. An inference that has a confidence of 20% should obviously not be acted on without further investigation, but if the confidence measures aren't published, how would anyone know?

There are many, many more situations in which ethical concerns can come up in the application of AI for HR. This should not be interpreted as a criticism of AI in HR. On the contrary, there are many more ethical and beneficial applications of AI in HR than there are potentially negative. The bottom line is that AI is a powerful tool, and as with any powerful tool, caution, diligence, and oversight are required to minimize the potential for harm.

As a final exercise in our discussion of ethics in AI for HR, we would like to examine the Code of Conduct for the Society for HR Management (https://shrm.org/). Specifically, let's look at the section on "Use of Information."

Use of Information

Core Principle

HR professionals consider and protect the rights of individuals, especially in the acquisition and dissemination of information while ensuring truthful communications and facilitating informed decision-making.

Intent

To build trust among all organization constituents by maximizing the open exchange of information, while eliminating anxieties about inappropriate and/or inaccurate acquisition and sharing of information.

Guidelines

1. Acquire and disseminate information through ethical and responsible means.
2. Ensure only appropriate information is used in decisions affecting the employment relationship.
3. Investigate the accuracy and source of information before allowing it to be used in employment-related decisions.
4. Maintain current and accurate HR information.
5. Safeguard restricted or confidential information.
6. Take appropriate steps to ensure the accuracy and completeness of all communicated information about HR policies and practices.
7. Take appropriate steps to ensure the accuracy and completeness of all communicated information used in HR-related training.

How might we implement this Code of Conduct to incorporate a more data- and AI-centric view of the world of Human Resources in the Enterprise? What is missing from this Code of Conduct?

Finally, some Questions to Ask: You are an executive or decision maker in an enterprise with HR responsibilities. There are vendors and pundits pushing AI everywhere and you have to make decisions about what to build, what to buy, how to change your organization, and what to ignore as hype. What questions should you ask?

■ What is the real value of this technology to my overall enterprise? Is the technology set up to measure and report on this value?
■ Does the technology give me the information I need to take action? (If not, walk away.)
■ How do I measure the effects of the technology? In money? In employee retention? In corporate culture advancement?
■ Does the technology use data that I already have access to?
  – Who owns the data? (for example, benefits details such as medical conditions can't be shared with an employer)
  – How must the data be protected?
■ How much effort is required to set up the technology? To maintain it in the long run?
■ Do I need to have analytics experts on my staff who can understand the capabilities and limitations of the technology?
■ Does the product link seamlessly with the HRMP or other enterprise software that I am using?
■ How do I ensure that I am not feeding the system biased data, leading to undesirable results?
■ Does the technology provide a way to compare how my organization is performing relative to other organizations? (This is classic benchmarking.)
■ Who in my organization actually uses or interfaces with the technology? What is the cost in terms of my peoples' time?
■ If you intend to build a model internally, what data do you have to train it, and what does that mean in terms of the quality of the model?
■ How often are you going to have to retrain your model to maintain its accuracy?
■ Do I really need AI to do this or is there a better way? (Sometimes fancy technology is not the most direct path to a useful and reliable solution.)

- What is the reaction of the employees going to be? (To avoid a negative result you need to make sure new AI tools do not create fear or a sense that Big Brother is watching.)
- Was the algorithm trained with data that is representative of my workforce or employment circumstances?
- Does the product adhere to the rules of where you are operating? (For example GDPR in Europe, CCPA in California.)
- Does the technology clearly protect the privacy of your employees, your leadership, and the company itself?

Conclusions

We can easily conclude from this chapter that discourse around the implications of AI is already part of the Human Resources landscape. Further, there are already AI solutions taking root in the HR Department, from improving the quality and effectiveness of job descriptions to optimizing training for individuals.

It is also clear that we are on a journey in which the prevalence of AI solutions in HR is likely to grow dramatically. AI is good at dealing with unstructured data, and humans generate huge amounts of unstructured data in the form of speech, writing, photos, and video. Furthermore, algorithms are not intrinsically biased, and their "motivations" can be probed much more easily than those of human decision makers, so the opportunity to dramatically improve the fairness, and therefore ultimate value, of hiring activity in the enterprise must not be ignored.

There are two major challenges to this. First, because algorithms learn from data, and data is collected by humans, there is a significant risk that we created biased algorithms that simply reinforce the human biases that already exist in hiring. Second, the process of collecting and storing sensitive data about employees, and the development and deployment of algorithms trained on this data can result in the exposure of private data if not done properly. Both of these risks can be addressed, for example by rigorous training of algorithm developers and users, and in order for AI and HR to mix safely, they must be addressed.

The opportunity to improve the entire lifecycle of employees in the enterprise through the disciplined use of AI cannot be overlooked, and if done well will be an exciting journey for HR personnel, management, and employees alike.

Notes

1 Dan-Olof Rooth, Automatic associations and discrimination in hiring: Real world evidence, Labour Economics, Volume 17, Issue 3, 2010, Pages 523–534, ISSN 0927-5371, https://doi.org/10.1016/j.labeco.2009.04.005.
2 Stijn Tonk, "Towards fairness in ML with adversarial networks," Go Data Driven, https://blog.godatadriven.com/fairness-in-ml, retrieved September 25, 2021.
3 U.S. Bureau of Labor Statistics, "Job Openings and Labor Turnover Survey," https://www.bls.gov/jlt/, retrieved 2020.
4 Nick Otto, "Avoidable turnover costing employers big," https://www.benefitnews.com/news/avoidable-turnover-costing-employers-big?brief=00000152-14a7-d1cc-a5fa-

7cffccf00000&utm_content=socialflow&utm_campaign=ebnmagazine&utm_source=twitter&utm_medium=social, retrieved September 25, 2021.

5 G Sheppard, "Work-life balance programs to improve employee performance," Walden University Scholar Works, 2016, 1–329.

6 Bidwell, Matthew. "Paying More to Get Less: The Effects of External Hiring versus Internal Mobility." Administrative Science Quarterly 56, no. 3 (September 2011): 369–407. https://doi.org/10.1177/0001839211433562.

7 National Retail Federation, "Retail shrink tops $50 billion as cyber threats become more of a priority," press release, June 6, 2019, https://nrf.com/media-center/press-releases/retail-shrink-tops-50-billion-cyber-threats-become-more-priority.

8 Ibid.

9 Chai R. Feldblum and Victoria A. Lipnic, "Select Task Force on the Study of Harassment in the Workplace," June 2016, https://www.eeoc.gov/select-task-force-study-harassment-workplace#_Toc453686303.

10 Alexis A. Fink and Michael C. Sturman, "HR Metrics and Talent Analytics," in The Oxford Handbook of Talent Management Edited by David G. Collings, Kamel Mellahi, and Wayne F. Cascio, (Oxford: Oxford Handbooks Online, September 2017), DOI: 10.1093/oxfordhb/9780198758273.013.25.

11 Ibid.

12 "15 Best Organizations and Associations for Human Resource Professionals," https://www.humanresourcesmba.net/best-hr-organizations-associations/.

Chapter 5

Customer Experience Management

Kirk Borne
DataPrime Inc.

Contents

DOI: 10.4324/9781351032940-5

Introduction

The Platonic Ideal of the Customer Experience actually exists. We've found it many times, often in the form of a one-of-a-kind retail institution, such as an owner-operated jeweler, a third-generation café, a family-run lady's boutique. As businesses around them flicker in and out of existence, these institutions glide through the decades, with category-defying margins and patrons who would sooner switch churches than shop elsewhere. In the owner-operated boutique, the owner knows what we look good in, and what to gently steer us away from. In an owner-operated camera store, sticker prices are merely an opening bid, cheerfully ignored to win a marginal sale or reward a loyal customer. The menu in the best cafés is no more than a suggestion; if your four-year-old wants her egg sandwich "deconstructed" (boiled egg on the side), then it shall be so.

Those category-defying margins allow the owners to open new outlets; but usually, the profit per square foot will be much lower, and further expansion will be discouraged. Of course, we live in a world of counterexamples, brands that seem to occupy every block in every city we visit. However, even in the most successful cases, it's hard to replicate all the magic of the original. Owners are hard to scale! How can a business scale the level of attention, of flexibility, of *service* that we see in these "ideal stores"? It's hard to do this within the confines of the manuals and standardization that built the big chains. Analytics and machine learning (ML) can't replicate the "owner magic," but they can help the business to understand and better serve the customer, allowing larger organizations to move closer to the Platonic Ideal we have described. This is consistent with a common definition of ML as the study of computer algorithms that improve automatically through experience and by the use of data, which is then deployed to power AI applications.

Customer Experience

Beyond Relationship to Engagement

A company might legally be considered a person. However, a bundle of physical and intellectual property is an unlikely participant in anything as warm and fuzzy as a relationship. And yet, consumers do develop visceral reactions to their favorite brands, forming attachments and expectations that do seem to accord a mere corporation with personhood.

We instinctively expect our friends, acquaintances, and colleagues to remember past interactions. The more successfully that our marketing imbues a brand with identity and personality, then the more we shift customer expectations toward this standard. The power of a brand is that instead of seeing a website or a sales assistant, the customer sees *the company as a partner in their journey*, and expects "the company" to remember them and act in a way that is consistent with their mutual history. Since "the company" is essentially a legal invention, this can be a tough illusion to sustain.

Machine learning combined with customer data can help us to meet these expectations, to respond to a customer in ways that reflect their tastes, intentions, and needs.

AI powering the Digital Marketing Funnel

Awareness (Discoverer), Interest (Curious), Intent (Motivated), Conversion (Decider), Loyalty (Customer), Advocacy (Fan)

One universal truth of humans is no one likes to feel they are being sold something, and another truth is "The psychological equivalent of air is to feel understood" says Steven Covey. (Preferably that would be fresh air, not hot air.) These two truths are the cornerstones of the transition from bricks and mortar to digital retail. Most readers will have spent enough time in a store to be able to recognize the intentions of other shoppers without conscious effort. When our "store" is a website, how can we approach this level of intuition about our visitors, and how can analytics help us to convert them into loyal customers?

In a world where the customer experience is informed by data about each unique potential customer, forward-thinking companies are modifying the customer journey to reflect an understanding of that person they are speaking too. That includes a shift in focus from content to context—not only focused on what the customer appears to be interested in, but also when, where, how, and with what else. The shift could be as simple as modifying the color scheme of the landing page depending on the time of day the customer is accessing the site, or as "small data"-driven as integrating the potential customer's name into the landing page on the first visit. When AI is used to automate this shift in a personalized way for each customer interaction, then scaling the online business to the Platonic Ideal of customer experience becomes reachable.

The Discovery Phase

There are still web stores that behave like a digital version of a catalog, leaving it to the user to flick through product listings. The obvious analytics play for customers entering our funnel is to try to show the customer whatever they are most likely to buy. The search terms a customer uses are a great starting point, but only a starting point. Using additional information on a specific customer can help improve the relevance of what we show them.

Automatically incorporating extra customer information into the online interaction is what turns a search into an AI-powered recommendation. Personalization in the discovery phase with useful and relevant recommendations can immediately frame the customer experience as a relationship, not as a "sale." Such positive engagement can linger far beyond that moment—even if it does not end in a sale this time (conversion), the customer will "remember" to return to this site the next time. That's loyalty. When the experience is worth talking about (especially in online reviews or social networks), then that's advocacy (becoming your fan in the marketplace). Customer data make that possible when used in ML algorithms to automate customer offers through AI (which can be construed in business applications in another way: as actionable intelligence).

Recommendations are easy in the special case of a small number of products that many people purchase repeatedly, and their value might seem less obvious for such "staples" which the customer will buy in any case. The real value of giving prominent placing to these products is the time that you are saving your customers; the value to *you* is that you are offering a very difficult-to-replicate experience, effectively offering each customer a "shop" arranged for their personal convenience, according to their unique preferences, something a competitor without the same history with that customer cannot replicate. Making sure customers have easy access to the things they already know they want to buy is a powerful way to protect revenue and defend against churn. AI may not be necessary to identify these obvious offers, but AI can respond "intelligently" to themes and trends in customer interests and intents as a function of numerous factors, including time of day, day of the week, season, product category, customer browse patterns, and other digital "breadcrumbs," thus making these slightly less obvious offers both surprising and delightful.

Where recommender engines can further boost customer revenue is in the "long tail" of your product offerings, products that a given customer might purchase rarely or only once, and which have low total sales volume. This is also the most technically challenging regime—on what basis can we possibly infer that a never-before-purchased product will delight a customer? Without algorithms, the lack of purchase data will miss this sales opportunity. Without the wider collection of other customers' data, even the most cunning algorithms won't be able to connect the dots that lead to these rare offers. Consequently, successful recommendation engines become powerful revenue generators when they blend information from multiple sources with the application of algorithms that are designed to find interesting product associations (links in the product graph that may have surprisingly few "degrees of separation").

Other AI approaches that assist the discovery phase in moving the customer from interest and intent to conversion and loyalty include natural language processing, location intelligence, low-dimensional embeddings, and reduction in uncertainty through feedback loops. Most of these work in a higher-dimensional space of customer and product parameters that the human brain cannot easily explore but an AI algorithm can rapidly exploit.

Product Descriptions

Modern natural language processing is powerful enough to compare text *semantically* rather than merely lexically so that a machine can measure the similarity between two product descriptions. This involves converting the text to something called an embedding—essentially, the machine learns to place each description in a high-dimensional space such that similar things are close together and disparate ones far apart. Whereas our own three-dimensional physical space only gives us three axes along which we can arrange our things, a higher-dimensional space allows many more ways for things to be similar *and* different.

Conveniently, recent advances in machine learning allow the *images* of products to be given their own embedding, *even one which is shared with textual descriptions*. Placing text and images in a common frame of reference is a powerful basis for both recommendation and search—we can look for products that are *visually* similar to something a customer has bought or browsed in the past, or that have similar descriptions, or both.

Customer Territory

In a similar way, customers themselves can be converted to embeddings, by assigning them coordinates in a sort of high-dimensional atlas of customer behaviors and interests. As with product descriptions, customers with similar habits and tastes should be placed in close proximity in this "customer space." The limiting factor in this sort of "location intelligence" will be your team's ability to integrate disparate information on a given customer, including their purchasing history, their geographic location, their visits to your website, and even seemingly insignificant details like the precise *device* they used to visit the site (for example, in some regions, Apple users have been found to have a greater propensity to spend). What is most critical here is access to quality customer data across different enterprise databases. As always, a successful AI strategy begins with a successful data strategy.

Birds of a Feather

Recommendation engines—which, after all, are just search engines that run without receiving explicit user instructions—can use these customer and product parameter spaces to find near neighbors for both customers and products. If you've got a big product catalog, then most items will always be rare purchases for most customers, so data on individual items will typically be quite thin. Embeddings are therefore used to map those sparse data into information-packed condensed representations. Consequently, "birds of a feather flock together" in our product and customer embeddings, thereby allowing a recommendation engine to make connections between similar products and between customers with similar wants. Identifying the robust mapping between customer personas and product categories in a complex data space is a routine job for an AI algorithm.

Getting to Know You

An ideal recommendation engine goes further than merely sorting your catalog to bubble the likeliest items to the top of the list. Good sales assistants don't merely respond passively to questions from shoppers but ask questions that help them better understand how to serve the customer. Similarly, a good recommendation engine will attach uncertainty estimates to its model of the customer and can use these to make recommendations that serve to reduce the uncertainty (is this customer interested in *playing* football or *watching* it? new boots or a new TV?). Views and clicks are a means of making a sale *in the current moment* but they are also a way to learn more about a customer and so increase future sales. This type of validation through feedback reduces uncertainty and model error—a basic feature of machine learning and AI applications.

For many companies, it will make sense to buy an AI-based recommendation engine-as-a-service rather than build from scratch. New firms that specialize in providing recommendations as a service can give you a relatively short path to higher customer engagement and increased revenue. Companies like Recombee[1] have flexible solutions that can be tailored to suit a variety of businesses and provide fine-grained recommendations that balance showing customers more of their favorites with helping them to explore and discover new products. Whether building in-house has a higher ROI than an off-the-shelf solution is a question each business will have to answer for itself.

The Interest Phase

Customers often like to explore alternatives before committing to a purchase. During this phase, it can be useful to offer customers ways of signaling their interest. "Save for later" or "click to compare" buttons give the customer something that helps them with their shopping. It also helps us avoid a kind of miscommunication that can happen when these options are not present. For example, customers may add items to a shopping cart not because they want to buy now, but because they don't want to lose track of it while they make their minds up; from an analytical perspective, this makes it harder to distinguish the committed from the curious. Depending on the nature of your business, a high-quality newsletter, a YouTube channel or an Instagram feed may be effective ways to build interest in an undecided customer, and each of these offers a chance to learn more about your customer base.

For example, newsletters can be both a powerful marketing tool to build new interest and a great way to learn more about your customers' existing interests; when a customer opens a mail, tracking tools allow us to connect this action with previous contacts with the same customer, building a clearer picture. Even the *failure* to open newsletters is informative (perhaps last month's content wasn't quite as compelling as it might have been). All of these actions or inactions produce signals (data) that can be collected and then fed into improved AI models of a customer's interests and intents.

The Conversion Phase—Closing the Sale

The abandoned shopping cart is a perennial frustration: losing a customer right at the end of the sales funnel is more painful because their abandoned cart shows us exactly what they looked at, thought about, and rejected. We can see exactly how much they *nearly* spent.

AI can't save all these sales, but it can help. In our ideal store, the owner, seeing a customer hesitate, can sweeten the deal with a freebie or a discount. Perhaps we can make a bundle offer, include a "free gift" or give a special deal on shipping? Returning to the customer models that are so essential to successful recommendations, machine learning can use the information we collect on our customers to estimate their responses to different offers. Collecting feedback (data) on the success or failure of these "experiments" provides continuous training and improvement of the AI model.

Each offer made and accepted or rejected then becomes a new training sample to further improve our models. Good clean training data examples are the fuel for AI algorithms—the more the better. Readers who use Amazon may have noticed small changes in the prices of products that they looked at but didn't buy; the authors have no privileged knowledge of those internal pricing algorithms, but this is exactly the kind of behavior we would expect to see from an AI trying to close a sale: each of us has our own "demand curve," a function of our preferences and our needs at a given point in time, and estimating the shape of this curve at a given point in time is exactly the sort of heuristic problem that machine learning excels at solving.

An example of this for a customer journey is bundling of services in which you are addressing the customer's bigger goal with a complete solution vs. a one-time sale. Successful companies in the health and wellness space have done well in recognizing the need for a holistic approach, and are creating ongoing online digital content subscriptions to bundle with supplements, coaching, and food delivery systems. This allows companies to increase margins with a SaaS offering, to increase the touchpoints with their customers to reduce churn (as well as to produce a richer map of the customer journey), and to increase the likelihood of the customer achieving their goals over time. This requires a good understanding of the customer persona being engaged, as a 25-year old single man likely has different constraints to wellness compared to a 45-year old working mom. AI allows the brand to provide personalized and relevant experiences that are targeted to each customer's unique persona. This will likely yield better click-through rates, targeted advertising campaigns, and ultimately more sales conversions.

AI powering the 5 E's of Experience (Connected to the Marketing Funnel through Maslow's Hierarchy of Needs)

When we consider the various dimensions of customer experience, we must return to the basis set of needs that drive many human decisions and actions. That set is collectively referred to as Maslow's Hierarchy of Needs. These include Self-Actualization,

Esteem, Love and Belonging, Safety Needs, and Physiological Needs. When customers shop and ultimately buy, they are (in some measure) satisfying one or more of these fundamental human needs. For example, a powerful motivator in marketing is FOMO—the fear of missing out—which ties directly into one's need to feel like you belong, that you are accepted, and that you are not being left out of something that others are experiencing. When a product helps you feel empowered, or esteemed, or safe, or healthy, then that is clearly connected with those deep human needs. Consequently, the compact version of the traditional marketing funnel touches those same points indirectly (and emphatically) through five stages: awareness, consideration, conversion, loyalty, and advocacy. Those five stages (sometimes more than five shades are included) in the marketing funnel are specific objectives of different marketing campaigns. How the modern marketer reaches those objectives is what we will now address. This is where data and AI can inform and inspire different experiences that propel the customer along the marketing funnel, by finding those "moments" that link with the customer's core needs. As a nod to the five components of Maslow's hierarchy and the five stages in the marketing funnel, we explore here five dimensions of customer experience: Encounter, Expectations, Empathy, Engagement, and Emotion.

Encounter (Create Awareness Among Your Stakeholders)

Most experiences that consumers have today are informed by their digital data footprint they have left behind. This helps marketers to craft the right message for the customer persona through each experience with their brand. With digital touch points ranging from text to social media, influencers, email, and beyond, the opportunities to reach new customers are widely expanding.

One of the most powerful convincers is the "social proof" afforded by a friend's endorsement of a particular product (one author here can trace decades of "cider appreciation" back to a university friend's recommendation; another author owes his uninterrupted loyalty to one specific brand of athletic shoes to a recommendation from a fellow runner three decades ago). Although the phrase can seem a little overused, social media "influencers" can be a powerful ally in building awareness. First though, you have to find them! Follower count alone is too crude a metric to help you find the right people: you need to identify people who are already passionate about the market segment you care about, and have used this passion to build a following. Major platforms like Twitter offer APIs that, in conjunction with natural language processing (and, yes, machine learning) can be used to identify potential influencers in your sector, the people with Kevin Kelly's proverbial "1,000 true fans"[2]. AI can help with such awareness campaigns on multiple platforms, to identify specific customer personas, for any number of diverse products and services. This "awareness building" consequently satisfies the need to belong, hence slaying that fear of missing out.

Expectations (Identify Your Stakeholders' Needs)

Companies can identify and attempt to meet customers' expectations by building customer personas that map to the needs that potential customers express in social media, in online interactions, in search histories, through web beacons or cookies, in their response rates to email or Call-to-Action (CTA) campaigns, and more. Digital footprints (sometimes referred to as digital exhaust or trails) provide a rich motherlode of data points to measure customers' interests, expectations, and needs. These needs are not Maslow's needs, but they are specific product needs, product requirements, desired features of products, price expectations, and more. Nevertheless identifying these needs is ultimately a pathway to tapping into Maslow's needs.

Persona-building is not the same as profiling customers' psychographics, which is a qualitative methodology used to describe consumers based on psychological attributes.[1] Psychographics have been applied to the study of personality, values, opinions, attitudes, interests, and lifestyles. While some of that goes into building a customer persona, the data sources and methods (AI and machine learning) go well beyond traditional demographic data analysis.

Reaching into the AI and machine learning toolkit, marketers can use clustering analysis to identify segments and personas in the customer population, use network (graph) analysis to identify frequently co-occurring needs (this product, in that color, with this form factor), also use graph analysis to identify influencers and to track marketing attribution, use sentiment analysis to measure the strength of customers' concerns and/or convictions about their existing product versus their ideal product, apply regression analysis to predict consumer interest and demand, and so on.

Empathy (Meet Your Stakeholders at Their Place of Need)

Tools that help customer experience teams with ticket management, such as Intercom or Zendesk, have been an essential mechanism for engaging concerned customers and to help reduce churn. They are collecting rich amounts of data about the customer's pain points, and companies such as Productboard are adding API integrations to make the most of this information by leveraging AI to show empathy with the customer by surfacing the following customer issues:

- Feature requests
- User pain points
- Questions due to usability issues
- Un-met user needs
- Comments that touch on features in competing products

This is invaluable information for product engineering teams, informing both product enhancements and bug fixes to reduce churn. Often the distance between the customer-facing teams (experience teams, sales, and marketing) and the internal facing teams (engineering) can be difficult to close. Collaboration and shared data points can help, especially when there is a match between the two teams' objectives. Just as AI has been used to match people in online dating apps, based on shared interests, similarly an enterprise AI can match customer-facing teams with the right engineering teams, at the point of customer need. Demonstrating that degree of responsiveness to the customer is further evidence of empathy.

The good news is that these benefits are not just for large enterprises. Even small and medium-size businesses can benefit from AI. As these enterprises scale up, these AI capabilities will be invaluable in keeping the development and engineering teams still in synch with the voice of the customer, as they probably were when their business was first conceived and launched. If nothing else, a social network analysis of your organization can reveal who is talking with whom and where significant collaboration gaps exist. Connecting those dots (or the lack thereof) with the customers' areas of concern is an interesting example of using AI as a recommendation engine for cross-enterprise functional engagement with the customer.

Engagement (Generate Interest and Curiosity Via Data-Informed Experiences)

Once data has been collected on a customer's interests, needs, and/or concerns, then it is imperative to engage with that customer. Engagement can be triggered by customer data (of the types mentioned earlier) and can take the form of specific actions or interactions on the customer's behalf. Enterprises are already employing AI to identify actionable alerts in many other data streams, including cyber incidents, market research, social sentiment analysis, employee satisfaction surveys, and even employee churn. Passive inaction on those enterprise-related alerts is bad business management. Passive inaction (nonengagement) on customer-related alerts is bad customer experience management.

Positive action means active engagement with the customer. After encountering the customer and identifying some of their expectations, then it is time to lift their interest and curiosity. Data informs how, what, when, where, and to whom the engagement should move forward. The engagement should be matched to customer expectations and needs. Again, AI can play the matchmaker here. Having customer personas is good. But, having a playbook of engagements for each person is even better. Training an AI with examples of successful (and unsuccessful) engagements, so as to deliver the right experience at the right time to the right customer, is best. Successful engagement moves the customer forward on the marketing funnel, toward conversion and loyalty.

Emotion (Apply Sentiment Analysis to Discover How the Experience Made Your Stakeholders Feel)

> People will forget what you said, people will forget what you did, but people will never forget how you made them feel.
>
> *–Maya Angelou*

As portrayed in culture, emotions and analytics appear to be in opposition—Kirk versus Spock; Dr. Watson versus Sherlock Holmes. Unless your customer base is drawn exclusively from the planet Vulcan however, an awareness of your customer's emotional response to your product and your company is important, and so we ought to try to measure it and understand it. Rapid feedback to your customer engagement (through live data) is ideal, but any sort of timely feedback is imperative. Sentiment analysis can deliver this. It is a type of AI that applies machine learning to training data that is primarily language (hence, natural language processing on social media posts or product reviews or emails or customer calls to the contact center), with labels on each training example indicating positive, negative, or neutral sentiment. The model is applied to new customer messages automatically, generating actionable alerts on messages that warrant a response.

Many a product trades at least in part on the positive emotions it creates, and even the most workaday utilitarian offerings need at least to avoid pushing customers into the arms of competitors. The most successful brands in the world today are really selling an experience. The physical product delivers that emotional lift, and Maslow is correct once again. But a product that is placed on a store shelf (or on an online e-commerce website) in a shrink-wrapped package alone does not generate that emotion. It is the data-driven customer engagement that aligns the product with all of the interests, intentions, desires, and needs of the targeted customer population. They will then want this. They will need this. They may not remember (or know) the details of your marketing campaign, but they will never forget how you made them feel.

A warning to the reader: although we are confident that emotions are real and important, that **does not** automatically make them accessible and legible to an observer. Companies selling new products targeting the security and recruitment sectors are making strong claims for the ability of machine learning to discern emotions and even personality traits through video of subject's expressions. These claims are surprising, given an extensive literature in the social sciences that demonstrates the difficulty that humans—presumably under extreme evolutionary pressure to be good at making sense of other humans—experience in making these assessments of other humans. Your baseline assumption should be that when people do not want to make their feelings visible, they will hide them very successfully. Glance at the commuters who may well surround you as you read: a wall of blank inscrutability is the facial uniform whether you are in Berlin, London or San Francisco.

Luckily, the converse is also true: if someone wants you to know how they feel, they'll show you. The value that businesses place on emotion is visible to the public in the form of the devices and surveys used to find out "how we did today." The difficulty with eliciting feedback in this way is that this voluntary feedback is typically given by a self-selecting sample, mostly people who are feeling especially happy or angry.

Angry customers—especially vocal, *publicly* angry customers—can be a great opportunity for a business to demonstrate a strong commitment to good customer experience. *If* you can take someone who's angry and make them happy, you've got a very powerful tool for convincing prospective customers to join you. A five-star review from a former detractor is worth a hundred from committed fans.

Emotion is hard to elicit from tabular data; perhaps a customer is cooling on your hotel chain, or perhaps they just aren't traveling as much these days. It's much easier if your customer has written to you; of course, customer service tickets aren't going to be a sea of positivity, so looking for negative emotions there is going to be a "water is wet" nondiscovery. However, machine learning *can* help you discover "topics" that are important sources of customer anger. When we discussed how AI can help with the "Discovery" phase of a customer's interactions, we mentioned that raw text can be converted to "embeddings," a kind of map which placed similar products close together. A similar process can be applied to customer tickets, so that complaints on similar issues cluster close together, even if customers use different words to describe the same underlying problem. Thanks to machine learning, we can do an analysis that lets us ignore irrelevancies (like the vagaries of spelling, punctuation, grammar, terminology) and focus on important similarities, and we have an example of these capabilities later in the chapter.

Recommender Engines and Personalization

Humans inherently have a bias that other people think and see the world as they do. When I see someone looking at a plate of food I dislike, I think they must be disgusted when they are actually delighted. In business this applies to how we anticipate people will behave. For example, I ask someone "how do you know what your employees want and need in order to remain loyal to your business?" Commonly the leadership with answer with "we know what employees want." "The challenge is that everyone has a different viewpoint for what will make the workplace work for them," says Carolyn Peer, CEO of Humaxa. With the workforce continuing to evolve, the needs of employees are no longer a "one size fits all" situation. Some employees value flexibility in their schedules, some value career advancement, and for some it could be pay; and these needs may evolve and shift over time. Employers know what factors go into the trends, but unless you are personalizing for each person, you are guessing what any particular person might value. This guessing and lack of personalization can lead to expensive results including spending money on things that don't work, attrition, and poor performance. Technology that is requesting feedback on a real-time basis from employees and using AI to surface emerging trends in the workplace culture, training needs, and building communities can help to improve outcomes for employees and ultimately increase results to the bottom line.

History of Customer Personalization

Over the past decade, the largest changes have been to Google and Facebook themselves. With AI being introduced into software platforms for email automation and ad buying it has become a competitive advantage for the advertising industry to understand the algorithms to help enterprises make the most of their return on ad spend (ROAS) investments. This has expanded a company's ability to reach and target potential customers, which was not feasible a decade ago, which in turn has been revolutionary by increasing how profitable campaigns can be. "It is an everyday part of life as an ad agency owner to change the customer's user experience, including what they see and how they see it. More messages are personalized and positively benefit the potential customer," says Anthony Acceterro, CEO of Launch Titans. "Also, the way brands communicate with customers via email is optimized. AI continues to enable improvements in the landscape." Investments by tech companies like Google and Facebook AI have enabled much finer-grained targeting for the marketing and advertising industry, getting the right message at the right time to the right potential consumers creating opportunities for many companies to find their loyal customer base and scale up with a significantly lower bar for entry into the market.

Examples in Marketing (Customers)

People are adding more and more touch points in their own customer journey, typically 4–5 before a sale (Facebook, Pinterest, Google Ad, Instagram Influencer, etc.). Some ad agencies are innovating to help enterprises better understand, if their marketing spends are working by creating analytics for tracking and attribution of return on ad spend. "By building out data warehouses to do customer business intelligence visualizations and dashboards, we are helping enterprises hyper-target their customers. For companies that already have revenue in the hundreds of millions, we can help them decide where to put their ad investments. By shifting their dollars to what is converting, these companies can make \$10M in revenue just by optimizing ad spends," says Anthony Accenturo. The customer experience does not end at the sale. Savvy marketers are engaging customer both before and after the sale to help with customer loyalty, and in the case of subscription-based products, to reduce churn. By staying engaged with the customer data, companies can continuously optimize messaging. Companies are now working with agencies to craft the customer experience and build big automation to create that experience across platforms. A customer may hear about a product from their favorite influencer on Instagram, then see an ad pop up on Google for it, then see it surface in their Pinterest feed, get an SMS nudge for it, and then get a Facebook ad. This leads some customers to believe their phones are spying on their conversations, but in reality it is more likely attributed to companies building their psychographic profiles and tracking the buying behavior of their cohort to provide them nudges for the right products at the right time.

Examples in Services (Digital Users)

Safety is one of the foundational layers for Maslow's hierarchy of needs. In a world that amplifies our awareness of threats, it is hard to measure risk accurately. We are living in times where we are rich in information but poor in wisdom. An example of a service that is helping to separate the true threat signals from the noise is the use of AI in threat scans in schools. The market for school internet filtering products is almost 20 years old, and mandated as part of receiving federal funds via the ERATE program. There are significant players in the market including IBoss, Lightspeed Systems, Familyzone, and others. The market is innovating to reflect the current threat landscape in schools, where students are more likely to be a threat to themselves than others. In 2015, suicide took over as the leading cause of death for young people. According to the CDC, 1 in 10 girls will attempt suicide before the end of high school. Internet filtering and alerting systems have taken the first step in flagging keywords if a student is using school issues devices to research how to commit suicide, but 4 out of 5 young people post on private channels before hurting themselves. Artificial Intelligence is being leveraged across school accounts to pick up these early warning signs in order to stay aligned with the ways kids are expressing calls for help today (Google Docs, Social Channels, Chats). Companies including Bark Technologies are reporting over 20,000 self-harm situations detected and escalated to adults, while more traditional players like Lightspeed have announced their Relay system to expand beyond search for insights into threats. Artificial Intelligence is not replacing the need for school counselors, teachers, and school safety officers;

instead, it is helping to focus the attention of these limited resources on the students in most need of support at the right times to help intervene with resources before a student has moved from ideation to attempts.

AI for Workforce Automation (Employees)

Chatbot assistants are doing things that people no longer have to do, so that people can now focus on more meaningful value-added tasks. One place this innovation is showing up is in the human resources function at companies. There are a significant amount of tasks that are repetitive and are well suited for computers to take action on, including helping employees serve themselves key information on company benefits, training, mentoring, and policies. This frees up the HR resources to focus on more pressing issues of diversity and inclusion, leadership development, and creating agile engaged workforces to meet the demands of the modern workplace.

Humaxa is a company that is helping to modernize the employee survey and providing valuable insights to leadership on employee engagement. One interesting result they have found is that "People are 25% more likely to provide feedback to an interactive chatbot assistant than a survey or person. It is difficult to get people to open up about sensitive issues in the workplace. The more sensitive the topic is, the more value a chatbot assistant can provide, because people are more willing to engage with a fun, available, anonymous chatbot then a person and or survey. The more sensitive the topic, the more a person is willing to disclose it to a chatbot assistant instead of a person (Trust in leadership, Diversity & Inclusion, Influence on decisions). The assistant's ability to take action even when the person remains anonymous, builds trust and helps employees to provide real feedback, etc., on leadership's performance." (Carolyn Peer, CEO Humaxa.)

AI for Competitive Intelligence & Business Development (Executives and Strategists)

Far overhead, bus-sized satellites with the ultimate in high-end sensors and optics circle the Earth, ceaselessly transmitting intelligence to ultra-secretive national security agencies. Sixty years since they first launched, state-owned satellites have been joined by new intelligence-gathering constellations, this time in the service of business.

Traditional satellites are excruciatingly expensive machines, precision-built in clean rooms in a sort of ultra-high-end artisanal process. With very high launch costs, failures were unacceptable, leading to many (expensive) layers of redundancy. We have no direct way to know the cost of military-grade spy satellites, but we can get a reasonable proxy by looking at the cost of roughly comparable civilian hardware like the Hubble Space telescope and the ESA's Earth Observation satellites—costs on the order of several hundred million dollars *per satellite* is a reasonable guess.

If traditional satellites are the "Rolls Royce" of space, today's space industry is having its "Henry Ford" moment with the convergence of several developments. In a rough parallel with how the standardized shipping container made transport faster and cheaper, the "cubesat" (more formally "U-class") standard for "microsatellites" made it easy for launch providers to mount, power, launch, and dispense large numbers of satellites. This format, based on units of "1U"—10cm x 10cm x 10cm cubes of "usable volume"—allows for larger satellites too, as long as they are multiples of 1U in size—for example, the Bay Area startup Planet builds and flies "3U" satellites—satellites that measure just 30cm x 10cm x 10cm when stowed. This small format—with its low cost of failure—encouraged engineers to take risks with consumer-grade sensors and processors. These mass-produced components, vastly cheaper than their aerospace-grade[3] equivalents, proved surprisingly hardy in low-Earth orbit, where the challenging environment of a hard vacuum, high radiation, and temperature extremes had ruled out their use in more costly traditional satellites. The cost revolution has allowed upstarts like Planet to launch enough satellites to re-image the entire land surface of the Earth at high resolution every single day, with improvements in data transmission allowing each tiny satellite to downlink a terabyte of data per day, with Planet operating 140 such satellites at the time of writing. It is even possible to order short *videos* of locations of interest (LOI!). The growth of an ecosystem of companies offering automated analyses based on feeds from companies like Planet suggests that the range of commercial uses for this type of data is expanding rapidly.

Add that flood of data points to another major cost component of traditional satellite surveillance: the vast teams of expert analysts required to study all that imagery and turn it into useful intelligence. Recent advances in machine vision have allowed significant portions of image analysis to be mechanized: Deep Learning can be used to convert raw pixels into information that means something to end-users—like traffic flows on highways, occupancy of parking lots at specific offices or retail outlets, container volumes at ports, output levels from power stations, estimates of crop health and crop yields, even the volume of oil being held in tank farms (whose gigantic cylindrical tanks have domed roofs that float up and down on the stored product).

It is now perfectly feasible for business to perform feats of analysis—for example, daily updates on customer volumes at every single outlet of a competing fast-food chain—that might previously have been beyond the capabilities of a super-power. Combined with more "traditional" information gathering, a corporation could observe the launch of a competitor's ad campaign and measure the resulting change in customer volume on a daily basis, conceivably learning the effectiveness or otherwise before their competitor received updated numbers from the managers at its outlets.

When we consider the first step in customer experience management, awareness, the biggest challenge in a crowded and highly distracting digital marketplace is standing out in the crowd. Your unique value proposition and product uniqueness may be brilliantly played, but if your potential customers are looking elsewhere, distracted by the next shiny object, then your marketing voice won't be clearly heard. Competitive intelligence is a key to standing out in the crowd, having your marketing voice rise above the drumbeat of digital innovation everywhere. Competitive intelligence gives you information that informs prescriptive action: optimizing your messaging in a way that acknowledges what else is out there and showing your value in relation to those others.

Selling online is a brutally competitive business. Consequently, it is not only intelligence about a competitor's products that is essential for you to make the case for your product. An awareness of competitor's pricing and inventory is also essential.

Every little bit helps, since that last bit might just be the one that helps push your conversion program across the finish line. That's why new sources of information, like the microsatellites mentioned above, can be a game-changer. Collecting this information is much easier than it was in the days of bricks-and-mortar, when many providers started offering software to scrape rival's websites. Information scraped from physical sites (not just websites) via satellite is out-of-this-world competitive intelligence.

The New Hyper-Personalization

"The top 1% of your customers are worth 18 times more than the average customer," according to RJ Metrics. This drops the tried and true methods of bulk marketing campaigns, A/B testing to large groups, and the days of a standard message into the dust bin of marketing history. So how does a company go about identifying and targeting those key customers in their funnel? "The good news is that retail marketers can immediately integrate machine learning and AI personalization solutions into their existing marketing automation stack, including leveraging their existing email service providers. Doing so delivers exponential accuracy and better results, which immediately impact their bottom lines. Imagine, using intelligent insights to better engage customers to deliver value that can make every consumer upwards of 18 times or more valuable." (Brian Solis, in Forbes: *Extreme Personalization Is The New Personalization: How To Use AI To Personalize Consumer Engagement.*) By focusing on the right audience and creating bespoke actions to drive conversions and revenue, companies can see a direct impact to their revenue. This is extremely important in the early days of companies where revenue growth is a key performance metric requested by investors. Marketing is often perceived as a black box with a lack of clarity for business owners regarding the return on investment. Agencies often struggle to quantify the value they are providing brands, that is where companies are innovating on analytics for Return on Ad Spends (ROAS) and hyper-personalization trends.

Contextual: IoT = The Internet of Context?

With the proliferation of sensors on everything (including wearables, handheld devices, smart homes, smart cars, smart shoes, as well as our personal accounts on social networks), this Internet of Things (IoT) is providing a vast data stream of insights about individual customers, not only what they are doing and what they like, but also where and when (and maybe even why) they are doing and liking those things. This "Internet of Context" provides more powerful forecasting capabilities for marketers. The insights provide a time/location/context dimension to delivering the right content (product or service) to the customer at the right moment in the space-time continuum. For example, I may have purchased a heavy wool sweater in the past, but not likely to buy one during the summer nor even in winter if I am traveling to the opposite hemisphere of the Earth (where it is summer!).

Context is king now. Content is a close second in priority, but context is everything. Literally, it is everything—i.e., everything else that's not the obvious thing. I may be a person of a certain age group, gender, and economic class, but if I am going to a sporting event, I am among a legion of fans who have two strong emotional things in common: a love of the sport and a love of their team. That specific (and strong) context changes my preferences and interests dramatically compared to other times, days, locations, and contexts of my life. Content-based recommender engines have been around for decades, but context-based recommenders are coming of age and can expect to have a very long lifespan in the marketer's arsenal.

Context can deliver on the promise of hyper-personalization for an engaging customer experience. The personalized product offer is not only tailored for me, but for me in the exact current situation in which I am placed. Sensors provide the contextual data that make hyper-personalization possible. The Internet of Context is the marketer's new best friend.

Geospatial: Location Analytics

In the age of Google, billboards might sound like a rather atavistic advertising medium, but a new breed of digital billboards is merging our physical and digital worlds. Going from an ink-based to an electronic display allowed billboard owners to do market segmentation—to let advertisers buy particular times of day, or particular days of the week, but also opened up new question for marketers: which slots should they buy?

Billboard owners now have a powerful new analytics capability to help them sell their slots: billboards that turn the tables on passers-by, watching us as we watch them. This is done not by recognizing our faces but by recognizing our phones. As mobile devices pass within range, electronic signatures are hoovered up and cross-checked against vast databases prepared by data-brokers. The data-brokers have prepared for this moment by embedding tracking technology in apps and websites, allowing them to share with the billboard much more than just your identity— depending on the apps installed on your phone, the billboard might now know your age, gender, approximate address, income bracket, occupation, hobbies, gaming habits. Your phone is a far more revealing window into your life than your face!

Such detailed information allows digital billboards to bring precision marketing à la Google or Facebook to the physical world: to offer advertisers the opportunity to identify and target particular sorts of people at a particular place and time. That is hyper-personalization and Internet of Context on full display to a watching world, especially to the potential (and very surprised) customer.

Cognitive Analytics: Next-best Action, Based on a 360 View of the Customer

Cognitive analytics refers to the analytical process of discovering the right question or right action that the data inspires. For a potential customer, this means discovering the next-best action from the 360 view of the customer. That comes from the combination and synthesis of all data sources, including historical trends, real-time behaviors, predicted outcomes, and measured responses.

Cognitive analytics moves beyond answering the given questions or taking the pre-planned actions, such as "knowing what product we should recommend to this customer." Instead, it flips the script and demands that the marketing process be dynamic, in response to what the in-coming data are telling us in this moment. The data should inform and inspire us to discover the questions that we should be asking: Why is this customer here? What is the customer's intent now? What is the new pattern of behavior? What are these outliers in their product views? How has their persona segment shifted? Is their persona drifting in real-time, perhaps as they explore new products in your online catalog? There's nothing wrong with you planting "Easter eggs" and shiny objects of your own along the customer's journey. Surprise and delight are powerful emotions for customer engagement, conversion, loyalty-building, and advocacy. AI can be implemented that look for these "moments" in the customer journey data, which then engages the customer "in that moment" with new, even unexpected, experiences.

Cognitive analytics is one of the five phases of analytics implementations. These are:

1. Descriptive Analytics = Hindsight: facts gleaned from historical data patterns (recorded data). **Passive**.
2. Diagnostic Analytics = Oversight: facts observed in live sensing of streaming data (tracking data). **Reactive**.
3. Predictive Analytics = Foresight: learning and inferring what is likely to happen next ("seeing the future") based on historical data and new (previously unseen) data (training and test data) – **Proactive**.
4. Prescriptive Analytics = Insight: learning from contextual clues and inferring what steps to take to optimize an outcome, in essence "changing the future" that the predictive model presented (context data) – **Predictive Reactive**.
5. Cognitive Analytics = Right sight: identifying the right question to ask, the right decision to make, the right action to take, at the right time, in the right context, for the right customer ("360 view" data) – **Interactive**.

In this analytics landscape, prescriptive and cognitive analytics may appear to be the same or very similar. However, in practice, prescriptive analytics (optimization) is based on inferred models (a "formula") and insights learned via signals (data) from a broad demographic in the population. In other words, a verified marketing campaign with validated CTAs. Conversely, cognitive analytics is hyper-personalized to the individual at that moment. It can (and probably should) be based on known actions to take when certain patterns appear in the "360 view" data, but sometimes those signals are unexpected and always those signals are personal to that customer. This is the time for reviewing and acting on your "5 E's of Experience" checklist.

Cognitive analytics is the best paradigm for data-driven discovery and decision-making in customer experience management because it does not answer the pre-planned questions, but it discovers the questions that should be answered. Machine learning algorithms can find those emergent patterns and make inferences from them, then AI can implement an action in response to those patterns and inferences.

The Growing Role of AI in Customer Relations

Easier Support Ticket Management

In a rapidly scaling company, ensuring a reliable and positive customer experience is key. The business to consumer (B2C) industry is leveraging automation tools for replying via chatbots to commonly asked questions, and routing tickets to customer experience team members in a streamlined way. AI solutions are starting to emerge as plugin API's for the common help desk software platforms (ZenDesk, Intercom, etc.). These solutions are recognizing the large amount of training data available in these tickets and helping to break down the silos and close the gap between customer support and engineering to provide timely customer feedback for product management and providing empathy in the customer interaction. This allows engineering to prioritize and improve on the user experience to reduce churn and increase revenue.

Spoken and written communications between the business and the customer have previously been amenable only to relatively simple statistical analysis. That is not to say that straightforward summary statistics don't deliver value: if the number of customer support tickets is spiking, then you've got a problem. However, modern machine learning makes it relatively easy to do better. Using advanced natural language processing techniques from the field of Deep Learning called "language models," we can convert data like free text fields into vectors called embeddings and open new doors for analytics. These techniques make it much easier to get insights into data that is hard to systematize—like customer tickets.

"Show, don't tell" is a great story-telling principal, so to make things really clear, we'll use support tickets from a real company, Endava[4], which in partnership with Microsoft anonymized and released a set of nearly 50,000 customer support tickets (you'll notice that in the examples we take from the dataset, the tickets read a little strangely because this preprocessing has removed names, and has also stripped out punctuation and made all words lower-case). These "data preprocessing" are common and essential to help the models run efficiently and effectively.

To illustrate the potential of embeddings, we used "sentence transformers"[5], a machine-learning-based programming library from the Ubiquitous Knowledge Processing Lab, a research lab within the Technical University of Darmstadt, Germany. These researchers extended BERT[6], a state-of-the-art Deep Learning-based approach to natural language processing developed by researchers at the Google AI Language Lab into a model they call "Sentence BERT." While the original BERT is a general-purpose model, used for tasks like text classification and question answering, Sentence BERT is trained very similarly to a facial recognition model so that it learns representations of sentences that are optimized for facilitating search.

The tickets in the Endava dataset[7] were originally submitted as emails, and most tickets have both a subject line and a short body, usually about 40 words long, with a few as long as 70 or 80 words. Using sentence transformers, we encoded each body as a vector of 768 floating-point numbers, then ran a clustering algorithm called "k-means" to look for common topics within the dataset. This is an "unsupervised" machine learning technique that doesn't require training data: the user just picks an arbitrary number of groups (we settled on 20 segments), and the algorithm tries to partition the data evenly into however many clusters the user has specified.

Although we never *trained* the language model on our customer support tickets, clustering the tickets this way quickly revealed a variety of leading reasons for creating tickets (in fact, because Sentence BERT is based on a pre-trained BERT from Google, it's hard to say exactly what the model has and hasn't seen beyond "very large amounts of English text"—similar models have even displayed rudimentary knowledge of chess, because the code that fed them harvested text denoting moves in chess games[8]).

Table 5.1 Purchase order samples were very similar, with most scoring very highly on a 0–1 similarity scale

Title	Body	Cluster, Score
new purchase po	Thursday pm purchase po dear purchased audio please log allocation please take consideration mandatory receipts section order receive item ordered how video please explorer kind regards administrator	0.91
new purchase po	December pm purchase po dear purchased remote control please log installation please take consideration mandatory receipts section order receive item ordered kind regards administrator	0.91
new purchase po	purchase po dear purchased fitness polar loop please log allocation please take consideration mandatory receipts section order receive item ordered how video please explorer kind regards administrator	0.91

Distinct clusters immediately formed around common business activities, with the tightest cluster forming around purchases. Note that we clustered on the body text, without using the title. The "Cluster Score" column needs a little explanation: it gives us a number for how close each data point is to the center of the cluster it has been assigned to. However, this is not a distance measure but a similarity score on a scale where zero would indicate "completely dissimilar" and a score of one indicates a perfect match (Table 5.1).

Other little clusters formed around "life events," with a distinct group of a couple of hundred employees preparing to leave. More interesting were the clusters of problems: even this cursory analyses revealed two distinct sets of issues around a time carding system, both with thousands of tickets—potentially a valuable indication of a major pain point. Similarly, large clusters revealed other common issues—password problems got its own cluster, and so did issues with Windows updates.

More interestingly, it's possible to invent a search query, encode it as a vector, and find similar tickets. Using the search string "*laptop frozen*" we can easily surface the most similar tickets. Although the absolute similarity scores are not very high compared to those we saw when clustering, both the titles and the bodies seem very relevant for our query. Note that the *exact phrase* is not present in even these the most similar results—but they bubble to the top anyway as being the most similar items (Table 5.2).

Matching our query against the short-but-descriptive titles results in even closer matches (notice the much higher scores in the "similarity" column); we can also test the power of language models by trying a phrase with a similar meaning but different words. Searching for titles using the query "computer unresponsive" gets the results shown in the following table. Notice that a title like "laptop freezes" is scored as being just as similar as "computer freezing," despite the lexical difference (Table 5.3).

Table 5.2   Language models make it easy to search for similar meanings, instead of just similar spellings

Title	Body	Similarity
laptop not working	laptop working hello could you please be kind have look laptop stopped working thanks best regards accounts receivable accountant ext	0.59
laptop freezes	sent Wednesday July laptop freezes laptop en data misc la si la crash tot se screen data stress minim si el ca se la ca hardware senior software engineer en	0.54
windows laptop freezes	laptop freezes hello currently having problem with laptop unable use because entire operating freezes laptop needs be restarted could you please help with issue best regards	0.53
endpoint security service issue	sent Thursday February endpoint issue importance high hello guys experiencing almost today performance issue with laptop runs very very slow can even click mouse does ignore can you please investigate with priority best regards lead ext	0.53
on laptop crashed	sent November laptop crashed hello dear laptop seems be crashed used work slowly for last several weeks stopped responding possible replace with tester	0.50

Table 5.3   We can see here how the language model lets us match phrases that have similar meanings, even though all of the actual words are different

Title	Body	Similarity
laptop freezes	sent Wednesday July laptop freezes laptop en data misc la si la crash...	0.81
computer freezing	sent Tuesday July computer freezing hi recently had laptop rebuilt kept freezing since...	0.81
computer freezing	computer freezing hi recently started having issues with laptop...	0.81
laptop keyboard freeze issue	... hi for two days always afternoon laptop keyboards freeze blocked can type anything...	0.78
laptop freezing	... ll be able move mouse for minute or two then freeze...	0.77

From this example, it is easy to see how language models—by allowing us to measure the similarity of two pieces of text in terms of "semantic distance"—can help us improve the customer experience both by giving us a macro-level overview (identifying common problems) and at the micro level by making it easier to search for similar problems that may already have been solved, making support staff more productive, or perhaps even enabling users to solve more problems themselves.

Big Data Is the Fuel (The Input) That Informs the Enterprise About the Customer: Sources (Digital Devices, IoT, Data Lake,…)

Digital Identity Verification Technology is a place where innovation in AI is streamlining the customer experience with sellers. Passwords are a point of friction in the experience of most people (as we saw in our "customer tickets" example). From oversimplification of passwords (hacking risk), forgotten passwords (friction meter rising), and passwords used across platforms (churn risk), many people are struggling to keep it all straight. Churn (or "flight risk") is very real in this situation—when users are fighting a complex system, the usual choice between "fight or flight" can easily become "flight." Resolving ongoing password issues are a significant drain on a corporate IT staff. "Users contact help desks about 28 times per year (approximately 20% of all help desk calls) for password issues costing upward of $179 per user every year, according to a recent Forrester report. According to a recent Verizon report, 81% of data breaches were due to stolen and/or weak passwords," says Josh Whatley, CEO of UnifyID, in the Beyond Passwords White Paper, which is focused on innovating beyond passwords to reduce friction in the customer experience.

Whatley goes on to say, "sensors can gather other data that is more passive, but no less powerful. A subset of these includes the way you grip the phone; the Wi-Fi access points with which you generally come in contact; your typing speed and style; the movement of the phone as you sit down (and the corresponding length of your femur); your walking gait. The combination of all those sensor-acquired data points becomes a digital model for what makes each user unique. It delivers a remarkably unique picture of any given user, with 99% accuracy." Leveraging trends in IoT, Cloud, and Big Data, this innovating company is helping the way business to consumer companies are engaging with their current customers to reduce the frictions associated with passwords for identity verification when existing customers are needing customer support. As we saw when analyzing customer tickets, passwords represent a significant paint point for users (and a resource drain for support teams).

Machine Learning Is the Tool (The Value-Creation Lever) to Gain Insights from the Customer, in 3 Ways

Supervised Learning (Predictive Analytics): Forecasting Customer Needs

"Supervised learning" means a Data Scientist sits close by the server and scrutinizes it intensely while it learns… no, of course it doesn't mean that! The supervision needs to come from a dataset that has matched pairs of "samples" and "labels." For example, a company might collect a set of customer-written reviews and rate each one as positive, negative, or neutral. Once enough data is available, a machine learning model can be given the reviews and attempt to correctly predict a label for each. An algorithm compares the model's output to the label, and penalizes the model for its errors, typically punishing larger errors more harshly: the labels are a "supervisory signal," so the accuracy of labels will be a limiting factor for a supervised learning project. If 80% of your labels are wrong, don't expect the machine to give correct results for 90% of new samples.

"If it sounds too good to be true, it usually is" holds true in this domain. For example, those labels will often have been applied by humans. Studies show that humans can struggle to consistently agree with each other *or even with their own previous decisions*. This is true for "crowd workers," it is true for medical consultants, and it will prove to be true for your firm. You'll need to make sure your team can give you solid numbers for label quality, and this will give you your first indication of the "quality ceiling" for any models your team might train when they've got enough of those labels. Sometimes, the source of a label is a customer action—perhaps your label is "SportsEnthusiast," and you apply it when a customer makes a purchase in that category, and hope to then predict this enthusiasm from other, nonobviously-sporty purchase. Reducing your involvement doesn't mean these labels are perfect: although the label may be applied correctly by your software stack, you cannot exclude a remaining source of error: nonenthusiasts buying for a loved one ("yes, I bought a box set of the Peppa Pig series for my 4-year-old niece, but good luck cross-selling me a 100-piece crayon set").

How much data are "enough"? A popular misconception is that "big data" is a pre-requisite for a supervised learning project. The number of samples a project requires varies as widely as the applications, but commonly ranges from hundreds to hundreds of thousands, and as new techniques emerge, the number of required examples keeps dropping. Despite the necessity for labels, supervised learning remains the most commonly deployed form of machine learning.

Supervised learning can help forecast customer needs if your team can identify signals that help predict what a given customer will buy. This might involve data you have collected on a customer, or from similar customers, or even from a third party:

> Websites like Clearbit store bulk data from B2B companies, so they know who the potential customer is on the first access point to their website. In some cases, companies can reflect a snapshot of the potential buyer's SaaS solution right on the homepage for their solution. On B2C transactions there are privacy laws that are upheld to prevent as much innovation there. But by applying location data, companies can use local weather information to change the color of the website themes to automatically reflect the mood the location of the customer accessing them.
>
> Anthony Accenturo, CEO Launch Titans

Unsupervised Learning (Discovery Analytics): Segment / Pattern / Trend Discovery in Customer Behaviors and Experiences

Some trends are easy to spot—if a product keeps flying off the shelves, we need to buy more of that. Not everything can be tracked as easily as a Stock Keeping Unit (SKU) though. For example, customer tickets can describe the same problem or frustration in as many ways as you have complainants, making it harder to spot commonalities. Supervised machine learning can't help you look for *new* things that you don't have labeled data for.

Fortunately, there are other techniques that can help. Earlier in the chapter, we described the use of embeddings for recommendation engines. Similar tricks allowed us to create embeddings from pieces of text and thus more effectively investigate customer tickets. Crucially, although we did need data (lots of customer tickets), we didn't need to use any labels: so we were actually using *unsupervised* learning (also referred to as "self-supervised learning," to make clear that the data, in and of itself, provides some guidance to the "learner"). Sometimes unsupervised learning is referred to as "the data becomes the model."

When we used "k-means' clustering, we applied an "unsupervised" technique—we didn't tell our computer *what* it should find, only that we wanted it to split the data into a certain number of segments, with each segment containing items that were similar to each other. Those segments then informed our actions ("the model"). We could just as well have applied the same approach to a customer's history of purchases—all kinds of data can be converted into embeddings to allow us to measure similarity, and so to cluster our data samples, which then informs our product recommendations ("the model").

Once clusters are found (like the common problems with passwords/windows updates/time tracking software), it becomes possible to track their evolution over time and establish the direction of trends. In our customer service tickets example, we could:

- Use the discovery of the "password problems" cluster to make the decision to try a product like UnityID as mentioned in an earlier section
- Track the evolution of the cluster over time
- Review the data to see if our new "passwordless" tool improved the trend

In a retail scenario, the same approach could be used to form clusters of related products and track demand over time. Trend analysis like this is another example of unsupervised (self-supervised!) learning. In fact, forecasting the future evolution of any trend is a sufficiently large and complicated problem to have its own field ("time series prediction"). From the perspective of artificial intelligence or machine learning, the attractive thing about time series is that you don't need to label the data—your "supervising signal" is whatever happens next in the time series—just wait to see if the future matches your predictions (continuing along the same trend seen in the preceding slices of data). Thus, predictive analytics can actually be either supervised learning (based on labeled training data) or unsupervised learning (based on patterns in the data: "the data becomes the model").

Another example use case that is getting an AI update is an old analytics stalwart, the customer survey. The purported strength of surveys is that they enable businesses to justify decisions based on hard data about customer's experiences. However, the traditional many-page multiple-choice query forms have many drawbacks, starting with their dismal completion rates: 3% is typical, so you'll be trying to make good decisions using feedback that ignores the views of 97% of your customers. There's obviously a very real risk that the diligent 3% aren't representative. Remember this: surveys were multiple-choice *because that was what we could analyze*. What's changed is that AI gives us a better approach: short surveys that allow free-form narrative answers. These can gather just as much information, but more quickly, and with a much higher completion rather (perhaps as high as 20%). Machine learning is the missing ingredient that empowers organizations to analyze this volume of open-ended text at scale.

In particular, unsupervised learning on free-form text allows us to avoid the other problem with multiple-choice surveys: an unchanging and limited set of responses. In narrative-based surveys, customers can give us responses that we never anticipated or thought of or had room for (on the multiple-choice survey questionnaire). Unsupervised learning can then cluster the concepts, topics, concerns, and sentiments from free-text answers, thereby giving us far greater insight into the customer experience and also delivering another significant customer experience benefit, as stated here:

> *"Extensive multiple-choice close-ended question surveys are now fading out and becoming a relic of the past. They were used by analysts because it made their job of quantifying customer feedback easier. Open-ended survey questions were overlooked because it was challenging to analyse and quantify text data at scale. But the irony is that [engaging] customers through multiple-choice surveys is the worst customer experience ever."*
> —**Sam Frampton, Chattermill**

Reinforcement Learning for Prescriptive Behavioral Analytics: Adapting, Improving, Optimizing Customer Experience

The key to supervised learning is labeled data—sample "questions" with "known-good" answers, in sufficient quantity that the model can go on to correctly label newly collected data. For example, you may have data on customers who decided to take their business elsewhere: predicting churn is a good use-case for supervised machine learning, because you'll also have data on customers who *didn't* leave.

Suppose that you have already trained a perfect churn-prediction model, and you use it to detect a customer that is about to churn (or you see this "prediction" in the data trail after the customer has already left). What next? Do you simply let the customer leave and take their business to your competitors? Or do you intervene to achieve a better outcome (change the future to reach an optimal outcome)? Of course, you would want to prevent the churn, if possible. We can turn to the data analytics (specifically, prescriptive analytics) to address the questions: What interventions will be most successful at retaining the customers that your model predicts are about to leave? And what can you do to win back those that did leave?

Not too surprisingly, this discovery process brings us back once again to the Maslow Hierarchy of Needs and the five E's of customer experience. Can you encounter, engage, and empathize with that customer in a way that meets (or exceeds) their expectations and satisfies their basic emotional needs to feel empowered, esteemed, wanted, safe, and healthy? The digital data trail along the customer journey can deliver the insights, through ML, that we need in order to reach that customer and grow their loyalty to your brand. For example, don't underestimate the power of FOMO (Fear Of Missing Out)—if you make them an offer they can't refuse, perhaps showing some statistics that demonstrate how so many of your other customers are already enjoying the benefits of that offer, then that might be quite sufficient to retain (or regain) their loyalty.

Reinforcement Learning is a type of supervised learning that we use when we know what success looks like (i.e., the reward for taking the right action, e.g., a drop in churn rate), but we do *not* necessarily know the right actions that will get us there. The best publicized examples of reinforcement learning (RL) are when machines beat human champions at games like Chess or Go: we (and the machines) know the rules of the game and know how to assess when someone is winning (or won) the game. To some extent, we can estimate who has the stronger position at any intermediate point during a game, but we do not have a dataset that tells us the optimal next move for each possible board state. In many real-world scenarios, that would be impossible. For example, Go has about $2x10^{170}$ legal board states, roughly equal to the total combined number of atoms in 10^{90} replicas of our own universe, containing an estimated 10^{80} atoms each—thus, the storage costs of such a dataset would be ridiculously budget-busting.

Most machine learning models are effectively learning a very sophisticated template that matches patterns in data samples to pre-specified classes of objects or behaviors. On the other hand, RL models are *policies*, which attempt to prescribe an *action* to take in a given state, so as to move closer to some reward (winning a game of Go, placing a workpiece on a jig, or keeping an autonomous vehicle centered in its lane). As the name "reinforcement" implies, there is a feedback loop that penalizes or rewards (reinforces) different actions (specified by the policies), using a pre-specified penalty/reward metric. The modeling process follows a series of actions through to their logical conclusion, hopefully as efficiently and effectively as possible: in many fewer steps than the number of possible steps in the system, while achieving the highest possible reward (success!). Although most machine learning models actually in production today are performing some form of classification or regression, it seems likely that in the longer term, RL will become a dominant approach, being able to learn and apply policies that will unlock vastly greater value across numerous application areas.

Returning to our about-to-churn customers, we could attempt to optimize our retention efforts by defining an "action space" and using RL to train a policy to select actions that minimize churn. This will be easy to get wrong[9]—great care needs to be taken with both the action space and the "reward function." For example, reducing prices to zero, or making them negative, will maximize customer retention, but at the cost of other metrics you care about! Such obvious business rules can be encoded in the RL policies. It may help to anthropomorphize machine learning models and think of them as clever but devious and inclined to cheat. RL can be considered a gamification of the machine learning process, and (as always) someone (or something) may learn how to game the system.

One challenge with RL is that it tends to be extremely data-hungry—models may require a great many rounds of "play" to reach good performance. One way to satisfy this requirement is to have models train in a simulator, an approach that is (thankfully!) extremely popular with teams developing self-driving cars, which typically drive vastly more miles in simulation than in real traffic. When creating a simulator is difficult or infeasible (customer behavior?), a learning approach called "off-policy learning" may help. A term of art, "off-policy" simply means that the model can learn from watching decisions play out even when those decisions are different than the choices it would have made itself: an analogy is that one could improve one's chess skills by playing ("on-policy") or by watching others playing moves we might not have considered ourselves.

Although it's quite early days for the use of RL in customer experience management, we're excited by its potential because, in beating human champions at games of deep strategy like Go, this technology has demonstrated an ability to take a long-term view: to learn to take actions today in service of a payoff that might be quite distant from the present. Thinking about the customer experience, many actions we take to make customers happy are a net cost at the time we take them. For example, when the customer interacts with a bank teller or a customer service agent or a concierge, or spends their loyalty club reward points, the vendor is usually making a loss on that transaction, in service of improving the customer's happiness and longer-term value (loyalty). Optimizing that risk-reward balance sheet in an intensely data-driven way is what makes RL an exciting and important technology in the future of customer experience management.

Analytics as the Outcome (i.e., the Business Product)

In this era of massive data collection and utilization, we often hear organizations declare that they are "Data-first" or "Data-driven." Similarly, as AI takes over the business conversations, particularly in the area of customer experience management, we hear organizations say that they are "AI-first. This is not much different than organizations saying that they are "Technology-driven." The problem with those statements is that they focus on the wrong things: data are the input (fuel) and the output (exhaust) of your business processes, technology is an enabling tool, and AI is an approach toward automating, optimizing, and moving your business "at the speed of data" (which is coming in fast and furious).

Instead, business organizations that succeed (in fact, sports teams and battlefield operations that succeed) are those that focus on strategic long-term outcomes, the ultimate goal, the "north star" that you are aiming for. The outcomes determine success or failure. In the digital business world, the outcomes are the analytics. Analytics are the products of applying machine learning algorithms to incoming data, enabled by technology, in order to produce decisions and actions that are automated, augmented, and amplified via AI. Hence, a better mantra for business success is to be analytics-first, or analytics-driven, while being data-informed and technology-empowered. This is definitely true for customer experience management. The customer doesn't care what databases you own, which cloud service provider you use, or what mathematical algorithms you apply. They care about quality products and services (outcomes!).

Analytics are the products, the outcomes, and the ROI of your data, data science, machine learning, and AI investments. Analytics products come in many forms. For example, a product might be a recommendation engine, a predictive model, a prescriptive model, a cleaned shared dataset, a metadata-enriched data catalog, an open-source software package, a (Python or R) code notebook, an API, cloud services, visualizations and dashboards, data stories (narratives), personalized web portals, gamification of user experiences, or other data-driven services. All of those products should be aligned with the business mission statement and aimed at achieving business goals, objectives, and success.

Acquiring more data or more automation is not a business mission statement. However, delivering best-in-class customer products and services in XYZ industry is a clear mission statement. As a powerful example, just look at Google's mission statement, which has not changed since the organization's early days in the 1990s: *"To organize the world's information and make it universally accessible and useful."* That's it! And yet that simple statement has been the "north star" for a corporation that today has a market value of approximately one trillion US dollars.

Note the customer-centric words in Google's very short mission statement: "universally accessible" and "useful." In the analytics-driven enterprise, optimizing customer experience outcomes are (or should be) part of the mission. Customer experience management is fueled by data, enabled by technology, optimized by machine learning, and boosted by AI. AI is a powerful enabler, accelerant, amplifier, and aide in delivering superior, just-in-time, hyper-personalized customer products and services.

Getting all parts of the organization on board with AI is made easier, while reducing inherent resistance to change, when AI's focus is aimed directly at achieving the business' mission and desired outcomes. Such a focus explicitly connects the AI strategy, activities, and related corporate messaging with what matters the most to everyone in the enterprise: outcomes! Customer experience management should be tightly nested within those AI conversations.

Notes

1 Recombee, "Artificial Intelligence Powered Recommender as a Service," accessed September 26, 2021, https://www.recombee.com/.
2 Kevin Kelly, "1000 True fans," The Technium, accessed September 26, 2021, https://kk.org/thetechnium/1000-true-fans/.
3 For jaw-dropping tales of the cost of "aerospace-grade" components and SpaceX's ability to build their own reliable-but-inexpensive alternatives, see the excellent "Elon Musk: Tesla, SpaceX, and the Quest for a Fantastic Future" by Ashlee Vance (Ecco, January 24, 2017).
4 Endava, company website, accessed September 26, 2021, https://www.endava.com/.
5 Nils Reimers and Iryna Gurevych, "Sentence-BERT: Sentence Embeddings using Siamese BERT-Networks," arXiv:1908.10084v1 [cs.CL] 27 Aug 2019.
6 Jacob Devlin, Ming-Wei Chang, Kenton Lee, and Kristina Toutanova, "BERT: Pre-training of Deep Bidirectional Transformers for Language Understanding," arXiv:1810.04805v2 [cs.CL] 24 May 2019.
7 Karol Zak, et al., "support-tickets-classification," (2021), GitHub repository, https://github.com/karolzak/support-tickets-classification.
8 Scott Alexander, "A very unlikely chess game," blog, January 6, 2020, https://slatestarcodex.com/2020/01/06/a-very-unlikely-chess-game/.
9 Machines are not always exempt from Goodhart's Law ("When a measure becomes a target, it ceases to be a good measure"). Wikipedia contributors, "Goodhart's law," Wikipedia, The Free Encyclopedia, https://en.wikipedia.org/w/index.php?title=Goodhart%27s_law&oldid=1042238131 (accessed September 26, 2021).

Chapter 6

AI in Financial Services

Jonas Christensen

Contents

DOI: 10.4324/9781351032940-6

Introduction

Making predictions based on probability has been a cornerstone of financial services since the earliest prototypes of banking arose circa 4,000 years ago when Middle-Eastern merchants began the practice of giving grain loans to farmers and traders. The loans were given based on a borrower's ability to repay with interest, which required merchants to assess the qualities of individual borrowers, as well as the inherent risk of their venture. This could include the quality of the soil for a patch of farm land or the dangers of a particular trade route. Although the specific risks being assessed by lenders have changed vastly since then, it still remains that lending money profitably is about assessing the likelihood of the borrower's capacity to repay the funds in the future.

Until recent times, such predictions relied largely on the lender's knowledge of a borrower's personal credentials and the inherent risk of their income-generating activities. Even as banking corporations grew larger in line with industrialization, credit decisions predominantly relied on the knowledge and expertise of the local bank manager. In local communities, lending decisions would typically be based on bank staff's intimate knowledge of their customers.

In 1956, an engineer named Bill Fair joined forces with a mathematician called Earl Isaac to create a standardized and objective way of assessing the credit worthiness of prospective borrowers using data inputs. Their company, Fair, Isaac and Company, today known as FICO, came up with the FICO Score which has underpinned consumer lending in the United States for many decades.

As the size and sophistication of the financial system grew in line with the proliferation and processing power of computer technology, so did the regulatory requirements around risk-taking in financial institutions. Internal credit risk functions grew in size and sophistication, and became data hungry as a result of needing to quantify probabilities of default and set risk tolerances. With increased knowledge and experience of utilizing data warehousing and statistical modeling, risk functions began applying quantitative statistical analysis and modeling to other risk management disciplines such as market risk and financial crime.

Market risk functions would typically produce probabilistic models and simulations to assess the likelihood of certain outcomes—often founded in liquidity stress testing. Deterministic models such as linear regressions or scorecards would be used to produce binary-outcome results such as whether to approve a loan or flag a suspicious transaction for further investigation.

The first frontier of quantitative data science in financial services focused mainly on various risk management disciplines. Since then, predictive modeling and analytics have spread throughout the organization and are now used to drive decisions across all lines of business including sales, marketing, operations, finance, and HR.

The growth of data collection, storage, and usage in financial services has coincided with the rise of large scale and personal computer technology. The introduction of online self-service banking, electronic payments, mobile wallets, accounting system integration, and 24-by-7 access to banking services has transformed the way consumers interact with financial services.

Today, financial institutions collect and house vast amounts of demographical and behavioral customer data that can be used to create a deeply personalized view of customers' needs and wants. As you will learn throughout this chapter, the evolution of AI in financial services is a true paradigm shift that creates a once-in-a-generation opportunity to differentiate against competitors through personalization and customer intimacy at scale.

The next evolution of data science will see banks and fin-techs build operational excellence through automation and deep personalization using AI and ML. Traditionally, data analysis in banking has relied on systems-generated data stored in a structured format; however, modern data science has evolved to be able to identify patterns in many different types of information. Interpretation of unstructured data sources, such as text, sound, images, and video, allows data scientists to build predictions, classifications, and recommendations that are contextual and highly personalized.

Why AI Should Be Used to Create a Competitive Advantage in Financial Services

No company can succeed today by trying to be all things to all people. It must instead find the unique value that it alone can deliver to a chosen market.
—The Discipline of Market Leaders, Tracy & Wiersema 1995

In 1995 Michael Treacy and Fred Wiersema published their book "The Discipline of Market Leaders" in which they describe how businesses can create a sustainable competitive advantage through three so-called value disciplines: Operational Excellence,

Product Leadership, and Customer Intimacy. Businesses must remain "competitively adequate" in all three disciplines but can only create and maintain a lasting competitive advantage by being market leading in one of the three disciplines.

In a nutshell, the three dimensions can be described as follows:

Operational excellence—through operational efficiency and standardization, businesses can provide consistent, low cost and hassle-free products and services to customers.

Product leadership—through product innovation and branding, businesses are able to charge a premium for their product or service.

Customer intimacy—by building close relationships and end-to-end solutions for customers, businesses are able to create a loyal customer following with a high lifetime value (Table 6.1).

With the aim of delivering superior profits through operational excellence at scale, banking giants such as Citibank of the United States and UK-headquarted HSBC have created global behemoths with the balance sheets of small nations. Other banks such as ING of the Netherlands and Banco Santander of Spain have driven their global expansions through product and service innovations, customized for local markets.

Interestingly, there are limited *standout* examples of financial services firms competing on customer intimacy. Although banks collect vast amounts of demographical and behavioral data on their customers, much of this data lies dormant or at least underutilized. In comparison, many of the technology companies that have dominated the NASDAQ Composite Index since the turn of the last century have achieved their market dominance through product and service offerings based on data-driven Customer Intimacy. Just think of Amazon's ability to recommend contextually relevant products or Netflix's curated list of content based on your past behavior.

Table 6.1 Provides specific examples of businesses competing in each of the three dimensions

Value Disciplines	Operational Excellence	Product Leadership	Customer intimacy
Basic concept	Low cost, hassle free	Superior/ innovative products	Delivering value to specific customer segments, creating loyalty
General examples	Aldi Supermarkets, mining giants	Apple, Nike	Amazon, Netflix, Google, Facebook, Spotify, Uber
Banking examples	Citibank, HSBC	ING, Banco Santander	Some fintechs, (traditional) community banking

Creating a competitive advantage: Since the turn of the century, many Silicon Valley tech companies have used data and analytics to create a competitive advantage through "Customer Intimacy." In the process, these companies have disrupted industries and impacted the way we live our lives. Financial institutions are the custodians of vast amounts of personalized data that could be used to create a similar "Customer Intimacy" revolution based on AI and machine learning.

Similarly, we will assert that the biggest opportunity for differentiation in financial services lies not in Operational Excellence or Product Leadership, but in utilizing the unique customer data harnessed by every modern financial institution. In fact, one could argue that the only true competitive advantage of any financial institution is the data it holds about the behaviors, needs, and wants of its customers, because no one else has this information. This is an advantage that is about to diminish significantly, as we will discuss later in this chapter.

So, What's Holding Back the Banks?

Although the world is blessed with thousands of well-capitalized banks, employing some of the most impressive human talent available, most banks are laggards when it comes to applying AI and ML techniques at scale.

Paradoxically, financial services businesses have some of the richest datasets available *and* are trusted custodians of this data, but so far have not yet taken advantage of this unique position. Instead, banks and other financial institutions are playing catch-up in the big data game that is currently being led by big tech giants such as Google, Facebook, Alibaba, Amazon, and Netflix. Although these tech giants operate in other industries (for now), they are typically used as examples of companies that have managed to create superior personalized customer experiences using data, analytics, and AI.

So, why haven't financial institutions taken advantage of their unique position yet? Although every financial institution is a product of its own unique evolution, the progression toward Artificial Intelligence-driven banking is typically stifled by the following factors:

1. **Legacy tech and processes:** many long-standing financial institutions have built their IT infrastructure over several decades. As a result, it is not uncommon for a large bank to be running hundreds, if not thousands, of different IT applications, some dating back to the 1970s. This mish-mash of systems (and underlying coding languages) brings about a host of challenges that make it difficult to experiment iteratively with AI and machine learning (ML) models via customer-facing channels.

2. **A bias toward compliance:** Banks are heavily regulated entities, and may be subject to fines, laws-suits, or other sanctions if they do not comply with regulations and their own terms and conditions. Furthermore, the average politician is well-aware of the fact that banks are as commonly disliked by the constituency as they are systemically important to economic stability. As a result, the mere suggestion that one should "let the AI model decide" on customer outcomes without any human intervention, is likely to send shivers down the spine of most traditional banking executives.

3. **Closed-loop thinking:** financial institutions are typically closed-loop systems where only limited information leaves or enters the organization. Compare this to a modern tech business—such as eBay, Facebook, or Amazon—where you will find application program interfaces (APIs) and open-source code consuming customer data and delivering value and functionality for a networked set of entities. This is an important consideration because it typically means that

financial institutions are storing many terabytes of unused data that otherwise could be consumed in a network (however, as we will discuss later, this is about to change).

4. **High barriers to entry for disruptors:** There is nothing like healthy competition to keep everyone on their toes. However, it is both difficult and expensive to set up a financial institution from scratch, and as a result, most of the world's large-scale financial institutions are many decades old. These incumbents are typically consumed by the aforementioned tech and compliance challenges that leave limited capacity for needle-moving innovation.

These four points have kept the financial services industry occupied for the last few decades, and as a result, innovation has mainly focused on creating digitized/ self-service options for customers, rather than experimenting with augmentation of customer experience using data.

The Open Banking Revolution that Will Change Everything

Until now, financial institutions have had the luxury of being able to choose if and when to use their unique customer data to create more personal and relevant experiences for their customers. However, with the advent of mandated consumer data rights such as the General Data Protection Regulation (GDPR) and Payment Services Directive (PSD2) in Europe and Open Banking initiatives appearing in many countries around the world, banks will soon be forced to "use it or lose it."

A basic philosophy of Open Banking is to unlock competition by (1) giving consumers full ownership and portability of the data they create (e.g., credit card transactions) and (2) mandating banks and other payments providers to follow one standard for facilitating data sharing through APIs. That way, customers can port their data between banks and nonbanks that have been approved to participate in the data-sharing ecosystem. In theory, this will break down the barriers to entry for new financial service providers.

The UK has been one of the first jurisdictions to implement a mandated Open Banking regime. Other nations, such as Canada, Australia, and Singapore, have followed suit with their own Open Banking regulations, but with an additional "Open Data" phase that will allow accredited organizations outside the banking sector to participate in the ecosystem (e.g., utilities, telecommunication companies, and government entities).

In an Open Banking world, if a bank chooses to leave unique customer data unused they can be certain that a plethora of competitors will be lined up to give their customers personalized, relevant and intuitive experiences using the same data. Consumers need financial services, but they won't necessarily get these directly from banks in the future. In a world where data can be transported instantly between many platforms, it is entirely likely that the "banking experience" will be handled by a nonbank.

Figure 6.1 shows the impact of this change from the consumer's point of view. Historically, consumers have had to shop around between several banking providers to get the best price or service in the market. As a result, many consumers have their banking spread across multiple banks—or they are simply paying a premium

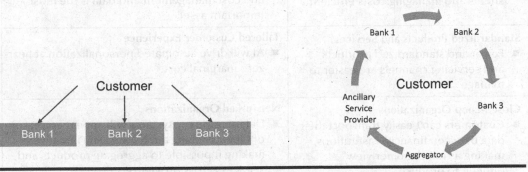

Figure 6.1 Data regulations across the globe are putting data ownership into the hands of consumers and making it much easier to compare banking products and switch providers. As transparency goes up, so must banks' ability to act in the best interest of customers. AI makes it possible to use customer data to identify and act on unmet customer needs that sit outside the traditional realms of banking.

for having all their banking in one place. In a networked banking economy, account aggregation can happen on top of products from many providers, which in turn increases transparency of pricing and makes it easier to switch from one provider to the next.

We are already seeing signs of this trend in China, even though the country has not implemented a regulatory framework around Open Banking. China's relaxed rules around consumer data privacy and the popularity of APIs among technology companies and financial institutions have led to mass adoption of AI-driven banking aggregation in the world's most populous nation. Tencent's WeChat app, which is used for social media, messaging, payments, and much more, has become the main interface between consumers and their banking needs. WeChat and Alipay, the two dominant payment apps in China, accounted for 93% of all payments in the country in the last quarter of 2018. As a result, the conventional banks are increasingly becoming balance sheet and transaction system providers for these customer-facing interfaces.

These changes in the financial services industry are no less than seismic, and we believe that for most banks it will ultimately mean one thing: AI or die.

Surviving and Thriving with AI

The societal trends, technological advances, and regulatory changes impacting the financial services industry will necessarily alter the business models of most financial institutions, big and small. Some organizations will take the lead on business model innovation and survive and thrive as a result. Others will ignore the signs and react

Table 6.2

Today Financial Institutions Thrive on:	Tomorrow's Financial Institutions will be built on:
Accumulation of Assets ■ Scale is built on increasing balance sheets and managing costs efficiently	**Accumulation of Data** ■ AI solves the trade-off between customization and cost management and data is the most important asset.
Standardized Products and Services ■ Fewer and standardized products and servicing channels are easier to manage	**Tailored Customer Experience** ■ AI will drive automated personalization at near-zero marginal cost.
Closed-Loop Organizations ■ Customers can't easily transport their data between financial institutions, making a "full customer view" difficult to produce.	**Networked Organizations** ■ Data sharing ecosystems will appear as a result of Open Banking and Open Data initiatives, making it possible to aggregate products and services across providers
Switching Inertia ■ Switching banks is a cumbersome and complex process for most individuals and organizations	**Click to Switch** ■ Barriers to switching will be reduced by API-enabled data sharing ecosystems and increased pricing transparency

too late or simply not have the resources to keep up. These organizations will likely be bought up by stronger organizations or wither away.

With the introduction of AI at scale, those who survive and thrive will compete on two fronts: (1) operational excellence through process automation and optimization, and (2) customer intimacy through personalization at scale. Table 6.2 describes how AI is likely to reshape financial services business models significantly in the near future.

May the Best Network Win

In a world where data sharing and portability has become the norm, individual customer data is no longer a unique source of competitive differentiation. Instead, financial institutions will have to find their feet in data-sharing ecosystems that house many different products and services.

Financial institutions should take heed of the importance of the "network effect." The network effect in a phenomenon whereby the value of a network goes up as more participants take part in the ecosystem. It is not a coincidence that all the large technology companies mentioned previously in this chapter have achieved their market dominance by taking advantage of this effect. For instance, more products on Amazon's platform will attract more users, and more users will attract more products. The same goes for Facebook, Google, Spotify, Netflix, Uber, or any other network platform provider. In financial services, the likely winners will be the proprietors and participants of the most popular platforms, whether they are incumbent banks or new entrants with a speciality in aggregation and experience design.

Another uncomfortable challenge for incumbents to contend with in an Open Data paradigm is the fact that data sharing and collection regulations and requirements become increasingly complex to live up to. At the same time, banks need to establish and manage a range of new partnerships in order to build networked platform solutions. Regulations in Europe already stipulate that financial institutions make available customer financial data to bank and nonbank third parties who are accredited to participate in the mandated data sharing ecosystem. This creates a situation where large technology firms can access financial data and combine it with other data it may hold on consumers—a luxury that is not reciprocated for banks. WeChat, often called "the App for Everything," is already giving us a glimpse into this future. As an example, Chinese consumers can invite friends to dinner, book a table at a restaurant, look up the menu, order, and pay—all within the WeChat interface.

As a result, the financial services industry and individual organizations will undergo substantial cultural and structural changes in the next decade. Financial services businesses will not only have to think differently about how they can compete for customer loyalty, but also how they organize their people, processes, and technology to compete in a data-rich economy.

Figure 6.2 highlights the impacts on financial institutions from the shift toward an AI and Open Banking revolution. So far, we have discussed the implications of AI and Open Banking on customer experience. However, as we will discuss in

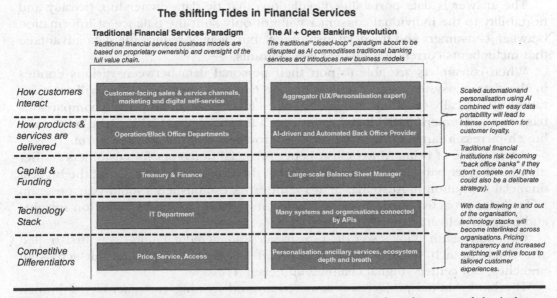

The shifting Tides in Financial Services

	Traditional Financial Services Paradigm *Traditional financial services business models are based on proprietary ownership and oversight of the full value chain.*	The AI + Open Banking Revolution *The traditional "closed-loop" paradigm about to be disrupted as AI commoditises traditional banking services and introduces new business models*	
How customers interact	Customer-facing sales & service channels, marketing and digital self-service	Aggregator (UX/Personalisation expert)	*Scaled automationand personalisation using AI combined with easy data portablility will lead to intense competition for customer loyalty.*
How products & services are delivered	Operation/Black Office Departments	AI-driven and Automated Back Office Provider	*Traditional financial institutions risk becoming "back office banks" if they don't compete on AI (this could also be a deliberate strategy).*
Capital & Funding	Treasury & Finance	Large-scale Balance Sheet Manager	
Technology Stack	IT Department	Many systems and organisations connected by APIs	*With data flowing in and out of the organisation, technology stacks will become interlinked across organisations. Pricing transparency and increased switching will drive focus to tailored customer experiences.*
Competitive Differentiators	Price, Service, Access	Personalisation, ancillary services, ecosystem depth and breath	

Figure 6.2 Banks will have to adjust their entire operations to take advantage of the industry revolution brought on by AI and Open Banking regulations. In a more networked industry, financial institutions will have to open up the "data vault" and become part of an ecosystem involving customers, competitors, and delivery partners.

subsequent sections of this chapter, AI will also have a radical impact on the way financial institutions manage their internal operations. AI has the ability to improve the efficiency and impact of almost every part of a financial organization.

The New Banking: Customer Empathy at Scale

We all know the stereotypical description of a banker: the cigar-smoking fat cat who makes big bucks by gouging the little guy. There are many surveys out there confirming this public view, and plenty of bad press on banks to put fuel on the fire. The stories of Wells Fargo opening millions of accounts in the names of customers without their knowledge, British banks manipulating the LIBOR reference rate, Australian banks charging fees to deceased customers and money laundering scandals across the US, Europe, and Russia cause both the public and regulators to seriously doubt the morals of financial institutions. A 2018 global study by Ernst & Young established that only 21% of consumers trust traditional banks to tell them when there is a better product or service available for their needs or situation[1]. The trust in traditional banks to provide customers with unbiased advice is not much better, coming in at 1 in 4. Although this image is difficult for banks to shake off, we believe that AI and ML will bring about a new kind of bank: a bank built on customer empathy at scale.

When used at scale, AI can solve the trade-off between customization and cost management because it provides the ability to identify and action individual customer needs without (costly) human intervention. But why will this customization be built around customer empathy as opposed to maximizing shareholder returns?

The answer is data portability. Regulations that tie data ownership, privacy and portability to the individual consumer will not only shift the balance of information between consumers and financial institutions, but heavily reduce the data advantage that incumbents currently have over new entrants.

When consumers are able to port their personal data between various entities in the data ecosystem, information transparency and data utilization will increase rapidly. Practically speaking, activities like product, service, and pricing comparisons based on consumers' individual data become a lot easier, and picking "the best of the bunch" across a range of financial services providers will become the norm.

An example of using AI to deliver better financial outcomes for customers (rather than just bigger bank profits) can be found at the Commonwealth Bank[2], the biggest financial institution in Australia. In 2015, the bank established a multi-year program to facilitate proactive, needs-based conversations with customers based on insights and triggers delivered through AI and ML.

Commonwealth Bank's so-called Customer Engagement Engine was first trailed at a single branch, using a single laptop, but has since been rolled out across all branches, call centers, digital channels and even ATMs.

The bank's initial project was centered around helping customer-facing branch staff have more relevant conversations based on customer needs and behaviors. Rather than branch staff having to scour customer accounts for information during a customer interaction, the Customer Engagement Engine presents the most relevant information for the conversation based on individual customer profiles.

The AI-based program has allowed the bank to move from one-dimensional product-based conversations to interactions that focus on customers' overall needs and financial wellbeing[3]. For example, the Customer Engagement Engine will prompt customers to use expiring credit card rewards points and show them how to get the most value out of their rewards.

In another, more prominent case of delivering customer empathy at scale, the bank proactively identifies government subsidies that customers might be missing out on, such as welfare payments, utility bill support or car registration rebates. With the evolution of Open Banking and APIs, Commonwealth Bank will soon be able to connect up to government sites and allow customers to claim government benefits through their mobile banking app or internet banking platform. An opportunity worth AU\$ 10 billion a year to its customers, according to the bank[4].

Furthermore, the bank has used this same program to create so-called intelligent routing for over-the-phone conversations. When a customer calls in, their immediate needs will be identified and linked up to "next best actions" identified by the AI decisioning engine. This allows the bank to systematically match the conversation to the best available agent for that conversation.

During the conversation, the bank will use natural language processing (NLP) in real-time to track the quality of the conversation, and make suggestions to the customer consultant based on what has worked before in similar conversations. NLP also allows the measurement and optimization of a plethora of variables that may affect the call such as call length, types of greetings used by staff, music on hold, tone of voice and individual customer consultants' ability to fulfill customer needs.

New ideas for customer outcomes-focused features are often generated through internal competitions among staff. This strategy allows front-line staff to have influence on the focus areas of AI and ML development, which in turn creates a deeper understanding, trust, and acceptance of AI and data-driven initiatives across the organization.

Commonwealth Bank has been able to build these examples of AI-driven customer experience on the vast amounts of data it already holds on its customers. When Open Banking and Open Data regimes are fully rolled out in Australia, the bank will be well-positioned to expand this approach across many external data sources.

AI Use Cases in Financial Services

Every financial institution will have countless use cases for deploying AI and this number will only increase with an organization's ability to record, store and utilize data from internal and external sources.

Simplistically, use cases fall into three categories: operational excellence (doing things cheaper, faster), customer experience (personalization), and risk management (avoiding the downside). Although these categories can we viewed as distinct from each other, they often overlap. For example, deciding whether to give a prospective borrower a loan is a credit risk decision, but it is also an example of a very personalized customer experience event. Thirdly, the speed and ease at which the decision is made not only affects customer satisfaction, but also the cost of running the business.

In the following use case examples (and there are many more than we can fit into this book), we will illustrate how each of these three categories can become a point of differentiation using AI.

Credit Decisioning

Deciding whether or not to lend to a prospective borrower is one of the most foundational elements of banking. On any given day, a bank will make many individual credit decisions that aggregate up to form the basis for the organization's profitability in the short and long term.

There are many parameters to be assessed: Will the customer be able to afford repayments on the loan over the loan period? What if interest rates rise? Can the customer be counted on to manage their finances responsibly? Are they even who they say they are? These are just a few of many assessments made before deciding to lend to a customer.

Operational Excellence: the loan origination process is often expensive for lender and borrower alike. Verifying a prospective customer's identity, assessing their income and expenses, current debt, repayment history, and estimating the market value of collateral security are all activities that require a relatively high degree of effort to complete. This drives cost to the lender and ultimately these costs are passed onto the borrower through direct service fees or indirectly through interest rates.

By applying AI and ML techniques throughout the credit assessment process lenders can cut down the lead time and human effort significantly. Firstly, facial recognition and identity verification algorithms can be deployed to verify the legitimacy and accuracy of documents supplied by the prospective borrower, making document handling and verification a much quicker job.

Secondly, automated property valuations can be used to estimate the value of a property in cases when borrowers want to issue "top-up" lending or Approvals in Principle. Automated valuations will be based on a range of data inputs such as previous sales of the same or neighboring properties, the market performance in the local area, land and property size, and potentially even photos of the property to assess its condition.

Customer Experience: responsiveness and speed of delivery are key pillars of any successful customer service strategy; however when it comes to waiting for an outcome of a loan application, customers are often particularly sensitive to delays or confusion in the process.

Whether the customer is an individual borrowing money for their first home or a business wanting to finance new machinery, the process of seeking finance is often stressful and time sensitive. A quick turnaround on a lending application can be what makes all the difference to a customer when choosing their financial institution.

ML can be used to estimate the probability of default at the application stage, but can also be used to manage the customer's credit risk throughout the lifecycle of the loan. A typical example of this is identifying customer behaviors that indicate financial stress. Acting on early indicators of financial stress can not only be a powerful way to reduce the risk of default, but also a great way of building true loyalty and rapport with customers. When used responsibly, AI can be an incredible tool for identifying and helping vulnerable customers at a time in need. Financial distress often occurs as a result of significant life events such as illness, job loss, bankruptcy, divorce, or death and customers in these situations may be incapable of or embarrassed to contact their financial institution for support. In these cases, AI allows organizations to build true customer empathy at scale by identifying potentially distressed customers before they end up in bankruptcy or default.

Risk Management: An old maxim in banking is that the profit is made before the loan is issued, which of course refers to the critical importance of a robust credit decisioning process. Although banks also incur costs in running their operations, it is indeed true that good or bad credit decisions can make or break a bank. If you're wondering just how essential this step in the lending process is, simply cast your mind to the global financial turmoil of 2007 to 2009, which resulted in government-funded bailouts of $498 billion in the United States alone[5]. The financial crisis was largely caused by lax credit rules and subprime lending tied to an overheated US residential property market. The systemically relaxed borrowing practices of US mortgage lenders, combined with falsely rated securitization trusts pushed not only banks, but whole nation states into financial crisis. Greece, with a population of just fewer than 11 million people, has received bailout funds from other nation states totaling $360 billion since 2010[6]. There is no doubt that the credit decisioning process is a foundational pillar of banking.

As mentioned previously in this chapter, analytics, and data science practices have been popular in credit risk modeling for many decades so should we really expect cutting-edge AI and ML techniques to outperform what is already trailed and tested? The answer is yes.

The rise of AI and ML is a result of the convergence of a few technological advancements. Firstly, the exponential rise of computer power allows us to crunch datasets and mathematical problems (which is really what AI and ML is at its core) that have previously been difficult—and therefore expensive—to solve.

Secondly, cloud computing allows us to access huge amounts of computer power on a needs-only basis, without having to build huge in-house data centers that cater for the maximum possible load needed. This makes complex algorithms significantly cheaper to run.

Thirdly, the availability of powerful computers at an affordable rate allows us to run more complex and sophisticated statistical techniques that can detect much deeper relationships in large datasets. This results in considerably higher rates of accuracy than traditional modeling methods such as regressions, clustering, or Monte Carlo simulations. With higher prediction accuracy and increased complexity of models, a new challenge arises: the interpretability and explainability of *why* the model outputs are what they are (dealing with this challenge will be discussed in detail in Chapter 10 of this book).

As banks dig deeper into their data and learn what are good predictors of future credit default events, they will be able to segment their credit scoring even further. This will reduce the risk of writing bad loans, but also strengthen the case for so-called positive bureau scenarios where a holistic assessment of a prospective borrower's behavior is made. For example, a lender might look favorably upon a prospect who is low income, yet always pays her rent, utility bills and debts on time and is considered frugal by nature.

A deep understanding of a borrower's individual behavior and associated credit default risk can also be used by lenders to offer risk-based pricing. In this case, the lender would offer an interest rate that includes the individual's probability of default as a risk premium.

To illustrate this, let's assume a simplified example, where a prospective borrower applies for a car loan with Bank A. Bank A deems the probability of default to be 6%

given the lender's behavioral profile. On top of that, the bank has set its "risk free" return on funds to 5%. Thus, the total interest offered to the borrower becomes 11%. This approach is not revolutionary in itself, however, the uplift in prediction accuracy makes a big difference to the precision of this approach. The key to this sort of pricing mechanism lies in the interpretability and explainability of the model and prediction. The reasons why one customer might receive a different price to another has to hold up with the organization's own fairness principles, as well as with the regulator or in a court room.

Liquidity Management

Just like credit decisioning, liquidity and cash management should be considered foundational pillars of financial services. At the most basic level, banks are simply clearing houses between those who have excess funds and those who need to borrow to meet their funding needs. Bank profits are made on the difference between lending and deposit interest rates. Therefore, holding too much liquidity will impact profits negatively because the extra deposits are not earning a positive return. Conversely, a lack of funding may mean that the bank will have to pause lending or seek more expensive funding sources.

Operational Excellence: Effective funding and liquidity management can have a significantly positive impact on a financial institution's bottom line. The mix of funding sources, the time to maturity of various funding and hedging instruments, and the price sensitivity of funding and lending activities all play a part in the complex puzzle of making assets and liabilities balance in the most profitable way.

At the same time, Treasury has a fundamental role in managing the risk profile of the organization. Banks have to meet funding mix and adequacy requirements as outlined in the so-called Basel III regulations. Following the global financial crisis of 2007-2009, these worldwide regulations were put in place to ensure stability and adequate liquidity in the financial system. The Net Stable Funding Ratio (NSFR) and Liquidity Coverage Ratio (LCR) sets out minimum requirements for stable funding in terms of the type of funding sources and the amount of liquidity required to be held by individual financial institutions. These factors make liquidity management a mathematical optimization exercise tailor-made for AI.

The use of AI to manage liquidity is being aided immensely by a global push for instant and real-time payment schemes. Many of these schemes are driven by domestic initiatives, but cross-border initiatives such as SWIFT GPI will essentially allow banks and their customers to send funds around the globe in a matter of seconds or minutes. The ability to perform real-time payments at a local and global level reduces friction from payment delays and cut-off times, which in turn opens the door to just-in-time liquidity management.

Producing accurate cash-flow forecasts is a fundamental challenge for most treasuries, let alone in real-time[7]. However, by combining real-time cash-flow data with market yields on liquid assets, ML models can be trained to balance the risk-reward trade-off between placing excess liquidity with the central bank, in highly liquid assets or in illiquid assets such as loans or term deposits.

By using Robotic Process Automation for the placement of cash across different assets, the treasurer's role becomes more strategic in nature. With focus shifting away from manual intervention in cash management, treasurers will be able to spend more of their time evaluating alternative cash-flow scenarios based on large volumes of data attributes and records. Because AI tools can bring together a much broader and deeper set of data inputs, model outputs will inevitably deliver a more holistic understanding of the drivers and risks associated with future cash flows.

Put simply, AI, ML, and automation will allow treasury to focus on the strategic and analytical activities that add incremental value to the business. Ultimately this will lead to more efficient use of funding and capital reserves at higher yields.

Customer Experience: As banks become more efficient balance sheet managers they likely become more profitable as well. This incremental profit can be passed on to shareholders in the form of dividends or retained earnings or be invested back into the business through better or cheaper products and services.

Risk Management: Liquidity management is as much a risk management exercise as it is an exercise in funding a bank's lending activities. The aforementioned opportunities to optimize cash-flows and funding pools will also benefits the bank's liquidity and funding risk positively.

Management of Physical Cash

Physical cash management refers to cash held by the financial institution, for example at branches, inside ATMs or a central storage facility. Management of physical cash can be treated as a supply chain optimization problem: to meet demand, cash may need to be ordered from a central bank (responsible for printing physical notes and coins), while factoring in delivery timeframes. Of course, customers will also deposit cash, which creates an inflow that can support the outgoing cash demand.

Below, we will discuss how AI can be used to optimize liquidity and cash management, while balancing customer experience and operational risk. Again, the upside that AI and ML brings stems from the ability to gain a much more granular understanding of historical factors and causes of supply and demand.

Operational Excellence: Physical cash is expensive to manage. Not only does it need to be handled, transported, and stored safely—when it is in physical form it is not earning a return for the business. Conversely, being unable to meet customer demand at a branch or ATM will create customer frustration. After all, cash should always be available at the bank. This is an optimization problem perfect for ML.

Because physical cash transaction patterns are made up of thousands, if not millions of micro events, it is difficult for the human eye to detect underlying patterns that may shift supply and demand. However, with modern data science techniques such as neural networks, banks can identify supply and demand patterns based on a wide variety of data inputs such as local area demographics, weather patterns, major shopping or cultural events, cash delivery timeframes, and any other variables that may contribute to the supply and demand for physical cash. For instance, if the weather is nice will more people in the local area go to the shops? Will the demand for cash increase as a result? Will we see an influx of cash deposits from the shops? What about that local football game on Sunday? Does it increase the demand for cash? Does it matter whether the game is played at 3 pm or 6 pm?

A sophisticated cash management strategy underpinned by ML can be used to optimize cash management at a granular and localized level, without the need for human "local area experts." Being able to scale such an activity effectively across thousands of outlets is only possible with AI.

Customer Experience: Bank customers expect quick and easy access to cash when they need it. Gone are the days where people patiently line up in long queues to cash in their pay check or withdraw funds from their accounts. Today, cash withdrawals should be safe, quick and readily available. Some banks have used AI technology to make it easier and more secure to retrieve cash from ATMs—sometimes even without a card. In 2019, CaixaBank of Spain introduced facial recognition to access cash via ATMs. Among the biggest benefits of this service is the increased security that comes with physical identity verification rather pin code entry. 66% of customers highlighted this as a key reason for using the service[8].

Risk Management: Although the demand for physical cash has been in consistent decline for many decades, management and handling of notes and coins still carries a lot of risk for banks. Historically, bank and money transport robberies were a major risk for financial institutions; however, that risk has reduced markedly in line with financial institutions holding less physical cash and other preventative measures. To put this into perspective, total annual US bank robberies (which includes robberies, burglaries, and larcenies against physical locations and money transports) reduced by 60% from 2003 to 2018[9].

Although the general population is using less cash than ever, one major challenge has been amplified in line with globalization and increased interconnectivity of financial institutions across national borders: money laundering. Physical cash is still very much alive in the underworld, and for many criminal organizations the global financial system provides the infrastructure to transfer funds around the world—as long as they can avoid the banks' financial crime detective processes.

Money laundering scandals can be a very costly for banks. There is often significant reputational damage associated with money laundering, but that is only half the story. The financial penalties applied by financial regulators tend to be enormous.

In 2018 Commonwealth Bank of Australia agreed to pay AUD 700 million (USD 535 million[10]) to settle a money laundering case involving years of systematic filtering of cash proceeds from criminal activities through the bank's ATMs. Over a 7-year period, a criminal syndicate used the bank's "Intelligent Deposit Machines" to deposit millions of dollars into fraudulent accounts and immediately transfer the funds overseas[11].

The money-laundering syndicate used a network of fraudulent accounts to deposit amounts of $9,900 or $9,850—just below the $10,000 threshold that requires banks to report transactions to AUSTRAC, Australia's anti-money laundering and counter-terrorism financing regulator[12]. In the end, the bank was alerted to the money laundering issue by a watchful staff member at a Sydney branch, who noticed one of the syndicate members returning to deposit large sums of cash on a regular basis.

This is a great example of a problem that could have been solved using advanced data science techniques. In theory, the bank had all the data it needed to discover the systematic criminal activity much earlier. Although the syndicate used several fraudulent accounts and many branches to place their deposits, the pattern was very recognizable: amounts just below the $10,000 threshold were deposited, the money would be moved around shortly after and eventually be transferred overseas.

The bank had another powerful dataset on hand, perfect for ML: the ATMs were fitted with video cameras and therefore the individual fraudsters were being filmed as they went from branch to branch doing their deposits. Had the bank used ML to link suspicious transactions to the appearance of individual depositors, it could have identified the criminal activity much quicker and without the reliance on an observant staff member to raise the alarm.

Payments

Payments have been one of the most exciting areas of financial services innovation since PayPal first launched its payments services in the late 1990s.

Although payments and transactions have historically been viewed as low-value activities compared to other core banking disciplines such as lending, deposits, and trading, many fin-tech start-ups are targeting the payments space as their entry point. Because incumbent banks typically see payments as a low-value (in direct comparison to say lending) and highly complex part of their service offering, opportunities for innovation in this space have been left untapped and available for entrepreneurial fin-techs to target.

Artificial intelligence is often the driving force behind fin-tech business models and payments—or rather the behavioral data associated with these payments—are the foundational inputs to AI-based fin-tech strategies. Payments generate a lot of data which in theory can be used to derive consumer behavior, needs, and preferences, which in turn can be used to create very personalized banking experiences.

At the same time, the rise of mobile banking and the app economy has paved the way for an increased consumer preference for instant access to information about their finances as well as an expectation that payments and transactions can be performed smoothly and instantly during all hours of the day.

Operational Excellence: In today's world of finance, most payments occur smoothly and automatically. However, when payments fail due to data inaccuracies or manually entered data, it is often a cumbersome affair to identify and correct a transaction. On top of that, banks must meet mandatory reporting requirements for payments as part of the industry's anti-money laundering framework.

Data gathering using AI-validated transactions can help automate and streamline these back-office processes, which in turn allows banks to scale the number of transactions without having to increase operational staff levels.

Customer Experience: It is no wonder data-driven start-ups and fin-techs have their eyes on payments as a source of true competitive differentiation. The information generated by transactions can be combined with other data sources to create a rich picture of customer needs, preferences, and life events. The data can be used to create deeply personalized and contextual experiences that create customer loyalty on another level. The opportunities are only limited to the imagination of those in charge of building out the required infrastructure.

Tink—a Swedish AI-platform-as-a-service provider specializing in financial services—gives us a glimpse into the near future of data-driven, personalized banking. Tink's technology uses transaction narratives to provide users with proactive price comparisons across everything from insurance and mortgages to everyday items like utilities and music streaming providers. Payments are also used to populate Tink's personal financial management tool, which not only classifies transactions into spend categories, but also helps users change behaviors or stick to budgets through proactive nudges and alerts[13].

Banks with a retail and commercial footprint have a unique opportunity to create value for their customer base. For instance, by understanding customers' transaction behavior, banks will be able to provide retail customers with personalized offers from merchants in their ecosystem. In other words, banks can leverage their data to create direct benefits for their retail customers in the form of personalized discounts and specials, while also assisting their commercial customers in generating sales from the bank's customer base. A real-life example of such as service is Mogl, an app that lets users access real-time restaurant and merchant discounts and rewards based on their location. The app uses location data to present personalized offers based on users' location and individual preferences, and uses real-time debit or credit card transaction data to provide instant cash-back or other rewards[14].

As banks become experts in leveraging transaction information, they will have the opportunity to on-sell this capability and offer transaction analytics as a service to merchant customers. This value-add service can provide merchants with spend pattern insights but also give them specific tools to target customers with relevant and timely promotional offers. In other words, banks have a substantial strategic opportunity to build ancillary products around the data that is generated by their core business and turn data into a secondary business.

Risk Management: Traditional fraud detection typically relies on a process of flagging transactions for manual review. This conventional, "man-made" logic for identifying potential suspect transactions is expensive, cumbersome, and difficult to scale without having to employ more financial crimes analysts. Furthermore, it inadvertently slows down the implementation of real-time payment systems because of the need for a human-eye check. AI has the potential to significantly reduce fraud and malicious activity in the payments system. Through ML techniques, financial institutions can combine vast amounts of data from many disparate sources and build a more accurate real-time detection engine that can increase the accuracy of detection manyfold. Furthermore, intervention can be automated, making the system scalable.

AI and ML also open the door to anti-fraud coalitions across the industry. In the future, financial institution can combine datasets and algorithms and collaborate to catch fraudulent activity being performed across many entities.

Self-Driving Finance

Achieving personalization and empathy at scale is the ultimate frontier for banks in a world where finances are driven by data and AI. Customers will be ultra-loyal when they are being cared for across all elements of their financial life. The financial institutions (or new market entrants) that first master the art of aggregating and contextualizing customers' financial needs and behaviors will thrive on this loyalty.

In contrast, financial advice delivered via traditional means is often generic, subjective or incomplete, leading to sub-optimal outcomes for the individual consumer or business seeking advice. Just consider the following three scenarios:

1. **Generic**—self-service advice found on banking websites is often based on generalized articles or calculators that use average assumptions.
2. **Subjective**—visiting the branch or ringing the call center is likely to deliver advice based on the agent's limited knowledge of the customer's context. At the same time, the agent may simply be unable to give certain types of advice from a regulatory compliance perspective.
3. **Incomplete**—financial advisors may be acting based on incomplete information as the customer might have financial products outside the advisor's organization.

AI and Open Banking will break up this paradigm and shift the competitive dynamics toward those who are best at providing excellent customer experience and personalized outcomes.

Self-driving finance is based on automation of routine or simple tasks such as bill payments, savings behavior, or opening of new bank accounts. On top of that comes automated advice pertaining to the customer's full financial life, including retirement planning, loan refinancing—or in the case of business banking, items like cash-flow management and corporate finance. For incumbent financial institutions there is a great risk that they will simply become financial product providers, unless they choose to compete on AI at scale.

Customer Support & Conversation Automation

Financial services customers have progressively become more reliant on self-service banking options, since the arrival of the first ATMs in the 1960s. However, there are situations where customers still need to have a conversation with their bank to solve their needs. AI is having a big impact on how customers interact with their banks in these situations, making conversations quicker, easier, and more secure for customers and banks alike.

A common technology is so-called conversational AI which underpins chatbots and virtual assistants in banks across the globe. Through natural language processing and generation, chatbots and virtual assistants are able to respond to queries in conversational language. This technology is typically used to service customers who want to perform simpler tasks such as balance enquiries, money transfers or have questions about loan applications or other processes. However, conversational AI is rapidly evolving and more advanced versions of the technology is helping customers complete complex loan applications at the convenience of their own schedule, outside branch and call center hours.

In 2018, HSBC went one step further and placed seven humanoid robots in their Fifth Avenue branch in New York City[15]. The robots, which all respond to the name Pepper, have been developed by SoftBank Robotics and can be programmed to interact with customers across many different industries. The humanoids, about 4 feet tall, are able to do more than just help customers with basic banking queries—they also tell jokes, pose for selfies and perform dance moves. Whether the robots will replace human staff or remain a charming novelty remains to be seen.

Biometric authorization is another form of AI used widely for making identity verification safer and more seamless. For instance, most banking apps are capable of using the pre-packaged fingerprint and facial recognition technology in smartphones to verify the customer's identity. AI is also used in call centers to verify identities through voice recognition technology.

An example of this is HSBC's Voice ID program, which allows customers to verify their identity by saying "my voice is my password" rather than recounting or typing in a phone banking password. The program gained some notoriety in 2017, when the BBC successfully fooled the system by letting a twin emulate his brother's voice[16]. The case exposed a number of vulnerabilities in the configuration, including the fact that the twin had unlimited attempts to verify his identity using voice. It took him 8 tries to get through. Despite BBC's famous doppelganger act, HSBC has been able to reduce identity fraud significantly using the technology. In other words, voice biometrics are still more secure than traditional authentication systems based on pin numbers or passwords.

Other British banks such as NatWest, Metro Bank, Monzo, and Starling allow customers to open new bank accounts using photo ID such as a driver's license or passport combined with a selfie photo or short video[17]. A real-time biometric check then confirms whether the selfie matches the image in the ID document.

AI as a Fraud Tool

The continued digitization of financial services has created a complex trade-off between fraud prevention and customer experience. Today's banking customers demand faster services like instant local and cross-border payments, 24-by-7 access to their accounts, and straight-through opening of new facilities. In turn, these faster services decrease the likelihood of detecting and recovering losses from fraudulent activity, because everything happens in a matter of seconds rather than days.

However, the risk of fraud and data breaches is not only confined to banks' internal systems and channels of interaction. In today's digitized and globally interconnected world, customers routinely store personal and payment information such as names and addresses, birthdays, phone numbers, credit card numbers, and passwords across a multitude of entities and digital platforms. Unfortunately, it is not uncommon to see huge data breaches at these entities, where criminals gain access to vast amounts of personal information that can be used to carry out fraudulent activity. Some known examples of data breaches that exposed personal information include Yahoo in 2013 and 2014 (3 billion and 500 million accounts, respectively), eBay in 2014 (145 million users), Equifax in 2017 (148 million users), and Marriot International in 2018 (500 million customer records)[18].

The sheer scale of these data breaches makes cyber-crime an extremely profitable business for those sophisticated enough to avoid getting caught. As an example, hackers pocketed an estimated £9.4 million from on-selling 244,000 credit card numbers stolen in a cyber-attack against British Airways in 2018[19]. These credit cards belonged to customers from a large number of countries, making it difficult for British Airways and card providers to put in a concerted effort to prevent fraudulent activity in a timely fashion.

Another pertinent reason for banks to embrace AI for fraud prevention is that many new and creative fraud schemes are based on ML and AI. As fraudsters become more sophisticated in their approach, traditional fraud detection methods such as human-manufactured rules engines will struggle to keep up with their adversaries. Rules engines will typically cover the most common fraud techniques, because these have been identified and subsequently coded into the rule sets, resulting in a lagged response between new fraud methods and prevention. Conversely, self-learning algorithms can quickly pick up and incorporate new trends and techniques, provided they are supplied with appropriate data.

Another common challenge with traditional fraud identification methods is the high rate of so-called false positives—events that have been flagged incorrectly as fraud. False positives often require the same amount of investigative effort as true positives, so they are a costly by-product inaccurate detection.

An example of this comes from Nordic banking giant Danske Bank[20]. Like other modern banks, Danske has seen the lion's share of its customers move from traditional branch-based banking to a digital self-service ecosystem involving internet banking, mobile apps, ATMs, and call centers. This shift toward a larger number of digital channels has increased the risk of fraud exponentially. As a result, the bank was struggling in the battle against fraudulent activity on two fronts: the fraud detection rate was sitting at only 40%, while the number of false positives was (a very costly) 1,200 per day. In fact, only 0.5% of all cases investigated turned out to be true fraudulent activity.

To tackle these issues, the bank instigated an AI-based fraud prevention project in partnership with Teradata. Over a 5-month period, several deep learning models were deployed to continuously improve on the status quo—a so-called "champion/ challenger" approach where new "challenger" models try to beat the "champion" model. The immediate results were significant: the AI models improved the fraud detection frequency by 50% while also reducing the false positives by 60%.

Unique Opportunities in Corporate & Institutional Banking

Large-scale corporations are inherently complex—and so are their banking needs. On any given day, a typical large corporate customer will take payment for products and services through a physical or online merchant facility, pay invoices to suppliers, bill customers for products or services provided, receive payments for previously issued bills, handle physical cash at several locations, sign contracts involving small and large financial transactions, require finance for materials, machinery or property, manage employee credit card and discretionary spend programs, make multinational funds transfers, manage liquidity and cash flow, buy and sell financial instruments to hedge against currency and interest rate risk, perform M&A activities and much more. While doing these activities, organizations want to account for every dollar leaving and entering the organization and also protect themselves and their customers against fraudulent activity performed by scammers or employees.

AI and advanced analytics open the door to many new opportunities for institutional banks to help their corporate customers understand and manage this complexity. Take for example the basic, yet traditionally resource-intensive task of matching outstanding invoices to payments received. Many corporations find the process of matching payments slow and error-prone because it is often difficult to obtain the remittance information needed to reconcile invoices. In 2018, Citi Bank's corporate division tackled this problem by making a strategic investment in HighRadius, a developer of AI-driven invoice and payments-matching software[21]. The service allows Citi's corporate customers to reduce labor-intensive tasks and eliminate errors caused by manual entry, while also increasing cash utilization due to better cash flow forecasting and more timely liquidity management.

This example highlights how banks can forge strong partnerships with their corporate customers by designing AI-enabled services and features that can streamline, automate and inform the multitude of banking-related touchpoints throughout corporate organizations. AI and ML techniques are needed in this equation, because they drive specificity without increased human labor to perform basic tasks—it is basically the corporate version of personalization and empathy at scale.

Institutional banking is complex and multilayered, yet margins are thin. Competition (and customer negotiation power) in the big end of town is strong, and in many cases institutional clients will be low value or simply unprofitable even though their business may create hundreds of millions of dollars in revenue for their bank.

The institutional banking arm of ANZ Bank—a large multinational bank with operations in 36 countries—faced this challenge in 2016, when it set up its first-ever data science team[22]. Initially, the bank used analytical insights to identify and remove unprofitable customers from its books. This improved the operational efficiency and overall profitability of the division, but also demonstrated the value of insights-driven decision-making to internal stakeholders.

The initial success gave the bank confidence to put further resources behind data science. The bank built a team of 10 data science interns recruited from a local data science meetup and began testing a long list of hypotheses. Through a series of data science experiments spanning several months, the bank discovered that it could create a Data-as-a-Service (DaaS) product for institutional clients, using spend data from its retail division. For example, the bank used retail customer spend data from McDonald's outlets to create demographic profiles of the best and worst-performing suburbs for McDonald's, localized market share reports, and other consumer insights products. The bank also provided McDonald's with the best locations for new stores by identifying suburbs with a similar demographical make-up and spend behavior to those suburbs with the best performing stores.

Initially, the analytics service was provided for free, but bundled with highly profitable financial products. Over time, the bank has turned the DaaS offering into a stand-alone product that can be accessed through a web portal and various APIs that communicate directly with customers' IT systems.

AI and Algorithmic Trading

Since the 1980s, the capital markets divisions of banks, retirement funds, hedge funds, and other institutional investors have increasingly turned their eyes toward AI to solve for speed and accuracy in their trading operations. On top of that, many market players look to algorithms to find and take advantage of profit opportunities that are not visible to the human eye.

In this section, our goal is to highlight some key areas in which AI is relevant to trading. This is not a book on algorithmic trading (of which there are more than 500 for sale on Amazon.com right now), but we will touch briefly on the foundations of algorithmic trading in order to create the appropriate context to think about where AI fits in.

The challenge with writing about algorithmic methods in trading is that few if any organizations are willing to share their trade secrets in this area. The result is that we are limited to writing generally about the kinds of problems being solved by AI with few specific examples. The good news is that we can be specific about the techniques used to develop trading algorithms so that it is possible to understand the process to build and apply the technology.

There are two main application areas in trading that are performed with the aid of algorithms, and which can benefit from advances in AI: Speculation and operational efficiency. Let's take a look at both.

Speculation

The goal of speculation is to generate profits directly from trading activities. Given that the vast majority of transactions in the markets are initiated with the idea of making a profit, speculation is an important area to understand but also a difficult area to actually profit in. The underlying assumption is that you must find a way to get an advantage in order to consistently profit. Presumably, our incredible AI algorithms will be our advantage, but the playing field has continued to become increasingly challenging.

In the early nineties, when I (Bob) co-founded a quantitative futures trading company, we were able to consistently generate profits with a portfolio of pretty good algorithms and a seven-foot-tall Order Execution Specialist in the futures pit at the Chicago Mercantile Exchange (CME). We could identify when to buy and sell to make a profit in a few hours, and he was able to execute our buy and sell orders quickly and efficiently so that all of our profits weren't eaten up by "slippage" (poor pricing on transactions). The markets were pretty efficient, but not so efficient that it wasn't possible to find valuable prediction algorithms. That began to change in 1997, with the introduction of the S&P500 e-mini, an S&P500 futures contract that was traded on the new CME Electronic Exchange. Suddenly, trades could be placed 100% electronically, and sales and pricing information became almost instantaneous. It took a few years for this new environment to impact the efficiency of the market, but the trend for algorithmic trading, and especially high-frequency trading, to increase the efficiency of the markets had begun. This trend has continued to the present time, and as a result, it is much harder to profitably speculate on the markets, with or without the aid of advanced algorithms and AI.

So how do we get an advantage? To profit consistently in trading we have to know something that others don't. In some cases, this secret knowledge can be a fact (e.g., it's going to rain in Kansas next week, damaging corn crops and increasing the price of corn), or it can be the knowledge of how to interpret a fact (a new Department of Labor Statistics measure came out and it showed a decrease in unemployment. Will market prices go up or down because of this?).

Can we use AI to know something new or different and thus gain a trading advantage? Sure. But remember that the markets are a great big picnic, covered with an army of ants (including some very well-funded ants) who are all looking for the next algorithmic crumb to pick up and carry off. Speculation is not easy money.

To see how we might use AI to gain an advantage in trading, it's worth looking at the two main subareas of speculation, arbitrage, and prediction (which many practitioners call statistical arbitrage, or StatArb).

Arbitrage

Arbitrage is the process of generating a trading profit that is in principle risk free by simultaneously buying something for a low price in one place and then selling it in another place for a higher price. For example, if the price of a stock in Exchange A $10.00 and $9.90 in Exchange B, then we could generate ten cents per share by simultaneously buying shares in Exchange B and selling them in Exchange A. Sounds simple, and in principle it is. The challenge is that prices are constantly moving so we might not be guaranteed to get our prices if we don't move fast (i.e., we need an algorithm to automate the detection and execution of the trade!). Additionally, we have to profit after transaction costs are considered and we can't buy or sell too much of the stock or we will impact the pricing ourselves. Of course, we are not alone in chasing arbitrage—there are many, many other speculators looking for such opportunities with automated tools. The conclusion is that arbitrage could be a good way to make profits in the market with a fancy algorithm, but we need to find a more complicated arbitrage opportunity to be consistently profitable.

Here's where AI comes into play. Recall that arbitrage depends on being able to buy and sell equivalent assets at different prices. Then the development opportunity may be in the definition of equivalent. It is possible in principle to use ML to scour markets for unusual arbitrage opportunities such as combinations of assets and derivatives (such as options or swaps) that are essentially equivalent. Such AI systems would be constructed to both recognize such equivalencies, detect when pricing is out of alignment so that an arbitrage opportunity exists, and to execute a properly-sized trade to profit from the anomaly. We have no doubt that there are quantitative trading firms out there that are running such algorithms today.

Prediction and StatArb

Prediction is bread and butter for ML, as we have seen elsewhere in this book. Remember also that we have argued that prediction in AI includes both predicting the future and predicting the value of something that can't be measured directly (even if it has happened in the past). The interesting question for the purposes of this section is, what can we predict so that we know something that others don't?

It's always possible that one might develop a powerful deep-learning-based AI system that is so good at time series forecasting that it can use transfer learning to continually develop new interpretations of market data and stay one step ahead of other traders. In general, especially given that there is only a finite amount of historical trading data around to train algorithms with, this may not be the best approach. More interesting approaches may be in the extraction and interpretation of unstructured, nontraditional data. For example, as our ability to interpret vast amounts of text accurately, and with good contextual awareness, it is currently possible to develop algorithms that scan news, social media, and other sources to identify information that might provide a statistical advantage while trading. This is an area which, although many organizations are already actively pursuing it, the pace of change of the underlying AI technology is creating opportunities for innovation.

Operational Efficiency

An interesting area of opportunity for AI in trading is in the second major application area of operational efficiency. There are many financial transactions in which a complex set of trades must be carried out in order to achieve an underlying corporate objective. Some of these transactions might be part of a larger speculative activity, for example, the need to buy a huge number of shares of a specific stock without impacting the price too much. They may also simply be part of the business operations of the organization, such as the need to rebalance a portfolio to remain in compliance with the stated guidelines of a retirement fund of institutional portfolio.

It is possible to train an AI agent to efficiently execute large trades. Why is this important? If the typical trading volume of a stock is 6 million shares per day and an offer to sell 500,000 shares showed up in the queue at the exchange, the price would go down dramatically. In general, this is simply because of supply and demand: Someone wants to sell a "huge" number of shares, so the supply is high and the price will go down. Mechanically, the electronic market is structured so that there are bidders offering to buy different amounts of stock at different prices below the current market price. There might be 10,000 shares bid for at the current price and then 10,000 bid for a few cents below the market price. A sell order for 500,000 shares would quickly eat through all of these bids, effectively decreasing the price at each new level. In fact, the impact of such an order could be to create a small panic in the stock (This can happen for large buy or sell orders, but tends to create bigger waves when it is a sell order). That's not good for a company that is trying to sell the stock at the original price. The AI approach is to train an algorithm to carry out such a large trade in smaller chunks, organized strategically to disguise the fact that a large order is lurking behind these smaller sales. There is an operational advantage in this type of strategy simply because such an agent can carry out its work efficiently, usually optimally, and without the need to pay a human to work the order.

In many financial organizations, complex portfolios must be maintained with highly constrained characteristics. For example, a retirement fund may be committed to maintaining a certain relationship to the S&P500 Index. As valuations in the index change, and indeed when the composition of the index itself changes, a fund that is indexed to the S&P500 will need to buy and sell large amounts of stock to maintain the proper composition. An agent, as described above, would be appropriate to develop to handle such rebalancing. Furthermore, many fund strategies are far more complicated than just maintaining a relationship to an index, and can include a variety of complex derivative instruments and a requirement to maintain fixed ratios of measures other than price or value. For example, a portfolio might be constructed in such a way that increases or decreases in interest rates do not directly change the value of the portfolio. To maintain a portfolio of complex financial instruments with this constraint is much more easily done by an algorithm. In fact, an AI approach can incorporate automation and prediction to allow for significantly better overall performance of each transaction.

Methods: Supervised Training and Simulation

How do we build such algorithms? Interestingly, the basic methods haven't changed much since the 1990s. Depending upon the question we are trying to answer and the data we have at our disposal, we are either going to do supervised learning or simulation, or a combination of both.

Supervised Learning

Supervised learning, as we have seen elsewhere in this book, is the process of feeding an algorithm examples of inputs, along with the desired responses. We then tune the parameters of the algorithm in order to coerce the algorithm into "answering" correctly when it sees these inputs. The expectation is that the algorithm will have learned something generalizable that can be used to answer the question when it is shown data it hasn't seen before.

For time series forecasting the input is generally some subset of the recent values of the time series and the label is the next value. Of course, it's also possible to include other information, including data from other time series, as part of the inputs. There are many ML models that can be used for time series forecasting, including recursive neural networks and neural networks with hierarchical attention models, which would be considered to be in the AI category.

Another example of input and label might be text from the Internet about a specific economic topic or company and the label would be the price change over the course of a day or part of a day. Again, supervised learning can be used to develop a model that will predict the price change based on the input text. The assumption of course is that there is a reliable, predictable relationship between the text and the price change that can be exploited. Deep learning and traditional ML regression such as logistic regression could be useful in an example like this.

The list of examples could literally go on forever. Any question that would generate a trading advantage if you could answer it, would be appropriate to expose to this approach.

Simulation

Having a trained prediction model is 9/10 of the battle, but there is an additional tool that is important for the development of trading models: simulation. In the development of trading models, the most famous simulation approach is backtesting, but there are other appropriate areas to apply simulation.

Backtesting refers to the process of estimating the profitability and riskiness of an algorithmic trading strategy by simulating how it would have done in the past on historical data. There are a number of software platforms for performing backtesting, and it is likely that most quantitative trading houses will have their own bespoke backtesting platforms, but the principle is always the same. You program the trading rules or plug in the forecasting algorithm and run it forward over time in a historical data set. Your simulation can include factors such as the timing of the model, variations in what price you will get when you place a trade, commissions, how you will exit a position, and other factors. This approach allows you to see how well an algorithmic approach might work in the real world, although it is still always a significant overestimate of the likely profitability of the strategy.

Simulation can also be used to assess risk. For example, by simulating possible future pricing streams one can estimate how much risk one might take on each trade to maintain a desired risk profile. The idea is that the simulation will include some possible future worlds in which a big variation occurs, allowing you to see a broader range of risk profiles. This is especially important since backtesting is dependent upon the one and only real-world history that is available to you (i.e., what really happened) and so your model parameters can end up being purpose-built to do well in the past, but with little hope for profitability in the future. In fact, a trading model that is not highly profitable is likely to be very expensive to operate in the long run because there will always be huge adverse periods that can rack up large losses, even in a marginally profitable trading strategy. Simulation can really expose such risks.

Simulation is also handy for studying the overall properties of portfolios and complex hedges. The approach is to create future pricing streams for all assets in the portfolio and then observe the overall behavior of the system. Such an analysis can reveal flaws in your portfolio construction assumptions, especially when considering complex strategies. The caveat is that you have to be careful to include realistic correlations between prices in your portfolio. Without that, simulation will underestimate large portfolio fluctuations that happen when the underlying components move together under certain circumstances. If your price simulations neglect this, you will have more risk than you think you do.

Warnings, Caveats, and Advice

"Past performance is no guarantee of future results." There is a lot of snake oil out there in the world of trading. There are more than 50,000 books on trading that are not about algorithmic trading and are therefore, in our opinion, highly suspect in terms of their veracity or value. It is reasonable to infer that there is a lot of selling of spurious information about algorithmic trading and AI as well.

Look for products that provide tools to facilitate model training, backtesting, simulation, and portfolio management, but not the actual models themselves. Very few algorithms that are available for sale are anything more than someone else's failed experiment.

For the enterprise, the most useful application area of trading is in the operational efficiency arena. If your organization needs to buy or sell large quantities of a commodity, or hedge the risk of high-value operations that depend on market factors, then building AI algorithms to help manage these buying, selling, and hedging activities can be very worthwhile.

AI for Central Banking

Central banks around the world are also embracing the opportunities created by the advancements in computer power, big data, and AI. Broadly speaking, central banks are concerned with AI across three domains:

1. AI and ML techniques can be used to combine many disparate datasets, thus creating the foundation for more timely and accurate measures of economic conditions;
2. AI and data policies such as Open Banking will have large impacts on the financial services industry and the economy more broadly. Central banks must keep abreast with these impacts and adjust economic policy accordingly;
3. Most central banks have a supervisory role to play within their jurisdiction, and must maintain a balance between innovation and system stability.

Traditional macroeconomic data such as consumer confidence, unemployment, or inflation are often subject to error. Some data are based on surveys of household and business attitudes, whereas others are collected from various government entities. Because data inputs are often collected gradually and disjointedly, there is always a trade-off between timeliness and accuracy in estimating current and future economic conditions.

However, through advanced analytics and AI, central banks can combine a variety of microeconomic data inputs to get early readings on macroeconomic trends or verify macroeconomic forecasts across a range of correlating factors. As an example, the European Central Bank uses microeconomic data from private-sector sources to supplement their macroeconomic forecasts or get earlier readings on shifts in the economy. Often these are somewhat disparate dataset that—when combined—have a strong correlation with the direction of the overall economy. Examples include Google search terms on unemployment or car sales being used to "nowcast" macroeconomic conditions, online price data being used to verify price index and inflation estimates, and credit card and ATM transaction data being used to forecast GDP growth. The ECB also uses text mining of financial news reports and central banking communications to gauge economic sentiment[23].

For many central banks, AI brings about a dual challenge of fostering innovation in financial services, while maintaining stability and security within the financial system during a time of rapid change. Incumbent financial institutions are investing in large-scale digital transformation programs to be able to take advantage of data-driven decision-making, and new market entrants often base their entire business models around digital offerings underpinned by AI (hence the name "fin-tech").

This rapid change in technology and increase in complexity creates an unprecedented situation for all participants in the financial ecosystem. While conventional econometric, statistical and scorecard-based modeling techniques often fall short of AI and ML in terms of accuracy, they are a lot easier to document, supervise and audit. As a consequence, financial services firms, central banks, and other supervisory organizations have a new-found challenge of ensuring accurate, stable, and ethical AI in financial services.

To tackle these challenges, central banks around the world are establishing in-house AI teams with broad-ranging responsibilities. As an example, the Bank of Italy established a multidisciplinary team on Big Data, Machine Learning, and Artificial Intelligence in 2018[24]. The team combines skills in economics, econometrics, statistics, and computer science to provide traditional central banking intelligence such as economic forecasts, unemployment and inflation estimates, and consumer sentiment, but also functions as a center of excellence for supervisory activity related to Big Data and AI.

Salvatore Rossi, Senior Deputy Governor of the Bank of Italy said, "All this is beneficial to competition and productivity in the financial industry, provided that the new entrants are properly supervised. Technology can help to innovate financial products and services currently provided by the traditional industry to the benefit of consumers. However, given all the well-known interconnections between operators in the market, the repercussions of technological innovation on the system's stability are not clear. Public institutions like central banks and other financial supervisory authorities should examine the matter carefully."

How to Identify Your Best Use Cases

There are hundreds, if not thousands, of applications of AI and ML in financial institutions, but the most promising opportunities will differ from one organization to the next. This plethora of options can make it challenging for organizations to agree on where to begin their AI journey.

Furthermore, it is difficult to accurately predict which data science initiatives will have the biggest payoff down the track. Not only will predictions be limited by the knowledge of those who make them, but may also be biased by the personal goals of individuals involved in the prioritization exercise.

Generally speaking, the best use cases will fulfill the following requirements:

- The use case has a clearly defined outcome, and obvious business value that can be quantified and measured post implementation of the AI initiative. Examples of such defined outcomes could be identification and reduction of customer attrition or identifying suspicious transactions with a greater level of accuracy. In both cases, measures of success can be clearly defined upfront.
- There is a clear link to the organization's overarching strategic imperatives. Linking use cases to important organizational goals will ensure stakeholder buy-in, support, and willingness to go the extra mile to make the project a reality.
- The project has an engaged business sponsor. Effective AI implementation often requires systems configuration, process implementation, staff training, change management, and communication with senior management across the organization. Without an enthusiastic business owner to partner with the data scientists, AI projects are unlikely to reach their full potential.
- The data needed for the exercise is already "plumbed" and ready for use in a modeling exercise. If a use case requires a large upfront effort to acquire, conform, and prepare data, it will be better left for future endeavors.

Building AI at Scale in Financial Services

By now we have established that there are plenty of use cases for AI in financial services, but unfortunately building AI at scale requires a lot more than just hiring some smart data scientists and hoping for the best.

To create a successful AI transformation, financial institutions will need to focus on five essential components that all need to be managed:

1. Picking use cases that are highly relevant to the future success of the organization. These are activities that have a large strategic and/or monetary impact.
2. Empower analytics and data science functions with the right mandate, skills, and tools to deliver on the promise of AI.
3. Building a data and digital ecosystem that is able to create and consume AI output in real-time.
4. Integrating AI and ML output into systems and processes across internal and customer-facing channels.
5. Creating a culture of data-driven decision-making and customer empowerment through AI. This cultural transformation requires a push from the data and analytics community and a pull from the wider organization (Figure 6.3).

Picking the Right Use Cases

If the executive leadership of an organization is bought into the long-term potential of AI, it is likely that data science experiments will get support and funding. However, even if the c-suite believe in the potential of AI and advanced analytics in financial services, the proof is in the pudding. AI initiatives need to deliver value for the business and customers. Therefore, getting AI off to a good start requires some practical proof points that show the value and potential of investing further.

The key to success is to focus on use cases that meet the following four criteria:

1. It is aligned to the overall strategic imperatives of the organization
2. If successful, it will have a measurable impact on one or more important value metrics like increased revenue, reduced cost, enhanced productivity, increased customer satisfaction, or improved risk control.

To create a successful AI transformation...

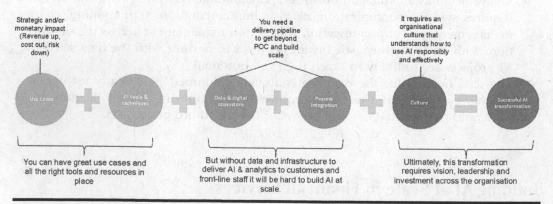

Figure 6.3 **Successful AI transformations require a strategic vision for AI, the technological capability to produce and consume appropriate AI outputs, and cultural adoption of AI as an understood and accepted part of business operations.**

3. The value can be proven through a proof of concept trial, with minimal upfront investment in data and technology

4. There is a community of engaged business stakeholders who will rally to make the initiative successful.

Successful delivery of use cases is not just about building something that works from a technical perspective. An equally important part of the exercise is winning the hearts and minds of colleagues at all levels of the business. In other words, picking initiatives that will have a measurable impact, and where a number of senior business stakeholders have skin in the game, is fundamental.

Empowering Analytics & Data Science Functions

Getting started with AI is much more than just setting up the technical infrastructure, hiring some data scientists, and telling them to get on with it. Of course, data scientists with the right technical expertise and business acumen are absolutely necessary, but without a sharp focus on delivering on the most important strategic priorities, distraction is waiting around the corner.

When it comes to hiring the right team members, it's easy to fall into the trap of looking for the AI unicorn: an individual with data science skills, strong business acumen and great leadership, communication, and organizational skills. After all, that is exactly the skillset needed to create the technical and cultural transformation underpinning AI at scale. In reality, such individuals are few and far between, so banks must focus on building their own talent pipeline and creating *a unicorn team* rather than *a team of unicorns*.

To be successful in delivering end-to-end AI projects, analytics teams must be able to manage the delivery pipeline from data acquisition to implementation of AI outputs and processes. Increasingly, analytics teams will go from advising the business through insights and recommended actions, to running the business through algorithms and data-driven process automation. This requires data science disciplines to be complemented by additional skills and expertise such as experience design, process design, project management, and change leadership.

Even with the right function in place, it's easy for analytics and data science teams to get side-tracked by the many seemingly urgent and important initiatives and burning fires that are always happening within a financial services organization. Data science and analytics professionals are often highly intelligent and multi-talented individuals with a unique ability to understand data and turn it into viable recommendations—a skillset that is often in high demand within the business. Therefore, banking executives must empower their analytics teams with the ability to focus on only the most important strategic imperatives.

A case in point is Toronto Dominion Bank's 2018 acquisition of Layer 6, an AI technology business specializing in customer experience design[25]. TD Bank bought Layer 6 to jump-start its AI progression with an established *unicorn team* of AI specialists, but also took every measure to make sure the Layer 6 team would focus on only the most important tasks. Rather than moving Layer 6 onto TD Bank premises, the team has remained in separate offices. If bank staff want to meet with the AI team, they have to go to Layer 6 offices, not the other way around. Before new workloads can enter a project for prioritization, strict commercial and customer experience hurdles have to be met. TD Bank has recognized that their new AI team is the pick of the litter. The best thing they can do to set the team up for success is to make sure the unhelpful interruptions never happen.

Designing the Data and Digital Infrastructure

Henry Ford, the founder of the Ford Motor Company who is frequently credited with developing the assembly line mass production practice, once said: "if I had asked people what they wanted, they would have said faster horses." This quote is often used to illustrate how technical evolution is only limited by the (lack of) imagination of those who operate at the forefront of innovation. Henry Ford's story bears many parallels to the situation of AI in financial services today. AI has the potential to revolutionize the way financial services think and operate, and it's up to the innovators in this space to take advantage of this opportunity.

Just like Henry Ford had to convince the cynics about the bright future of the automobile, banks must prove the value of AI in order to justify further investments. And just like Henry Ford needed his mass-produced automobiles to be accompanied by infrastructure such as gas stations, roads, and repair shops, banks need to invest in the data and digital infrastructure required to operationalize AI at scale.

In order for banks to progress beyond the proof-of-concept stage with AI initiatives that focus on personalized customer experiences, enterprise systems must be implemented and configured to be able to receive and utilize AI outputs in real-time. For example, if a customer visits the credit card page on the company website, a product recommendation engine should pick up this event straight away and update its recommendation as a result. This requires an operational data and systems infrastructure that is different to traditional data warehousing. Designing data and digital infrastructure that can make real-time updates requires banks to think more like the big Silicon Valley technology companies such as Facebook and LinkedIn. Their newsfeed algorithms need to be able to update in line with user activities and cannot rely on data that is processed in overnight batch jobs.

However, as banks begin to upgrade their technical infrastructure to take advantage of AI outputs, they must do so with a clear view of how outputs will be used and the expected returns. The end-state vision must be detailed enough that value can be quantified and measured as the technology is rolled out. Therefore, the link between AI proofs of concept and technology investment should not be overlooked. Banks should take an agile approach to building out their data and digital infrastructure based on the needs of specific use cases, so that value can be realized quickly.

When it comes to tools used to perform ML and other advanced analytics techniques, banks need to take advantage of the plethora of open-source tools already available in most organizations. Furthermore, data scientists should be empowered with tools to analyze unstructured data sources like weblogs, clickstreams, text, images, voice and video recordings. Some of the richest customer information lies in customer interaction data such as live-chat, call recordings, and email messages, but it requires the right analytical tooling and skills to make sense of.

Culture Is Half the Story

Successful AI transformation is as much about creating a cultural transformation as it is about developing and deploying algorithms in real-time. With limited precedence for this kind of transformation in financial services, one thing is certain: CEOs and other senior executives play a pivotal role in making the transformation a success.

CEO leadership is required to create two assets underpinning success: a transformation strategy that takes into account culture and governance and a robust analytics function capable of delivering AI value proof points while educating the business on what is possible.

The analytics community will need executive support to create the "push" for advanced analytics. An analytics push encompasses much more than just providing analytical outputs to the business. To progress toward AI at scale, banks must set the aspiration but also define standards for data definitions and quality, as well as translate their strategy into AI principles. There are a lot of outputs to deliver and many mindsets to change. The CEO must set the ambition for the organization and communicate it widely and often. Only with the right analytics mindset pervading throughout the organization can AI be adopted at scale.

As the organization matures and the analytics mindset becomes commonplace, the "push" from the analytics function should be balanced by a "pull" from the wider organization. However, an increasing demand for analytics is not in itself a measure of success. Rather, the measure of success should be an increased demand for *the right kind of analytics*. Great analytics stem from high-quality questions, not data. The organization must be able to ask the questions that really matter, and pick the solutions that will have an impact, rather than doing analysis for the sake of it. Value and impact must be at the forefront of every analytical endeavor.

When the focus on value creation is consistent from task to task and project to project, the organization gets trained to take advanced analytics seriously as a business discipline. In reality, the speed of the transition toward AI is heavily reliant on individual organizations' ability to shape the combined skillset of their workforce to take advantage of the new paradigm.

A New Kind of Analytics Leadership

The evolution of advanced analytics and AI in financial services also creates the need for a new kind of analytics leader. Historically, analytics leaders have been functional experts tasked with the important role of *describing, enlightening, and advising the business* on data and insights. However, with the ascent of advanced analytics and AI, analytics leaders will increasingly be *running the business*. In a highly digitized world, the combination of technology, experience design, and AI-driven decisions will replace or augment human interactions at scale. In turn, analytics functions will be interacting with customers and colleagues through the models and algorithms they implement—this is a big shift in remit and responsibility.

For analytics leaders, the job becomes increasingly complex as a result. In order to technically implement AI at scale, analytics leaders at all levels of the organization will need to over-index (to use an analytics term) on strategic thinking, change management, intrapreneurship, and a range of other leadership traits. This is no small feat and it requires financial services organizations to invest in their analytics talent pipeline.

Over time this evolution will necessitate data and analytics to have a seat at the executive table. If advanced analytics and AI are going to augment or replace large parts of customer and employee experience, the discipline should be on par with other functional specialities such as IT or Finance. Moreover, as advanced analytics and AI becomes a foundational strategic lever, other c-suite executives should also roll up their sleeves up and get a meaningful understanding of how raw data becomes valuable output.

The elevation of analytics to the highest ranks of the organization draws many parallels to the promotion of corporate IT functions in the past. As personal computing became increasingly widespread in the office and at home in the 1990s, information technology became a foundational strategic lever in financial services.

Today, Chief Information Officers are essential members of any banking executive committee. Banking staff are expected to be computer literate and the organization's tasks, communication, and ways of working are largely designed around computer technology. Similarly, future banking staff will be expected to be analytics literate and the organization and tasks will be designed to enable data-driven decision-making and automated processes based on AI (Figure 6.4).

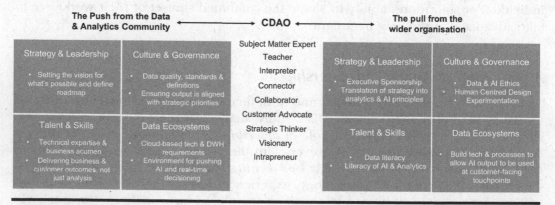

From Advising to Running the Business

Figure 6.4 **The role of Chief Data & Analytics Officer will become increasingly important as financial services firms progress their AI maturity. The cultural change required to create a successful AI transformation is large and the CDAO must have full support (and involvement) of the CEO and executive management.**

Does Your Business Intelligence Have Artificial Intelligence?

The advent of AI and ML doesn't just provide financial institutions with better ways to understand relationships in data, it also has the power to revolutionize the way we present and interact with the data itself.

An organization's analytical maturity can be assessed in four stages using Gartner's Analytical Maturity Model.

1. **Descriptive Analytics**—is backwards looking and describes what has happened. Reporting and measurement of outcomes falls into this category.
2. **Diagnostic Analytics**—tells us why or how something has happened. This is the analysis that tells us why a customer churned or how some customers come to be more profitable than others.
3. **Predictive Analytics**—is future looking, with an element of forecasting involved. Examples include revenue forecasting or churn propensity modeling.
4. **Prescriptive Analytics**—Prescriptive analytics goes beyond predicting outcomes and recommends a course of action. Some typical examples include image recognition, chatbots, or self-driving cars.

An organization with a nascent analytics capability will typically operate in the realm of descriptive and diagnostic analysis, which basically entails understanding what has happened and why. This type of analytics is backwards looking by nature (Figure 6.5).

Organizations with a basic business intelligence (BI) and reporting setup will typically rely heavily on spreadsheet-based reports and individual requests for data extracts that require manual handling by a team of analysts. This creates a situation where analysts and data scientists get pulled away from transformational and impactful work, in favor of helping the organization get the basics done.

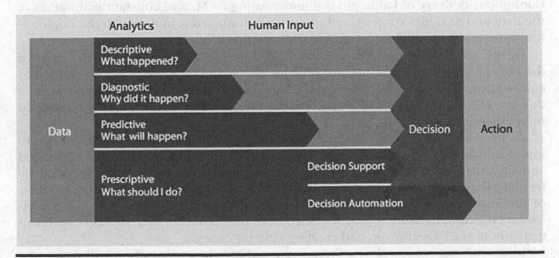

Figure 6.5   Gartner's Analytics Spectrum illustrates how various levels of analytics can be used to augment, support, or automate human decision-making.

On the contrary, organizations with more advanced BI and reporting capabilities will spend a larger proportion of time and resources doing predictive and prescriptive analytics. Therefore, it is imperative for any financial institution to get its BI suite up to modern standards. That way, time and resources can be freed up across the business to focus on the prescriptive and predictive parts of analytics and data science. Put simply, you must do BI before you can do AI.

Luckily, today's modern BI tools such as Tableau, QlickView, Power BI or Yellowfin BI come with inbuilt AI and ML capabilities that give end users of reports and dashboards the ability to do "self-service AI." Modern BI tools can not only visualize data, but also explain why something happened, alert end users to important trends, generate written reports on datasets, and much more. In short, the descriptive and diagnostic parts of analytics can and should be largely automated, thereby redirecting human resources toward more advanced analytics. See Chapter 8 for a detailed overview of visualization.

Getting to AI Adoption at Scale

The five foundational components of successful AI transformation are equally important but they don't necessarily happen concurrently or at the same speed. In reality, there are several "chicken and egg" problems to overcome: how do we get the resources to build out the technical infrastructure required to use AI at scale, when we haven't proven the value yet? How do we create a culture of data-driven decision-making augmented by AI outputs while we build our algorithms? In the following section, we will look at how financial institutions can balance these competing priorities and sequence activities to achieve AI adoption at scale.

At a high level, AI success is predicated on two concurrent processes that go hand in hand to deliver the technical framework and the organizational culture required: Continuous delivery of value proof-points relating to AI, and constant maturation of the data and analytics strategy and governance framework in line with the organization's maturing AI capability. Figure 6.6 shows this sequencing.

In the initial stages of AI implementation, it is important to plant the AI seed through proofs of concept, but a solid data and analytics strategy is also needed to communicate the end-state vision and roadmap for AI. The strategy should include delivery milestones and the investment in people, technology, and processes required to get there.

As the organization's AI capability moves up the maturity curve, it is important to invest in data and analytics literacy across the organization. Many of the structured and unstructured data points that AI and ML models rely upon are generated by frontline staff so it's important that there is a broad understanding and appreciation of the importance of data quality at all levels of the organization. Data and analytics literacy training is also vital for dispersing the AI vision and strategic roadmap throughout the organization and creating cultural change.

Increased data and analytics literacy throughout the organization will result in a greater demand for advanced analytics and AI outputs, so it's important to quickly follow up with some AI deliverables. The most obvious use cases—the low-hanging fruits—are often centered around creating internal efficiencies or automating

The Path to AI at Scale

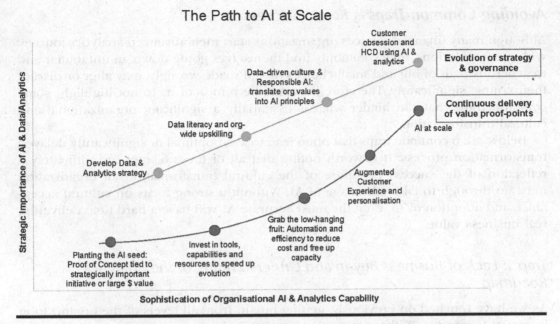

Strategic Importance of AI & Data/Analytics (y-axis)

Customer obsession and HCD using AI & analytics

Evolution of strategy & governance

Data-driven culture & Responsible AI: translate org values into AI principles

Continuous delivery of value proof-points

Data literacy and org-wide upskilling

AI at scale

Develop Data & Analytics strategy

Augmented Customer Experience and personalisation

Grab the low-hanging fruit: Automation and efficiency to reduce cost and free up capacity

Planting the AI seed: Proof of Concept tied to strategically important initiative or large $ value

Invest in tools, capabilities and resources to speed up evolution

Sophistication of Organisational AI & Analytics Capability (x-axis)

Figure 6.6 To succeed with AI at scale, organisations must focus on establishing appropriate processes, capabilities, governance and strategic linkage while also experimenting with AI delivery on the ground. As the organisations learns, the strategic importance and sophistication of its AI capability will increase accordingly.

processes, as opposed to focusing on augmented or personalized customer experiences. Internal processes are more controllable and often follow standard procedures, so they are a good target while the organization learns how to produce and present AI outputs effectively. Additionally, letting staff interact with outputs and experience the benefits of AI first-hand is critical for AI adoption and culture change.

As financial institutions move up the AI maturity curve, so should the development of the AI strategy and governance. With a more data literate workforce and some AI experience under their belt, organizations should prepare to take the next step toward building AI at scale by translating their corporate strategy and values into AI principles.

This is a very critical step in the progression toward AI at scale as it gives employees the design principles needed to innovate, implement and iterate with AI models without the need for arduous approval and governance processes. On the other hand, failing to translate and understand corporate values in the context of AI can lead to significant unintentional damage to an organization's brand as well as customers, staff, and society as a whole. For example, banks need to decide when and how algorithms are allowed to make decisions and when a human should be involved.

With an AI strategy and principles in place, financial institutions will be ready to tackle more difficult AI challenges such as automated and personalized product and service recommendations. At this point, human-centered experience design principles are critical to ensuring that AI outputs are appropriately connected to the context of customers and front-line staff. Through the combination of technology, experience design, and AI, financial institutions will be able to deliver personalization at scale without breaking the bank.

Avoiding Common Traps is Key to Success

Although many financial services organizations start their advanced analytics journey with great ambitions, they commonly find themselves going down an unfamiliar and treacherous path of big and small choices that, if made wrongly, may alter or disrupt their course significantly. Therefore, it would be remiss of us to not highlight some common traps that can hinder what is essentially a significant organizational and cultural transformation.

Below are 6 common traps that often lead to a suboptimal or significantly delayed transformation process. It is worth noting that all of these 6 traps are ultimately a reflection of the success or failure of the cultural transformation an organization must go through to take advantage of AI. Without a strong focus on cultural acceptance and adoption of AI, even the most accurate AI will have a hard time delivering real business value.

Trap 1: Lack of Business Buy-in and Understanding of the Analytics Roadmap

As we have touched on previously, getting buy-in from all levels of the organization is crucial to success. Without executive support and sponsorship, the analytics community will never get the investment in tools, technology, and people required to move forward. An equally important part of the journey toward AI at scale is winning over the hearts and minds of business leaders by solving their problems using AI. That way, the organization will start to trust the algorithms and see them as much more than a "black box." In other words, the analytics community should focus on building "teams with no name" by banding up with cross-functional allies who believe in the vision and have real problems to solve using AI.

Trap 2: Forgetting to Train the Rest of the Business in Analytics

Business-wide Data and analytics literacy is another central component of creating this "grass roots" excitement about the potential of advanced analytics and AI. Without the right "pull" from the wider business for data-driven solutions, embedding AI and ML will be an uphill battle. Additionally, if the organization is relying on a small group of people to think and innovate around advanced analytics; chances are that many of the best use cases will go unnoticed.

To avoid this trap, banks should focus on two elements. Firstly, there is formal training on data, analytics, and AI across all levels of the organization. Secondly, employees outside the analytics function need to feel part of the action. Earlier in this chapter, we described how Commonwealth Bank of Australia use internal competitions to foster participation and buy-in from frontline staff. This also ensures that use cases and final solutions have a strong connection to the everyday reality of the end-consumers of AI outputs.

Trap 3: Treating the Analytics Team(s) As an Internal Consultancy

Many organizations dream big but fail to set their AI delivery teams up for success. The common scenario is as follows: the organization starts out well by hiring some data scientists and setting up the right technical infrastructure. However, before long, data scientists are working on a plethora of urgent and important projects that could benefit from the highly sought-after technical skillset of these experts. As a result, the analytics team ends up working like an internal consultancy, jumping from project to project rather than building on the long-term vision for advanced analytics and AI. The solution is simply to make these disruptions go away so data scientists can focus on the most important strategic imperatives.

Trap 4: Being Stuck in the Pilot Stage

Delivering impactful AI projects is essentially a three-step process:

1. Identify an appropriate business problem and build an AI solution;
2. Test the solution via a pilot project and iterate if needed;
3. If the solution works, industrialize it.

Industrialization of the final solution often requires some sort of tech change and ongoing management of the process from an expert team. For example, a bank might trial a retention tool that identifies with a high level of accuracy who is likely to attrite, and when. The pilot proves successful and the bank reduces customer attrition by several percent as a result. Now comes the final challenge: industrializing the tool in a process that requires minimal maintenance for maximum impact. The team that delivered the pilot might have been a mix of internal and external experts across data science, data engineering, technology, experience design, and project management, and these people usually need to move on to the next project. Therefore, banks must not just have a team of cross-functional builders, but also a team that can handle the ongoing management and continuous improvement of existing solutions. Even fully automated solutions need ongoing supervision to make sure everything is performing as intended.

Trap 5: Giving up After False Starts

Commonly, this situation tends to arise when a model prediction or recommendation has not been linked to the right solution. Designing and implementing an effective intervention is at least as important as the prediction. For example, the data science team might have identified customers who are likely to refinance their loan with a competitor with a high degree of accuracy. However, if the chosen intervention is not effective (customers didn't want it) or unprofitable (e.g., through deep discounts), it is likely to cast doubt on the project as a whole, including whether the prediction was actually accurate in the first place. Too often, high-quality algorithms remain unused because end users don't trust them or don't know how to apply the outputs effectively.

In anticipation of such events, banks should prepare all involved parties for the inevitable failure through upfront communication, and lots of it. Everyone involved must understand that advanced analytics delivery is not a linear process, but rather a practice of learning through trial and error. In the team sport of analytics, it is important that one failed attempt to deliver value from an AI use case doesn't discourage the team from trying again. Furthermore, post-implementation reviews are an important part of building team cohesion and connectivity between those who build, deploy and use the AI outputs. The key to winning the hearts and minds of everyone involved—even when results are not as desired—is creating a set of shared goals that link up the cross-functional team.

Advanced analytics is not a silver bullet for solving all your biggest problems with ease. Instead, banks can solve many smaller problems that add up to a significant impact. This is especially true when it comes to enhancing or optimizing internal processes. More often than not, a failed use case will create valuable lessons and clues for the next iteration.

Essentially, analytics should be seen as the Research & Development arm of financial institutions. Analytics doesn't necessarily require huge multi-million-dollar investments with no option to stop. Instead, pilot projects should be used to experiment, learn and iterate until the next valuable proposition is identified.

Trap 6: Building Huge Data Infrastructure Without the End in Mind

A typical murmur from data scientists and analysts is that if only the data was cleaner or better structured they would be able to do so much more. With this notion in mind, many financial institutions spend years building the "perfect" data infrastructure, without a clear view of how it will be used or the expected return on investment. To avoid this trap, banks should focus on building out their data infrastructure based on specific use cases, so that value can be realized quickly. This agile approach to data storage and usage gives analysts and data scientists what they need quickly and saves the organization from lengthy and expensive data transformation projects based on an unproven vision of the future. The tools and technologies are evolving so rapidly in this space that multi-year enterprise data warehouse projects are likely to be outdated by the time they are complete.

Don't Go Alone, Use Partnerships

Although novel at first, many of the AI features discussed in previous sections of this chapter quickly become part of customers' expectations for how a bank should work. Financial institutions should be very cognizant of just how quickly technology features can move from leading-edge to being part of consumers' baseline expectation. Keeping up with the competition requires constant investment in flexible technology to an extent that is prohibitive for many financial institutions.

AI-based Software-as-a-Service companies such as Tink, Frollo, and Sitecore, or AI technologies like IBM's Watson, can deliver ready-made and scalable software solutions for a fraction of the cost and effort required to build a solution in-house. For small and medium-sized organizations, it will often make sense to partner with specialized solution providers. This, in turn, requires a flexible, API-based technology infrastructure that can handle real-time data sharing across applications.

Similarly, most financial institutions starting their journey toward AI at scale will benefit from external assistance in getting their foundational infrastructure in place. This includes upskilling staff, creating the right data and technology infrastructure, and delivering the first end-to-end use cases. However, it's important to note that financial institutions should not outsource their advanced analytics completely. It is imperative for the future sustainability of any financial services firm to retain a high degree of AI knowledge and skill internally.

A Note on Responsible AI

As AI becomes more commonplace in financial services, financial institutions should prepare themselves to meet progressively higher standards for how they use customer data responsibly.

Specifically, banks should expect to be weighed and measured on three factors:

1. Banks' systemic importance to society and de-facto power over the individual means that they are expected to use AI for good.
2. Banks must be able to *prove* that they are using AI for good, including avoiding (and proving avoidance of) bias in AI models.
3. Data privacy regulations will put additional requirements on how bank data is used within third-party networks. As a result, banks will require oversight of how customer data is used within data sharing ecosystems that they subscribe to.

The acid test for these three points is not whether banks can demonstrate responsible data use in a court room. Rather, success should be measured in terms of a positive societal impact from AI in financial services. This ties back to the concept of customer empathy at scale, discussed in previous sections of this chapter.

In order to be capable of delivering responsible AI, banks must focus on five components:

1. **Ethics & regulation**—banks must comply with relevant regulations, but also live up to implicit ethical expectations from the broader community.
2. **Bias & fairness**—AI and ML algorithms must behave in accordance with ethical expectations and every effort must be made to remove underlying bias in the models (e.g., discrimination against certain parts of the population).
3. **Interpretability & explainability**—banks must be able to interpret and explain their AI output. Accurate but unexplainable algorithms will carry too much risk for banks and customers alike.
4. **Robustness & security**—a robust AI and data sharing framework must be put in place to make sure customers' personal data is kept secure and used only for intended purposes.
5. **Governance**—banks must establish appropriate governance around design, development, deployment, and maintenance of AI solutions to make sure points 1 to 4 are met without fail.

Points 2, 3, and 4 relate directly to the performance of AI solutions, whereas points 1 and 5 ensure appropriate use of data in accordance with regulatory and ethical expectations. Table 6.3 illustrates the difference between having a responsible AI framework that works versus deploying AI without appropriate forethought.

Table 6.3　The difference between good and bad AI

AI Performance	Good	Bad
Bias and fairness	Personalization	Discrimination
Interpretability and explainability	Transparency of AI	"Black Box Decisions"
Robustness and security	Intimacy	Compromised privacy

Good AI is not just about complex maths and highly predictive algorithms. Companies must actively decide on a plethora of ethical conundrums as they decide what responsible AI looks like.

AI-Driven Banking: A Peek into Capital One's Journey

Capital One is regarded by many as a pioneer in the financial services industry when it comes to the application of analytics, AI, and data-driven decision-making. Capital One's transformation toward its AI vision is very impressive, considering that the firm is not a small fin-tech start-up, but the 10th largest bank in the United States by assets, employing over 50,000 people. The bank was the first company in the world to introduce the role of Chief Data Officer to its payroll in 2002, labeling itself as the first big data company[26]. Today, Capital One is one of very few organizations that can reasonably call themselves AI-driven. However, to get to this point, the bank has undergone a large-scale transformation, spanning almost a decade.

In 2011, the bank embarked on a multi-year transformation program that touched every corner of the organization's technology, process, and culture. On the technology front, Capital One moved to an Agile software delivery model and hired thousands of employees into software engineering and digital roles, with the goal of becoming a cloud-first and open-source-API based organization. Although the bank didn't have a complete end-state vision for how the organization would look and feel many years into the future, the underlying principles of being fast and nimble for customers guided them along. The strategy was based on a belief that real-time AI and ML would transform the business and customer experience.

Capital One's former VP of Machine Learning & AI, Nitzan Mekel, summed up the bank's AI-driven customer experience strategy[27]:

> The whole relationship between a customer and a bank changes because now we can be a real advocate for them in the most direct possible way, while before there was just this big gap and a customer was, for lack of a better word, sort of a number. Now we can understand their context.

Today, the company culture is very much founded in data-driven decision-making. As the company's CIO Robert Alexander described it:

> Every time we make a decision it's an opportunity to use machine learning—what customers to market to, what products to offer them, what terms accompany the relationship, what rewards to offer, what spending limits to put in place, how to identify fraud, and so forth.

Because Capital One is truly AI-driven, the organization understands the importance of having a data-driven culture, underpinned by a robust framework for transparent and responsible AI. Internal investment in data management, ethics, privacy, and security is substantial, but focus goes beyond the confinement of its own organization. In fact, the bank sees it as its responsibility for foster the right ethical framework for complex applications of AI across financial services and society as a whole.

In 2019, David Castillo, VP of Capital One's Center for Machine Learning, explained:

> We have done a lot of work on explainability; we are a leader in the industry on deep learning transparency issues. We are involved in cross-industry explainability forums involving competitors, academics, legal experts, technical experts, and regulators—trying to address bias and responsible AI. We've made substantial progress in what is called 'global attribution mapping,' where we attribute influence to particular features in models. We're also focusing on the visualization of deep learning. We're having conversations with regulators about the journey toward explainability.

Capital One has become an industry leader in the application of AI in financial services, but the bank is still well-aware of the looming risk of disruption from new market entrants. CIO Robert Alexander explained the bank's approach to staying ahead of the competition: "Why hasn't legacy banking been disrupted by tech firms? It probably will be at some point. But we have an opportunity to disrupt our own industry."

The Future of Financial Services

The global financial services industry is undergoing a once-in-a-generation transformation driven by the following 5 forces: (1) digitization of products and services; (2) mass proliferation of data; (3) the availability of cheap computer power and storage; (4) a networked economy, enabled by the internet and APIs and (5) a regulated change toward consumer data right and portability of data.

In order to keep up with this seismic shift, big changes must necessarily take place inside incumbent financial services organizations. Technology platforms will need to be modernized to be competitive in an API-driven economy. Systems and processes will need to be configured to allow for AI-based solutions to be implemented. Employees will need to learn and adapt to an extent that exceeds any past transformation. Some skills will be in short supply, leading to stifled progress. Financial institutions will need to figure out how to utilize their vast amounts of data for the greater good of the customer, before someone else does it for them.

For incumbent financial institutions, it will be essential to establish an extensive network of partnerships across multiple sectors, including government entities and private enterprise. As financial services move from standardized product offerings to improving financial outcomes for customers, vast societal benefits will likely ensue.

The winners will be companies (banks and nonbanks) that manage to establish a lead in using AI as a competitive differentiator. As we have learned from the likes of Google, Amazon, Netflix, Uber, LinkedIn, and many others who have managed to create a network at scale: those who scale first are rewarded by a virtuous cycle of compounding advantages that are difficult to beat.

Notes

1   https://www.ey.com/Publication/vwLUAssets/ey-trust-without-it-youre-just-another-bank/$FILE/ey-trust-without-it-youre-just-another-bank.pdf

2   https://www.itnews.com.au/news/cba-system-suggests-20m-customer-conversations-a-day-493688

3   https://www.itnews.com.au/news/cba-prompts-600000-customers-to-spend-unused-credit-card-points-533051

4   https://www.itnews.com.au/news/cba-primes-app-for-10bn-welfare-payments-claw-back-531017

5   https://mitsloan.mit.edu/ideas-made-to-matter/heres-how-much-2008-bailouts-really-cost

6   https://qz.com/1311113/how-much-money-has-greece-received-in-three-bailouts/

7   https://cib.db.com/docs_new/Realtimetreasurywhitepaper.pdf

8   https://www.finextra.com/newsarticle/33388/caixabank-rolls-out-facial-recognition-at-the-atm

9   https://www.fbi.gov/investigate/violent-crime/bank-robbery/bank-crime-reports

10 Based on USD/AUD exchange rate as at 4 June 2018.

11 https://www.afr.com/companies/financial-services/money-laundering-scandal-what-cba-admitted-to-and-why-it-happened-20180604-h10xm3

12 https://www.afr.com/companies/financial-services/commonwealth-bank-safe-haven-for-criminal-activity-20170804-gxp54g

13 https://tink.com/use-cases

14 https://www.mogl.com/what-is-mogl

15 https://www.cnbc.com/2018/06/26/this-bank-is-staffing-branches-with-humanoid-robots-that-dance-take-s.html

16 https://www.bbc.com/news/technology-39965545

17 https://www.theguardian.com/business/2019/jun/20/natwest-is-first-big-uk-bank-to-let-customers-open-account-with-a-selfie

18 https://assets.kpmg/content/dam/kpmg/xx/pdf/2019/05/global-banking-fraud-survey.pdf

19 https://www.dailymail.co.uk/news/article-6387001/Russian-hackers-9-4m-British-Airways-data-breach.html

20 http://assets.teradata.com/resourceCenter/downloads/CaseStudies/CaseStudy_EB9821_Danske_Bank_Fights_Fraud.pdf

21 https://ctmfile.com/story/citi-deploys-ai-to-boost-corporate-smart-match-platform

22 https://www.datafuturology.com/podcast/2019/8/6/set-yourself-multi-year-professional-challenges-with-felipe-flores-founder-amp-podcast-host

23 https://www.bis.org/ifc/publ/ifcb50_25.pdf

24 https://www.bis.org/review/r181213c.pdf

25 https://www.theglobeandmail.com/business/article-inside-tds-ai-play-how-layer-6s-technology-hopes-to-improve-old/

26 https://www.forbes.com/sites/tomdavenport/2019/07/10/from-analytics-first-to-ai-first-at-capital-one/#632988392f1b

27 https://blogs.nvidia.com/blog/2018/10/12/ai-in-your-wallet-capital-one-banks-on-machine-learning/

Chapter 7

Artificial Intelligence in Retail

Shantha Mohan
Integrated Innovation Institute, Carnegie Mellon University

Contents

DOI: 10.4324/9781351032940-7

Introduction

Retail according to Merriam-Webster dictionary is *to sell in small quantities directly to the ultimate consumer, and also the industry of such selling*. The retail industry has several stakeholders. We can classify these primary stakeholders as those who supply the goods (suppliers), those who sell the goods (retailers), and those who consume the goods (consumers). In addition, there are other secondary stakeholders including those who provide financing, transportation, packaging, advertising, contract manufacturing, and also wholesalers, distributors, and regulators of the industry. Artificial intelligence (AI) (and machine learning (ML)) can be beneficial to all these different stakeholders. Machine learning can be used to find patterns in the flows and behaviors of all people, products, and processes associated with those stakeholders' functions. Those learned patterns can then be applied through AI implementations to drive and optimize (automate and augment) known processes. AI (with ML) can create and enable entirely new ways of doing business. It does this by learning about the problem space and the data associated. The retail industry is undergoing seismic changes because of advances in these digital technologies, and those who embrace them stand to benefit tremendously. Now and in the future, it could mean the difference between thriving or withering away. A 2018 McKinsey Global Institute report on AI[1] predicts that the most potential value in retail will be gained in the areas of marketing, sales, and supply chain management. In this chapter, we will look at some use cases of AI/ML in the retail industry.

Chapter Overview

We first look at the retail industry landscape and how geographies, products, and channels contribute to different challenges depending on the specific slice of this landscape. We then discuss the importance of data in retail applications and discuss what is different today that necessitates the use of AI/ML. Retail use cases follow this, starting with the customer, and going all the way back to the design of products.

There are some aspects of retail that are not included in this chapter such as customer satisfaction and future of work in the retail industry.

Customer satisfaction and customer experience are critical to successful enterprises. This is covered in Chapter 5.

A McKinsey report on automation in retail[2] says, more than 60% of most automated jobs are in retail, and disruption in this industry is inevitable. Entry-level jobs will be the most affected since they have the lowest skill levels and high turnover. Traditionally, retail is the place where youngsters learn to work. We can expect this to change.

Please see Chapter 4, HR and Talent Management, for a full treatment of AI/ML and the future workforce.

The Retail Industry Landscape and Challenges

When we talk about retail, we need a context: where, what, and how.

Geographies (where), products (what), and channels (how) all contribute to defining the retail industry landscape. In this section, we will look at each of these contextual elements and how they define the retail problem space and the relevant solutions that AI can enable.

Geographies

The retail domain is vast and varied. It also has unique characteristics depending on geography.

The evolution of retail parallels that of the evolution in technology, and the advances in tools and technology happen at varying speeds across the world. In the western world, the retail ecosystem evolved with the invention of the cash register, credit cards, electronic cash registers, information systems, world-wide-web, e-Commerce, and social media. The technological advances made the big box retailing a norm in the developed world as early as 1962, when the first Walmart opened[3]. The developing world has taken a long time to adopt these technologies. Only now the big box retailing is taking hold in developing countries like India. Even today, supermarkets in India struggle against traditional store formats of retailing such as local kirana shops and pavement vendors.

E-commerce is adopted to varying degrees across the world. Thanks to global connectivity, technologies enabling e-commerce are getting quickly adopted in developing countries. In fact, China has adopted e-commerce to a greater degree than the Western world.

The problems of the developed world differ from those of the developing world. In the developed world, many retail innovations are focused on how to automate and reduce dependency on humans. An example of this is Amazon's Go store[4]. In India, where labor is cheap, retail innovations focus on taking advantage of this resource. An example of this is the use of kirana stores for the last mile delivery of goods ordered online. While the focus of the developed world is personalization, in the developing world, being able to provide goods at affordable prices and reaching consumers in remote locations take priority.

Some unique supply chain challenges in the developing world are being addressed with machine learning. Indian e-commerce retail leaders such as Flipkart in India implore the data scientists to develop AI algorithms that solve retail problems specific to India[5]. The story of dealing with the unstructured postal addresses of India is[6] fascinating. Flipkart (majority stake acquired by Walmart in 2018) wanted to address the problems related to last-mile delivery. The Indian postal addresses are based on a system developed in the 1970s and do not quite lend themselves to being comprehended geospatially. When filling in the shipping address, Indian consumers are not very consistent in the information they provide. Flipkart's data scientists worked on creating an address classification system that can overcome this problem by using probabilistic separation of compound words, elimination of bogus addresses, and intelligent machine-learning (ML) models.

Products

The invention of barcodes in 1974[7] was a huge step in identifying products uniquely and quickly to speed up selling in supermarkets. An equivalent identification in the world of fresh produce and bulk products is the Price Look Up (PLU) code. Such products must be weighed to identify the amount to charge the buyer. These are what I would call the last holdouts in full automation in stores such as the Amazon GO, even though many stores have self-checkout lines, but require some human intervention.

Depending on the type of product being sold, the customer journey varies and so are the challenges associated. The biggest challenge in selling physical goods is supply chain management. How do you get the product from its source to its destination as efficiently as possible? This is the topic of supply chain management, as described in Chapter 3. An important aspect of managing supply chain is the understanding of the product characteristics. Does the product have a long life, like that of an appliance and not sold as often as a product like razor blades? Does the product demand last only for a short time like that of a fashion apparel, or does it have a steady demand such as the one for athletic socks? Is the product perishable like fresh produce or is it a staple such as cooking oil or cans of soups? Is the product needed only during specific times of the year and hence seasonal, such as umbrellas?

With virtual goods (also called experience products), such as airline tickets and streaming media, the biggest challenges are customer satisfaction and experience-delivery. After buying the service, the customer has physical experiences—that of the actual travel, or watching a video or hearing music—and executing to customer satisfaction becomes a key retail challenge.

Channels

Products can travel through multiple touchpoints in different channels before it gets to the consumer. Prior to e-commerce, the physical retail stores served as the end point of a product's journey before a customer took it off the physical store-shelf. A customer walks into such a store, picks the products she wants to buy, pays for the products with cash or credit card, and leaves the store with the products. In the e-commerce world, the customer browses a virtual store, picks the products she wants, adds them to the virtual cart, pays for them with a card, and provides a shipping address to which products are delivered a few days later.

The challenge of keeping the product available on the shelf is a problem applicable to both the physical and virtual stores, yet the way the challenge is addressed depends on how the channel functions. With a physical store, a customer who doesn't find the product on the shelf can substitute with a different product, or may go to another store thus costing the retailer (and the supplier) a sale. The product fulfillment is instantaneous. With e-commerce, product availability and product fulfillment are decoupled, allowing for many options. At the time of purchase, the customers have multiple options of getting the product shipped home, or shipped to a store nearby from where you can pick it up (click and collect) after a few days, or have the option of visiting a physical store where the product is in stock. The problem of optimizing the supply chain has now become complex and using AI/ML to address this challenge is very attractive.

Importance of Data

Collaboration

We cannot implement AI/ML without quality data. Retailers have actual demand data and customer behavior data. Suppliers have product data and supply data. Putting them together can create a huge opportunity for both retailers and suppliers.

The retailer collects the most granular consumer data at the point of sale. They can also collect behavioral data, store or online traffic data about the consumer, the physical inventory at a store location, orders placed, and arrival timing of goods at the store from warehouses. For big retailers with multiple stores across the world (such as Walmart), each store forwards this set of data to a company data store. The data store then becomes the system of record. Helpdesk conversational data and social media data can augment the traditional POS and inventory data.

The supplier has the product data with each product uniquely identified and product attributes that help analyze product desirability, price, and cost. When the supplier offers the product through their own e-commerce site, they also get a share of consumer data and behavior of consumers on the site.

Understanding the journey of a product from the time of creation to when it reaches the consumer can generate tremendous benefits for suppliers, retailers, and consumers.

If a supplier of a product sells directly to end-users, the journey is straightforward, and the supplier can use the information about the sales performance of a product to understand how to tune prices or cut costs. But when multiple hand-offs occur prior to the product reaching the consumer, knowing the complete journey of the product becomes important in understanding how to supply the product and to take into account demand fluctuations.

For virtual products, similar data-sharing opportunities arise. Often the sales (sourcing) platform is different from the delivery (consuming) platform. Linking data sets that measure supply, demand, satisfaction, feedback, and even marketing data (e.g., results of A/B testing of product features, prices, and preferences) can provide great business insights to the different stakeholders in the virtual product lifecycle. Amazon is highly successful in owning all pieces of a virtual product lifecycle by creating an ecosystem in which they own the product data (including the product itself in some cases), the sales (supply/demand/location) data, and the consumer (preferences, intents, and experience) data.[8]

Types of Data

Traditional enterprise data comes from the various enterprise systems used in running a retail business. A typical set of information systems at a retailer would include:

- Point of sales (POS) systems at stores
- e-commerce system
- Finance and Accounting
- Human Resources
- Supply Chain Management (SCM)

- Revenue management
- Customer Relationship Management (CRM)
- Sales/Revenue Management

At a supplier, besides the above, there are information systems to manage manufacturing. They generate product data that include quality attributes.

Traditionally these data are augmented with syndicated sales data bought from companies such as Nielsen, which provide data from consumer panels, competitors' sales data, and benchmarks across the industry.

Traditional enterprise systems are applications built with a foundation of a relational database. The data stored in these databases are *structured* and organized with rows and columns in a database table.

AI/ML algorithms running on today's hardware can deal with enormous structured data sets, while traditional applications falter in terms of responsiveness and time to insights.

Now consider new data sources that are changing the retail world today. These new data sources provide unstructured data.[9] The magnitude of data available from these sources is mind-boggling. Modern data collected involve the customers' behavior on e-commerce websites. Some are from the retailers' and suppliers' social media sites such as Twitter, Facebook, and Instagram. Besides this, one can acquire data from other business entities through private data exchange transactions[10]. Going beyond direct exchange of data, one can buy data from third-party vendors such as Acxiom, Oracle, and Experian who provide thousands of attributes of millions of people in the USA, Europe, and elsewhere in the world[11]. These third-party data providers track all of us using unique identifiers. Here is a sample of attributes that define the identity of a consumer:

- Name, gender, birth date, Social Security Number
- Postal address, phone number, email address
- Credit card number
- Device ID, Google ID, Facebook ID, Microsoft ID, Apple ID, Amazon ID

After establishing an ID, it becomes very easy to track every movement of a consumer, whether they are buying a product at a physical store or a website. All the transactions of a customer become input to a data store and form the basis for behavior analysis.

What do you do when you don't have enough data to train ML models? This is where *synthetic data* comes in. It is data that is artificially created instead of being generated by actual events, a fancy name for simulated data. Software engineers use simulated test data all the time to test for error conditions and corner cases. Taking that a step further, if a set of data can be created that can form the seed of the training data to train ML models, then the need for having real-world data becomes less pressing. Companies such as AI. Reverie help create annotated synthetic data with their simulation platform used in training computer vision algorithms.

Supervised learning models require labeled data for training. You can think of the process of training as something similar to humans learning to tell the contents of a can by the label on it. Just as one can learn a lot by looking at a label on a can of soup, ML algorithms can learn a lot about the features of the data to use in the algorithms from the labeling. This labeling of unstructured data is usually accomplished by humans working with specialized software tools. There are many companies offering third-party labeling services. There are also a lot of companies that offer tools (open source and commercial) to help in the labeling process.

Here are some examples of how ML uses new data sources in retail, some of which are explored further in the section on retail use cases:

- Recording of sales-calls can be fed into an ML algorithm to identify effective sales processes. They can be used to train sales agents in doing a better job of selling.
- Help desk interactions can help analyze customer sentiments. We can use them with other customer data from traditional systems such as Customer Relationship Management (CRM) systems to better serve customers and increase satisfaction.
- Weather data and special events data can be used in a demand prediction model for managing the supply chain efficiently to improve product availability.
- Social media data can be harnessed to understand behaviors of different demographics better and be able to do targeted marketing that addresses specific needs.
- Logs from machines on the shop floor collect data from sensors that can be used to predict maintenance activities. Preventive maintenance is traditionally applied to all equipment to avoid hitting quality limits, while ML-enabled predictive maintenance can determine if it is even necessary to perform the activity, thereby avoiding costly unnecessary maintenance in some cases and performing timely maintenance only in essential cases.
- Physical stores equipped with AI-driven wireless can combine store-specific data made up of Wi-Fi logs with customer-specific data (gleaned by identifying the customer from their smartphones) to serve the customers better by greeting them by name, providing personalized recommendations, helping them navigate the store, and offering real-time promotion/product discounts.[12]

Data Quality

Data quality is such an important topic that it deserves a whole book, or at least a whole chapter, but this section will just touch upon the topic.

A 2019 article in TDWI talks about the importance of data quality in implementing solutions using AI/ML[13].

It quotes an IBM senior vice president's interview in the Wall Street Journal:

> about 80% of the work with an AI project is collecting and preparing data. Some companies aren't prepared for the cost and work associated with

that going in. And you say: 'Hey, wait a moment, where's the AI? I'm not getting the benefit.' And you kind of bail on it.

In addition to the common data quality problems, here are some sources of poor data quality in the retail environment:

- Coding of a retail item
  - Coding a UPC to a vendor is sometimes wrong.
  - Retailers think about "Items"; suppliers think about "UPCs," and the relationship is many-to-many in several cases
- Retailer data warehouse might have trouble keeping up with changes in the "real" world resulting in trickles and restatements (delayed and corrective data feeds from individual retail stores of the retailer)
- Item attributes are incorrect
- The checkouts at POS terminals are notorious for scanning the wrong products (impacting OOS/phantom inventory). A typical example of this is an item that comes in many flavors or colors. If someone buys items of different colors, a salesperson might scan one of them and enter the transaction for all them against that one scanned UPC. This affects inventory accuracy. The UPC that was scanned shows up with less inventory than physically available at the store, and the UPC that was not scanned shows too much inventory. The impact ripples all the way back to the suppliers in misreading the product demand signals.

It is common to find missing values and missing attributes in traditional retail data. Data gathered from social media adds another level of complexity. Selecting the right set of data elements to use is another data cleansing problem.

The data cleansing task is 80% of the work required to implement a quality solution[14], including that of an AI/ML-enabled one. Data quality problems include duplicate or unwanted data, errors introduced because of poor data transfers, and typos.

We can clean unstructured text data using unsupervised ML algorithms such as K-means-clustering and exclude data that doesn't fit the norms for quality data. We can examine the problem data clusters to see how we can correct or omit them altogether.

Master data management (MDM), used to manage the identity of products, customers, and other entities sourced from multiple systems, is a critical aspect of data quality. Machine learning can speed up the process of data unification. Tamr reports of a case study involving Scotiabank[15] that says:

> *"just over six months, Scotiabank ingested and profiled 35 large data sources with 3.7 million rows of data to produce 325,000 clusters of customer records. The team is now able to onboard a new system from landing data to mastery in just 5-7 days, and create a new Golden Record in a maximum of 2 days."*

Quality data is critical for implementing any system that uses data for providing intelligence on all aspects of retailing.

Retail Use Cases

The use cases will make more sense with the understanding of the traditional supply chain process and the modern omnichannel process.

The traditional retail supply chain starts with product design, manufacturing, packaging and shipping. Distributors receive the products, store them in their warehouses and ship the products to individual stores. A distributor could be the captive to the retailers or a third-party. The stores typically draw products based on the demand expected at the stores. The end-point in the chain is the customer (Figure 7.1).

Today, the retail supply chain is not so straightforward.

A *multichannel* supply chain provides the product to customers through many channels that are not integrated (Figure 7.2).

In an *omnichannel* experience, customers are served seamlessly across all available channels and the supply chain becomes more complicated (Figure 7.3).

Suppliers not only distribute the products to retailers but also use their warehouses to satisfy customer demands from their own e-commerce portal. Retailers serve their customers physically from their stores, but also use stores as the last-mile delivery point, fulfilling orders placed on their e-commerce portals.

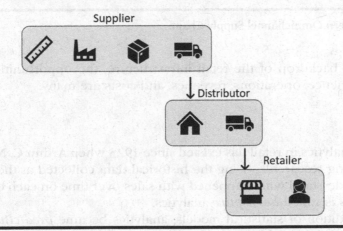

Figure 7.1 Traditional Retail Supply Chain.

Figure 7.2 Multichannel Customer Reach.

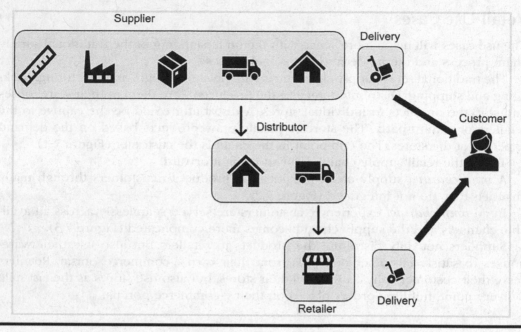

Figure 7.3 Modern Omnichannel Supply Chain.

Against this backdrop of the retail infrastructure, the opportunities to optimize customer experience, operations, revenues, and costs are many.

Analytics

The usage of analytics in retail has existed since 1923 when Arthur C. Nielsen, Sr. pioneered marketing research[16]. Using the historical data collected at the point of sale, retailers can understand what happened with sales over time on each of the products being sold. This is called *descriptive* analytics.

With the addition of statistical models, analytics became *predictive*. The statistical forecasting models could predict demand so that retailers and suppliers can plan production, distribution and levels of inventory of products. The next level of analytics is *prescriptive*, which provides retailers and suppliers with recommendations on what actions to take to achieve business goals with better outcomes. The focus of AI/ML is on predictive and prescriptive analytics.

With unsupervised learning, an ML model could identify patterns in customer behavior. This type of machine learning is used when you want to discover and characterize different segments in your data. A typical retail use case is to segment the consumers by age groups by forming clusters in order to target specific segments with specific promotion campaigns. Algorithms that can do this include K-Means Clustering, Hierarchical Clustering, and Gaussian Mixture Model. The prescriptive ML analytics include recommender systems that use clustering algorithms and then prescribe specific actions to take.

The ML algorithm type known as reinforcement learning has a behavior that maximizes a specified output by learning to perform desirable actions. Unlike big data use in unsupervised learning, the system learns on the job by correcting itself based on a series of actions that maximize the reward. Robots are classical examples of this ML algorithm's use.

Deep learning algorithms take machine learning to another level by being able to execute complex multilayered models known as neural nets. We typically use these types of algorithms when unstructured data augments typical structured data available in retail. Some of the most common data types used in deep learning are images (including videos) and text (such as documents, conversations, and social media posts). Deep learning can infer content, context, and meaning from these complex data types. Such applications are increasingly common in retail.

Sphere of Influence and Big Data

Many of the retail use cases have existed since the beginning of trade. So what is different about them now? *The history of retail: A timeline*[17] is a fascinating account of how technology and innovations have shaped the retail industry.

Another way to look at the retail industry is to look at it using the sphere of influence concept (Figure 7.4).

Manual: Systems that supported retail evolved in parallel. Prior to computerization, retail transactions were manual. They were captured in register books and stored in personal storage. Retail clerks manually entered the information. Even today, in developing countries the mom-and-pop stores use this method. The reach of such retailers is small, limited to the neighborhood. The amount of data that is used to satisfy the customer and to run the retail business is limited.

Software Enabled: With computerization came electronic medium to store the transactions. Over time, information systems were developed to capture transactions and manage trade. The data associated with this sphere of influence grew. With the invention of databases, and later data warehouses, data analytics was possible

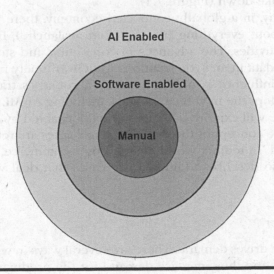

Figure 7.4   Sphere of Influence.

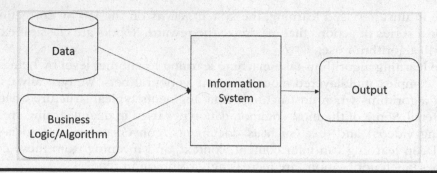

Figure 7.5 Traditional Information System.

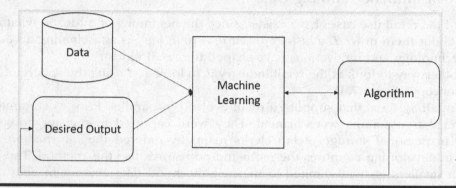

Figure 7.6 AI/ML Enabled System.

on terabytes of data generated by retailers such as Walmart to make business decisions and meeting customer satisfaction. The analytics, however, could go only so far because the systems were rule-based and if the system encountered a situation that was unknown, it broke down (Figure 7.5).

AI Enabled: Today, in a globally connected economy, there is an opportunity to collect more data about everything (the *big data* avalanche), from customer interactions to system activities. The advances in computing and storage allow users to make use of the big data in analytic solutions to deliver timely business intelligence. Now the sphere of influence is only limited by a country's trade policies and the retailer's ability to adopt the new technologies, including AI/ML (Figure 7.6).

In this section, we will explore use cases in retail enabled by AI/ML. All use cases need an anchor of the concept of the *user*. Some use cases are retailer centric. Others are supplier oriented. In today's world enabled by e-commerce, many suppliers are also retailers. We also describe additional use cases that deal with the operational aspects of retail.

Customer Behavior

Customer satisfaction drives demand. There are several ways in which AI can enhance customer experience and thus increase demand for the products that retailers offer. Besides understanding customer behavior, AI can also help influence it. Specifically,

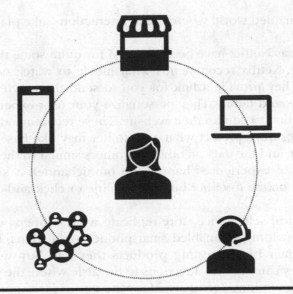

Figure 7.7　Customer Touchpoints.

behavioral analytics is not only descriptive, but it can also be both predictive and prescriptive. In this context, the concept of customer journey takes on the meaning of "customer trajectory, influenced by forces both internal and external." This is analogous to a comet moving through the Solar System, or a healthcare patient progressing through a medical situation with all of its diverse touch points. Retailers have access to this type of AI-enabled behavioral analytics by analyzing diverse sources of data including (Figure 7.7):

- Point of sale transaction data
- Helpdesk interactions
- Social media interactions
- Product search histories in weblogs
- Facial recognition/profile data

ECommerce and Brick and Mortar stores have different ways of collecting customer behavior data. Harmonizing the data collected from disparate sources is key to building customer behavior analytics. Identifying a customer uniquely across all the data points can enable several use cases. In the section on types of data, we talked about the different types of data that now enable uniquely identifying a specific consumer.

Personalization is a key use case enabled by behavior analytics. If the retailer has a 360-degree view of the customer, they can then provide recommendations specific to that customer.

When the retailers had a 1–1 relationship with customers, which even today exists in countries such as India, it is common to find a retailer recommending a product he thinks the customer is bound to buy. This has multiple benefits. One, the retailer gets to make a sale, which could become a repeat sale, two, it shows the customer how much the retailer cares about them, thereby increasing customer loyalty, and three, it makes the shopping experience a delight for the customer. How do you replicate that in the technology-enabled world where social interactions take place on the Internet? AI / ML can help.

Companies such as Netflix have been using AI for quite some time in their recommendation engine[18]. Netflix recommends what movie to watch next based on your viewing behavior. They provide a link for you to send the movies as recommendations to your friends and family. They personalize your user experience in how they present the information to you on their website. These recommendations come about because the ML algorithms predict what a customer may like based on the data specific to the customer, and the data on other customers similar to the specific customer.

Today, many retail experiences happen on omnichannel. A shopper goes from browsing a product online to either buying it online or click-and-collect it in a store near her.

How can a physical self-service store replicate what happens with recommendation engines? By providing AI-enabled smartphone applications, many *smart stores* can help the customer by suggesting products they can buy when the customer enters the store. They can provide directions to the aisle where the product is located. They can call out promotions personalized for the particular shopper. Thus a mother who has been buying diapers can be provided with coupons for buying wipes or baby toilet items. The program powered by AI can keep track of the customer's journey with her baby over the years to suggest products appropriate for the age. This would also work for children's clothing. Historically, retailers have used shoppers' aggregated data from syndications to understand sales patterns and in many cases only with sample data. Now with the power of computing, and storage, retailers can collect the data, on their own, and also buy from third parties and use it at the most granular level of each customer, and their transactions, and such data is key to creating AI-powered personalization.

Combining the power of augmented reality (AR) and AI, Nike personalizes shoes the customers buy[19]. Based on customer data, Nike determined that most consumers buy wrong-size shoes. This contributes to returns and unsatisfied customers. To solve this problem, Nike turned to augmented reality (AR) and machine learning. An app called "Nike Fit" helps the customer get a hyper-accurate measurement of her feet using AR, feeds it into an ML algorithm to provide the best recommendation unique to that customer. Buyers can use Nike Fit at home or in stores.

Similarly, AR-enabled and AI-powered "smart mirrors" in clothing stores (discussed later in this chapter) can show your reflection in the mirror augmented with an image of you virtually wearing your choice of new garment[20]. You can literally see yourself in the clothes before you buy, and even before you physically try on the clothes. No more 15-minute trips to the changing room for each garment—instead you can see how it looks in seconds. The customer shopping experience and delight in such a case is incredibly enhanced. An evolution of this concept is to recommend (through the AR mirror) other articles or styles of clothing to the customer that they may not even have been aware of.

Recommendation engines need to be tuned carefully to achieve desired results. Recent research[21] that made use of an open-source collaborative filtering algorithm found that recommendations could affect views and conversions in different ways depending on the attributes of the products. For instance, the study found that the impact on product views is greater for functional, basic-necessity products compared to luxury products. This was also true for experience products compared to search products. The paper states that in order for recommender systems to be more effective, the descriptions of the products have to be more detailed. Other research indicates recommendation engines could affect the discovery of niche products[22]. The premise is that if you keep recommending popular products, then niche products have no room for growing and tend to stay that way, or even worse, become obsolete due to very little revenue. Part of the research around AI-powered recommendation engines is focused on how to select which niche products to present to (and hopefully surprise and delight) the customer.

Vendors such as Amazon are going one step further in personalization by anticipating the demand from a specific customer. By combining the buying data of a customer with what they browse on the website, Amazon anticipates the customer's next order using predictive technology, and uses this information to prepare such anticipatory orders ready to be shipped at a moment's notice using patented shipping methodology[23]. Such orders for items occasionally bought are error prone because of the inherent inaccuracies involved in predictions, but it could work very well for repeat orders such as weekly groceries. It has been a few years since Amazon filed the patent, and there has been little talk about this in recent years. It may be several years before this approach matures.

Retail Management

Managing Demand

Demand management is all about understanding what the market needs during specific time periods are in order that they can be fulfilled with the right product. Demand prediction in today's world of exacting customers, omnichannel capabilities, a tremendous amount of data, and new technologies is an enormous challenge and opportunity.

Knowing the demand for products helps both retailers to order just enough products in order to reduce the cost of inventory. It helps suppliers to produce just enough products to fulfill the orders from retailers, but in today's world also help the supplier's own e-commerce operations. The other side of the coin is product availability. Retailers and suppliers want to make sure the product is highly available, preventing out of stock (OOS).

Dealing with the new product launches (no historical data available) requires qualitative forecasting based on market research, surveys, and industry expert opinions among others.

When there is plenty of data available from past years, we can use many quantitative methods such as trend analysis and econometric models.

Forecasting

Automating the planning of manufacturing and shipping is key to delivering a frictionless experience to the end customer. Accurate forecasting is vital to this process. See Chapter 3, AI for Supply Chain Management, for an exhaustive treatment of the subject of forecast. In this section, we will limit our observations to demand prediction in retail.

Traditional predictive analytics used in the retail industry rely heavily on historical data. Limitations in compute power forced the prediction to be at an aggregate level and caused the use of hierarchical implementation of the forecast. At the most granular level are forecasts by day (sometimes by hour!) of demand at a specific store. The demand for products at a physical grocery store is different on different days of the week, time of the day and month of the year. It is important for planning and ordering purposes to know this at the product level. For fresh produce, this is critical in order to reduce waste. For seasonal products, it is important to know the base demand versus peak demand. However, this level of detail may be difficult to include in a weekly or monthly demand forecast. Demand forecasts use aggregations to generate forecast by week and the next level can then predict the demand for each day.

Inputs to the traditional forecast models typically include historical actual demand and patterns of demand such as trend seasonality. More advanced users consider external factors such as weather pattern forecasts and stock market predictions. In a more complex implementation, a forecast of events that could affect demand can be included. For example, if a new housing development is coming up near a grocery store in six months, it would be important to take into account the increase in demand due to increased shoppers. More sophisticated models would consider competitors' reactions, product substitutions, and market baskets. A key input to the forecast model is planned promotion. Industry studies support the fact that promotional lift could be substantial—accurately predicting demand for these periods (called Trade Promotion Forecasting (TPF)) makes for the difference between a successful promotion campaign and a dismal one.

Traditional time series forecasts work well for short-term predictions, well-known demand trends, and seasonality. However, they fall short when more factors need to be considered, such as product characteristics and external factors.

Forecasting for retail demand is highly complex because different types of products need different prediction algorithms. Predicting demand for fashion apparel differs from predicting demand for consumer packaged goods (CPG) or fresh produce. Feature-rich ML algorithms such as gradient boosting and deep learning take advantage of their ability to work with big data and can increase the prediction accuracies substantially. Advanced ML models such as recurrent neural networks (RNN) and long short-term memory (LSTM) can consider numerous features and create predictions at a granular level with high accuracy. Those are the same algorithms that are used in Deep Learning applied to natural language understanding (conversational AI), which is not surprising since time series (historical product demand and sales data) and natural language (words in sentences) are examples of sequential data types, where past data values can be predictive of future data values.

Out of Stock (OOS) and Availability Management

Forecasting is only one aspect of having the right products at the right time in the right store or warehouse. Even the best forecast cannot prevent retailers from running out of products on the shelf because of unforeseen actions in the store. By some estimations, products are OOS more than 8% of the time in physical stores, and more than 14% in e-commerce stores.

OOS is a much-studied topic for fast-moving consumer goods (FMCG), starting with a research paper in 2003[24]. The authors updated their findings in a 2008 report that was funded by a grant from the leading CPG company, Procter & Gamble[25]. As explained in that report, the loss of revenue for retailers (and the suppliers of the products) is only one component in the total cost of OOS. For instance, dissatisfied customers leave the store to find the product elsewhere and may switch completely to a competitor. For suppliers, the added "cost" is losing the customer loyalty, if the consumer decided to switch brands. The authors of this report also noted that the time lost in answering customer questions about the OOS item costs a typical grocery store close to $1000 per week (in today's inflation-adjusted dollars). For the shopper, the added "cost" is the time spent trying to find the product elsewhere or choosing another product to substitute it.

There are various reasons for stock outs. Some of the most notable ones are:

■ The inventory system is out of sync with reality. It reports there is inventory in a store, when in fact there is none. This is the phantom or ghost inventory problem. One of the contributors to this is the scanning of like-products (different flavors of a drink for example) to one UPC code
■ There is inventory in the store, but it is not on the shelf. This is a shelf-stocking problem.
■ Product is not accurately characterized leading to wrong products being ordered.
■ Forecasting accuracy is less than ideal.
■ Incorrect Trade Promotion Forecasting
■ Manual store practices that don't adhere to shelving policies.

Many leading CPG companies along with their collaborating retailers have invested in programs dubbed *Perfect Shelf* in an effort to improve OSA (On-Shelf Availability). Perfect Shelf contains the specific product a consumer wants in the right store, at the right time, in the right quantities, at the right value. However, manual audits and outdated inventory systems have prevented from attaining the goal. Traditional OOS algorithms have seen successful for the time they were designed for. However, in today's fast-changing world, AI/ML has the potential to go far in preventing OOS, understanding the root causes, and recommending or triggering actions to reduce them and improve OSA.

Computer vision technology is being used in retail stores to help combat OOS problems. Shelfie[26], an Australian company, provides a solution in which cameras mounted on shelves take images of the retail shelves and send the data over to the cloud. A combination of computer vision technology and ML algorithm analyze the image data to detect shelves with missing products. This analysis is sent to the store personnel who can take appropriate actions which might include bringing any stock that might be available elsewhere in the store to re-stock the shelf, or ordering the out of stock product, or inspecting the shelf to make sure it is organized properly.

AI-driven drones are being developed[27] to provide in-store shelf visibility of products, promising to reduce out of stock. The Pensa aerial drone system uses autonomous drones, computer vision, and AI to provide real-time shelf view with analytics built on top of these technologies. The drones are autonomous and can spot empty shelves while flying near the ceiling to lowering themselves then to capture details of what products are missing, with appropriate situational awareness to mind the store traffic.

Marketing

The function of marketing has undergone tremendous changes since the Internet revolution. Businesses can reach more and more consumers through digital marketing. The amount of information businesses can gather has grown exponentially. Traditional information systems struggle to make sense of so much data. The technological advances in the ability to make sense of unstructured data, the tremendous advances in computing power, and the democratization of algorithm use via cloud computing contribute to the use of AI in automating the marketing process (Figure 7.8).

Prior to the *big data* revolution, the amount of data that could be analyzed to understand market trends, and the tools that could do the analyses have been limited. The evolution of database technology made big data possible. Analytical databases such as Vertica and technologies such as Hadoop made big data analysis possible. ML algorithms speed up transformation of big data into market insights.

The four pillars of marketing are *product, price, place, and promotion*. AI /ML can play a part in each of these pillars.

Product and Market research

Market research for a new product line used to take months and weeks for a team of researchers. This time lag is no longer acceptable in today's fast-paced world. Enterprises expect to have all the market intelligence available quickly. That involves automating each of the steps involved in market research. With AI, new insights can be discovered in minutes or even seconds. AI can help identify differentiating product characteristics compared to existing products and competitors' products.

ML algorithms can help quickly balance product portfolios. For a business selling a single product, it is easy to understand the actions required to make the product successful. But when enterprises sell many products, it is important to understand the facets of the complete portfolio of products that contribute to the success of the company. Companies such as Procter & Gamble, Georgia Pacific, Nestle, Apple, and other big companies use portfolio management, especially when considering new product introductions. Portfolio management helps with competitive positioning and product investment decision-making, including obsoleting poorly performing products. There are a few popular techniques used in product portfolio management

| Product | Price | Place | Promotion |

Figure 7.8　Pillars of Marketing.

such as Boston Consulting Company (BCG)'s growth-share matrix, and McKinsey & Company's GE-McKinsey nine-box matrix. The growth-share matrix was created in 1970, and more recently there has been a proposal to make it more relevant to the current nature of businesses[28]. It advocates continually evaluating product portfolios by evaluating new products and markets, taking risks with products that are questionable with controlled experiments done in a methodical way quickly, and growing promising ones to become starts of the portfolio. It also calls for milking the cash cows quickly and retiring them to keep the portfolio fresh. Speed is critical. By investing in feature-rich ML models this can be achieved.

A key step in developing or modifying new products is *A/B testing* or *split testing*. Automating A/B testing with ML capability allows e-commerce businesses to run more tests, with more variables in a short time frame. In addition, AI-enabled tests can be run with adjustments continuously. Vendors such as Sentient Ascend and Evolve Technologies champion conversion rate optimization (CRO) using AI-powered testing tools. However, continuous adjustments may run counterproductive to letting a test run its course[29].

AI enables automation to create huge productivity gains for those who use it. But, beyond productivity, traditional rule-based systems were limited to using structured data. Besides the customer data available from the enterprise systems, social media data is valuable in identifying what kind of product features customers find useful. Social media sites such as Twitter, Facebook, and Instagram have rich sets of data. This set of data is useful for not only sentiment analysis, but it can be also converted into meaningful attributes that can augment the traditional data attributes to mine useful marketing information. Taking it a step further, AI can come up with the recommendations for what the new product line should look like.

Carrying the right assortment of merchandise at the right stores is a major problem for apparel retailers. Products that sell well in stores in upscale locations differ from those that sell in stores in middle-class neighborhoods. The apparel chain store H&M resorted to machine learning to identify the right assortment for each store, instead of stocking all stores with the same merchandise[30]. Using store receipts and loyalty card data and returns data, the algorithm looks to provide assortments recommendation tailored for each store.

Pricing

Dynamic pricing is yet another important AI use case enabled by customer data by matching supply and demand. Dynamic pricing could be targeted at a specific customer, offering her special discounts; or it could adjust pricing depending on the availability of the product or service and the demand for it. The dynamic pricing concept is as old as retail. In the days before money was invented, people bartered. And what they bartered varied from one person to the next and one circumstance to another. With the invention of money, a seller could charge a price for goods. Dynamic pricing has long existed in industries such as airlines, with pre-internet technologies using business rules. In fact, many legacy systems were built using rules. The inherent limitation of rule-based systems is that they need to be programmed for every scenario possible. Now consider AI-based systems. They are continuously training on the data as data gets accumulated (note that the ML models must be continuously updated with new knowledge gained). Companies such as Amazon and Uber have been using AI to set their prices. Most of us have used Uber or Lyft. The ride-share companies constantly tweak their prices depending on demand. Time of the day, location popularity (such as a league championship game), and other factors that increase the demand for rides will influence pricing.

Amazon's dynamic pricing works similarly. A customer browsing an item in the morning may see a price different from the one when browsing for the item in the evening. The dynamic pricing algorithm takes into account the changing demand for the item, competitor's pricing, and the customer location. Amazon's vendor community also uses AI for pricing their wares.

Using dynamic pricing has several operational challenges. Not surprisingly, keeping up with competitors' process is the topmost challenge.

Dynamic pricing does not work for all products and you must first determine if you should apply dynamic pricing. It is also important to make sure your ML models comprehend the minimum and maximum price limits. A run-away dynamic pricing algorithm is akin to a flash crash in the stock market driven by momentum-chasing trading algorithms that operate without such limits. Nobody wants to see those things happen, neither the customer nor the retailer. An excellent application of machine learning along with other optimization techniques is described in the paper *Analytics for an Online Retailer: Demand Forecasting and Price Optimization*[31].

Dynamic pricing does not mean personalized pricing, which is to charge each customer a different price, a practice that is considered discriminatory. Amazon tried personalized pricing in a test on DVDs in 2000 that led to disastrous results and has apparently stopped using demographics or personal data in dynamic pricing algorithms.

Placement

Marketing strategies depend on geographies, demographics, and channels. From a macro decision of what products to sell where, to how the product is positioned in a brick and mortar store or e-commerce store are decisions that have huge impacts on sales.

PepsiCo, one of the major consumer packaged goods (CPG) has developed a cloud-based data and analytics platform called Pep Worx[32] that allow their partner retailers' stores to position their products by using fine-grained proprietary analytics, some of which are enabled by machine learning. Stores of all sizes, serving different demographics, can customize which products they offer depending on the information about the customers who shop there. We talked about the importance of collaboration between retailers and suppliers, and Pep Worx is a great example of that, with usage by retailers such as Circle K, Kroger, and Dollar General.

Retailers such as Walmart are investing in solutions that ensure quality of products customers buy. Eden[33] is an AI system used for optimizing the delivery of fresh products. Eden combines a digital library of food standards with millions of pictures of fresh produce in algorithms used to direct the delivery from source to destination. For example, by understanding the freshness characteristics of bananas, Walmart can prioritize delivery of those batches closer to ripening to nearby locations. AI computer vision algorithms can play a major role in such applications.

Promotion

Promotions today are personalized, and no longer dependent only on transactional data. Most effective marketing strategies today exploit users' emotions, experiences, and real-time feedback.

Marketing to individuals using AI is prevalent in the retailing of beauty products. The marketing solution involves identifying personal characteristics through cameras on mobile or stationary devices and then be able to combine that with the vast amount of data in an ML application to suggest appropriate beauty products. Sephora, a retailer of beauty products uses scans of customer faces and combine it with a shade library to create a color code called ColorIQ[34]. This helps the customer choose the right shades for themselves, and it also helps the brand's marketers to not push inappropriate products to the customer.

Timely analysis of market research data to understand segments of the market allows marketers to target a group of consumers with specific, targeted promotion campaigns. When the marketing message is highly relevant to a specific segment of the population, the response from that population is high. Segmentation is not a new business process. However, with ML capabilities, micro-segmenting is possible. Micro-segmenting is only possible if there are many features (a high variety of customer characteristics) to segment on (also known as deep hierarchical clustering). This is one of the strongest value propositions of "big data"—high-variety data sources that deliver deep insights into those micro-segments, whose analysis is only possible through the algorithmic assistance of ML / AL. Combining data that already exist in operational systems with data from social media, market researchers can create insights using ML models. Understanding the effectiveness of promotions involves looking at past data to identify what promotions worked, and whether it was worth promoting considering the expense involved. To analyze past performances of promotions, retailers (and brand owners) must collect data on their promotions. Traditional promotion data includes:

■ Historical sales, regular and promotional
■ Campaign-specific data such as promotion price, where promoted, what special packaging if any, what physical placement in the store, and what e-commerce strategies used, etc.

Today, we can augment these data sources with social media data from Instagram, Facebook and Twitter. This augmented data can then be used to construct feature-rich ML models that can provide rich insights into the promotions quickly. When a promotion is associated with a new product launch, one doesn't have historical data; but we could use historical data of a like-product. The absence of historical training data for the predictive models is an example of a "cold-start problem," which unsupervised ML excels at addressing. Like-products will cluster together in the product data catalog, and clustering is one of the foundational techniques of unsupervised ML. An artificial intelligence is only worthy of the name AI if it can intelligently identify those likenesses in the old and new products' characteristics (data features).

Pricing is a critical element of promotions. Companies such as Wise Athena[35] offer AI solutions that can price CPG products continuously. CPG companies can use the

AI capabilities offered by Wise Athena to automatically pick the best features that describe the products. The models include cannibalization[36] and cross elasticity[37]. A case study indicates[38] that a cleaning supplier in Latin America with hundreds of unique products benefited by being able to predict volumes and margins in what-if pricing scenarios.

Demand Fulfillment

In the case of physical stores, demand is fulfilled when the shopper loads their shopping cart, and brings it to the register to pay for the items. In the case of e-commerce, the retailer has to either ship the product to the customer's shipping address, or have the customer pick it up from a store of choice. In both cases, the fulfillment of demand requires operational effort. Retailers are starting to experiment with several strategies to address the automation of demand fulfillment. Containing labor cost seems to be the main motivation behind these advances. However, smooth customer interaction (friction reduction in the customer experience) also seems to be a goal. In this section, we look at a few representative use cases where AI/ ML is starting to make inroads.

The technology underlying these use cases include computer vision, voice technology, and ML algorithms that activate and control robots, autonomous vehicles, and drones.

In early 2019, the CPG giant PepsiCo started pioneering roving robot vending machines called *Snackbot* to deliver snacks from their *Hello Goodness* line in college campuses. Students order snacks using an app. While these robots are autonomous, they need human support for error correction and restocking. Students are quite ready to act as ambassadors to keep the robots roaming. It helps that the robots have a friendly look. They can navigate rough terrains, curbs, and sidewalks, can operate using low-cost camera and sensor technologies, and are water and weatherproof. It will be interesting to see how this pilot progresses.

In 2016, the retailer Lowes deployed robots in their San Francisco stores to help customers navigate the aisles and act as customer service agent to help answer customer questions. Customers can interact with the robot using a touch screen and also with voice. If a customer has trouble finding an item, the LoweBot can direct them to the right location in the store. This implementation of AI presumes that the human customer service agents will now have more time to deal with complex customer issues. There has been little progress with this initiative since the initial reports.

Sobeys, one of the largest grocery chains in North America introduced AI-powered shopping carts in their Glen Abbey location in Oakville, Ontario, in October 2019. These smart-carts from a company called Caper are intended to improve a customer's shopping experience by sensing the items being included in the cart with the use of cameras and sensors, but also provide personalized suggestions for additional products to buy, offer shopping discounts and recipes. The customer still needs to scan their products and interact via a touchscreen, then check out with the built-in payment card scanner.

Another grocery retailer Kroger launched an autonomous vehicle delivery in Scottsdale, Arizona in August of 2018, and added two more locations in Houston, Texas in March 2019. These autonomous vehicles have no drivers to take control if needed, but each vehicle is followed by a human-driven car while the pilots are underway. Other retailers testing autonomous vehicle delivery include Amazon, Walmart, and Draeger's Market chain in San Francisco.

Drones are also being developed for use in the last-mile delivery. Amazon pioneered drone delivery in 2016 with Prime-Air. Walgreens is using drones for drug delivery[39]. It could take a while before drone delivery becomes common due to the regulatory nature of the technology space.

Designing the Stores and E-commerce Websites

Product Matching

One of the difficult problems in e-commerce is product-matching. E-commerce sites such as Amazon and Walmart host thousands of sellers offering hundreds of millions of products. When introducing new products, the retailers must match their products to existing products in order to avoid posting duplicate product listings. When showing a list of products on a product page to a customer, products that satisfy a certain criterion must be grouped and listed together. Universal identifiers such as UPC, GTIN, ISBN work well for most products, but sometimes they may not be accurate. The e-commerce website of Walmart[40] evaluates the title, description, images, and price of a product and uses ML algorithms to arrive at a match/no match decision on a product.

Companies such as Malong Technologies[41] in China offer specialized scenario-based visual search and tag capabilities using machine learning. Their solutions cater to retail sectors including apparel, wine, and furniture.

Store Design

Almost every major retailer is investing in the store of the future that is AI-enabled. Many brands are investing in stores that use AI/ML to provide superior customer experience.

Nike Store of the future[42] describes the store of the future, *House of Innovation*, that works seamlessly between the Nike app and physical store. When a user enters the store, the user has the option to use their smartphone to access the retailer or supplier's app that can help them choose what they want to buy. Customers can scan QR codes of garments on a mannequin, and have recommendations provided to them with appropriate size, and colors. When the user asks to try them out, they are directed to a fitting room where the clothes are waiting for them, with a live attendant to help with any changes in choices. This is made possible by vision technology and AI/ML.

A similar use of AI can be found in Fashion AI Concept Store in Hong Kong owned by Alibaba[43], the major e-commerce retailer in China. Using *smart mirrors*, users are given personal attention and recommendations in their clothing choices.

7Next, an initiative of the convenience store giant 7-Eleven, is a response to the growing trend in automation in the retail industry. In November 2019, it opened an employee-only store that is completely automated. It uses computer vision technology and deep learning algorithms running on custom-built hardware. During development, the project got a fast start with the help of AI.Reverie[44]'s simulation platform that produced synthetic data to seed data for training the algorithms. Hundreds of cameras capture every movement of the customer when she enters the store. Numerous sensors track the shelf for product activities. Shahmeer Mirza, the Machine Learning Engineer and Team Lead for 7Next at 7-Eleven, explained the challenge posed by the data from these sensors and the many iterations it took to get the ML models working with high fidelity. 7-Eleven has created an app that shows the experience of a shopper who enters the store. At every visit, a unique QR code is generated for the customer to secure the transaction, who then scans the code at the entrance to the store to create virtual cart and proceeds to shop. When the customer walks out, they are charged for what they added to the cart and provided a receipt.

A Wall Street Journal article[45] talks about the many cashier-free-store trials underway by retailers around the world. Specialty stores such as convenience stores that can be imagined as giant walk-in vending machines could be successful using the cashier-free approach.

Retailers are starting to use solutions such as Standard Cognition[46] as the in-store automation platform with different goals in mind:

- Frictionless customer experience from the time they enter the store to when they leave it
- Reducing costs
- Extending store hours to 24x7 in locations such as hospitals

In addition, retailers are also considering using the capability for real-time inventory and planogram compliance. The solution uses only over-head cameras to accomplish the AI-powered checkout, unlike other solutions that also need sensors, and it prides itself on being able to address the concerns of privacy, scalability, user experience, and flexibility while providing retailers with insights on how the store is operating.

Product Design

Modern product design can be made efficient using *Generative Design*. The designer inputs the design goals, requirements, and constraints into a program that then provides design options that are evaluated by humans. A key advantage is that a lot of designs can be created by the system in a short time when compared to humans. Generative designs also comprehend and create some designs that are considered impossible when using traditional manufacturing processes, but made possible using additive manufacturing. They can also optimize the manufacturing process, thus reducing costs.

Pinar Yanardag and Emily Salvador use generative design techniques to create *The Little Black Dress*. Their company LBD-AI.com now offers jewelry designed by AI[47]. A key message from this company is the collaboration between humans and AI.

The project *Reimagine Retail* was a collaboration between IBM, fashion designer Tommy Hilfiger and the Fashion Institute of Technology (FIT) Infor Design and Tech Lab[48] that demonstrated the use of AI in fashion design. The students used IBM's AI capabilities, including deep learning trained with fashion data. It will be interesting to see how this project evolves and scales.

Many food companies are turning to AI for creating new products, new recipes, and new flavors. McCormick, the seasoning company is working with IBM's AI platform Watson to develop new food products using AI. New food products are usually derived from existing products by applying new specifications which are sent to hundreds of developers who then experiment with removing an ingredient or adding one. Since the algorithm can comprehend a lot more information (such as food trends) than a human about all the different aspects of creating a product, and learn with every iteration, it can help a less experienced developer produce with same number of iterations something equivalent to what takes an expert (with 15 to 20 years of experience). The algorithms may also generate a huge number of recipes and create a product that a human might not have considered. Other food companies that use AI include the food giant Conagra which uses AI to spot trends in consumption and usage as well as social media data to develop new products and PepsiCo's Frito-Lay which uses AI to produce new flavors of chips. It is to be noted that the use of AI in these applications still requires human oversight and involvement. One cannot launch new products without a human taste-testing and tweaking the recipes.

Manufacturing

The use of automation in manufacturing is not new. Starting with the first industrial robot installed by Unimation at General Motors in 1961, there has been steady progress in automation. Compared to such industrial robots, today's robots implement advanced machine learning and deep learning capabilities to aid and control all aspects of manufacturing. A fascinating use case that demonstrates this comes from PepsiCo's Frito Lay division, which was awarded a patent for the technology[49]. Adaptive machine control has been used by Frito Lay since the 1990s since the quality of the potato chips is very important to maintain brand differentiation. Today, several ML algorithms are used to understand and manage the quality of the chips. The texture of the chip and weight are data points that are inputs to algorithms that are used to determine if the process is under control for optimal production of chips. Predicting the weight of the chips using an ML algorithm has also been a cost-saver, eliminating expensive weighing equipment.

Identifying defects that are too microscopic to see, using purpose-built AI solutions, has been reported. These solutions combine the computer vision capability with ML algorithms to enable detection of liquid leaks, air leaks, microscopic surface defects and scratches, and defects in packages, among others. Landing AI claims to do defect detection with only a small amount of data using their small data technology[50].

Georgia Pacific uses machine learning to optimize the complex production process involved in making paper. These papers are used in products you and I use every day—bath tissues and paper towels. A case study reported by Amazon Web Services[51], states that ML models built on raw production data are used to provide feedback to operators for adjusting production machine speeds and augmenting novice users' ability to run production.

AI-enabled machine controllers are being developed for packaging of products. An example of this is the Omron's AI Controller which monitors the signals coming from a packaging machine and in real-time control the machine's operation in order to prevent abnormal operation. In order to do this, it collects data in real time of 5000 measurements per filling of one bottle of a product. These real-time measurements are used by the AI engine to determine if the process is under control. The Overall Equipment Effectiveness (OEE) has been shown to increase with the use of the AI controller. The use of deep learning and random forest algorithms have been shown to predict and improve OEE with high accuracy.[52]

Responsible Retailing

Retailers and suppliers are aware of their contributions to the carbon footprint from their activities. Every time a product gets shipped from one distribution center to another, and to the store, and eventually to the customer, the transportation activities contribute to the carbon footprint. The plastic used in packaging of the products contributes to environmental deterioration. These are but two of the examples of where retailers and suppliers have the opportunity to retail responsibly.

The fashion industry is considered one of the worst offenders in sustainability for various reasons. Some of these have to do with textile manufacturing processes that use large amounts of chemicals which pollute the environment. The behavior of customers who buy fashionable garments and discard them is also a contributor. Yet another reason is the returns logistics. Online purchases apparently have a high rate of return due to the practice of customers ordering multiple sizes and returning those that don't fit. The logistics involved in these returns give rise to wasted transportation resources that contribute to the carbon footprint. AI-based recommender systems and virtual fitting rooms (VR experiences) can help the customer choose the right size before buying and thus help reduce the number of returns.

With the advent of e-commerce, parcel delivery has become a significant contributor to waste, thus impacting sustainability. Orion (On-Road Integrated Optimization and Navigation) by UPS[53] is an example of managing delivery efficiently with algorithms. Orion takes into account each driver's experience and gives them workable routes for each day of delivery, considering over 200,000 routing options for each route of each driver. It is to be noted that this is a hard problem, and UPS drivers in Manhattan still use an older system.[54]

Consumers' expectations for year-round availability of fresh produce is another contributor to the issue of sustainability. In addressing this need, retailers are sourcing globally, and creating supply chains that contribute to the carbon footprint due to increased transportation. Efficient supply chains can address the problem of reducing carbon footprint. AI algorithms can include a feature of contribution to carbon footprint when designing supply chains. Tradeoffs to be made between achieving customer satisfaction and reducing carbon footprint can be considered by identifying suppliers closest to the customers. AI can assist local growers in identifying the "best" products to grow that will satisfy such constraints within their reachable market.

It is interesting that while AI can help reduce carbon footprint in various ways, it can also be a contributing factor. Horizon, the EU Research & Innovation Magazine[55] reports: *"training a large AI model to handle human language can lead to emissions of nearly 300,000 kilograms of carbon dioxide equivalent, about five times the emissions of the average car in the US, including its manufacture."* However, it should be noted that the study quoted in the article[56] says, *"In particular, they found that a tuning process known as neural architecture search, which tries to optimize a model by incrementally tweaking a neural network's design through exhaustive trial and error, had extraordinarily high associated costs for little performance benefit. Without it, the most costly model, BERT, had a carbon footprint of roughly 1,400 pounds of carbon dioxide equivalent, close to a round-trip trans-America flight for one person."* Alerting the AI solution providers to algorithm costs will hopefully galvanize them to design algorithms responsibly. It is to be noted that reducing the emissions can be accomplished by using data centers that take advantage of cheap renewable energy and ease of cooling because of where they are located. There are varying opinions on the estimated risks of these smart technologies, which are the subject of ongoing discussions within the AI community.

Future of AI/ML in Retail

What this chapter has done is to touch upon the use cases being explored or addressed in the retail industry today. Many of the use cases are at varying degrees of maturity.

In the 2016 video *State-of-the-Art AI: Building Tomorrow's Intelligent Systems*[57] Peter Norvig, research Director at Google talks about the maturity of AI systems compared to that of traditional software systems. Compared to traditional software, we don't have modularity with machine learning. We don't have versions that correct bugs or enhance the capabilities, and the result is probabilistic. Data is fundamental to machine learning, and continuous update to training data and models that use that data is necessary to keep up with changes in the world in which the algorithms operate and to deal with the ensuing feedback from this world. And because data is fundamental to machine learning, the data chosen to train the algorithms must be representative of the problem domain and not introduce bias. Maturity in the tool-set we use to develop ML algorithms is a prerequisite to scaling. As Peter says:

> *"The problem here is the methodology for scaling this up to a whole industry is still in progress.... We don't have the decades of experience that we have in developing and verifying regular software."*

In retail, the maturity of those systems that do not deal with humans physically (for example, the back-office systems such as efficient supply chain algorithms, or recommendation systems) is higher when compared to those that do (for example, cashierless stores are good for some, but not all types of stores).

Tremendous progress in innovation is being made every day in AI and ML algorithms. Those in the retail sector who are aware and take advantage of those innovations stand to benefit.

While waiting to go through the process of publishing this book, COVID-19 struck. The impact of this unprecedented event has been devastating to all including the retail sector. There were already major trends in the retail landscape such as the customer preference for e-commerce, last-mile delivery solutions, click-and-collect, and abandoning of malls. COVID-19 has accelerated these trends. Subsectors within retail have experienced changes in different ways. Grocers have seen tremendous demand due to panic-buying, while retailers catering to discretionary items such as the apparel have seen enormous lowering of demand. Supply chains have been disrupted, and labor shortages have increased. Retailers have had to be concerned with the safety of the consumers and employees.

What will be the role of AI in post-COVID-retail? There are indications that the panic-buying (consumer behavior has proven to be anything but normal) and increase in online shopping have unearthed some of the limitations of current ML algorithms used in e-commerce[58] to deal with the kind of volatility experienced during the pandemic, not only in the customer-facing recommendations, but also the backend decision-making to do with inventory and fraud detection. The lessons learned about the buying patterns during the pandemic will help strengthen the algorithms. Automation solutions such as Standard Cognition, and the 7-Eleven's 7Next are bound to see growth and proliferation due to social distancing, for both consumers and employees. Many of the implementers of AI are learning that you can't just set it and forget it. The solutions need constant attention from humans, and in situations such as the pandemic would require humans to step in and take control and steer the solution in the right direction.

Acknowledgements

Ed Dixon reviewed an early draft and provided valuable feedback.
Kirk Borne did an extensive review and his suggestions for revisions made a tremendous difference to the quality of this chapter.

Notes

1 "Notes from the AI frontier: Applications and value of deep learning," McKinsey Global Institute, retrieved September 22, 2021, from https://www.mckinsey.com/featured-insights/artificial-intelligence/notes-from-the-ai-frontier-applications-and-value-of-deep-learning

2 Steven Begley, et al., "Automation in retail: An executive overview for getting ready." McKinsey Company, May 23, 2019, retrieved September 22, 2021, from https://www.mckinsey.com/industries/retail/our-insights/automation-in-retail-an-executive-overview-for-getting-ready

3 Stephanie Braun, (May 8, 2015). "The history of retail: a timeline." Lightspeed, retrieved September 22, 2021, from https://www.lightspeedhq.com/blog/the-history-of-retail-a-timeline/

4 Wikipedia, "Amazon Go," retrieved September 22, 2021, from https://en.wikipedia.org/wiki/Amazon_Go

5 Sumanta Dey & Bijoy Venugopal, "Flipkart wants data scientists and engineers to build AI for India: Sachin Bansal," retrieved September 22, 2021, from https://stories.flipkart.com/flipkart-ai-india-sachin-bansal/

6 Bijoy Venugopal, "With AI & ML, Flipkart is addressing the uniquely Indian problem of problem addresses," retrieved September 22, 2021, from https://stories.flipkart.com/ai-ml-flipkart-indian-address/

7 Gavin Weightman, "The History of the Bar Code," retrieved September 22, 2021, from https://www.smithsonianmag.com/innovation/history-bar-code-180956704/

8 CB Insights, "Amazon Strategy Teardown: Amazon's Barreling Into Physical Retail, Financial Services, Healthcare, And AI-Led Computing," retrieved September 22, 2021, from https://www.cbinsights.com/research/report/amazon-strategy-teardown/

9 Rupert Goodwins, "AI weaves value from unstructured data," Raconteur Publishing, retrieved September 22, 2021, from https://www.raconteur.net/technology/unstructured-data-ai-ml

10 Lotame, "1st Party Data, 2nd Party Data, 3rd Party Data: What Does It All Mean?" retrieved September 22, 2021, from https://www.lotame.com/1st-party-2nd-party-3rd-party-data-what-does-it-all-mean/

11 Cracked Labs, "Corporate Surveillance in Everyday Life – Linking, matching and combining digital profiles," retrieved September 22, 2021, from https://crackedlabs.org/en/corporate-surveillance/#6

12 "Retail," Juniper Networks, retrieved September 22, 2021, from https://www.mist.com/retail

13 Wayne Yaddow, "AI and BI Projects Are Bogged Down With Data Preparation Tasks," TDWI, retrieved September 22, 2021, from https://tdwi.org/articles/2019/08/16/diq-all-ai-and-bi-data-preparation-tasks.aspx

14 Armand Ruiz, "The 80/20 data science dilemma," InfoWorld, SEP 26, 2017, retrieved September 22, 2021, from https://www.infoworld.com/article/3228245/the-80-20-data-science-dilemma.html

15 Mike Gurican, "A Probabilistic, Machine Learning Approach to Data Unification", Jun 19, 2019, retrieved September 22, 2021, from https://www.tamr.com/blog/a-probabilistic-machine-learning-approach-to-data-unification/

16 "Celebrating 95 years of Innovation," Nielsen, retrieved September 22, 2021, from http://sites.nielsen.com/timelines/our-history/

17 Stephanie Braun, "The history of retail: a timeline," Lightspeed, May 8, 2015, retrieved September 22, 2021, from https://www.lightspeedhq.com/blog/the-history-of-retail-a-timeline/

18 Allen Yu, "How Netflix Uses AI, Data Science, and Machine Learning — From A Product Perspective," Becoming Human: Exploring Artificial Intelligence & What it Means to be Human, retrieved September 22, 2021, from https://becominghuman.ai/how-netflix-uses-ai-and-machine-learning-a087614630fe

19 Gunseli Yalcinkaya, "Nike app uses AR and AI to scan feet for perfect fit," May 9, 2019, retrieved September 22, 2021, from https://www.dezeen.com/2019/05/09/nike-fit-app-ar-ai-trainers/

20 Martin Rakver, "Helpful Uses of Augmented Reality in Clothes Fitting," Augmented Reality, retrieved September 22, 2021, from https://smartglasseshub.com/augmented-reality-clothes-fitting/

21 Dokyun Lee & Kartik Hosanagar, "How Do Product Attributes and Reviews Moderate the Impact of Recommender Systems Through Purchase Stages?" Published Online: 1 May 2020 https://doi.org/10.1287/mnsc.2019.3546

22 Himan Abdollahpouri, et al., "Managing Popularity Bias in Recommender Systems with Personalized Re-ranking," Cornell University, retrieved September 22, 2021, from https://arxiv.org/abs/1901.07555

23 Patent US8615473B2, "Method and system for anticipatory package shipping," retrieved September 22, 2021, from https://patents.google.com/patent/US8615473B2/en

24 Thomas W. Gruen & Daniel Corsten, Desperately Seeking Shelf Availability: An Examination of the Extent, the Causes, and the Efforts to Address Retail Out-of-Stocks, International Journal of Retail & Distribution Management 31(12), December 2003, https://www.researchgate.net/publication/36385147_Desperately_Seeking_Shelf_Availability_An_Examination_of_the_Extent_the_Causes_and_the_Efforts_to_Address_Retail_Out-of-Stocks

25 Thomas W. Gruen & Daniel Corsten, "A Comprehensive Guide to Retail Out-of-Stock Reduction in the Fast-Moving Consumer Goods Industry," retrieved September 22, 2021, from http://www.uccs.edu/Documents/tgruen/OOS%20Guide%202008%20Revision.pdf

26 Shelfie, "Stopping Stock-Outs," retrieved September 22, 2021, from https://shelfieretail.com/

27 "Powerful AI System Provides Real-time Shelf Visibility and Learns as it Goes," Pensa Systems, retrieved September 22, 2021, from https://www.pensasystems.com/technology/

28 Martin Reeves, et al., "BCG Classics Revisited: The Growth Share Matrix," June 4, 2014, retrieved September 22, 2021, from https://www.bcg.com/de-de/publications/2014/growth-share-matrix-bcg-classics-revisited.aspx

29 Amy Gallo, "A Refresher on A/B Testing," Harvard Business Review, June 28, 2017, retrieved September 22, 2021, from https://hbr.org/2017/06/a-refresher-on-ab-testing

30 Dan Alaimo, "H&M turns to big data, AI to tailor store assortments," RetailDive, May 9, 2018.

31 Kris, J. Ferreira, et al., "Analytics for an Online Retailer: Demand Forecasting and Price Optimization," HBS Scholarly Articles, retrieved September 22, 2021, from http://nrs.harvard.edu/urn-3:HUL.InstRepos:26964422

32 Russell Redman, "Using data to help retailers get closer to customers," Aug 31, 2018, retrieved September 22, 2021, from https://www.supermarketnews.com/marketing/using-data-help-retailers-get-closer-customers

33 Parvez Musani, "What's for dinner tonight?" Walmart.com, March 1, 2018, retrieved September 22, 2021, from https://corporate.walmart.com/newsroom/innovation/20180301/eden-the-tech-thats-bringing-fresher-groceries-to-you

34 Hilary Milnes, "How Color IQ, Sephora's shade-matching skin care tool, boosts brand loyalty," Digiday, April 13, 2016, retrieved September 22, 2021, from https://digiday.com/marketing/color-iq-sephoras-shade-matching-skin-care-tool-boosts-brand-loyalty/

35 "Where CPG companies come to optimize their pricing," Wise Athena, retrieved September 22, 2021, from http://wiseathena.com/

36 "What is Market Cannibalization?" Corporate Finance Institute, retrieved September 22, 2021, from https://corporatefinanceinstitute.com/resources/knowledge/strategy/market-cannibalization/

37 "Cross elasticity of demand," Wikipedia, retrieved September 22, 2021, from https://en.wikipedia.org/wiki/Cross_elasticity_of_demand

38 "Wise Athena: Setting the Right Price with Artificial Intelligence," CIO Review, retrieved September 22, 2021, from https://bigdata.cioreview.com/vendor/2016/wise_athena

39 "DroneDeliveryIsOneStepCloserToReality,"NPR.org,October18,2019,retrievedSeptember22,2021, from https://www.npr.org/2019/10/18/770898952/drone-delivery-is-one-step-closer-to-reality

40 Ajinkya More, "Product Matching in eCommerce using deep learning," Walmart Global Tech, Septemeber 11, 2017, retrieved September 22, 2021, from https://medium.com/walmartlabs/product-matching-in-ecommerce-4f19b6aebaca

41 Malong.com, retrieved September 22, 2021, from https://www.malong.com/en/home

42 "Nike House of Innovation preview," Nov 15, 2018, Engadget Video, retrieved September 22, 2021, from https://youtu.be/eecmQ3xhlZ0

43 Alizila Staff, "New Alibaba Concept Store Teases Future of Fashion Retail," Alizila: news from Alibaba, July 5, 2018,retrieved September 22, 2021, from https://www.alizila.com/new-alibaba-concept-store-teases-future-of-fashion-retail/

44 AI.Reverie, retrieved September 22, 2021, from https://www.linkedin.com/company/aireverie/

45 John Murawski, "Cashierless Stores Make Inroads in U.S.," Wall Street Journal, Aug. 12, 2019, retrieved September 22, 2021, from https://www.wsj.com/articles/cashierless-stores-make-inroads-in-u-s-11565602204

46 "AI-Powered Autonomous Checkout," Standard Cognition, retrieved September 22, 2021, from https://standard.ai/

47 "What happens when AI designs a Little Black Dress?" Little Black Dress, retrieved September 22, 2021, from https://lbd-ai.com/ https://lbd-ai.com/

48 Rachel Arthur, "Artificial Intelligence Empowers Designers In IBM, Tommy Hilfiger and FIT Collaboration," Forbes, retrieved September 22, 2021, from https://www.forbes.com/sites/rachelarthur/2018/01/15/ai-ibm-tommy-hilfiger/

49 Patent US9541537B1, "Quantitative texture measurement apparatus and method," retrieved September 22, 2021, from https://patents.google.com/patent/US9541537

50 "Leak Defect Detection," Landing.AI, retrieved September 22, 2021, from https://landing.ai/defect-detection/

51 "Georgia-Pacific Optimizes Processes, Saves Millions of Dollars Yearly Using AWS," AWS.Amazon.com, retrieved September 22, 2021, from https://aws.amazon.com/solutions/case-studies/georgia-pacific/

52 Ibtissam El Hassani, et al., "Artificial Intelligence and Machine Learning to Predict and Improve Efficiency in Manufacturing Industry," Cornell University, retrieved September 22, 2021, from https://arxiv.org/abs/1901.02256v2

53 "UPS On-Road Integrated Optimization and Navigation (ORION) Project," informs, retrieved September 22, 2021, from https://www.informs.org/Impact/O.R.-Analytics-Success-Stories/Optimizing-Delivery-Routes

54 Larissa Zimberoff, "Why Machine Learning Is a Delivery Driver's Best Friend," Fortune, February 6, 2018, retrieved December 12, 2019, from https://fortune.com/2018/02/06/machine-learning-delivery-driver/

55 Annette Ekin, "AI can help us fight climate change. But it has an energy problem, too," Horizon, The EU Research & Innovation Magazine, European Commission, 12 September 2019, retrieved September 22, 2021, from https://horizon-magazine.eu/article/ai-can-help-us-fight-climate-change-it-has-energy-problem-too.html

56 Karen Hao, "Training a single AI model can emit as much carbon as five cars in their lifetimes," MIT Technology Review, retrieved September 22, 2021, from June 6, 2019, retrieved September 22, 2021, from https://www.technologyreview.com/s/613630/training-a-single-ai-model-can-emit-as-much-carbon-as-five-cars-in-their-lifetimes/

57 Peter Norvig, "State-of-the-Art AI: Building Tomorrow's Intelligent Systems," EmTech Digital, May 23, 2016, retrieved September 22, 2021, from https://events.technologyreview.com/video/watch/peter-norvig-state-of-the-art-ai/

58 Will Douglas Heaven, "Our weird behavior during the pandemic is messing with AI models," MIT Technology Review, May 11, 2020, retrieved September 22, 2021, from https://www.technologyreview.com/2020/05/11/1001563/covid-pandemic-broken-ai-machine-learning-amazon-retail-fraud-humans-in-the-loop/

Chapter 8

Visualization

Leland Wilkinson

University of Illinois at Chicago, USA

H2O.ai

Contents

DOI: 10.4324/9781351032940-8

Introduction

A picture is worth a thousand words. This hoary favorite of designers and visualization gurus is not only false, it is silly. Pictures and words play complementary roles in human information processing and are not functionally comparable. Even if they were comparable, a single image cannot rival the message of the Shema verse in Deuteronomy, "Hear, O Israel: the Lord is our God, the Lord is One." Arguably, no image has been pondered as much as this single verse.

The picture/word comparison may be silly, but that is not because pictures are worthless. On the contrary, pictures, diagrams, graphs, and other visual forms convey a rich assortment of meanings that, like the Shema, cannot be reduced to simple concepts. Pictures indeed can reveal some meanings that would take many words to express. And they serve as delightful and useful adjuncts to text. Consider the following graphic plotting birth rate against death rate for assorted world countries. (These data on world countries, used in this and subsequent figures, are adapted from the CIA World Factbook dataset reproduced on the Kaggle Web site https://www.kaggle.com/fernandol/countries-of-the-world.)

- The distribution of birth rates spans almost twice that of death rates over the globe.
- The joint distribution of birth and death rates is curiously nonlinear (U-shaped regression line).
- The highest density of countries involves ones with relatively low death rates and low birth rates.

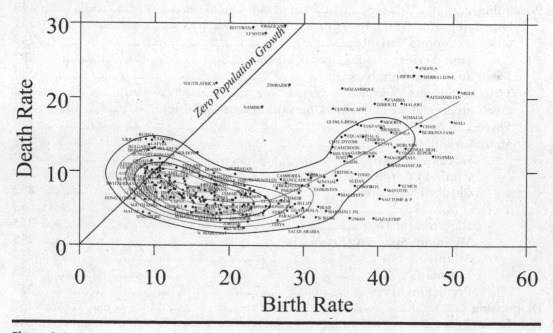

Figure 8.1

- A substantial number of countries in this dense area are losing population, especially in Europe.
- In general, high birth rates are associated with developing countries.
- A number of developing countries have rather alarming death rates coupled with high birth rates.
- The outermost contour is an approximate 90 percent confidence interval on the joint distribution of rates.
- With respect to that contour, there are many outlying countries, particularly in the high birth rate region.
- Botswana, Swaziland, and Lesotho are extreme outliers, with very high death rates and moderate birth rates.
- All three of these extreme outliers are losing population, which is unusual for developing countries.

That's not quite a thousand words, but it is clear that some graphics require more than a few words to describe them adequately. For these graphics, the "less is more" dictum of Mies van der Rohe is not appropriate. Edward Tufte, who popularized this visualization slogan, actually wrote "For non-data- ink, less is more. For data-ink, less is a bore."[1]. Going too far in either direction can obscure an important message. Furthermore, the precepts that apply to presentation graphics don't always apply to exploratory or other types of visualization. Many visualization gurus who love to quote Tufte think they can promulgate absolute rules for all circumstances.

Sometimes a single graphic won't reveal the whole story underlying the chosen variables. The following figure is designed to be viewed alongside the birth rate vs. death rate scatterplot. We see that the geographic distributions of both variables have important similarities (particularly in Africa and North America). Moreover, a cluster analysis of these two variables reveals three clusters that have coherent geographical distributions. Cluster 1 represents the developing nations, including the outliers. Cluster 2 represents mostly developed nations. And Cluster 3 represents the countries in between.

To tell a story from visualizations based on even a few variables (two in this case) may require several visualizations. And the principles involved may be different for each panel depicting this story. Consequently, this chapter will present and review principles involved in a wide variety of visualizations, many designed for the analysis of large datasets and/or designed to support inferences from AI models.

We begin by looking at exploring, which is usually the first step in developing useful models. Then we look at presenting, which includes the many graphics intended

Figure 8.2

for communicating results to an audience with the time to examine them in detail. Then we look at diagnosing models, which employ visualization to assess whether models are appropriate; statisticians invented most of these visualizations, motivated by the need to discover whether the assumptions underlying specific models are met.

Exploring

Experienced data scientists know that before developing and fitting any model, it is critical to examine data visually to detect possible anomalies and to derive cues for what model or aspects of a model is appropriate for the given data. Failing to do this risks the famous "garbage in, garbage out" mess that can lead to incorrect inferences, undetected biases, and false conclusions.

Surprisingly, some machine learning vendors and enthusiasts think that this sort of visual exploration is unnecessary or, at best, a fishing expedition. These enthusiasts appear to imagine that AI algorithms will automatically adjust for the kinds of quirks and exceptions that statisticians and scientists have worried about for centuries. They imagine that AI algorithms like deep learning networks and tree ensembles are robust against anomalies, missing values, and contaminations in data. Worse, some "AutoML" programs optimize goodness of fit without taking into account other factors that can affect the appropriateness of a model; they simply run several different ML algorithms and pick the one that makes the "best" prediction on a test dataset. As statisticians have long known, however, an incorrect model can sometimes fit data *better* than a correct model.

The term Exploratory Data Analysis (EDA) was invented by John Tukey[2], one of the most important statisticians of the twentieth century. Much of the motivation underlying his famous book titled with that term is contained in the following quote[3]:

> "Probability modelers seem to want to believe that their models are entirely correct. Data analysts regard their models as a basis from which to measure deviation, as a convenient benchmark in the wilderness, expecting little truth and relying on less."

By contrast, Tukey promoted visual inspection of data as a critical first step in any data analysis. Although a few EDA enthusiasts have urged us to "let the data speak for themselves," Tukey disagreed with that extreme as much as he did with the other extreme advocated by modelers. Instead, Tukey advocated a cyclical process to data analysis.

1. Examine data visually.
2. Infer and fit a candidate model to the data.
3. Collect residuals to the model.
4. Treat the residuals as new data and go back to the first step if residuals do not look random.

A data analyst should continue this cycle until there is nothing more to be found in the residuals. The analyst should also consider rejecting a model at any time that it becomes apparent that the fitted values are implausible. This cyclical approach results in models that draw new observations into the analysis at sequential steps instead of constructing one gigantic model to cover all possibilities. To see this approach in action, you can view several videos at http://stat-graphics.org/movies/

To facilitate this approach to data analysis, Tukey and his team at Bell Laboratories invented several visualization tools.

Linking

Linking involves establishing a link between two or more visual elements. For example, we might click on a bar in a bar graph and highlight all the points in a scatterplot that are members of that bar. Or, we might click on a point in a scatterplot and see a text box with information about that point. The purpose of this facility is to reveal relationships that would not be apparent in separate graphics. Of course, we could use color or other aesthetics to accomplish this, but that method would contribute to visual clutter. Linking provides on-demand information that is otherwise hidden.

Linking can also be implemented through *hovering*. That is, if we have a mouse or pointing device, linking can expose relations as soon as a cursor passes over an element. This capability can be useful for quick exploration and animation. It serves to engage a user who wishes to get a high-level view of a collection of relations.

Another type of link is called a "lasso." This is a tool that allows a user to freehand draw a bounding region around points or other elements. Once the boundary (lasso) is closed, those points are selected and elements in other graphics are highlighted.

Brushing

Becker and Cleveland[4] introduced this idea based on their work with Tukey. A brush is a region in a graph. Usually that region is a rectangle, but it could be a circle or another shape. After a brush is established (through a drawing gesture inside a graph's frame), it can be dragged in real time to highlight elements in other graphs. The rapid moving of the brush rectangle coupled with highlighting helps to reveal patterns in all linked graphics. You can see an example at https://vega.github.io/vega/examples/brushing-scatter-plots/.

Transformations

Tukey parameterized a simple class of models designed to deal with asymmetry in the density of variables[2]. The next figure summarizes his idea plus a derivation that became quite popular among statisticians.

This class of transformations has several benefits. Mainly, it tends to symmetrize highly skewed variables (such as income or counts). When we analyze variables that have been symmetrized after transformation, simple statistics like means and traditional statistical models do a better job of characterizing the density of the variables. Secondly, transformations can reveal that some cases that might be considered

Tukey Ladder of Powers (re-expressions)

Assume data are positive, or use $X + 1$ if non-negative

Tukey formula

$$X \longmapsto X^p$$

Box & Cox formula (derived from Tukey's idea)

$$X \longmapsto (X^p - 1) / p$$

Values of p

$p = 2$ yields X^2

$p = 1$ yields X

$p = .5$ yields sqrt(X)

$p = 0$ yields log(X)

$p = -1$ yields $1 / X$

For Box & Cox formula

$p = 0$ yields log(X) because $\lim_{p \to 0} (X^p - 1) / p = \log(X)$

Also, dividing by p in Box & Cox formula preserves polarity of X

Ascending the ladder ($p > 1$) spreads out large values and compresses small values.
Descending the ladder ($p < 1$) compresses large values and spreads out small values.

Figure 8.3

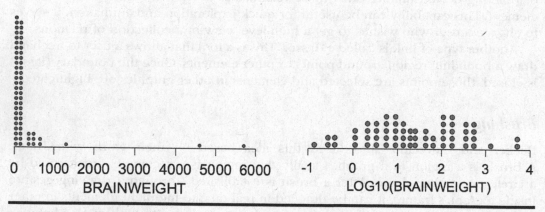

Figure 8.4

outliers are not outliers after the transformation. The following example involves data from a study of sleep patterns in animals[5]. The left panel shows a dot plot of the raw data brain weights. The two dots at the right correspond to Indian and Asian elephants. After the data are logged, it is apparent in the right panel that these animals are not outliers.

Interactive User Interfaces

Modern EDA user interfaces (UI) must be highly interactive. You can see an early example (Prim9) at (Figure 8.5)

Desktop EDA software first appeared on Unix systems[6]. You can see a video demonstration of XGobi, an early EDA system, here (Figure 8.6):

Figure 8.5   https://www.youtube.com/watch?v=B7XoW2qiFUA.

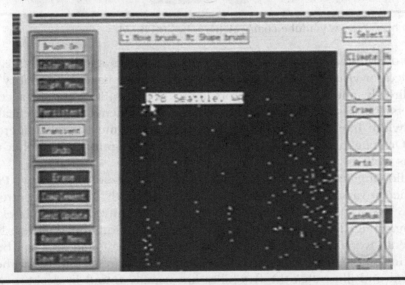

Figure 8.6   https://www.youtube.com/watch?v=n5i9RLCe1rQ.

A Tukey advisee, Paul Velleman, introduced EDA on the Macintosh in 1987[7]. You can view an example here (Figure 8.7):

More recent implementations of Tukey's ideas have exploited the real-time capabilities of interactive graphics libraries. The biggest challenge to interactive UIs has arisen from the need to explore big data. Contemporary implementations generally work in a client-server environment with client-side code enabling the interaction. Languages like JavaScript play a major role in these architectures. Display libraries like D3[8] and Vega-Lite[9] provide the interactive functions needed. But the main computational algorithms must be located on the server or on a large distributed network. Technologies like Graphics Processing Units (GPU) are required to handle

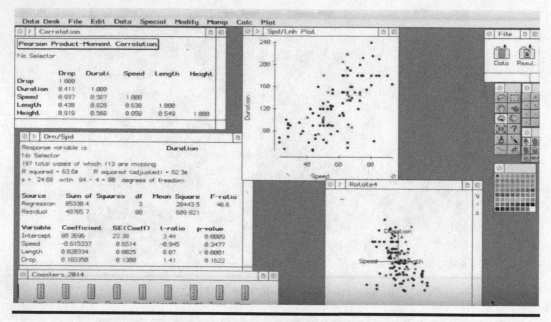

Figure 8.7   https://www.youtube.com/watch?v=D-zCrr43hLM.

very large distributed datasets. These multi-core systems handle the statistical functions needed for visualization. Because browsers do not have the memory to handle big-data directly, and because transport languages like JSON cannot accommodate big datasets (because transmission of billions of elements is impractical even on high-bandwidth Internets), the server-side calculations must involve aggregation of the data. On megapixel displays, we can work with significantly higher-resolution graphics as well.

The following figure shows one application developed by Prithvi Prabhu for H2O.ai. The canvas contains a high-resolution table plot[10]. The user controls for this application are on the left border of the screen. These involve capabilities for filtering, sorting, tiling (faceting), joining, and other operations on datasets. Notice the tear-off menu overlaid on the middle of the display. Menus like this can be dragged anywhere inside the browser window. This display system is tailored for the browser environment and illustrates the flexibility not usually found in desktop windowed systems. You can view a video here (Figure 8.8).

Presenting

Presentation graphics are generally static, intended to be printed or displayed on a computer canvas. Because they are static, they usually contain more detail than other graphics meant for a glance or to be queried dynamically. This is the category of visualizations that has many centuries of development and has been written about most widely[11].

The types of presentation graphics depend on their underlying mathematical models, as discussed in[12]. These models involve functions of variables. A variable

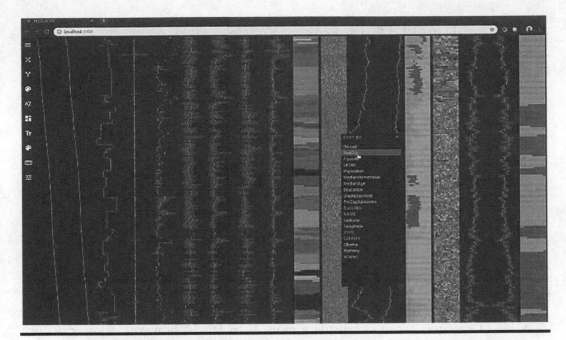

Figure 8.8   https://www.youtube.com/watch?v=D-zCrr43hLM.

maps a set of objects to a set of values. Age, for example, assigns a person (or some other object) to a number. When that number can range across an infinite set of values within some interval, we call it a continuous variable. By contrast, gender maps a person to a category. The set of possible categories is finite and consists of labels for a property (including discrete numeric labels). In that case, we call it a categorical variable.

This distinction makes a difference in visualization. Statisticians and data scientists worry a lot about the types of variables used in their models. Visualization people often worry less about this distinction than they should, perhaps because they fail to understand that every analytic visualization is based on an underlying model. Visualizations that are not based on mathematical models are best understood as diagrams. Useful as they are, diagrams are not the subjects of this chapter. Instead, we will look at various combinations of continuous and categorical variables and their associated visualizations.

One Categorical Variable

The simplest visualization we can do for a categorical variable is to display it in a table. Here is an example for the countries data.

Asia	E Europe	W Europe	Baltics	N Africa	Sub Sahara	N America	S America	Near East	Oceania

Figure 8.9

A	B	C	A&B	A&C	B&C	A&B&C

Figure 8.10

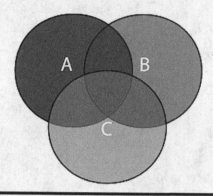

Figure 8.11

A list of categories can encapsulate more than labels, however. Some category lists encode a deeper structure. The most familiar one is the Venn diagram. Here, for example, is a list of categories representing sets. In this list, an ampersand (&) is used to represent intersections (∩) of those sets.

The Venn diagram for this list looks like this:

A Venn diagram is defined by a collection of regions (usually circles) that intersect in all possible combinations. For circular regions, the only possible Venn diagrams involve three or fewer circles (other shapes can accommodate more). When we are not constrained to represent all possible intersections, we can construct an Euler

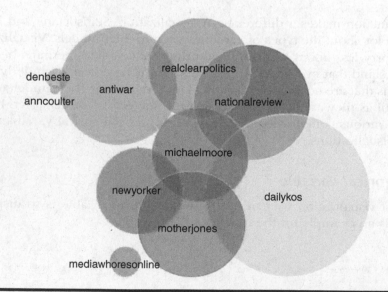

Figure 8.12

diagram. All Venn diagrams are Euler diagrams but not all Euler diagrams are Venn diagrams. The following figure shows an Euler diagram constructed from ten sets of categories. The circle sizes represent the cardinality (size) of each set in the data. Specialized computer programs are required to produce these diagrams from lists of categories and their intersections.[13,14]

The sets in this case were blogs by various political commentators. The elements of the sets were word lists of various sizes. The sizes of the circles were computed from the number of words in the lists and the sizes of the intersections were computed from the proportion of shared words. The word lists were pre-processed to remove stop-words, punctuation, and singular/plural variations). The R venneuler package (http://cran.r-project.org/web/packages/venneuler) was used to draw the diagram.

One Continuous Variable

We call most single continuous variable plots densities. In these plots, we are looking for the regions where we might expect to see most instances of values (modes). We also would like often to locate outliers and other anomalous values on a variable. The most popular type of density plot is the histogram. The following figure shows a histogram of population density from the countries dataset.

This histogram is so skewed that we can benefit from a log transformation before computing the histogram bins. The following figure illustrates the result. Transformations like a log or square-root often stretch a skewed variable into a more symmetric form. This allows us to examine more detail in highly dense regions that are obscured in the raw data. Another consequence of transformations is that points or histogram bins that appear to be outliers in the raw data are not outliers in the transformed. Notice the two bins greater than a billion in the previous plot are not noteworthy in the transformed figure. Beginning statistics students sometimes think transformations are a form of lying with statistics. On the contrary, failing to transform severely skewed distributions can be a form of lying with visualization.

Histograms are probably the most popular density display. They are ubiquitous in introductory statistics textbooks. Their popularity conceals a slippery character, however. Constructing appropriate histograms is an art that few of the tutorials explain.

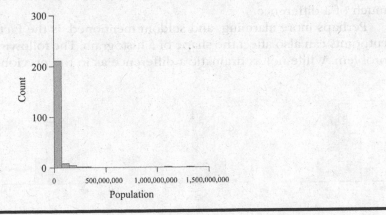

Figure 8.13

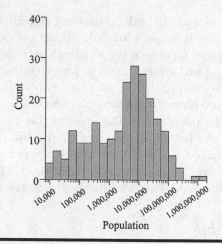

Figure 8.14

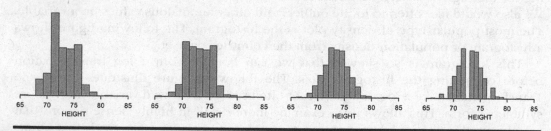

Figure 8.15

The first problem is how to choose the number of bins to fill with values. The next figure shows that this choice can affect the shape of the histogram. The only parameter that varies in these four histograms is the number of bins. There is considerable research on choosing an "optimal" number of bins to allow a histogram to reflect the true shape of an underlying density. These references are beyond the scope of this chapter, but well-designed software should take this problem into account. One can also vary the number of bins around the software's chosen estimate to see if it makes much of a difference.

Perhaps more alarming, and seldom mentioned, is the fact that placement of bin cutpoints can also affect the shape of a histogram. The following figure illustrates this problem. While not as dramatic a difference as in the previous figure, The cutpoints

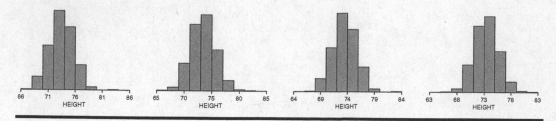

Figure 8.16

do affect shape. Some computer programs (e.g.,[15]) attempt to draw a compromise between cutpoints positioned at tick marks and reasonable shape. Programs that allow the bins to be located anywhere on the scale are less useful for many social science applications, where data are integer valued.

The kernel density display is one attempt to solve some of the deficiencies of histograms. It fits a continuous density distribution to the observed locations of points and is less susceptible to the bin width and bin location problems. Kernel density displays do require a parameter value analogous to the choice of number of bins, but their shape is usually less sensitive to this value. The following figure shows an example of a kernel density display for the population data. As with the other density examples in this section, we have log transformed the population variable.

The dot plot is another popular method for displaying a density, especially for small batches of data. It has been used frequently in medical studies, where it can be important to locate on a scale the exact value of certain points. The following plot shows a density for the population data. The dot plot is an ideal candidate for interactive graphics, where the user wants to be able to touch a dot and discover the case corresponding to that dot. In this figure, touching the dots at the rightmost end of the display would show China and India. Histograms, by contrast, cannot be used for this purpose because the bins may contain one or more cases located at different values inside a bin. The best one could do would be to display a list of values inside the bin. For similar reasons, dot plots are a preferred method for displaying outliers

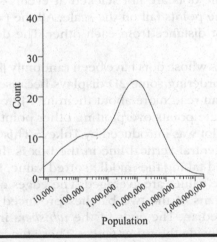

Figure 8.17

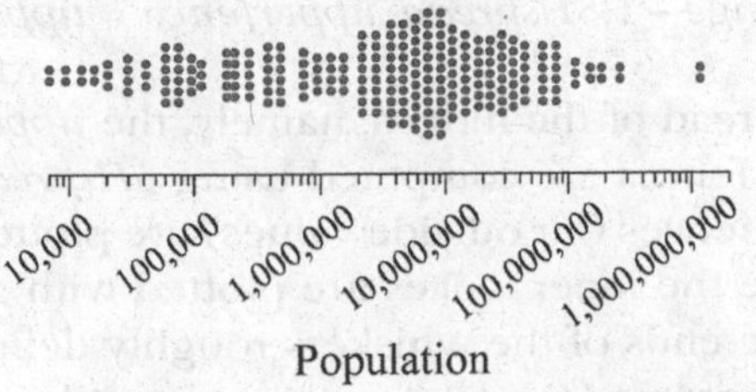

Figure 8.18

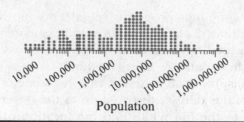

Population

Figure 8.19

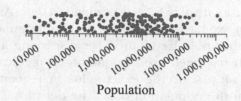

Population

Figure 8.20

because they are less likely to be swamped by other observations inside an extreme bin. Furthermore, bins containing only one extreme case in a larger batch of data would be so short as to be nearly invisible.

The following figure shows the histogram-shaped dot density plot. Although it resembles a histogram, the dots are not stacked at evenly-spaced intervals. Instead, they are located where the points fall on the scale. All the points in a given stack are within the width of a dot distance from each other. The details of this plot can be found in[16].

Jitter densities are plots whose dots have been randomly jittered instead of stacked. They can be useful for bordering some 2D displays because they take up little room in the canvas area. You can read more about them in[17]. Jittering can also be used on scatterplots to help alleviate points overplotting other points.

The box (schematic) plot was introduced by Tukey[2]. This plot is based on statistics called *letter values*. The central vertical line in the box is the *median*, computed by sorting a list of values and taking the middle sorted value. If the number of cases is even, then the two middle values are averaged. The edges of the box are the *hinges*, computed from the medians of the two batches produced when the sorted values are split at the overall median. The ends of the *whiskers* in the box plot extend to the most extreme values inside the *inner fences*. These fences are defined as follows:

lowerfence = lowerhinge − 1.5Hspread upperfence = upperhinge + 1.5Hspread,

where *Hspread* is the spread of the hinges, namely, the *upper hinge* minus the *lower hinge*. Finally, the outer fences are computed using 3*Hspread* in the same formulas. Values outside the outer fences (far outside values) are plotted with a small circle and remaining values outside the inner fences are plotted with asterisks. The sections of the box plot between the ends of the whiskers roughly delineate the quartiles of the data. Some box plot programs (e.g.,[18]) use these quartiles instead of Tukey's letter values.

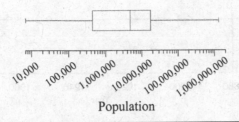

Population

Figure 8.21

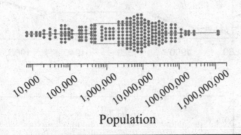

Population

Figure 8.22

Sometimes it can be useful to combine a dot and box plot, a graphic invented by Jerry Dallal. The following figure shows an example on the countries data. This plot can be useful for delineating the quartiles as well as the individual observations. If there are outliers in the box plot, the outlying dots will cover them.

Time Series

Time series data require specialized graphics. In most cases, time is represented on a horizontal axis and the data values are plotted on the vertical axis. Time itself may be coded as date-time values or the series might exist in a single column or row where the time values are assumed to be equally spaced.

The following figure illustrates four of the most popular time series displays. The top panel shows the traditional line graph, several centuries old. The data consist of number of patents issues by the US patent office in a five-decade interval. This type of graph effectively reveals trends, cycles, spikes, and outliers. Notice, for example, the plunge in patent approvals after the Great Depression. The second panel plots the annual points and fits them with a nonparametric loess smoother[19]. The advantage of this plot is to display simultaneously a plausible model and the raw data, similar to the plotting of a regression line on a scatterplot. The smoother does cover over the Great Depression dip, a consolation for investors who take a *very* long view.

The third panel plots the residuals from the loess fit. This type of plot makes an appropriate companion to any time series model because the non– homogeneity of the residuals is highlighted. It draws our eyes toward exceptions. The bottom panel simply substitutes an area element for the line element in the top plot. It does add contrast to the display and possibly makes it easier to detect various patterns in the time series.

The next figure emphasizes the fact that bar elements need not be uniformly distributed on an axis. Microsoft Excel and other graphics packages convey the message

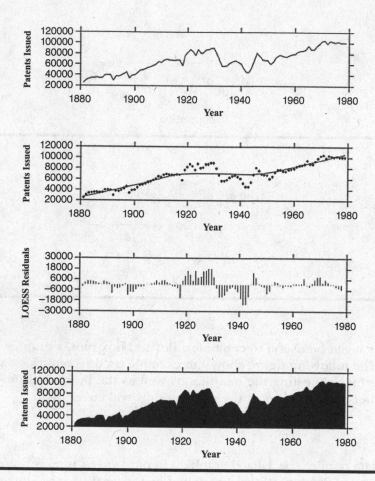

Figure 8.23

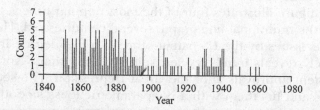

Figure 8.24

that bar charts are inherently categorical, but as[12] shows, this notion is an artifact of failing to separate the function of graphical elements and graphical scales. The data are based on dates of annual coal mining disasters[20,21]. We use the same narrow bars (spikes) that we used for the residuals plot above. This graphical template would be useful for plotting time series data that are even more unevenly spaced. This method would prevent the eye from interpreting the slopes of line segments in a line graph that vary simply because of the spacing.

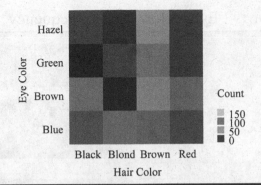

Figure 8.25

Two Categorical Variables

We saw that the simplest display for a one-way table of categories is a table of categories. The same goes for a two-way table. If frequencies for each category combination are available, then we can publish the frequencies inside each cell. A nice embellishment is to use a color or darkness scale to represent the frequencies. Here is a table of eye colors vs. hair colors. The data for this example are adapted from[22], who collected hair color and eye color reports from his class of statistics students. There are several excellent references on how to visualize tabular data[23,24].

The clustered bar chart is a popular alternative. It is suitable if each collection of bars across groups shows a coherent pattern and there are not too many bars in a cluster. Otherwise, this can be a cluttered display. If the total count in each cluster is primary and the counts within cluster elements is secondary, then a stacked bar chart that stacks the bars in each cluster may be preferred.

The following figure shows a clustered bar chart on the hair and eye color data.

If one wants to view the columns conditioned on the rows (or vice versa), then a table maps into a tree. The following display conditions eye color on hair color. For each hair color, it is easy to see the frequencies of each eye color associated with that

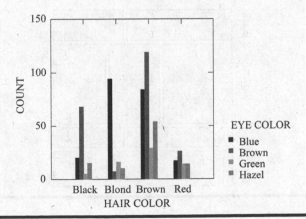

Figure 8.26

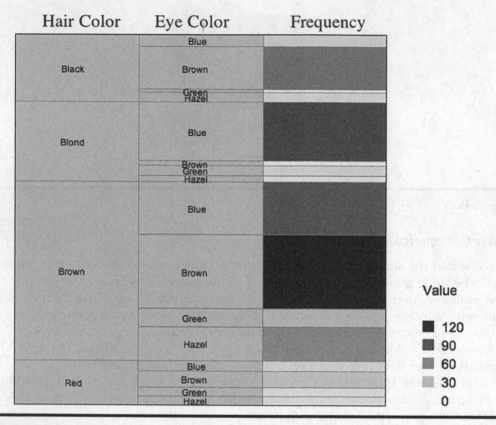

Figure 8.27

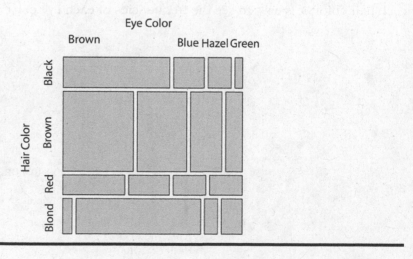

Figure 8.28

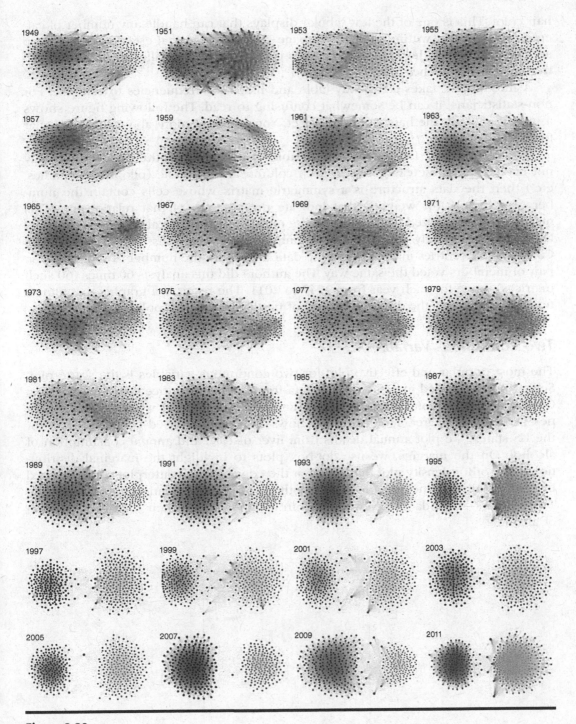

Figure 8.29

hair color. This is one of the few tabular displays that can handle any number of categorical variables (within the limits of page size or screen real estate. You just keep adding columns to the right and the cells get smaller and smaller as the horizontal tree structure branches out.

A mosaic plot takes a two-way table and maps the frequencies to cell size. For non-statisticians, it can be somewhat confusing to read. The following figure shows a mosaic plot for the hair and eye dataset. You can read more about this particular technical display in[25].

Suppose we have two categorical variables consisting of entities that may or may not be related. If the categories in each column are the same (people, companies, etc.) then the data structure is a symmetric matrix whose cells contain the number of instances (or weights) that indicate the strength of that relationship. This matrix can be analyzed with methods like multidimensional scaling (MDS) to reveal these relations clearly. The following example, from[26] concerns members of the US Congress. The entries in the cells of the data matrix are the number of times a given pair of members voted the same way. The authors did this analysis 60 times (60 such matrices), once for each year from 1949 to 2011. The result is a graphic that almost uniquely illustrates the dramatic history of partisanship in US politics.

Two Continuous Variables

The most popular and effective plot for two continuous variables is the scatterplot. Seeing points plotted in a continuous data frame helps us notice joint and marginal (separate) distributions of the variables. Embellishing the plot with marginal densities makes this clearer. The next plot shows an example based on health data for the US states. We plot annual deaths from liver disease and annual consumption of alcohol. On the margins, we use dot-box plots to highlight the marginal distributions. Any other density plot that can fit at the edges of the scatterplot could be used instead. Finally, we include a modal smoother[27] to indicate trend in the relationship. Two outliers—Nevada and New Hampshire—stand out for their high consumption of alcohol.

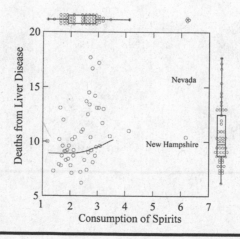

Figure 8.30

With large datasets, scatterplots become problematic. It can help to use hollow circles for plotting symbols to deal with overlap (as in the previous figure), but that approach has its limits. The following figure shows another approach. On the left is a conventional scatterplot of the results from a national survey on couples' relationships[28]. There were 3,035 respondents to the survey. It is difficult to see the internal structure of the joint density in its most concentrated region. The right panel shows an alternative. The points have been aggregated in hexagonal bins that together form a tiling of the entire frame[29]. Each bin is colored according to the number of points falling inside it. An amusing aspect of this display is that some respondents reported being in relationships that have lasted longer than their age. This plot is a "behold proof" of the necessity of using visualization to help clean data before doing formal modeling.

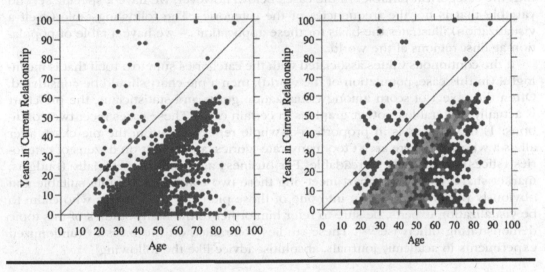

Figure 8.31

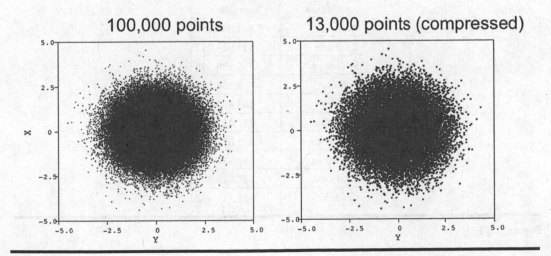

Figure 8.32

For extremely large datasets, other types of aggregation can be employed. The following figure illustrates an aggregation of 100,000 data points compared to the raw data in simple scatterplots. This aggregation was driven by a customized algorithm that resembles some varieties of cluster analysis[30]. Its virtue is that outliers, even singletons in huge datasets, are maintained in the aggregated display. Random sampling of the points would not necessarily reveal outliers in large datasets because of their relative infrequency.

One Categorical Variable and One Continuous Variable

There are several graphics suitable for this type of application. As in some of the previous graphics, there is often an implied second variable (frequencies) that accompanies the categorical variable. In the cases below, however, we have a specific second variable that is not the frequencies of the categories. The following table (itself a visualization) illustrates the basis for these applications – we have a table of population against regions of the world.

If the continuous values associated with the categories sum to a total that is meaningful (in this case, population of the world), then a pie chart should be considered. Often the object of scorn among visualization gurus and statisticians, the pie chart is actually preferable to other graphics in certain cases. These cases meet two conditions: 1) the interest is in proportion-of-whole rep- resentation; the pie chart, after all, is a whole. 2) There aren't too many cate- gories; a pie chart on dozens of categories (slices) is generally unreadable. For business applications especially (budgets, market share, etc.), a pie chart meet- ing these two conditions is quite suitable and obviously popular. If you run into one of those pie chart demonizers who claim to be visualization experts, be sure to refer him or her to the many studies of this topic demonstrating otherwise[31-36]. These studies contradict, on the basis of randomized experiments in academic journals, absolutist advice like the following[1]:

Region	Population
Asia	3,687,982,236
E Europe	119,914,717
W Europe	396,339,998
Baltics	7,184,974
N Africa	161,407,133
Sub Sahara	749,437,000
N America	331,672,307
S America	561,824,599
Near East	195,068,377
Oceania	33,131,662

Figure 8.33

"A table is nearly always better than a dumb pie chart; the only worse design than a pie chart is several of them, for then the viewer is asked to compare quantities located in spatial disarray both within and between charts [...] Given their low density and failure to order numbers along a visual dimension, pie charts should never be used."

Advice to visualization experts: never use the word never. And if you want to make pronouncements concerning the perception and cognition of graphics, learn how to do a randomized experiment and base your recommendations on evidence, not hand-waving.

So here, for better or worse, is a pie chart of the population data.

Violating the requirement that pie charts represent proportion-of-whole data is a good example of how to lie with visualization. Doing so may be encouraged when certain computer programs allow pie slices to represent averages or other statistics. The following example is from a local Fox news station broadcast[37].

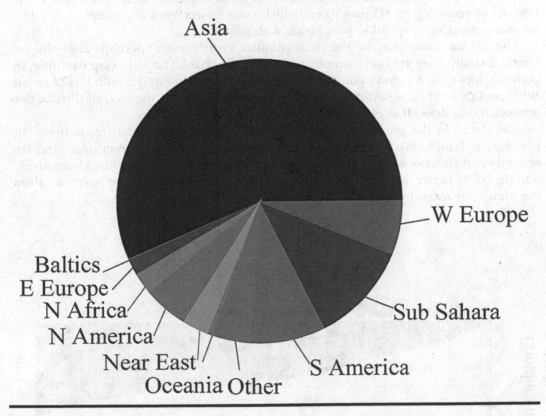

Figure 8.34

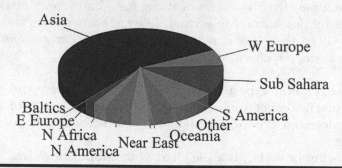

Figure 8.35

3D pie charts are even more reviled by "experts" despite their popularity with users, particularly in business. The evidence on their accuracy is somewhat mixed, however[38,39]. As long as the tilt is not severe, the errors in percep- tion of proportions are not likely to be large. Nevertheless, I would tend to avoid them since they are likely to perform somewhat worse than the standard two-dimensional pie chart. Instead of resorting to 3D pies to embellish your PowerPoint presentation, it might be more effective to sprinkle your slides with glitter.

The 2D bar chart may be the most popular visualization (perhaps after the pie chart). Usually, they are quite simple, with just a few bars. The following example, by contrast, has a bar for every country in the dataset — a huge graph with lots of detail. What makes it work is sorting by population, which reveals the overall distribution across all countries. It is clearly not uniform.

The detail in the graph stretches the limits of printed or video resolution. The best way to handle this problem is to split the chart or choose a larger page size. For several centuries, books have had foldout sections for graphics like this. Alternatively, and probably better, is to use interactive display tools like brushes or lenses to allow the viewer to zoom in to examine local regions of the graph.

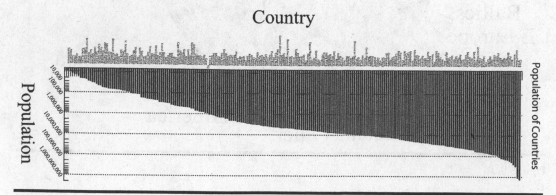

Figure 8.36

Three Variables

Statisticians tend to eschew 3D graphics of any kind. Many scientists and business people tend to use them when helpful. There are several contexts where 3D graphics make sense. The first is for mathematical functions. The following figure shows a 3D plot of the beta density function. The beta distribution has two parameters, but to render this in 3D we clamp them to the same values.

We could plot this function using contouring in 2D, but I would argue that most people would have more difficulty perceiving the overall shape of the function. Perhaps plotting the 3D surface and the contour plot together would achieve both goals. What is most remarkable about this plot, however, is how it shows the transition from arcsine distribution (the inverted U at the front) to a uniform distribution (in the middle) to an approximate normal distribution (the bell-shaped curve at the rear). Without such a visualization, it would be hard to imagine how such a transformation could smoothly occur.

The next figure contains a contour plot of literacy on top of the birth-death scatterplot. Literacy is mapped both to the symbol sizes and to the contour colors. Not surprisingly, the developed countries have a higher literacy rate. Using two aesthetics (size, color) to represent the same variable values is a helpful redundancy. We should not be afraid to do this because there is a long literature in psychology (beyond the scope of this chapter) that indicates redundant cues facilitate perception of patterns.

If we have three continuous variables that sum to a constant (1 for proportions, 100 for percents), we should consider making a ternary plot. This type of graph is

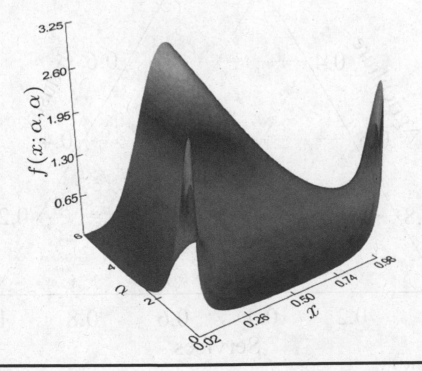

Figure 8.37

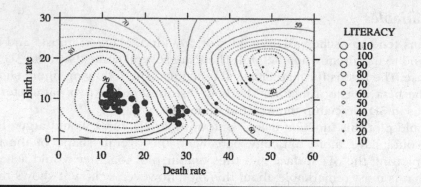

Figure 8.38

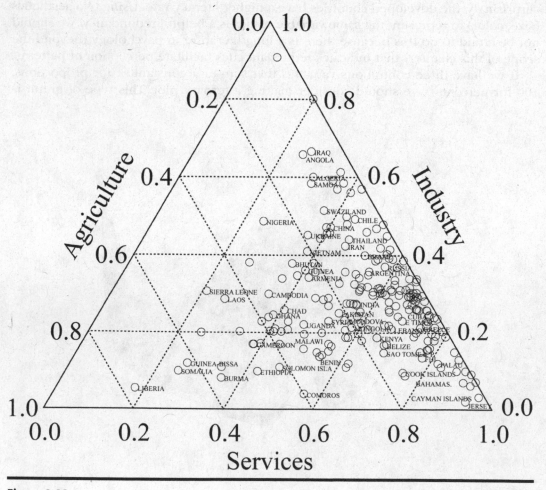

Figure 8.39

used widely in experimental design for quality control (e.g., three ingredients) and in some scientific fields (e.g., geology). The countries data do contain three such variables — the proportion of resources devoted to agriculture, industry, and services in each country. Constructing the plot involves some trigonometry, but reading it is mostly a matter of following the grid lines to each of the three axes. Liberia, for example, has a coordinate of (.769, .054, .177) on (Agriculture, Industry, Services), which places it in the lower left of the triangle. Cambodia comes close to having equal values on all three variables and is therefore near the center of the plot. Most countries concentrate on services, with lower values on agriculture and industry.

Many Variables

With many variables, we get into some rather complex visualizations. There is no satisfactory way to represent many variables in a single plot. We are sometimes forced to use several visual methods to portray the same data. And for those who like to interpret visualizations through story-telling, there are few comprehensible stories involving many variables. Nevertheless, this section introduces three of the best methods for approaching this goal.

Scatterplot Matrices

A popular display for visualizing pairwise relations in high-dimensional data is the scatterplot matrix (SPLOM). This plot consists of a collection of scatterplots arranged in the form of a symmetric or rectangular matrix. It will be symmetric if we wish to display plots of all pairs of variables. It will be rectangular if we wish to see only a subset of those pairs. On the diagonal or margins of SPLOMs we often add densities (e.g., histograms) of the variables.

The following figure shows a rather large SPLOM of a selection of the countries variables. This plot illustrates a common problem with almost every multivariate display—the exhaustion of real estate. In other words, with more than about 25 variables, we are unable to represent local features (single scatterplots in this case) in the usual display area. Furthermore, the SPLOM does not give us a good sense of the higher-dimensional structure of the points. It is, however, excellent at helping us to identify atypical distributions of points in the subframes. We see, for example, that Climate is mapped to only a few values and Phones is linearly related to GDP.

Parallel Coordinates

A popular multivariate display, especially among visualization researchers in computer-science, is called Parallel Coordinates. Despite its appearance, it is really a rather simple display. Plots of this form are more than 100 years old[40] and psychologists have long been familiar with profile plots to display test scores on inventories like the MMPI[41]. The display is simple because all we have to do is 1) draw a set of vertical parallel axes, one for each variable, 2) locate the values of a case on each of these axes, and 3) connect these locations with a single profile line. We do this for every case (row) in a dataset.

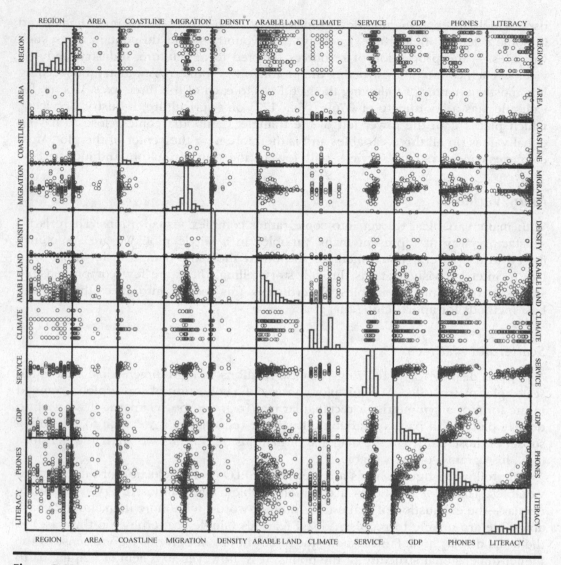

Figure 8.40

The person responsible for taking parallel coordinates to a different level, however, is Alfred Inselberg. As a mathematician, he recognized the implications of treating these displays as a coordinate system. (Coordinates are involved with locating points in space.) Inselberg's book on this topic is anything but simple[42]. It is the authoritative reference on this topic and worth reading if you can handle the math. For Inselberg, parallel coordinates are not a type of chart, but rather a foundation for exploring high-dimensional geometric objects.

One useful embellishment for parallel coordinates is to use cluster analysis to determine if there are any clusters in the data and, if so, highlighting the profiles in each cluster with a different color. A k-means cluster analysis of selected variables in the countries data indicates the possibility of two clusters. They are colored in the following figure.

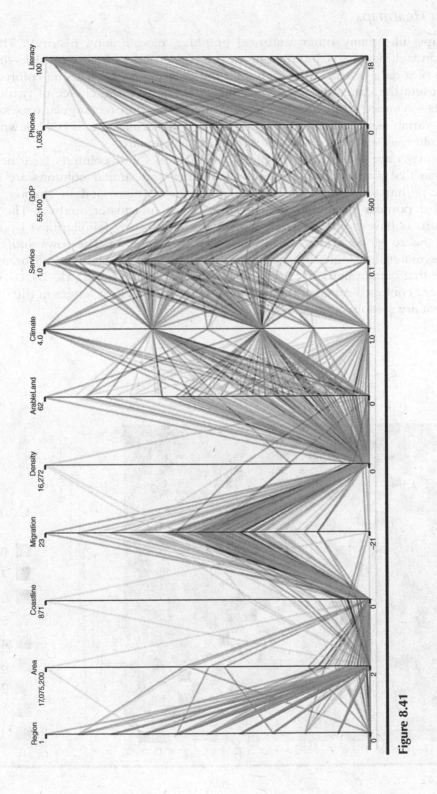

Figure 8.41

Cluster Heatmaps

Heatmaps, like many other statistical graphics, have a long history[43]. There are many kinds of heatmaps, but the one we are concerned with here involves the direct display of a data matrix. We simply plot the data matrix itself using colored pixels to represent the data values. As with SPLOMs, we have the choice of two types of matrices—symmetric (all variables against all variables) or rectangular (cases in rows against variables in columns). Imagine, if you will, shrinking a SPLOM down so that each scatterplot cell is nothing but a colored pixel square.

Heatmaps are most interpretable when the rows and columns have been permuted so that similar rows are near each other and similar columns are as well. Various permutation methods for this purpose are discussed in chapter 16 of[12]. The most popular permutation method is based on cluster analysis. The following figure is based on data from[44], involving confusions (similarities) by subjects among the 26 Morse codes for the letters of the alphabet. The rows and columns were permuted by single-linkage hierarchical cluster analysis. The red/orange cells indicate that certain pairs of letters, such as (J, P), (B, X), (Q, Z), (K, D), (G, O), and (C, Y), are confused relatively often. Also, there is a block of letters in the blue sections that are seldom confused.

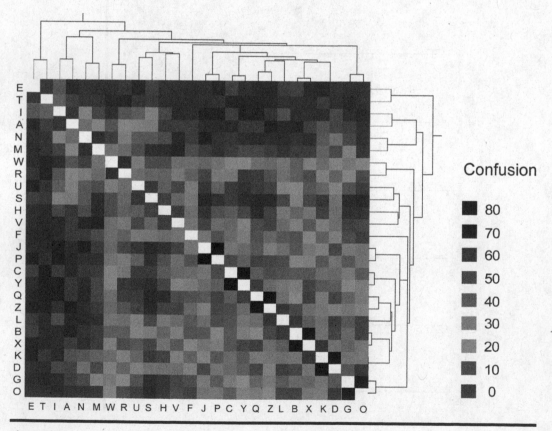

Figure 8.42

Trees

Trees are one of the most informative and useful graphic representations in all of visualization. They form the basis for a number of analytic models, such as cluster analysis and decision-tree methods. This section features a number of tree displays that are based on different underlying models. Sometimes trees that look similar visually can be based on radically different models.

Hierarchical Trees

Hierarchical clustering trees are perhaps the most popular of tree displays. Hierarchical clustering is a recursive joining or splitting class of algorithms that attempt to represent similarities or dissimilarities among variables or cases in a tree structure. In this model, objects (points or clusters of points) that are connected by short branches are similar to each other. The way to read the tree is to start at the leaves (on the left for

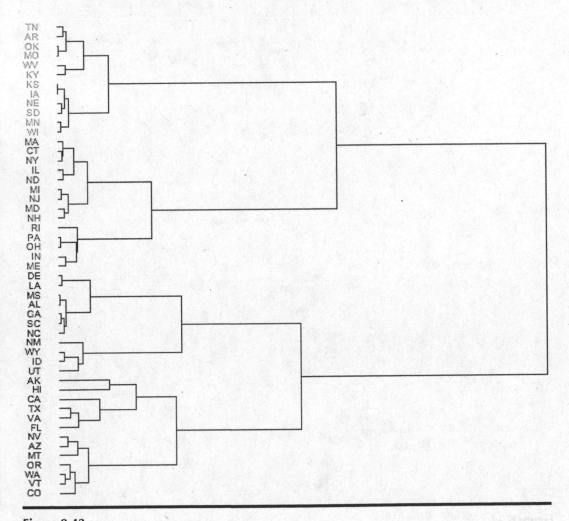

Figure 8.43

this horizontal tree). The modeled distance between two objects is represented by the highest (rightmost) node that contains both trees. Tennessee and Arkansas, for example, are closely related in this tree. Tennessee and South Dakota are less related. To see the distance between them, we have to look all the way up to the node that joins the (TN, AR, OK, MO, WV, KY) cluster to the (KS, IA, NE, SD, MN, WI) cluster.

It helps to represent significant clusters by coloring leaves by cluster IDs. The clusters are derived from the tree with a specific algorithm. Namely, we look for a relatively large branch from the parent node of the cluster to its grandparent node. In this case, we see three clusters, appropriately colored. Now, some clustering programs advise you to look for a single cutting distance (in this case, some vertical line) that can be used to separate clusters. By this method, one would expect four

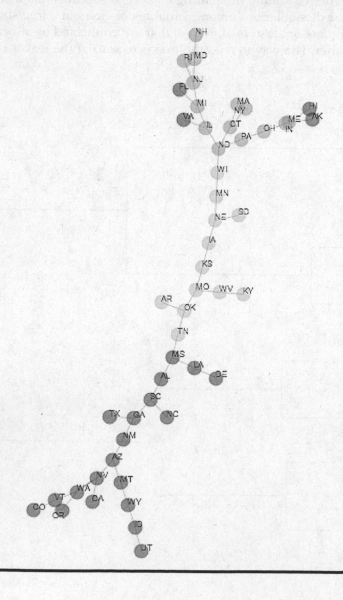

Figure 8.44

clusters that are derived by a cutting line somewhere in the middle of the tree. But the statistically more appropriate method used here says there are only three. That's because the bottom cluster (DE through CO) has a larger diameter (joining distance) than either of the other two. The joining distance algorithm used in most clustering programs is appropriate only if all the clusters have the same diameter.

Minimum Spanning Trees

The next figure shows an example of a different sort of tree called the minimum spanning tree. A spanning tree is an undirected geometric tree. Spanning trees have *n?*1 branches that define all distances between *n* nodes. A minimum spanning tree (MST) has the shortest total edge length of all possible spanning trees. This example has been computed on the same countries dataset as the hierarchical tree. There is a dualism between the hierarchical tree and this one. Cutting the MST at some branch (link) results in two subtrees that correspond to subtrees in the hierarchical tree diagram. In a perfect clustering, we would expect the colors in both trees to be distinct. Four states, however (FL, VA, HI, AK), are behaving differently from the others on these measures. Plotting both trees after a cluster analysis is a good rule of thumb for locating tight clustering solutions.

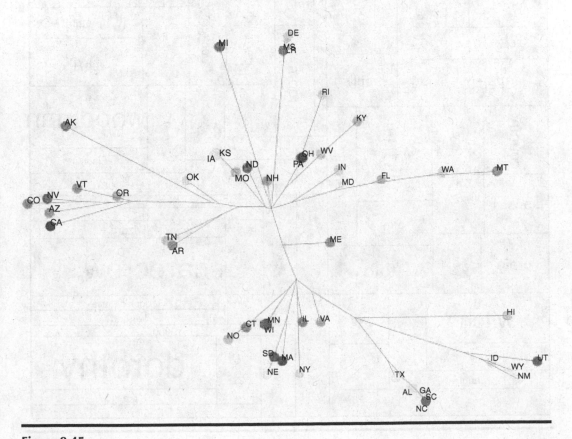

Figure 8.45

Additive Trees

Additive trees are useful for representing the distance between any two nodes as the length of the path (along branches) that join them. The layout is arbitrary because there is no common scale for the nodes as in the hierarchical tree. Instead, we observe the modeled distance between any two nodes by visually tracing the shortest path along the branches from one node to the other. The following figure shows an additive tree computed on the same countries data.

Treemaps

Treemaps are 2D graphics representing trees through nested rectangles. They originated as a way to display such things as a computer directory[45] and large analytic

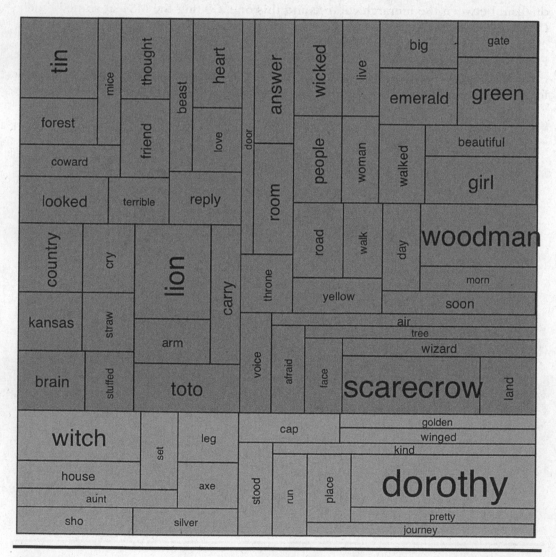

Figure 8.46

trees. The following figure shows a treemap from a hierarchical cluster analysis of "The Wizard of Oz." The two clusters colored in the treemap are located at the highest level of the tree. In the treemap algorithm, we next split each of these two with a vertical line boundary. Then we split the four resulting rectangles with horizontal boundaries. And so on.

This recursive splitting algorithm is similar to that used for decision trees constructed by recursive partitioning[46]. Consequently, the tree underlying the treemap is binary (each node has only two subnodes). When treemaps are used for representing other types of trees (with many nodes branching off a single node), there are several ad hoc algorithms for sizing the rectangles.

Martin Wattenberg's Map of the Market[47] is among the best examples of these alternate approaches.

Prediction Trees

The first prediction tree algorithm was called Automatic Interaction Detection (AID)[48]. Its purpose was to detect interactions (product terms) in a statistical model on data. For example, if we split by gender in a drug trial and find that males do better with higher dosages and females do better with lower dosages, there is an interaction between gender and outcome. The ingenious algorithm that Morgan and Sonquist invented was to do successive splits on predictor variables (like gender) such that the sub-populations after the splits improved the prediction of outcome on the dependent variable. The following figure shows the result of using this algorithm to predict the price of cars. Each successive split is summarized by the width of the branch joining the split node and its children. The leaf (final) nodes constitute the predictions. In the display used here, you can consider the observations (cars) as represented by marbles in each box. As you proceed down the tree, groups of marbles are separated by each split.

The algorithm does remarkably well in making predictions (especially when compared to regression or formula-based methods. In fact, the most effective prediction methods available today are built on this model. One is called Random Forests[49] and the other is called Gradient Boosted Trees (a form of Gradient Boosting Machines)[50].

Diagnosing

Before we get to visualizations in this section, let's take a look at the foundations of predictive modeling. First of all, we are restricting our scope to predictive modeling because there are other types of AI (e.g., pattern detection) that do not rest on these foundations. Predictive modeling, however, arguably comprises the majority of AI applications. In predictive modeling, we are given some criterion (credit risk, vulnerability to infection, product choice, voting, etc.) together with some potential predictors of this criterion (age, genetic markers, demographics, etc.). Our task in predictive modeling is to do two things:

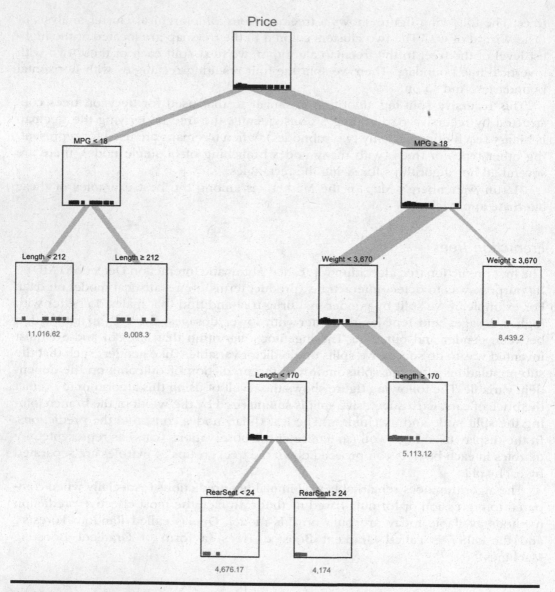

Figure 8.47

1. Given a set of values on our predictors, what do we expect is the most likely value (prediction) on our criterion?
2. How confident are we in that prediction?

In my experience with AI customer applications, there is considerably more attention given to 1) than to 2). Business people, bureaucrats, and scientists too often want a globally accurate prediction without consideration for confidence in individual predictions. Without explicit information on 2), however, I would argue that a solution to 1) is worthless. If this point of view is puzzling to you, I urge you to read[51].

We can measure the quality of a prediction in several ways. However, all of the widely-used measures of goodness of fit are global. That is, we say a model is "good" if the global aggregation of discrepancies between the predicted and observed values on our criterion is relatively small. AI computer programs (and classical statistical models) optimize the value of that chosen global fit over all the observed values.

But optimizing global fit does not insure that every given prediction is equally accurate (close to the observed value). Optimal models (in the goodness of fit sense) can make some bad (inaccurate) predictions along with good (accurate) ones. If every given prediction (within some established range) is relatively accurate, then the global goodness of fit is likely to be good, but that rarely happens in practice. So in modeling, we like global *and* local accuracy.

The discrepancies between the predicted and observed values on a criterion are called *residuals* in many AI and statistical models. (In some models, we denote discrepancies as *deviances*.) Plotting these discrepancies against the predicted values is the best summary of the performance of a model. The discrepancies can be either positive (the model is estimating values that are smaller than the observed values) or negative (the model estimates values larger than observed). If many more of these residuals are positive (or negative) in a given region of the predictor values, the model is *biased*. That is, it tends to over-predict or under-predict the observed values. As with accuracy, bias can be global or local. In either case, we don't like bias.

Summing up these considerations, we should always be looking for a model that is accurate and unbiased. We can't optimize both at the same time, but we can devise models that rest on a tradeoff between both. In any case, both measures are important aspects of modeling. Residual plots are the visualization method for evaluating both. With these ordinary-language definitions in hand, let's now look at some residual plots on real data. The next figure shows three different models predicting Literacy from GDP in the countries dataset.

The left two models are algebraic (linear and nonlinear). The linear model is of the form

$$y = c + bx.$$

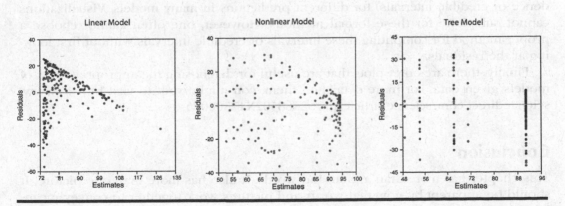

Figure 8.48

The nonlinear model is of the form

$$y = c \,/\, \Big\{ 1 + \exp\big(b(x-a)\big) \Big\}$$

The rightmost is based on a bootstrapped prediction tree. These fundamentally different prediction models are all elucidated by the same type of plot. That's because all of them compute predicted values and residuals. Looking in more detail, we see that the linear model (ordinary least squares regression) is a bad fit to the data. Even though the overall fit of the linear model is not much worse than that of the non-linear model (both have a similar spread in the residuals), the plots reveal that the distribution of the residuals for the linear model is anything but uniform over the estimated values. The nonlinear model residuals, while somewhat better behaved, are still not uniform across the estimated values. The prediction tree model has several noteworthy features. Unlike the algebraic models, there are only four bands of predicted (estimated) values. The first three have relatively comparable dispersion. The fourth prediction band (approximately 90 percent literacy) has less dispersion. Furthermore, it involves more skewness, which contributes to the bias of these predictions.

Why do we care about a relatively uniform and symmetric distribution of residuals across all the predicted values? Apart from the technical assumptions inherent in computing probabilistic inferences for ordinary least squares linear models (all the technical formulas statistics students hate), we care because those two conditions (uniformity and symmetry) allow us to trust our model's performance across a range of predicted values.

When a residual plot shows the two conditions are not well met, it can help us to understand where we should be careful in making predictions. The tree model happens to fit better than the other two. Its Proportional Reduction in Error (PRE) is .491, while the PRE (R^2) for the linear model is .263. If we choose the tree model, however, we have to qualify our predictions depending on where they fall in the overall distribution. We must understand that the tree-based predictions at the upper end of literacy are biased; they tend to overpredict literacy in that range. Worse, they are biased *and* skewed.

There are mathematical methods for computing the errors to be expected (confidence or credible intervals) for different predictions in many models. Visualizations cannot substitute for these formal methods. However, one often cannot choose a proper method for computing these intervals or credible intervals without first looking at the residuals.

Finally, there are other plots that are useful for diagnosing the appropriateness of models given data. For more details on them, you might want to visit https://www.sciencedirect.com/science/article/pii/S2468502X17300086.

Conclusion

This chapter has more than a thousand words. It also has more than one picture. It should be apparent by now that words and pictures work together to convey meanings that neither alone can convey. Most importantly, researchers and practitioners of machine learning and artificial intelligence need to understand the core issues in visualization and need to understand that technical visualizations are not simply pictures. Every technical visualization rests on an underlying mathematical model that must be articulated in order to comprehend its meaning. As such, visualization is not ancillary to AI. It is part of AI.

Notes

1 E. R. Tufte, *The Visual Display of Quantitative Information* (Cheshire CT: Graphics Press, 2016).
2 J. W. Tukey, *Exploratory Data Analysis* (Reading, MA: Addison-Wesley, 1977).
3 J. W. Tukey, "Comment on Emanuel Parzen [Nonparametric statistical data modeling]," *Journal of the American Statistical Association* 74 (1979): 121–122.
4 R. A. Becker and W. S. Cleveland, "Brushing Scatterplots," *Technometrics* 29 (1987): 127–142.
5 T. Allison and D. Cicchetti, "Sleep in Mammals: Ecological and Constitutional Correlates," *Science* 194 (1976): 732–734.
6 D. F. Swayne, D. Cook, and A. Buja, "XGobi: Interactive Dynamic Data Visualization in the X Window System," *Journal of Computational and Graphical Statistics* 7 (1998): 113–130.
7 P. F. Velleman, *Data Desk* (Ithaca, NY: Data Description Inc., 1998).
8 M. Bostock, V. Ogievetsky, and J. Heer, "D3 Data-Driven Documents," *IEEE Transactions on Visualization and Computer Graphics* 17 (2011), 2301–2309.
9 A. Satyanarayan, D. Moritz, K. Wongsuphasawat, and J. Heer, "Vega-Lite: A Grammar of Interactive Graphics," *IEEE Transactions on Visualization and Computer Graphics* 23 (2017): 341–350.
10 W. A. Malik, A. Unwin, and A. Gribov, "An Interactive Graphical System for Visualizing Data Quality–Tableplot Graphics," in *Classification as a Tool for Research. Studies in Classification, Data Analysis, and Knowledge Organization*, eds. H. Locarek-Junge, and C. Weihs (Berlin, Heidelberg: Springer, 2010).
11 J. R. Beniger and D. L. Robyn, "Quantitative Graphics in Statistics: A Brief History," *The American Statistician* 32 (1978): 1–11.
12 L. Wilkinson, *The Grammar of Graphics, 2nd Ed.* (New York: Springer-Verlag, 2005).
13 L. Micallef and P. Rodgers "eulerAPE: Drawing Area-Proportional 3-Venn Diagrams Using Ellipses," *PLOS ONE* 2014, https://journals.plos.org/plosone/articleid=10.1371/journal.pone.0101717.
14 L. Wilkinson, "Exact and Approximate Area-Proportional Circular Venn and Euler Diagrams," *IEEE Transactions on Visualization and Computer Graphics* 18 (2012): 321–331.
15 SYSTAT, *SYSTAT Version 13* (San Jose, CA: Systat Software, 2018).
16 L. Wilkinson, "Dot plots," *The American Statistician* 53 (1999): 276–281.
17 J. M. Chambers, W. S. Cleveland, B. Kleiner, P. A. and Tukey, *Graphical Methods for Data Analysis* (Monterey, CA: Wadsworth, 1983).
18 R Core Team, *R: A language and environment for statistical computing* (Vienna, Austria: R Foundation for Statistical Computing,Vienna, 2013), http://www.R-project.org/.
19 W. S. Cleveland, and S. Devlin, "Locally Weighted Regression: An Approach to Regression Analysis by Local Fitting," *Journal of the American Statistical Association* 83(403), September 1988: 596–610.
20 D. J. Hand, F. Daly, A. D. Lunn, K. J. McConway, and E. Ostrowski, *A Handbook of Small Data Sets* (London: Chapman and Hall, 1994).

21 R. G. Jarrett, "A Note on the Intervals Between Coal-Mining Disasters," *Biometrika* 66 (1979): 191–193.

22 R. D. Snee, "Graphical Display of Two-Way Contingency Tables," *The American Statistician* 28 (1974): 9–12.

23 A. Gelman, H. Wainer, W. M. Briggs, M. Friendly, E. Kwan, and G. Wills, "Why Tables Are Really Much Better Than Graphs [with Comments and Rejoinder]," *Journal of Computational and Graphical Statistics* 20 (2011): 3–40.

24 H. Wainer, "Understanding Graphs and Tables," *Educational Researcher* 21 (1992): 14–23.

25 M. Friendly, "Mosaic Displays for Multi-Way Contingency Tables," *Journal of the American Statistical Association* 89 (1994): 190–200.

26 C. Andris, D. Lee, M. J. Hamilton, M. Martino, C. E. Gunning, and J. A. Selden, "The Rise of Partisanship and Super-Cooperators in the U. S. House of Representatives," *PLOS ONE* 2015, https://doi.org/10.1371/journal.pone.0123507.

27 D. Scott, *Multivariate Density Estimation: Theory, Practice, and Visualization, 2nd Edition* (New York: John Wiley & Sons, 2015).

28 J. M. Chartrand, *National Sample Survey* (Unpublished raw data, 1997).

29 D. B. Carr, R. J. Littlefield, W. L. Nicholson, and J. S. Littlefield, "Scatterplot Matrix Techniques for Large N," *Journal of the American Statistical Association* 82 (1987): 424–436.

30 L. Wilkinson, "Visualizing Big Data Outliers Through Distributed Aggregation," *IEEE Transactions on Visualization and Computer Graphics* 24 (2017): 256–266.

31 J. G. Hollands, and I. Spence, "Judging Proportion with Graphs: The Summation Model," *Applied Cognitive Psychology* 12 (1998): 173–190.

32 S. Lewandowsky, and I. Spence, "The Perception of Statistical Graphs," *Sociological Methods and Research* 18 (1998): 200–242.

33 D. Simkin, and R. Hastie, "An Information-Processing Analysis of Graph Perception," *Journal of the American Statistical Association* 82 (1987): 454–465.

34 I. Spence, "Visual Psychophysics of Simple Graphical Elements," *Journal of Experimental Psychology: Human Perception and Performance* 16 (1990): 683–692.

35 I. Spence, "No Humble Pie: The Origins and Usage of a Statistical Chart," *Journal of Educational and Behavioral Statistics* 30 (2005): 353–368.

36 I. Spence and S. Lewandowsky, "Displaying Proportions and Percentages," *Applied Cognitive Psychology* 5 (1991): 61–77.

37 M. Bartosik, "Fox News Chart Fails Math," NBC, November 25, 2009, https://www.nbc-chicago.com/news/local/FOX-News-Chart-Fails-Math-73711092.html.

38 R. Kosara and D. Skau, "Judgment Error in Pie Chart Variations," Eurographics Conference on Visualization (EuroVis) 2016.

39 M. Schonlau and E. M. Peters, *Graph Comprehension: An Experiment in Displaying Data as Bar Charts, Pie Charts and Tables with and without the Gratuitous 3rd Dimension* (Santa Monica, CA: RAND Corporation, 2008), https://www.rand.org/pubs/working_papers/WR618.html.

40 M. Friendly, "The Golden Age of Statistical Graphics," *Statistical Science* 4 (2008): 502–535, https://arxiv.org/pdf/0906.3979.pdf.

41 J. R. Graham, *MMPI-2: Assessing Personality and Psychopathology 3rd Edition* (Oxford, UK: Oxford University Press, 1999).

42 A. Inselberg, *Parallel Coordinates: Visual Multidimensional Geometry and Its Applications* (New York: Springer-Verlag, 2009).

43 L. Wilkinson and M. Friendly, "The History of the Cluster Heat Map," *The American Statistician* 63 (2009): 179–184.

44 E. Z. Rothkopf, "A Measure of Stimulus Similarity and Errors in Some Paired Associate Learning Tasks," *Journal of Experimental Psychology* 53 (1957): 94–101.

45 B. Shneiderman, "Tree Visualization with Tree-Maps: 2-d Space-Filling Approach," *ACM Transactions on Graphics* 11, 92.

46 L. Breiman, J. H. Friedman, R. A. Olshen, and C. J. Stone, *Classification and Regression Trees* (Belmont, CA: Wadsworth, 1984).

47 M. Wattenberg, "Map of the Market," 1998, retrieved September 26, 2021, http://www.bewitched.com/marketmap.html.

48 J. Morgan and J. Sonquist, "Problems in the Analysis of Survey Data and a Proposal," *Journal of the American Statistical Association* 58 (1963): 415–434.

49 L. Breiman, "Random Forests," *Machine Learning* 45 (2001): 5–32.

50 J. Friedman, "Greedy Function Approximation: A Gradient Boosting Machine," *The Annals of Statistics* 29 (1999): 1189–1232.

51 C. O'Neill, *Weapons of Math Destruction: How Big Data Increases Inequality and Threatens Democracy* (New York: Crown Publishing, 2016).

Chapter 9

Solution Architectures

Edward Dixon
UCSF Center for Digital Health Innovation

Contents

DOI: 10.4324/9781351032940-9

Introduction

How does AI fit into the wider application or solution? How do we handle the computational demands? We introduce a simple classification scheme for AI architectures. By the end of this chapter you should have a good intuition of which architecture best matches the needs of your own business problems. You'll also have a deeper understanding of the best practices around developing and maintaining AI-based products, and be aware of the common pitfalls around spinning up a new AI product development team. For the purposes of this chapter, we will treat "machine learning" as a synonym for artificial intelligence, because of the dominance of this form of AI workload.

AI Inference Architecture Taxonomy

Data centers are an attractive default home for software—load aggregation maximizes capital utilization; centralization simplifies maintenance and upgrades—but deciding where to place AI workloads requires us to consider other factors:

Latency

Many traditional workloads have extremely undemanding latency requirements, such as batch processing of server logs, but AI makes it easier to build applications that interact with the physical world, where delayed results can have consequences that are a little more serious than a spinning hourglass. It's hard to think of a scenario where we wouldn't want a model that controls actual moving hardware to be as close as physically possible to the motors or actuators—"AI at the edge." Simple proximity though may not be enough:

- Inference times can vary on general-purpose hardware, especially if it also runs something other than a special-purpose real-time operating system
- Ultra-low latency (single-digit milliseconds or lower) can require the use of hardware accelerators such as FPGAs. This hardware in turn can impose its own restrictions in terms of the type and complexity of models that are supported.

Latency requirements may be less clear-cut in, say, a retail setting, where a model might be interacting with a customer or trying to target offers to specific demographics. It's a good idea to come up with a 'latency budget' to spend on the various components, and to validate the 'latency cost' assigned to network traffic between the store and the data center.

For web applications, latency has long been a concern, with website loading times receiving special attention. A famous (in-certain-circles) study at Google showed that changes in load times of as little as 100ms measurably reduced user traffic[1]. The solution has been to create content delivery networks, placing bandwidth-heavy content as close to every user as possible through purpose-built infrastructure, managed by specialized providers like CloudFlare[2]. Originally used for static content such as images, content delivery networks have evolved to include code that executes "serverlessly," allowing web applications to have "server" components that are deployed in a way that makes few demands of the application developer (no need to rent a particular server or VM, or even to create a container). It seems safe to predict the imminent appearance of services designed to move inference transparently to servers/accelerators close to users, keeping latency low, while maintaining the advantages of cloud-based deployments.

At the other end of the latency spectrum, you may have inference needs that are "important, but not urgent." For example, some teams have large datasets that they reanalyze in their entirety as better-trained models become available (perhaps your intellectual property team use NLP to look for prior art that might invalidate competitor's patents, scanning, and re-scanning all extent patents?). Since completing the work is not urgent and the work itself is intermittent, such a team might take advantage of spot pricing—a special low-cost pricing tier offered by cloud service providers, in which cloud compute instances are rented for as little as 1/7th the normal price (!). The catch? Instances can be taken back at any time, so whatever software is executed on these nodes needs an extremely resilient design. Multiple startups are working on software infrastructure to make this ultra-cheap cloud compute more accessible. Sufficiently large organizations may be able to exploit the internal equivalent of spot instances—underutilized servers. For example, as Facebook users in a particular region fall asleep, the servers that had been providing their news feeds switch to training machine-learning models, returning to their usual workload as the locals awaken.

Bandwidth

AI allows us to work with more complex, "natural" signals. Moving sales data back to a central data center for additional processing doesn't use much bandwidth, but what about processing video feeds from store cameras? Even locations with excellent high-reliability, fixed-line connectivity, may struggle to pass HD feeds from the dozen or more cameras of a small high-automation store, let alone the hundreds or thousands of feeds from a large one. The bandwidth requirements of your application may easily be the factor that determines where the computation needs to happen[3].

The ideal home for a machine-learning application, from a load-maximization perspective, is of course the data centers, where load aggregation will help you maximize capital utilization. If you are analyzing your brand's "mentions" on social media, or routing customer service tickets, "in the data centers" is an easy answer. However, as we've seen, product requirements around latency and availability will often rule this out. If your application helps farmers spot-treat weeds, then you probably don't want to bet on flawless connectivity right to the margins of every field, and edge-based compute is the only plausible option. For other applications, the answer may be more difficult; data centers are an attractive default home for software—load aggregation and centralization that simplifies maintenance and upgrades—but user expectations for latency and the limitations of connectivity will tip the scales toward Edge compute for applications that interact with the physical world.

Legal, Policy, and Security Constraints

Where data are allowed to be, even absent GDPR, will place additional constraints on location for many. Bringing the compute to the data is a simple solution, but it may not suit every service. Consider a machine-learning service that does inference on medical records. The customer may be unable to move records off their own data center for processing, but perhaps the service providers need to keep the application in their own cloud (to secure IP, or due to special hardware requirements). Technologies discussed in Chapter 10 (neural encryption, homomorphic encryption, multi-party computation) may need to be considered. Each of these has important limitations, but the research frontier is expanding rapidly in each case (multi-party computation is now very close to matching the accuracy of unencrypted inference, and has performance costs that are likely to be bearable for many real-world applications). The promise of these technologies is that they show ways to keep our data private *and* share it too (for example, to offload computation to a remote service without either the input or the output being intelligible to a third party, or to allow a machine-learning model to be trained on private data without leaking the particularities of that data). While existing implementations tend to have limitations in terms of performance (sometimes a performance penalty of several orders of magnitude), the pace of improvement is such that a transition from "mostly science" to "plain old engineering" seems imminent.

Popular Design Patterns for Deploying AI

Model as a Service

The pages of our planet's history are laid down as a sort of rocky layer cake; software design has been similarly layered, with application developers enjoying ever-greater insulation from the hardware. The latest manifestation is "serverless" code execution, as offered by all the main cloud service providers, whereby events such as requests to a URL trigger execution of a function. The neat thing from the perspective of the programmer is that they didn't have to configure a server, a VM or even a container. If demand is high, their cloud service provider will 'magically' spin up as many clones of the function as necessary; if low, then they'll pay very little (not having had to rent even a virtual server). This design pattern has been very popular, with the main cloud service providers offering their own versions, and lots of open-source projects spinning up to offer private cloud / hybrid cloud variations. If you think of a model as essentially an unusually large, compute-intensive function, then the design pattern looks like an obvious match (the more so since most models today don't have "side-effects" —the output of a given call is completely determined by the input).

Google, which has been a very early adopter of machine learning, and a company that applies it to an incredibly diverse array of problems (correcting misspelled search terms, choosing ads to match search queries, machine translation, image search, data center cooling optimization), made the decision to build software infrastructure to make it easier to deploy new models. The open-source version is called TensorFlow Serving. Unlike TensorFlow itself, this application has nothing to do with model training. Instead, it allows models to be deployed into a cluster to serve predictions via gRPC. One powerful feature is model versioning which enables "canary testing," a DevOps practice of allowing a new software release to handle only a small fraction of traffic at first, in case production usage differs in some important way from the test environment.

Google has also created a second open-source project called KubeFlow, which uses both TensorFlow and TensorFlow Serving as components.

> Kubeflow started as an open sourcing of the way Google ran TensorFlow internally, based on a pipeline called TensorFlow Extended. It began as just a simpler way to run TensorFlow jobs on Kubernetes, but has since expanded to be a multi-architecture, multi-cloud framework for running entire machine learning pipeline"
>
> ——KubeFlow Documentation

KubeFlow embodies the best practices for developing machine-learning products which have evolved within Google over many years. The idea is to remove the "deployment friction" that still bedevils many teams. With traditional approaches, teams tended to choose between approaches that prioritized ease of experimentation (Data Scientists trying inventive new approaches with great exploration tools like Jupyter Notebooks) *or* ease of deployment (pick one approach, hardwire it deep into the application, update very rarely). Effectively, teams had to choose the lesser evil, either slow, expensive, and error-prone integration of Data Scientist's latest invention, *or* products gently sliding into obsolescence. Instead, using KubeFlow Fairing, Data Scientists or machine-learning engineers can turn chunks of code (like a Jupyter Notebook, or maybe a Python file) into a docker image, allowing an easy path to either scaled-up training *or* deploying the trained model to server predictions.

The platform also facilitates converting the multiple steps involved in the typical machine-learning application into units called "pipelines," designed to enable easy re-use. For example, raw input data of different types might be processed by different models with their outputs, then used as inputs to another model. A pipeline for training might include model evaluation steps, very much like continuous integration in a conventional software project.

A key design goal is framework agnosticism, and so it supports training and inference with many different machine-learning libraries (TensorFlow, Chainer, PyTorch, MXNet) and inference with Seldon Core (Seldon Core, which supports any containerized ML framework, has as one component Intel's OpenVINO). With Seldon, KubeFlow gains the ability to perform sophisticated monitoring of machine-learning models in production, using other machine-learning techniques to check for unexpected errors, or to route traffic toward a better-performing model.

Summarizing, KubeFlow is the prototypical modern framework for "model as a service":

- Pipelines make for a modular approach, which facilitates easy re-use and allows very complicated services to be constructed quickly from simpler ones without re-work
- A sophisticated service guides experimenters through model selection (between a 6X and 70X speedup over a more naive approach typical of other services[4])
- It facilitates a hybrid approach, allowing the user to mix public and private clouds.
- It supports a heterogenous hardware environment:
  - CPUs (Intel users will experience significant performance lifts from OpenVINO)
  - GPUs
  - FPGAs (OpenVINO again)
- Sophisticated monitoring (Seldon Core) of model accuracy in production use

All major cloud service providers and many specialized new entrants are offering their own variations on "model as a service." Each provider seeks to create "stickiness" and protect their margins with custom frameworks and special features (Microsoft Azure, for instance, allows the creation of sophisticated machine-learning pipelines a drag-and-drop no-coding-required, interface), and increasingly these frameworks are backed by custom hardware such as Google's first-to-market TPUs, the AWS Inferentia chip, Microsoft's FPGA-based inference acceleration, that complicate comparisons. A possible equilibrium for users who worry about lock-in and longer-term support in such a fast-changing industry is to settle on a popular open-source framework like KubeFlow, that is sufficiently flexible to incorporate new frameworks and hardware as they become available. All this without forcing a move away from whatever has already been built.

Micro Service Architectures

A traditional application is a monolith, a single artifact (though it may "contain multitudes" within a single archive or JAR file). A tremendous success as a design pattern, its limitations have been gradually exposed as engineers attempt to serve customers at unprecedented scales. Modularity or encapsulation is the design principle that made endangered species of the global variable and the GOTO statement, and in doing so, enabled the code reuse that is now fundamental to software development.

Unfortunately, newer and 'better' tools give each new generation of programmers more invidious ways to violate encapsulation—violations that are only discovered when one attempts to re-purpose or replace some interesting component of a monolith. Without the discipline imposed by a truly independent existence, these design sins are hard to avoid. The penalties for such transgressions are large—valuable components must be refactored or re-use forgone.

The microservice design pattern takes reuse and scalability as primary virtues, and protects programmers from moments of weakness, much as object-oriented languages have done—by making it easier to preserve encapsulation than to destroy it. Instead of shipping as a single (perhaps very large) unit, an application is decomposed into a set of services, each with a public well-defined interface that constitutes a kind of contract with its users, promising them that, whatever might change internally, they can expect the same service on each "visit." The benefits to reuse should be obvious—each service, being independent, stands ready to be re-used at any time for some new application.

As well as allowing re-use, this pattern can make scaling a system to handle more traffic much easier as one simply instantiates more instances of whatever service is under pressure (rather than duplicating an entire application). If the interface has been well thought through, it also makes it easier to support an inevitable (long may it remain so!) fact of machine-learning life: there will very soon be a new and better model to be deployed. With proper support for versioning, microservices can make this easier, allowing each component to be updated at an appropriate frequency.

Perhaps even more important from a machine-learning perspective, is that this design choice also decouples the selection of languages and framework (so long as that interface/contract is preserved, "users" invoking the service are unaffected by minor details such as which language we wrote the service in, or whether we preferred PyTorch to TensorFlow). Software frameworks have had short half-lives in the past, but this seems to be even truer of machine-learning frameworks: with the microservice design pattern, your team doesn't have to commit to a single framework for all time.

This design pattern won't suit every application as communication can become a bottleneck, and teams sometimes get the level of granularity wrong. Not everything needs to be an independent service.

Lab vs. Production

Much of what we hear about machine-learning comes from computer scientists rather than software engineers; even when an article or a video comes from Google or Facebook, it typically comes from a research lab. These bear roughly the same relationship to production systems as a chemistry lab does to a pharmaceutical production line; the machine-learning lab is (and should be!) all about speed of experimentation, with almost all compute cycles spent on training new models and the barest minimum required for statistical validity expended on inference. This is exactly the opposite of production use, where almost all compute cycles will be spent on inference[5]. There are other differences too—hardware demand in the lab tends to be "all or nothing"—periods of high demand during training, with lulls while results are analyzed, while production use may be predictable days in advance to within a few percent. For these and other reasons, we will now explore the right software and hardware mix, for production use is quite different to what is required in the lab.

On Debt

Traditional software development has provided many practices to prevent the accumulation of 'technical debt'. For those unfamiliar with the concept, technical debt is an insidious burden that accumulates quietly when software developers make decisions that increase the amount of work they'll need to do in the future. For example, a useful piece of code might be copied and pasted to different places as it is needed—apparently saving time versus making it into a little library ("I just need it in this one other place"). Later, an engineer fixing a bug in *one* copy of the code will have to apply the same fix in many places (or, more likely, not know the copies exist. It will now take much longer to detect and fix all copies of the bug than it would have taken to do it correctly the first time. Extreme cases—a poor software architecture—can lead to 'technical bankruptcy' (when the cheapest option is to scrap an application and re-implement it—this happens!). "The road to perdition is broad and straight," but decades of collective experience have established best practices (modularization, automated testing, code reviews) that should minimize technical debt.

However, the design and operation of machine-learning-based systems creates new opportunities to accumulate 'technical debt' in ways that traditional measures won't prevent.

Data Dependency

A good example is 'data dependency'. In traditional software, we take strict measures to minimize the interdependence of code modules, using design principles like encapsulation. The idea is that the user of a code module should only need to know what data to supply and in what format to expect the results—the actual operations of the module are and should be a black box, and internal changes should not affect the calling module. If the reverse were true, then a single change inside a popular model or function could have widespread (and likely negative) effects.

This design principle is effective for traditional software, which operates in simple ways on structured data (if the data format or schema changes, versioning prevents catastrophe). However, when a machine-learning model is trained on a particular dataset, it comes to learn something much less visible—the statistical regularities or 'distribution' of the data. A good example is described in Chapter 5 of 'Online Harassment' (Springer, 2018):

> Google worked with the WikiMedia foundation[6] on a project designed to foster a less hostile working environment for wiki editors. A substantial dataset of posts from editors (more than 100,000) was collected and labeled by human workers (example labels included 'attacking', for posters using rather profane *ad hominem* arguments). The resulting dataset was used to train a machine-learning model that agreed very closely with the human consensus for each post (even trained humans don't always agree, so Google paid 10 people to review each post, and the model proved better at approximating the collective judgement than a baseline of a 3-human consensus). What may sound like online harassment—at least in terms of detection—was now a solved problem. However, when a model trained on the WikiMedia dataset was evaluated on a new dataset—posts from a Reddit forum for sports fans—the false positive rate was extremely high. What went wrong? The *schema* didn't change as, In both cases, the model was just being fed a short English-language paragraph, but the *distribution* was too different. Well, Wiki editors are bookish folk, and sound like

it, so swear words are a reliable signal of extreme exasperation, but sports fans use 'fucking' just to warn that a noun is on the way.

Another example comes from the experience of highly skilled engineers developing a machine vision-based system for industrial automation at a facility in northern Europe. After their new unit passed extensive (TÜV approved) testing, it was deployed to a factory in Spain whose well-designed building made excellent use of natural light. Almost immediately, the team learned that their machine—tested under fluorescent lights in a gloomier climate—had problems with bright sunlight gleaming on metallic surfaces.

In both cases, the 'debt' comes in a most insidious form that would leave no trace in conventional bounds, either checking or logging. Instead, these systems have a *data dependency*: they depend on new data being 'sufficiently similar' to their training data. Even more insidiously, data distributions can also change *over time* (perhaps your sales prediction system only trained on data from March to October, and is going to work brilliantly... right up to Black Friday).

To mitigate the data dependency risk:

■ "Downstream" models must be re-tested when an upstream module (code or model) changes.
■ In production use, "domain drift" models can be trained to check for differences between inputs seen in production versus the training and test sets.

Data Management

Datasets, especially cleaned and labeled datasets, are just as essential as tooling on a conventional production line, and may represent a substantial investment (it will have cost you something to collect, prepare and label). Astonishing as it might sound, in the absence of established processes, datasets are likely to be stored in a haphazard fashion, without any documentation, versioning or backups. Apart from the risk of losing valuable company assets, an unstructured approach may make it difficult or even impossible to compare competing approaches to your business problem. Datasets, especially the benchmark datasets used to measure quality, should be organized, and stored with the same care your team takes with source code.

This means that datasets, like code branches, need names, version numbers, and documentation. As your teams iterate, they are likely to collect data from different sources, try different labeling strategies or data cleaning strategies. Knowing where data came from—having "data provenance" —will be helpful later:

■ Data is what shapes your models into something useful; if you don't track the exact data that was used to train a given model, you won't be able to re-train it when the time comes. This will put you in roughly the same position as a software team who've lost the source code required to build the next version of their binary.
■ Bugs in production can sometimes be traced back to specific (flawed) training examples. If a given version of a particular model makes a mistake, your team needs a system that captures data provenance to detect mislabeled samples.

- Regulatory bodies may soon require you to justify decisions made by your model by enabling machine-learning audits.

Fortunately, you don't have to reinvent the wheel: instead, consider using products from companies like Pachyderm and Valohai that make good data management the path of least resistance.

Recruitment and Debt

Companies that are just getting started with machine learning are uniquely vulnerable to acquiring technical debt as they hire the people intended to establish culture and good practice within their machine-learning unit. For instance, you may be recruiting scientists with strong backgrounds in mathematics and modeling, but no experience of *commercial* software development. Such people are often expert in writing software at a particular scale—programs on the order of thousands of lines, written to a very particular standard (the Minimum Viable Prototype or 'just good enough to get the data for the next academic paper') and have no experience in designing large-scale software, or in engineering for testability and reliability (of course, the ideal candidate would be an expert software engineer *and* an experienced machine-learning researcher!). Recognizing the reality that such persons are almost non-existent, strong consideration should be given to having a newly hired researcher pair-program with an experienced software engineer: this should help to avoid expensive design defects *and* build new strengths in both individuals.

Recruiting for skills not currently present in your organization is inevitably risky—how well can you really evaluate candidate's skills? You may want to consider using an established consultancy firm to build the first version of your new machine-learning project. Of course, for the longer term, you'll want to build your own internal team as you seek to turn machine learning into a competitive edge for your company, but this may be a lower-risk way to get a good baseline system up and running.

Beyond the obvious technical skills, a most desirable quality in your Data Scientists or machine-learning engineers is a ruthless empiricism (common to strong Kaggle competitors!). In such a fast-changing field, you need to be prepared to abandon tools that have served you well and make the intellectual investment to understand new techniques. In traditional software, popular languages and frameworks might remain competitive for a half-decade, but this is most certainly not true of machine learning. A pragmatic "we'll use what works" attitude will help your team make the hard decision when their favorite model starts to slide into obsolescence. The contrasting "not invented here" culture will, over time, allow your competitors to open an insurmountable lead.

Some Design Considerations for the Production Use of Machine Learning

A research team might be expected to spend nearly all their computing power on training and to focus the software infrastructure they build on automating aspects of their research. Engineering teams who like a sound night's sleep, worry much more about achieving a high degree of automation in the testing and deployment of newly-trained models. They are concerned about the capacity of their systems to scale, to meet sudden changes in demand ("how will you scale this?" is a key question that Googlers ask of new projects). Architects will worry about how well their design will cope with the ultimate test of any architecture: how gracefully it will accommodate tomorrow's feature requests. Product owners will want to meet service level agreement metrics—latency, uptime? —while also keeping the cost of inference as low as possible. This chapter should help your enterprise make choices that allow success on all these dimensions.

The Machine-Learning Lifecycle

Making the training and deployment of the machine-learning models at the heart of your solution into a reliable and repeatable process requires software and workflows that go far beyond what is required to build an impressive demo—the difference between bolting a prototype together on a bench and running an assembly line.

Featurization

Before models can train or serve predictions, data usually needs to be transformed in some way—for example, breaking textual input up into words, a process called *featurization*—forms that make the data easier for a model to learn from. Despite the image of Data Scientists as wizards weaving new algorithms, "feature engineering"— experimenting with different approaches to preparing data *before* it is introduced to a model—is often their most valuable contribution.

Unfortunately, this step is also a notorious pain point when moving a successful model to production: it is quite common to have a Data Scientist code up their featurization step in Python or R, and for an engineering team to then re-implement this in a more performant language (Java? Go? C++?). This approach has drawbacks beyond the cost of writing (functionally equivalent) code twice:

- Ensuring that both implementations do *the same* thing to the data can be quite difficult, making the re-implementation surprisingly time-consuming, the more so since prototype code is unlikely to have good unit test coverage.
- Mistakes not caught during development will lead to "drift": model performance during production will be worse than claimed by the test statistics produced during training. These errors may be very insidious.
- This ad-hoc approach doesn't lend itself to re-use. Code that does a good job of featurizing a particular data source is valuable, but wrapping it up as an easy-to-reuse module makes it much more so, because it greatly lowers the cost of experimenting on a particular data type, increasing the chances that your team will be able to build new applications upon it.

Your team needs to commit to a method of doing featurization that:

- Doesn't require re-implementation (saving a lot of bug fixes)
- Makes featurization a discrete and re-usable component

- Supports versioning (so that your Data Scientists are free to keep innovating on featurization, without fear of breaking already-trained models in production).

Composition and Reuse

Another difference between demos or prototypes and the production use of machine learning is that, when used in products by experienced teams, machine-learning models become 'just' another type of software module. Just as traditional applications are unlikely to involve passing data through only a single step, machine-learning solutions involve passing data through at least two steps—data featurization and either inference or training. They can, however, be much more involved, with multiple models acting on a particular input, either sequentially or in parallel. Let's take an imaginary facial analysis service as an example:

- An incoming image would first pass through a featurization step (for an image, this often involves resizing it to a standard size and normalizing the brightness of the pixels).
- The "featurized" image could then be fed to a model trained to locate faces in the image
- Each face might then pass through *another* featurization step (for example, standardizing size)
- Faces could then be fed through a "face identification" model which turns each face into a numerical vector that can be checked against a database of known faces (another step, and one that involves more traditional code).
- Faces could also be fed (in parallel?) through an "attributes" model to obtain a high-level description (Male/Female? Approximate age? Smiling? Eyes open or closed? Pose?).
- A text generating model could then use the output of the face identification and attributes models to generate descriptions of the people in the photo ("A red-haired lady is frowning at an older man").

Considering this service, we can see elements that are highly likely to be subject to further experiment—a better face-finding model, say, *should* improve the whole service. However, it could also lead to challenges for downstream models, for example, by finding smaller faces or ones with more extreme poses—a kind of hidden dependency (perhaps the face identification model has only ever trained on faces that were straight-on to the camera, but a more effective face finder now catches even faces at very oblique angles). Detecting such dependencies can't rely solely on human diligence: really good test automation is vital to finding these issues and should be triggered by new versions of upstream components.

This example also makes it easy to see the value of a schema capable of describing the whole pipeline, so that exciting new variations demoed by Data Scientists can easily be replicated, further tested, and moved to production by machine-learning engineers.

Looking at our example from a product perspective, it is easy to imagine taking elements of this service and using them to create something quite new, without even re-training a single model: we could combine the face finder and face attribute models to build a photo booth that automatically takes shots *only* when users are present and smiling, or develop a car safety product to detect drivers falling asleep.

Facilitating just this type of re-use is the motivation behind the launch of "model zoos" by various organizations—offering not just source code or data files defining models, but also the machine-learning equivalent of software binaries: pre-trained models which will often have been trained on very large and challenging datasets, perhaps for an extended period.

Also targeting re-use, but at a different level of granularity, is the popularity of "pipelines"[7] in modern machine-learning frameworks. A typical implementation allows engineers to write a definition that ties together models and other software modules into larger structures—pipelines—like our example image processing services. You should expect:

- Out-of-the-box support for model versioning
- An agnostic approach to the specific machine-learning model type (your Data Scientists should be able to work with TensorFlow, Caffe, PyTorch, or the latest shiny new thing)
- Seamless support for hybrid infrastructure (you may or may not need to use a mix of public and private clouds, but you'll want to avoid permanent lock-in to either).
- Easy containerization

Training Models and Hardware Selection

Training machine-learning models are notoriously computationally intensive by comparison with many traditional workloads (my wife can tell if I'm doing machine learning from the roar of fans spooling up when training begins). The challenge, for a business, is that demand (and hardware utilization) from data scientists and machine-learning engineers tends to be highly variable—intermittent periods of high demand while experiments are being run, interspersed with lulls (new code gets written or new datasets get wrangled). If you have enough hardware to run all experiments in a short time, then you'll probably find it spends a lot of time idling.

Training at Home

How to give your machine-learning team plenty of firepower—at a reasonable cost? One answer is to make better use of the hardware your organization already owns. Companies like Facebook and Google experience large diurnal variations in usage (even the most devoted cat video fan eventually falls asleep), leading to idle capacity in their server farms. Containerization has allowed both companies to give idle machines a "night shift," switching from serving cat videos to training machine-learning models. In this way, vast numbers of otherwise under-worked CPUs have been made available to machine-learning teams[8].

The previously mentioned open-source project KubeFlow, gives other organizations a head start in imitating this strategy—as the name suggests, KubeFlow's mission is to enable machine learning on Kubernetes, allowing users to combine the power of many machines. As well as making it easier to run training on a cluster, it also uses algorithms developed at Google to improve experimental efficiency, effectively automating part of the experimental process. While the parameters "inside" a model are optimized by the machine-learning algorithm, values must also be chosen for values "outside" the model's learning process (like the type of model, or the number of parameters to use, or various model-specific options)— these are known as hyperparameters. As a result, teams who train machine-learning models have a lot of knobs to tune (accepting default values is an option too, but these won't usually be optimal for whatever the current business problem is). Since a particularly good choice of hyperparameters can significantly improve model quality, teams often simply try as many combinations of settings as their resources allow—a brute-force approach that, in the age of Deep Learning, where some models take hours or even days to train, is often too expensive to permit much of this.

Avoiding expensive exhaustive searches, Kubeflow's "Hyberband" feature automates and optimizes this hyperparameter tuning in two ways:

- Unpromising experiments (hyperparameter settings) are abandoned as soon as sufficient evidence accumulates that the model being trained will underperform (rather than just training for a set period).
- Each experiment is used to inform the choice of settings for the *next* experiment: rather than explore all settings exhaustively, Hyperband is actually seeking out more promising regions of "parameter space" and ignoring regions where the accumulation of evidence suggests no progress can be made. The original paper on the underlying algorithm ("Hyperband") suggests gains of between 6X and 70X versus random search[9]—that is, achieving similar results with older brute-force methods would take far longer.

Training in the Cloud

The main cloud providers and a host of startups, having heard the story about shovel-sellers and gold rushes, are competing vigorously for your business—or are they? GPUs have the lion's share of the training market at the time of writing (at least for deep neural networks) and given the ease with which code and data can move between clouds, you might expect prices to converge rapidly. Nevertheless, significant discrepancies exist between providers offering identical hardware—an arbitrage opportunity you should exploit.

A larger opportunity for cost savings exists in the pricing models used by cloud providers— "spot" or "preemptible" instances. In exchange for *being willing to lose the hardware at any time with no notice*, one can rent hardware for a small fraction of the usual rate. Enterprising startups are working on ways to combine fleets of ephemeral spot instances into reliable low-cost training platforms.

As with other assets, the "rent vs. buy" question often comes down to utilization; renting cloud GPUs for a couple of months of continuous training could well cost more than *buying* the same hardware outright. The Cloud makes the most sense when your needs are *sometimes* very great; specialized training hardware like Google's TPUs can allow you bring the equivalent of a hundred or more high-powered GPUs to bear on an experiment, getting quick answers that let your team move on to the next business problem.

Tracking Experiments

Any team working on a machine-learning-based product will quickly come to select key metrics by which all new models will be judged. Before very long, your team will hopefully have tried a great variety of approaches, with mixed results. Simply keeping track of what works and what doesn't is important—it will help your team avoid duplicated effort, and improve transparency for you. Previously, tracking of experiments relied heavily on the diligence of individual scientists and keeping track of experiments in a transparent way allowing for easy reproduction of results) was the exception. Inevitably, valuable knowledge was siloed and lost.

Enter modern cloud-based monitoring tools, which offer easy-to-integrate libraries that help teams monitor model training in real-time, with a high degree of flexibility to incorporate custom metrics (adding standard metrics to training code might take only a few minutes). The benefits to smoother collaboration between technical team members are obvious. Managers benefit too; instead of relying on generic and cryptic word-of-mouth updates at team meetings, any team member can access a real-time dashboard to help track progress on those key metrics.

Near-Term Hardware Developments

As with so many areas, Google's hardware accelerators are signposting the future. Based on a class of computer chip called an ASIC (Application Specific Integrated Circuit). ASICs sacrifice flexibility for performance and power efficiency in a specific role: a TPU is effectively an ASIC array, exploiting the highly parallel nature of matrix multiplication, the demanding operations at the core of modern machine learning. ASICs happen to be relatively cheap to develop (as compared to CPUs or GPUs) and a wave of ASIC-based accelerators are under development at hardware startups (like GraphCore, which has a partnership with Dell) and incumbents (like Intel, which announced ASIC-based inference accelerators at CES 2019): by the time you are reading this book, ASIC-based products are likely to be encroaching steadily on what has been a GPU dominated (NVIDIA dominated) market.

Inference and Hardware

A Data Scientist wants one thing from their hardware: the lowest possible training time. For machine-learning methods like Deep Learning, this has meant using NVIDIA GPUs, and more recently, purpose-built accelerators—Google's TPUs (Tensor Processing Unit). However, an architect selecting a hardware platform for production use—for inference—may be trying to maximize any of a range of objectives. At the time of writing, the best choice of hardware for inference is application specific.

For example, many applications are constrained by memory capacity or bandwidth rather than matrix multiplications.[10]

Images Per Dollar (Samples Per Dollar)

The dominance of NVIDIA in the training of neural networks might lead one to expect a similar dominance in inference. However, most organizations, even those using GPUs for training, use CPUs for inference, and one reason for this is cost. An Intel solution (Intel-optimized Caffe, running on an Amazon EC2 instance) achieved a cost of just $0.02 per 10,000 images processed in April 2018[11], less than 1/3rd the cost of the cheapest GPU-based entry.

Images Per Hour (Throughput)

The GPU's original purpose—sustaining a high frame rate for graphically intense computer games—has given it an architecture well-suited for high-volume inference (analogous to the GPU's roots, generating images at a high frame rate). However, the GPU faces new challengers in the form of custom-designed inference hardware which aims to keep the strengths of the GPU (massively parallel matrix multiplication), while also addressing weaknesses (e.g. memory capacity, memory bandwidth, support for low precision arithmetic, support for non-square matrices).

Lowest Latency

For many applications, latency is not particularly important: if an appliance scanning biopsy slides for cancerous cells takes an extra 100ms, the additional delay is unlikely to be clinically significant. However, websites serving search results do need to worry about the customer retention impact of even an additional 10th of a second. Although GPUs beat CPUs in sheer throughput, their design puts them at a speed disadvantage if the goal is to return a single response with the lowest possible delay. Benchmarks show CPUs achieving a latency of less than half the best GPU result[12]. For more specialized applications where latency needs to be consistently below 1 millisecond (typically robotics, aerospace or defense applications), specialized hardware (FPGAs or ASIC-based accelerators) may be necessary.

On the assumption that if machine-learning achieves widespread adoption, the demand for hardware to perform inference will greatly outstrip the demand for training hardware (in much the same way build servers are a niche by comparison with production servers), a considerable number of companies are bringing special-purpose inference hardware to market. At the time of writing, AWS Inferentia (based on Amazon's custom hardware) had just been announced, Google's TPUs were about to reach Version 3, and Dell had just revealed the shipping of the first samples of a new accelerator developed with the UK-based Graphcore. Intel is also close to shipping its own inference accelerators (born of the Nirvana acquisition). All of this is to say that this section of this book will age extremely rapidly. It should be assumed that custom-built accelerators will very soon outstrip both CPUs and GPUs on all measures except flexibility.[13] We mention this last attribute because there is no reason to expect that innovation in machine learning or deep learning research will slow.

Monitoring Machine Learning in production

As George Box[14] warned us: "All models are wrong but some are useful." Even the best model is only an approximation of some unattainable platonic ideal. This warning should ring in the ears of any engineering team preparing to deploy models into production!

Given that imperfections are a certainty (as with hand-written software), we need to give serious consideration to how we can effectively monitor models in production. With purely hand-written software, basic health indicators like CPU and memory utilization can be quite revealing—a sudden spike in CPU utilization, or steadily climbing memory allocation can provide warnings of previously undetected bugs. However, a model spitting out nonsense results typically has exactly the same CPU and memory footprint as one that is working well. While hand-written software makes it easy to add logging, and to use these logs to create dashboards, machine-learning models are not so amenable to traditional logging. Conceptually, a machine-learning model can be thought of as a (very large!) chunk of code written by an engineer who never bothers with log entries!

In a perfect world, all possible scenarios would be tested exhaustively during development, and indeed machine learning has an advantage over hand-written software in that automated testing is integral to creating models in the first place. Unfortunately, as Box stated, this does not guarantee failure-free performance in production, it just means that our models will fail in ways we haven't seen before! Of course, traditional software encounters unexpected inputs too, however, noisy failures—exceptions or crashes—at least alert us to a problem. The greater danger is a program or model that fails silently. How can we detect this condition? We can't rely on test data because if we could, the failure would have been caught and fixed before the model made it into production.

"Out of Distribution" Errors

Every model you deploy will eventually see inputs that are just too different from the data it trained on, so your team should have mitigation measures in place ahead of time. The simplest step it can take to reduce problems with edge cases is to allow classifiers a "none of the above" option.

One clever answer to this problem is to train another model, whose sole purpose is to try to distinguish data encountered during production, from data seen during training and testing. The intuition here is that a model can be trusted only when inputs are sufficiently similar to the examples the model was shown during training. Since most popular model types don't have the "insight" to make this distinction, one workaround is training another model on the task. Such a model is a binary classifier and tries to label each sample it sees as coming from either the training set or previously unseen production data. Assuming that the data used to train your model was representative of the sort of inputs seen in production, this task should be impossible. If this "familiarity" model can do better than a random coin toss, your team should review a sample of the new inputs with and consider whether the training data should be augmented.

Your team should also explore the possibility of using probabilistic deep learning, in which models learn not only to solve a problem, but to do so with a kind of statistical introspection that allows them to more fully capture their own uncertainty. This is still very much a cutting-edge area, but one with a lot of promise for improving solution robustness.

Competing Solutions

A complimentary approach is to treat the production deployment of machine learning as another experiment. The reader may be familiar with the concept of A/B testing—many websites show slightly different UI's to different users, measuring their response and ultimately sending more users to the most successful version of the UI. The apparent simplicity of this approach conceals a tradeoff so fiendishly intractable that it occupied optimization researchers for decades (the brilliant mathematician Peter Whittle claimed that, during World War II, a frustrated Allied scientist proposed that the problem be dropped over Germany so that Nazi mathematicians "could also waste their time on it"). The dilemma should resonate with anyone who has ever wandered the streets of an unfamiliar city, looking for a good restaurant. Better to keep walking, or to sit down and order? Exploration increases the available information and so the expected quality of the decision (meal!), but at some point, resources need to be re-allocated to exploitation. This has become known as the "multi-armed bandit problem"[15]. Fortunately, the last 70 years have seen huge progress, and modern solutions for deploying machine learning (for example, Seldon Core[16]) provide model selection based on a "multi-armed bandit" solver off the shelf. If you have a ready means to evaluate models once in production (perhaps they make a forecast that can be compared with what actually happens?), it may well make sense to deploy multiple models in competition and allow your deployment framework to re-allocate traffic between them as evidence accumulates.

In production, all but the simplest models must be expected eventually to encounter data for which their training has not prepared them. As with "traditional" software, if you never encounter any defects, you probably haven't looked hard enough!

"Why'd It Do That?": Explainability and Traceability

Whether your model's output is good or bad (but especially when it is bad!) you will find that your team needs to be able to review model outputs (predictions), perhaps simply to understand why a decision was made, to help resolve a customer issue, or as a business or regulatory requirement. Depending on your application, you may need to track each prediction made by a model in production: the input, model name and version (and the training dataset and associated hyperparameter configuration). Over time, this capability is likely to contribute significantly to improving the quality of your solution. While many organizations have built their own traceability systems, there is a new trend toward using purpose-built solutions.

"Model explainability" is comparatively straightforward for very simple statistical models (you might encounter these when your child is born and medical staff calculate an APGAR score to decide whether any immediate interventions are necessary or, later in life, your physician may calculate a Marburg score to decide whether you have heart disease). For such simple models, where the doctor just adds a few numbers, it is usually very easy to see what symptoms have tipped the diagnostic scales.

However, the models you deploy will likely be far more complex (deep neural network usually have *at least* millions of parameters instead of the 5–10 a simple medical model might have), and are often described as "black boxes."

Traditionally, teams had to choose between models that were easy to comprehend and models with acceptable accuracy. In practice, teams usually 'learned to love' the inscrutable models required to deliver human-or-better accuracy. Transparency is now receiving renewed focus, not least from working groups like the European Union's High-Level Expert Group on AI, which lists it as one of seven key principles for the "Ethical Development of AI."[17], is commonly cited as highly desirable by end-users, and seems likely to feature in any regulation of AI.

Setting the ethical motivation to one side (we've got a chapter for that), transparency has real value in model development as a validation tool. Sometimes, a model that gets an excellent test score is actually using a "signal" that will get it into trouble in production use. Infamous examples of models misled by a badly-constructed training set include one that learned to detect huskies with (apparently!) high accuracy by learning to say "husky" whenever presented with a picture that included snow, and an HR "career success" prediction model that showed a preference for employees called "Jared" who had also played lacrosse…

Knowing more about what elements of the input drove a decision is an attainable step in the direction of transparency to help you and your team be confident that the decisions your models make have a plausible basis in the data. Fortunately, recent progress has moved model explainability from an exciting research field, to a technology that engineers can integrate, even for models traditionally considered to be a "black box" (e.g. deep neural networks). For example, an image classification decision can now include an image showing the regions of the input that the model used to make its decision.

You should expect your team to evaluate existing commercial and open source offerings like Alibi[18] (rather than "rolling your own")[19]. Incorporating this functionality in your solution at an early stage will give your testing team a useful validation tool; later on, when you have real users, you'll be much better positioned to handle technical support queries (perhaps you'll even find a way to offer explanations for predictions directly to end users).

Security and the Design of Machine-Learning-Based Services

Piracy

Traditional software's endless war against piracy might have been alleviated by the shift toward Software as a Service, but offerings that depend on machine learning may expose themselves to a new type of risk. Unlike traditional applications, machine-learning models can be duplicated simply by feeding them (unlabeled) data and observing their outputs. Known variously as "model distillation" or "student teacher learning," this technique was originally developed as a way of condensing or distilling a very large model or ensemble of models into a single model (usually much smaller, perhaps 1–2 orders of magnitude fewer parameters).[20]

The significance from a security perspective is that the learning efficiency of the "student" model is extremely high; comparatively few samples are needed to reach a level of quality that approximates that of the original model (as compared to the amount of data required to train the original "teacher" model that is being copied). The rough intuition here is that the soft labels (think class probabilities) provided by a "teacher" model are far more informative than the "hard" labels usually provided by humans ("this image contains a house cat" versus "this image is probably of a house cat, but looks somewhat like a wildcat or a lynx, and faintly resembles a lion"), enabling the student to quickly develop good internal representations of the input.

In the context of a machine-learning service, your team should consider that allowing a customer to feed data to a model then observe the "raw" output (e.g. a vector of class probabilities) will allow the customer to quickly and very cheaply create a near-perfect "clone" of your service[21]. Since simple mitigations (for example, reducing the decimal places of class probabilities that you report) have little effect, an effective defense will need to be designed-in at a very early stage of your project (perhaps instead of offering model outputs, your service needs to use them to act on the user's behalf in some way, removing the need to expose your model's output directly?).

Malicious Inputs

Traditional applications are sometimes vulnerable to carefully crafted malicious inputs such as SQL injection attacks (crafted to attack a database using code placed in the text fields of an application), buffer overrun exploits (which allow malicious code created by the attacker to run within an application), and so on.

Machine-learning-based applications often have a conceptually similar weakness that allows attackers to manipulate them using a cleverly constructed "adversarial input." As with pirating models, the level of effort required to create an effective exploit may be much lower than with traditional applications.

Figure 9.1

So, what *is* an adversarial input? The technique involves taking a normal input (say, an image of a stop sign) and making a small modification, often imperceptible to a human, that "tricks" the model into making the wrong decision—for example, confusing it into thinking that the sign reads "go." A 2017 research paper "Robust Physical-World Attacks on Deep Learning Visual Classification"[22] actually demonstrated the real-world feasibility of such an attack, designing "graffiti" stickers (pictured) that fooled a classifier into identifying them as speed limit signs with a high success rate—despite the sign remaining perfectly identifiable to human drivers!

An even more extraordinary example (pictured below) comes from researchers at MIT, who were able to create a 3D-printed "turtle"[23] which was consistently classified by a Google-trained model as a "rifle." This extraordinary illusion worked from a variety of distances and angles—while remaining imperceptible to a human.

Subsequent research has demonstrated that "black box" (no access to the targeted model's code or parameters) can succeed, and that adversarial inputs that defeat one model are very likely to be effective against others. While scientists have made huge progress on defending against "adversarial input" attacks, many commercial systems likely remain vulnerable; teams building or maintaining systems based on deep learning need to consider possible attacks and mitigations as part of their secure development process. Since both attacks and mitigations are extremely active areas of research, teams that conclude that adversarial attacks are a concern for their product need to think of mitigation as an ongoing process, not a one-off "gate" to pass before release.

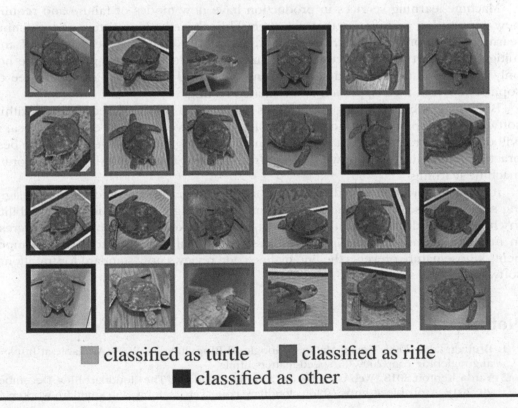

classified as turtle ■ classified as rifle
■ classified as other

Figure 9.2

Summary

Architecture selection for machine-learning applications is carried out under similar constraints to traditional software. However, the facility with which machine learning allows our computers to interact with the physical world—where latency, bandwidth, and uptime are at a premium—is beginning to shift the "center of gravity" toward edge computing, in contrast to the domination of the data center for traditional applications.

Hardware selection represents another source of complexity for the design of machine-learning based systems. Highly tuned inference engines make CPUs a compelling and flexible option (Intel's Cascade Lake processors can process more than 2,000 images per second, and achieve a latency below 2 milliseconds[24]), but application-specific requirements related to throughput or latency may point to accelerators.

Software architectures for machine learning often draw on recent trends like microservices, and benefit from containerization in the same way as traditional applications. The extremely rapid pace of change in machine learning raises the value of modularity (making it easier to accommodate tomorrow's shiny new thing). Machine learning is making a transition from a primarily scientific undertaking, to one with a growing body of engineering-focused best practices and tools. It enables your team to build and iterate rapidly while maintaining data provenance and without accumulating technical debt.

Machine-learning services in production have new modes of failure and require new monitoring techniques that are themselves based on statistics and machine learning. Additionally, they create new vulnerabilities that must be considered and mitigated as part of your secure development lifecycle. To assure products are not only accurate but robust and secure, teams will need to achieve a high degree of sophistication in their approach to automated testing.

Building machine-learning applications really is 'just' another specialization within software development, not an unattainable goal. However, as an emerging area, it will demand extra effort from your team in establishing your own version of the best practice consensus that is now emerging from the first firms to routinely incorporate machine learning.

If this chapter had to be distilled to a single paragraph, it would be this: designing solutions based on machine-learning means placing a high value on adaptability to change, in order to be ready to benefit from the exceptional rapidity of progress in machine learning. It requires a ruthlessly empirical approach to testing components whose nature prevents the line-by-line code reviews now standard for traditional software.

Notes

1 Brutlag, Jake. 2009. "Speed Matters." Google AI Blog. June 23, 2009. Available at https://ai.googleblog.com/2009/06/speed-matters.html.
2 Varda, Kenton. 2018. "WebAssembly on Cloudflare Workers." The Cloudflare Blog. December 20, 2018. Available at https://blog.cloudflare.com/webassembly-on-cloudflare-workers/.

3 An interesting strategy employed by some tech giants is to use machine learning to learn a compressed representation of the data. This might be a sort of neural replacement for traditional compression that simply gets a better compression ratio, or it could involve computing a much more abstract representation which uses far less bandwidth, but enables later processing by a number of different applications to enable a hybrid approach (perhaps an indoor system calculates this 'abstract' and uses it for targeted advertising, while a different application back at Corporate HQ uses the same representation to study style trends among store customers).

4 The Hyperband paper may interest more technical readers. Li, Lisha, Kevin Jamieson, and Afshin Rostamizadeh. 2018. "Hyperband: A Novel Bandit-Based Approach to Hyperparameter Optimization." *Journal of Machine Learning Research* 18 (2018): 1–52, Retrieved from https://arxiv.org/pdf/1603.06560.pdf.

5 Every rule has exceptions! For example, in algorithmically trading hedge funds, teams using machine learning to make investment decisions are in a continuous arms race with other teams doing exactly the same thing. I train a new trading model, my competitor trains another one to out-wit mine, I respond in turn, and so on. For each new model deployed, vast numbers of failures will have been trained and found wanting.

6 Wulczyn, Ellery, Nithum Thain, and Lucas Dixon. 2017. "Ex Machina: Personal Attacks Seen at Scale." *WWW '17: Proceedings of the 26th International Conference on World Wide Web*. April 3, 2017. pp. 1391–1399. Retrieved from https://doi.org/10.1145/3038912.3052591.

7 As a comparatively new concept, the nomenclature isn't quite settled yet. You may well see the same feature offered under a different name.

8 CPUs were not the traditional tool of choice for training deep neural networks. However, the gap versus GPUs has narrowed dramatically, partly due to software optimizations and partly due to new instructions like AVX-512. Readers can watch this race at https://mlperf.org/results/

9 Hyperband is based on Bayesian methods which model system in terms of distributions rather than point estimates-essentially, all possibilities are considered at once, but each new piece of evidence gradually reduces the probability assigned to most outcomes. Explicitly modeling uncertainty in this way creates greater experimental efficiency because it allows experiments to be concentrated on regions where certainty is known to be low (so additional evidence will be more informative than in regions of which we already know much). The reader is right to suspect close links with information theory. A classic example of their application was the location of the wreck of the USS Scorpion.

10 Park, Jongsoo et al. 2018. "Deep Learning Inference in Facebook Data Centers: Characterization, Performance Optimizations and Hardware Implications." ArXiv.org. November 29, 2018. Available at https://arxiv.org/abs/1811.09886.

11 "Inference Cost." Stanford DAWN Deep Learning Benchmark (DAWNBench). Available at https://dawn.cs.stanford.edu/benchmark/#imagenet-inference-cost.

12 "Training Time." Stanford DAWN Deep Learning Benchmark (DAWNBench). Available at https://dawn.cs.stanford.edu/benchmark/#imagenet-inference-time.

13 Your first stop should be the excellent MLPerf benchmark, carefully designed to reflect real-world loads as realistically as possible: https://www.mlperf.org/.

14 Fellow of the Royal Society, and son-in-law to Ronald Fisher, the man who essentially founded modern statistics.

15 The multi-armed bandit gets its name from an imaginary casino visitor who plays different slot machines, gradually settling on the ones with the best payouts.

16 SeldonIO. 2021. "Seldon-Core." GitHub. Accessed October 5, 2021. Available at https://github.com/SeldonIO/seldon-core.

17 High-Level Expert Group on AI. 2019. "Ethics guidelines for trustworthy AI." European Commission. November 17, 2020. Available at https://ec.europa.eu/digital-single-market/en/news/ethics-guidelines-trustworthy-ai.

18 SeldonIO. "Alibi." GitHub. Accessed October 5, 2021. Available at https://github.com/SeldonIO/alibi.

19 The open-source Alibi library provides implementations of several well-known methods for explaining model decisions.

20 A 2018 paper applied the same technique to the problem of training models using a very large cluster. Anil, Rohan et al. 2018. "Large Scale Distributed Neural Network Training through Online Distillation." arXiv.org. Available at https://arxiv.org/abs/1804.03235.

21 Interested readers looking for a concrete example are directed to an article—with code samples—that we co-authored: Dixon, Edward, Alex Ott, & Damilare D. Fagbemi. 2018. "Pirating AI." Medium. November 26, 2018. Available at https://medium.com/@damilare/pirating-ai-800a8da6431b.

22 Eykholt, Kevin et al. 2018. "Robust Physical-World Attacks on Deep Learning Visual Classification." *2018 IEEE/CVF Conference on Computer Vision and Pattern Recognition.* June 2018. Retrieved from https://doi.org/10.1109/cvpr.2018.00175.

23 Athalye, Anish et al. 2018. "Synthesizing Robust Adversarial Examples." *Proceedings of the 35th International Conference on Machine Learning, Proceedings of Machine Learning Research* 80:284–293. July 3, 2018. Available at https://proceedings.mlr.press/v80/athalye18b.html.

24 Narvaez, Paolo. 2019 "Intel Innovations Hardware Acceleration for Analytics and AI." *12th Extremely Large Databases Conference.* XLDB. April 3, 2019. Retrieved from https://conf.slac.stanford.edu/xldb2019/sites/xldb2019.conf.slac.stanford.edu/files/Wed_15.20_Narvaez_Paolo_Intel_XLDB19.pdf

Chapter 10

AI and Corporate Social Responsibility

Edward Dixon
UCSF Center for Digital Health Innovation

Lisa Thee
Oii Incorporated

Bob Rogers
UCSF Center for Digital Health Innovation
Oii Incorporated
Harvard University IACS

Contents

DOI: 10.4324/9781351032940-10

Introduction

History tells us that new technologies arrive in a wave of concern relating to their moral and ethical effects. This has been true of the printing press, the bicycle, and the telephone, and it is now true of Artificial Intelligence (AI). We explore popular concerns and the degree to which existing evidence supports them, discuss popular remedies, and conclude by offering recommendations grounded in experimental work on the moral component of human behavior.

In this chapter we ponder the challenges that prevent AI from being the panacea it could be: A list of things that might keep users of AI up at night, including:

- Threats to privacy that data collection for the sake of AI could create,
- Biases that can creep into AI algorithms, causing them to provide imbalanced or incorrect answers to the questions they are asked,
- Trust concerns that come up for us when we don't know why algorithms make the decisions they may,
- Liability that could be induced for users of algorithms due to inherent risks with technology or due to ignorance about regulatory obligations.

In this chapter we also seek to counterbalance these concerns by explaining some of the amazing technologies that have been developed to assist with these challenges by protecting privacy in data collection (for example, differential privacy), allowing the use of data without moving it (for example, federated learning and confidential computing) and advances in our ability to understand why algorithms make the decisions they make.

We round out this chapter with a how-to guide for AI leaders who want to help their organizations make a difference in the world with AI for Good. Not only do these examples provide inspiration for leveraging the power of AI to solve challenges our world faces, but they provide a great context for how AI systems can, and should, be built for any application.

Things That Keep Us Up At Night

As AI practitioners and users we must remain diligent in our efforts to ensure that the technology we develop or deploy does not do more harm than good. Challenges in this category, *things that keep us up at night*, include threats to our privacy (due to both the mass collection of data about us to develop AI and the risks to our privacy from AI technologies themselves), the presence of bias in our algorithms (we certainly don't want to encode racism or other negative biases in our technology), trust (how do we build technology that we can trust, and does that necessarily require that algorithms be able to explain themselves?), and liability (if something goes wrong, who's to blame?). Let's unpack these topics to understand how to manage some of the risks in the deployment of AI.

Privacy

Machine Learning (ML) can be used to automate mass surveillance, and, as we'll see, this is already happening in various ways around the globe. We examine common concerns, the extent to which they are being born out in practice, and the tension between the public's expressed desire for privacy and the demand for improved services (for example, in healthcare and in law enforcement).

The Surveillance Society

Crossing the border into a new country now requires providing fingerprints, a photograph of your face, a copy of your passport, and visa information to the government. The use of biometrics is rising in the public consciousness, often with negative associations (a little too reminiscent of police station mugshots?). Concern about the potential for misuse has led to extraordinary steps—like a ban by the City of San Francisco on the use of facial recognition by police officers, and in discussions on English-language social media, commentators are quick to identify facial recognition as a technology that might foster a slide toward authoritarianism. Do these fears have any foundation in reality?

Some governments are positively enthusiastic, funding huge networks of cameras and ML-equipped servers to process their feeds in real-time. These national surveillance systems read like the ACLU's worst fears made real (Figure 10.1):

- Cameras on the road network use number plate recognition to follow cars all over the country
- Facial recognition and pedestrian re-identification are used to track the public as they walk the streets

■ In some cases, algorithms to detect what people are doing are being put in place, raising concerns about the reach of government

In the US and the EU, ML and biometrics are also used by law enforcement and by industry, but with a different focus. The same hardware and closely related algorithms, instead of being used for blanket surveillance, are helping social media companies and law enforcement bodies to cope with a surge in the production of child sexual exploitation material (CSAM or child pornography)—both to remove this material from social media platforms, and as an aide in identifying perpetrators and victims. High-profile non-profits like Thorn champion technical innovation as a tool to create leads for investigators whose cases have no complainant, no crime scene, and no names, and as a way to protect the mental health of human analysts who spend their days reviewing images and videos of egregious crimes.

These differing applications of the same underlying technology suggest that—as with the printing press, the bicycle and the telephone—the applications primarily reflect the values of the societies that build them.

Of course, surveillance is not exclusive to states; companies like Facebook and Google have a business model built around data they collect on their users. A few decades ago, it would have been hard to imagine the level of information that these

Figure 10.1   Traffic and CCTV surveillance have become ubiquitous in many places.

companies can gather: People use Facebook and its subsidiary WhatsApp to communicate with family and friends, and use Google as an all-purpose oracle. With Google search seamlessly integrated into the address bars of browsers and interfaces of our phones, these companies have a perfect window into our interests. Nor is the tracking limited to our web activity: Apps on our phones allow Google and Facebook to track our movements in the physical world, a level of surveillance that exceeds the reach of even George Orwell's "Big Brother." All these data would be quite useless were it not possible for the collectors to use them—and use them they do. Every night as Facebook's users drift off to sleep, servers located in nearby datacenters gradually fall idle. Below some utilization threshold, they switch from serving up the latest cat videos to a new task: Learning to serve *more relevant* cat videos. In an eerie symmetry, as our dreaming brains sort through the events of the day, the server's fans start to spin again: using records of our interactions that day (what we liked, what we ignored, and so on), they train new models (deep neural networks) that try to predict what content we'll find most engaging. Every morning, we awake to an AI-powered newsfeed that is now *very slightly better* at capturing our attention.

As we now know, the models that vie for users are blithely amoral: they seek only to maximize our attention and make no judgments about what we consume. If anti-vaccine or "flat earth" conspiracy videos do the trick, soon they'll fill our feeds. The algorithms cater to all tastes: in 2019, YouTube was to be found to be helpfully steering a certain subset of users toward videos including incidental child nudity[1]. Our modern commercial surveillance networks are quite the opposite of Orwell's dystopia: they exist not to control, but to seek out and gratify our heart's desire.

Perhaps the strangest feature of this system, whose violations of privacy are no secret to the general public, is the contrast between consumers' stated preferences and their behavior. Users *could* leave Google for privacy-focused search engines like DuckDuckGo, or stop posting to Facebook. Although some advocates for privacy are doing exactly this, recent financial results for Google and Facebook suggest that almost all their users—whatever their stated concerns—are quietly acquiescing to the status quo.

But what about the future of retail, with its unstaffed shops, where every customer is scrutinized by dozens of cameras, all backed by powerful facial recognition? It's possible that this innovation will prove a step too far for consumers. However, consider your local convenience store or your pharmacy: if you are like me, the people that serve you every day know your face, often your name, and your children. They know you like to come in for a bottle of wine and an enormous sack of crisps on a Friday night; they know your contraceptive preferences, your favorite paper. Leaving that shop, perhaps you occasionally bump into people you know, if not on the footpath, then at the school gate, or in your gym (Figure 10.2).

Perhaps the truth is that for most of us, privacy is more about emotions than reason: buying a racy book or a packet of condoms on the Internet *feels* a lot more private than queueing to pay our neighbor at the till, even if, intellectually, we know that our purchasing history will be reflected in every banner ad our browser loads.

AI really *does* threaten our privacy; most readers of this book are already scrutinized by machines trying to understand you well enough to predict your needs. A sufficiently determined government could easily suborn the existing infrastructure to ascertain your likely voting intentions, your sexuality, or your religious beliefs, and

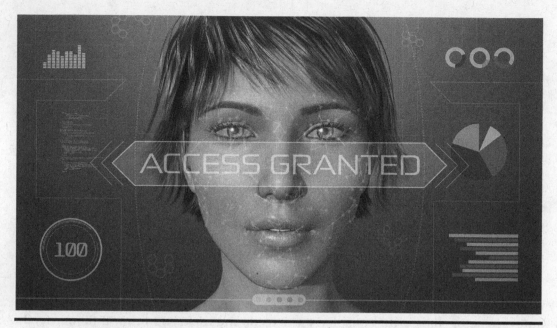

Figure 10.2 Facial recognition continues to be a powerful, but limited and controversial, technology.

use the traditional organs of the state to punish you for them. Of course, an authoritarian state could already do this quite effectively through old fashioned means—turning your colleagues and friends, even your relatives, into informers.

This technology really can be used to surveil and control; preventing that cannot be done through merely technical means. Builders of ML-based products may need to adopt a similar outlook to other manufacturers of "dual use" goods: a seller of fertilizer needs to wonder whether that new order for a few tons of ammonium nitrate is for a wheat field or a terrorist bomb plot; AI is *already* an immensely powerful component of surveillance systems, with great potential for good (identifying people who rape children) and equally great potential as a tool of repression.

In a country where this level of lack of privacy is an expected norm, where cameras are capturing your image at every move, how will countries that outlaw camera and smart city surveillance stay in pace with AI innovation? The root of all AI starts at ground truth with the data. Some countries have relied on for-profit companies to cultivate and make use of these data, primarily for use by advertisers and as clickbait. In other countries, governments have stayed in lock step with innovation and are leveraging their populations for labeled training sets. This could have a significant impact on the future progress of health care, personalized services, and user experience. One of the strongest advantages western culture has had is the pace of technological innovation, which could be flipped on its side with the data age. Once the technology is developed, no nation state will be able to prevent the spread of algorithms as customs can only control the movements of goods and not digital ideas. This will likely be one of the ethical quandaries of our lifetime. How do we set boundaries in an interconnected world? How do we keep AI in alignment with its intended use cases, and not reapplied for nefarious purposes?

In retail locations, there is no expectation of privacy as many stores have used a camera system for asset protection for years. One exciting application of AI in this environment is the ability to do facial matching for missing children, in addition to people with criminal records. Large retail chains are starting to experiment with this use case as a pro bono extension of their safety and asset security practices. Companies like FaceFirst are differentiating their product offering to retailers by providing them this feature for free when using the full suite of capabilities. Another place that retailers are experimenting with facial recognition matching is in the self-checkout area. To reduce friction for alcohol purchases at the checkout line, companies like Yoti are exploring facial recognition for age estimation. Currently, facial age estimation is not an exact science, often having a range within two years plus or minus ground truth. By selecting to allow anyone who is over the computer's age estimate of 28, this allows a large portion of customers who are clearly over 21 to have a more seamless and efficient self-service experience. For this use case to be successful, legislation will have to adjust to acknowledge that AI is an effective tool for age estimation, just like humans are good at determining a 30-year-old is not an 8-year-old.

Technology That Helps Protect Our Privacy

The good news is that all is not lost. As AI and algorithmic solutions to human problems evolve and potentially erode our ability to protect our data, new technologies are being developed to fight back. Privacy-preserving computing is a fast-growing area of technical development that is allowing algorithm developers to compute on data without explicitly seeing the data (Figure 10.3)

As we've discussed, many of the problems we would like to solve with AI require access to personal information—whether it be data about healthcare, habits, or interests. Much of these data are being produced on devices such as smartphones, smart

Figure 10.3   Privacy-preserving computing techniques hold tremendous promise in advancing AI with minimal impact on privacy.

devices, or machines in hospitals. Traditionally, training a model would require transferring these data to a central server. However, this raises numerous concerns about the privacy and security of the data — the AI lab now requires trust not only in its ability to develop good AI algorithms, but also in its ability to protect private data from accidental or malicious release or misuse.

When seeking to provide AI services in domains that require private data, while also seeking to abide by data privacy laws and minimize risks from the handling of private data, ML researchers have begun to harness solutions from privacy and security research, developing the field of private and secure ML. The field of private and secure ML is heavily inspired by research from the cryptography and privacy communities. It consists of a collection of techniques that allow models to be trained *without* having direct access to the data and that prevent these models from inadvertently storing sensitive information about the data.

Federated Learning

The first stop on our journey into privacy-preserving and secure computing for AI is federated learning, in which we train ML models on data that is stored in *multiple* locations. Instead of moving the data to the model, the model is sent to where the data is located, reducing the need to move data or to create large, aggregated datasets that could become attractive targets for hackers. The data remains in its source system (for example, a cell phone, or a hospital server). The model is sent to the device, trained locally on the local data on each device, and the new-and-improved model is then sent back to the main server to be aggregated with the main model. This preserves privacy in the sense that the data has not been moved from the device.

Federated learning also presents a practical alternative to moving around huge amounts of data. For example, predictive maintenance uses sensor data to predict when a machine, such as an engine, needs maintenance. Often, the amount of data produced by dozens of sensors monitoring 24 hours a day is simply inconvenient or impossible to move to a central server to train. In addition, federated learning makes it possible to no longer need to centralize the data being produced on edge devices such as smartphones. As this becomes a common privacy practice for apps, ask yourself if you really *need* to move customer's data onto a central database, or if you can take advantage of federated learning instead.

However, there is still a limitation: the content of the local data can sometimes be inferred from the weight updates or improvements in the model (for example[2],[3]). While individual clients are not able to reconstruct samples, an "honest-but-curious" server could. To prevent the possibility of inferring personal characteristics about the data, further techniques can be employed, such as differential privacy or confidential computing.

Differential Privacy

To help us compute the amount of our private information that is leaked by any kind of technology, including privacy-preserving computing, a technique called Differential Privacy has been developed.

Often, deep-neural networks—the most common ML models today—are over-parameterized, meaning that they can encode more information than is necessary for the prediction task. The result is a ML model that can inadvertently memorize individual samples. This means that sometimes, AI models could 'leak' these details later. Differential privacy is a framework (using math) for measuring this leakage and reducing the possibility of it happening.

For example, researchers at UC Berkeley, Google, and the National University of Singapore have demonstrated that a language model designed to emit predictive text (such as the next-word suggestions seen on smartphones) can be probed to release information about individual samples that were used for training ("my social insurance number is ..."). This exposes data owners to a risk to privacy from contributing their data to the training of a model, even if the data is never handled by the AI lab.

Recent advances in differential privacy provide a mathematically rigorous framework for measuring and reducing privacy leakage from trained ML models. When evaluating whether or not a model retains private information, the definition of privacy is crucial. Differential privacy, introduced by Cynthia Dwork, describes a claim to data owners: "you will not be affected, adversely or otherwise, by allowing your data to be used in any study or analysis, no matter what other studies, datasets, or information sources are available[4].

A critical aspect of this definition is the guarantee of privacy no matter what other studies, datasets or information sources are available to the attacker—it's been well-publicized that two or more 'anonymized' datasets can be combined to successfully infer and de-anonymize highly private information. This is known as a 'linkage' attack, and presents a serious risk given the abundance of data so easily available to attackers today[5],[6] (examples: Netflix prize, health records being identified). Differential privacy, however, is more robust than simple dataset anonymization in that it quantifies the risk that such de-anonymization can occur, empowering a data owner with the ability to minimize the risk (in some cases eliminating it entirely). Recently, Apple's ML Privacy Team demonstrated that when combined with (local) differential privacy, federated learning provides strong privacy guarantees for all participants[7].

Differential privacy works by the addition of a controlled amount of statistical noise to obscure the data contributions from individuals in the dataset. This enables all data contributors a certain degree of probable deniability as to whether they were in the dataset to begin with, and thus privacy-impacting inferences cannot be made based on predictions from the system. This is performed while ensuring that the model still gains insight into the overall population, and thus provides predictions that are accurate enough to be useful.

Inference Privacy

When training models on images, sometimes the area of interest itself is not sensitive or private material, but the image contains other information that *is* sensitive or private. For example, to train a model to detect smiles, perhaps it isn't necessary to include everyone's full faces in the training data. Research from UC San Diego has demonstrated that in this case, obscuring the parts of the image that are private (the rest of the face) and only training on the smiles is a privacy technique with negligible computational overhead. This technique is called inference privacy, and it's easy to think of many image-focused use cases for this in both the medical field and fighting crime. For more details on inference privacy, see[8] for example.

Keeping Your Model Private

Finally, while Federated Learning and Differential Privacy can be used to protect data owners from loss of privacy, they are insufficient to protect a model from theft or misuse by the data owner. Federated Learning, for example, requires that a model owner send a copy of the model to many data owners, putting the model at risk of IP theft or sabotage through data poisoning. Encrypted computation can be used to address this risk by allowing the model to train while in an encrypted state. The most well-known methods of encrypted computation are Confidential Computing (for example within a hardware-defined secure enclave), Homomorphic Encryption, Secure Multi-Party Computation, and Functional Encryption.

There are currently restrictions on the types of calculations that can be performed using homomorphic encryption, and the computation performance is still very far from traditional techniques. Secure Multi-Party Computation is computationally less intensive than Homomorphic Encryption, but requires a lot of communication between the parties, so bandwidth can be a bottleneck. A promising approach using Confidential Computing to protect both healthcare data and healthcare AI has been developed by BeeKeeperAI at UCSF. This is an active area of research, however, and these techniques will improve in the years to come (Figure 10.4).

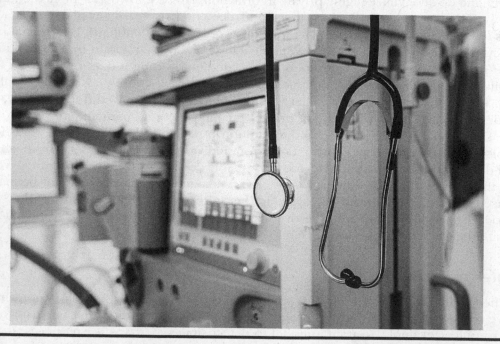

Figure 10.4 Patient data is especially sensitive. Without the ability to compute on private healthcare data, it is challenging to develop effective AI. Privacy-preserving and confidential computing may help alleviate this problem.

Privacy-Preserving Machine Learning in Practice and Business

In practice, private and secure AI is performed using a combination of these techniques, and each method has limitations and costs. Some techniques would be overly burdensome in contexts where data and model owners already trust each other (e.g. when an AI team inside a company trains models on company-internal data), while others would be insufficiently secure for contexts that need to protect data and models from the actions of malicious actors. An appropriate mix of techniques for a specific project can only be decided once the various trade-offs of techniques are clearly communicated to the data-holders and key stakeholders of the project.

When used where necessary, however, privacy-preserving methods have the potential to (1) greatly improve the performance of some fields of AI, (2) solve the impending data ethics issues surrounding some fields of AI, and (3) enable AI to be used in brand new, uncharted territory.

One way to think about the current and future potential of privacy-preserving AI is to split it into these three concepts:

1. It can allow you to do what you're already doing, but better, due to:
   a. Access to more training data due to increased ability to 'share' data: if you can access & train on 100 images of a rare cancer now, this will enable you to train on all 10,000 images across the country, or even across international borders, and thus have better models.
   b. Access to training on more globally representative datasets: today, many models fail to generalize to a wider dataset. PPML techniques could enable training on datasets from diverse, global sources, which is especially important for any healthcare or crime-fighting applications.
   c. Reducing the need to move huge amounts of data from phones, sensors, devices, etc. onto servers just to train.
2. It can allow you to do what you're already doing, but in a more ethical way—the law and the public are demanding an end to privacy-infringing practices, and as the legal system catches up, many current-day data collection practices could become illegal. By investing in the infrastructure to train in a privacy-preserving way, you're future proofing your business model against this eventual sea change. A good place to begin is to ask yourself if you really need to move customer's data onto a central database, or if you can implement federated learning instead.
3. The final and most exciting avenue to think about is that it will enable research and businesses that we currently can't do, for example because the data is too sensitive to collect in a non-privacy-preserving way.

Finally, it's important to note that not all uses of AI will need to implement privacy-preserving technologies. Some forms of data are inherently less sensitive than others, or perhaps the data is entirely public already (e.g. a linguistics researcher training on completely public tweets). However, as AI is used in surveillance, crime, healthcare, and beyond, privacy techniques will be crucial to ensure we can use AI for the benefit of humankind—without leaving even more problems in our wake.

Bias

As we've discussed so far, there are real choices that we need to make to determine where the balance between benefits and drawbacks of AI will settle in our society. This discussion mostly assumes that we understand the algorithms that we are using and that we are making conscious decisions about what we should and should not do. There is an additional consideration: What if our algorithm has undesirable properties that we are not aware of? How can this happen and what can we do to prevent the negative impacts of such ignorance?

One of the most common ways that algorithms can lead us to incorrect conclusions is through the presence of bias, which can creep into the data we are using to train our algorithms without our realizing it has happened.

Before we go one step further in this discussion, we must define what we mean by bias. In fact, one of the biggest challenges we are seeing in the public discourse on the ethics of AI is confusion and a lack of clarity around the meaning of the word "bias" in the context of algorithms. So first, a definition:

> Bias in algorithms occurs when they produce erroneous results because of incorrect assumptions, including assumptions about how well a dataset represents the facts about a target population.

One of the challenges in the public discussion around AI and bias is that algorithmic bias is often conflated with legal bias: In law, bias is an unfair act or policy stemming from prejudice, and is usually frowned upon from a legal and regulatory perspective.

If the assumptions or data underlying an algorithm are flawed in a systematic way, and the use of that algorithm then results in a legal bias (unfair act or policy), then we have crossed over from algorithm bias to legal bias. This is a situation that regulation, such as GDPR, seeks to prevent. A challenge in conceptualizing how this can play out is that it is **not** true that an algorithm that identifies a difference in the underlying data about different groups is inherently biased. We expect algorithms to tell us the truth about the data they were given, and sometimes the underlying truth does not reflect the world we want to see. Ultimately, it is how we apply these algorithms that determines whether they are causing bias in a legal sense.

Let's start by looking at how data can be biased, and why we must be vigilant about bias in our data. There are many ways that data can be biased. Different biases have different impacts and potential mitigations. Let's look at two of the most common data biases: Selection, or sample, bias, and prejudice bias (which we prefer to call context bias), and what we like to call *system-perpetuated bias*.

Selection bias occurs when data has been collected in a way that over- or under-represents important aspects of the underlying truth. Since algorithms can only learn from the data that they are presented, they will faithfully represent the incorrect truth contained in their data. An example in the world of HR might be a model to predict how likely a candidate will be successful in a role. To train such a model requires building a dataset of historical performance for employees along with whatever underlying attributes might be relevant to the prediction. Let's assume that undergraduate university is one of the attributes. If it happens that no past employees happened to have mathematics degrees, then it is hard to imagine that a candidate with a math degree will fare well in the model's assessment. This is likely to be a pure sampling bias: That is, the dataset is simply missing any data representative of math majors because there just didn't happen to be any. There's no *a priori* reason to discount mathematicians for the role being assessed, so this selection bias will impact the usefulness of the model.

If we pull this thread further, we may encounter a second, more insidious, kind of selection bias. Suppose that there is a reason that there have never been employees with mathematics degrees at the company. Have you ever wondered why there is no Nobel Prize for mathematics? There is an apocryphal story that claims this is the result of a love triangle between Alfred Nobel, a mathematician he was competing with, and a third party whose love they were both seeking[9]. While the evidence does not support this explanation, we could imagine a similar situation with the founder of a company in the role of Alfred Nobel. A personal bias against mathematicians in early hiring practices might result in a history at the company with no mathematician employees. That leads to a hiring model that does not predict good outcomes for mathematician candidates, hence no mathematicians get hired, and so the cycle continues with reinforcement from AI. Ultimately, since the real objective of the algorithm is to help the company find good candidates and compete, the algorithm fails the enterprise as the result of a nasty selection bias (Figure 10.5).

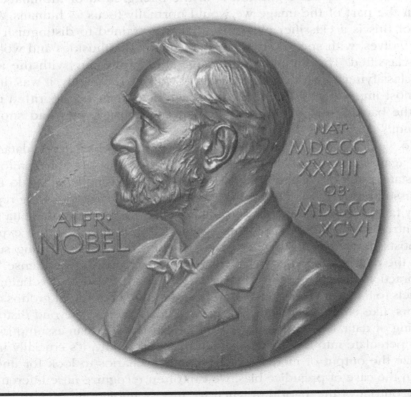

Figure 10.5 The Nobel Effect: If you have never hired a mathematician, will your algorithms learn that you shouldn't hire mathematicians?

The second major type of bias we must understand is prejudice bias, or what we prefer to refer to as "context bias." This occurs when an algorithm learns a pattern or makes a conclusion that is incorrect or misleading and which could lead to incorrect conclusions that run counter to our broader policies or beliefs. Consider an algorithm that is being trained to identify what sport is being played in a photograph. The input dataset will contain images of potentially many different individuals photographed in different phases of participating in various sports. The algorithm's sole objective is to correctly label each photograph with the sport that is being depicted. We are not normally able to constrain how the algorithm makes this decision or how it prioritizes the information in each image, so the raw frequencies of different attributes of images will impact the results. As a result, it is not only possible, but likely, that the algorithm will infer false associations. In the case of sports images, examples have been exposed on the Internet in which an image of an Asian who is not playing any discernible sport will be labeled as table tennis. Obviously, it is not desirable for an algorithm making decisions in a Human Resources context to make assumptions that would be considered racist if they were made by a human.

We call this prejudice bias because it is not usually known exactly what aspect of the data, in this case an image, is being used to make the decision, but the result appears to be prejudiced in some way. Sometimes, the information that is being picked up by the algorithm is in the background of the image and not actually in the part of the image we would normally focus as humans. A famous example of this is a classifier algorithm that was trained to distinguish between dogs and wolves, with special attention to ensuring that huskies and wolves were correctly classified. The initial results were quite promising, with the algorithm correctly classifying a majority of huskies and wolves. Ultimately, it was discovered that the most important distinguishing characteristic that the algorithm used was snow in the background of the picture. Wolves almost always had snow in the background![10]

How do we detect that our models are being fooled by bias in our data? How do we guard against using models that are propagating, and possibly reinforcing, an incorrect statistical view of the world? How do we build models that do not make incorrect assumptions in the face of biased data and data that is missing representation of key factors? Much of the responsibility lies in the hands of the data scientists we have entrusted to build or apply our algorithms. Well-trained and/or experienced data scientists have a highly tuned sense for when there is something suspicious lurking in the data, a capability we refer to as data scientist "spidey sense." It is not just best practice, but necessary, to look critically and the data that is being used to build models to look for under- and over-representation of different groups or underlying factors, like ethnicity, gender, or undergraduate degree. Beyond distortions in the sampling of data, it's important to also look for ways human assumptions might be able to percolate into the data collection process. Finally, it's crucially important to scrutinize the output of models under various scenarios to look for unexpected patterns. In the case of prejudice bias, we can often recognize false inferences if we look at the output of the algorithm when we give it ambiguous data. In the case of the sports recognition algorithm, images of people doing ambiguous activities tend to expose unusual or unexpected results.

Another methodology that is growing rapidly is the synthetic or simulated data approach. We can create datasets for which we know the correct labels, but which cycle through a large number of variations in underlying data, giving us the ability to fill in under-represented groups or to add different types of randomness that require the algorithm to base its decisions on more robust information. These data can be used to train algorithms, or they can be used to detect unexpected behavior in an already trained model. In either case, the use of simulated data can be a powerful tool to detect and to reduce the impact of data bias.

There is a caveat in our discussion of prejudice bias that we must explore further. Every inference by an algorithm should have a confidence level associated with it that represents how confident the algorithm is that it got the right answer. It is never advisable to use AI systems that don't provide confidence levels along with inferences. To understand the importance of this, recall our sports detection algorithm. A photograph of an Asian male depicting no discernible sport is labeled as table tennis. This is concerning until we note that the confidence level reported by the algorithm is only 20%. In this case, it is unwise to draw much of a conclusion about the prejudices that have been encoded into the algorithm. It is possible that every image, regardless of who is in the photo, that does not clearly identify a sport will be reported as table tennis with a low confidence level. Alternatively, it could be the background lighting or some other contextual feature that is driving a low-confidence inference of table tennis, and it has nothing to do with the ethnicity of the subject of the photo. Again, it is incumbent upon the data scientist or the person responsible for deploying an AI technology to be continually vigilant about the quality of input data and the implications of results.

So, we have asserted that no AI technology should ever be used if it does not provide confidence levels with results. Another important practice is to include ongoing feedback on specific AI outputs or inferences during the day-to-day use of the technology. This can be in the form of collecting feedback from users or customers:

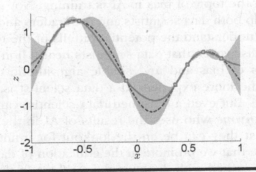

Figure 10.6   Good AI publishes confidence levels along with model outputs.

Source: Antro5 at English Wikipedia, CC BY-SA 3.0, https://commons.wikimedia.org/w/index.php?curid=52740780.

"We think this is table tennis: Did we get it right?" or it can be a behind-the-scenes QC process that is carried out by non-data scientists who can assess the accuracy of an inference or prediction. This is a powerful model that not only allows for the detection of undesirable results, but when the data is collected properly, it can be used to improve the accuracy of models (Figure 10.6).

There is one additional tool that we can use to improve the quality of our data and to remove some biases: simulated data. The process of creating simulated data that we can use to train our algorithms is a vast discussion that covers everything from simple methods to make computer vision more robust to images with different orientations to sophisticated, real-time simulations of physical processes for training autonomous systems to navigate the real world effectively. To understand how simulated data might apply to building AI models in HR, let's go back to our company that has some challenges in assessing and hiring mathematicians. The problem with our candidate assessment model was that it tended to penalize otherwise qualified candidates who had a math degree, ostensibly because the company did not have any data on the successes of past math majors. To address this with simulated data, we can create fictitious past employee profiles for math majors, based on our actual past data for other degrees, and include these data in our model training. We can ensure that the simulated data we create at least nullifies any negative effect in the model that would be caused by a lack of historical examples of mathematician employees. There is still a real risk for bias using this approach since the details of which historical profiles we use and our assumptions about what aspects of bias we want to control allow us to tune the system against or in favor of mathematicians as easily as making the impact neutral. The important point is that this approach gives us a knob to control rather than forcing us to accept whatever biased data we happen to have on hand. Furthermore, it is always possible to apply more than one model, incorporating different types of assumptions, to understand the range of appropriate scores each candidate might receive. There is always more than one way to skin a cat, we just must be aware that we are, indeed, skinning a cat. We would expect that third-party products for developing and applying simulated data will provide standard methods for addressing many of these issues.

One final word on the topic of bias in AI is training: Not algorithm training, but *human* training to help both data scientists and the leaders and engineers who apply models in practice to understand the potential pitfalls of the tools they develop. We have stressed in this discussion that data scientists bear a lion's share of the burden in identifying sources of bias and undesirable algorithmic consequences. This is absolutely true, and the more experienced a data scientist is, the better his or her "spidey sense" will be. But even a seasoned data scientist can be fooled. It is critically important that *anyone* who uses the results of AI in the enterprise be trained in Ethics for AI so that they can be on the lookout for unintended consequences. This is a core principle that we promote in the education of data scientists and other professionals who are tasked with deploying algorithms in the enterprise. A strong understanding of the statistical sources of bias, of the ways processes and humans can influence the data available to algorithms, and the dangers of mis-applying or misinterpreting algorithmic results will only increase in importance as the enterprise becomes more and more reliant on AI. Train your people.

Transparency, Explainability, and Interpretability in AI

Doctor: You can't trust an algorithm if it can't explain why it is making a recommendation.

Me: Uh...Can you explain why you make the decisions you make?

Doctor: Of course!

Me: That's funny, because in my AI career I have worked with clinicians who have been tasked with annotating different clinical findings in healthcare data. Everything from severity of a condition in an ultrasound to the correct or incorrect placement of a tube in the chest x-ray of an ICU patient. In general, I am lucky to see clinicians agree with each other more often than 65% of the time. And I've seen them disagree with their own previous annotations as much as 45% of the time. If they could really explain their decisions, I would expect that their decisions would be more consistent and repeatable.

We are not saying that doctors don't do good work, because they do, and under extreme conditions of urgency and uncertainty, and with a great deal at stake. The reality is that **humans** frequently don't know *why* they do what they do, even when they think they do. In fact, there is a vast body of research that bears this out. See for example[11]. (Figure 10.7).

So, what is our point regarding AI? There is much public and private discussion in which people assert that AI should not be used in many applications if it can't

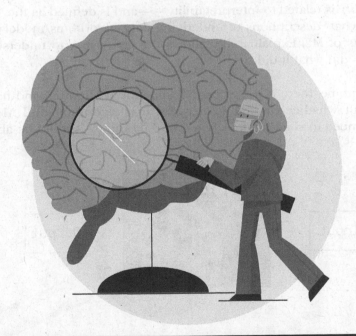

Figure 10.7   It's very hard to inspect human decision-making directly.

explain itself. In other words, people are demanding explainability, that is the ability for a non-data-scientist to be able to understand why the algorithm made its decision. Given that humans can't explain themselves, a lack of explainability is not a valid criticism of AI. In fact, because ML algorithms can be interrogated, probed, analyzed, archived for future review, and reconstructed (activities we would consider aspects of algorithm *interpretability*), they are far more likely to be accountable for any single decision than a typical human would be. Furthermore, given the very nature of ML, in which algorithms can continue to improve when exposed to new examples and information, we would argue that algorithms are much easier to improve than humans. Our general fear about letting AI answer important questions without explainability is misguided.

On the other hand, the truth is that there are situations in which we need to have a "why" to go along with the "what," and this puts an additional burden on the developers and users of AI and algorithmic approaches to these problems. In fact, this is why regulatory bodies all over the world have developed, or are developing, laws that include the right to an explanation. When these laws apply to the output of an algorithm, then it is important to understand what is meant by "explanation," so that our organization can remain in compliance. We will investigate this question shortly (Figure 10.8).

To facilitate our discussion let's review the definitions of interpretability and explainability that we put forth in Chapter 2:

Interpretability refers to methods and models that make the internal mechanisms, behaviors, and predictions of an ML system understandable to data scientists, ML, engineers, and technical users.

Explainability is related to interpretability – —and is defined as the "what," "why," and "so what" descriptions of underlying data, algorithms/models, or typically, the results of ML. Explainability allows the lay person to understand why the algorithm did what it did.

In the meantime, there is a tremendous amount of shouting and hand wringing going on about whether we should demand that algorithms and AI be "explainable," and we need to shed light on when our algorithms should be able to explain

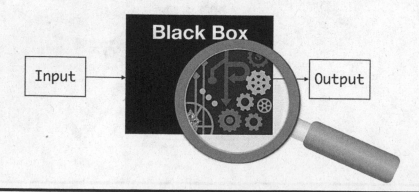

Figure 10.8 There are ways to make a black box talk: While it's not always a great idea to make algorithms self-explaining, it is far easier to inspect an algorithm than a human brain.

themselves, and what exactly we mean by this. In general, to understand what capabilities our AI systems must have, and therefore what technologies are needed to support them, we can break each situation down into one of the following questions:

Questions About Algorithms

- Can we trust this algorithm's output?
- Why did the algorithm make this decision?
- The algorithm made a mistake. What can we do to fix it?

Questions about processes

- Does this process comply with applicable regulations?
- Someone got hurt. Who is liable?

If someone needs to ask one of these questions about your AI system, either for ethical reasons, a practical concern, or because of a regulatory requirement, then your system may need to output more than just an answer. This additional output will not necessarily be an "explanation": It could also be a summary of inputs, an interpretable summary of the algorithm process, a saliency map of the most important inputs to the decision, or any number of other reports or artifacts. In other words, the questions above are more likely to require interpretability than explainability. Let's go through each of these questions and discuss the different methods to answer the question and look at the technical implications of each.

Can We Trust this Algorithm's Output?

Trust is a requirement for almost every algorithm that is worth developing and deploying. We don't go to the effort of building AI to solve problems that we don't care about, so we need to trust that the algorithm is doing what we intended. In practice, there are many ways to develop trust in an AI system in addition to explainability and interpretability.

Experience and predictability: Think back to the first few times you used a turn-by-turn GPS-based navigation system. You probably didn't trust it, and you suspected that your own intimate knowledge of the best ways to navigate familiar areas was better than what the GPS navigation software could offer. You probably even worried that the GPS might send you off on a big detour or take you right into a traffic jam caused by unexpected construction or a recent road change. But as you used GPS repeatedly and became more familiar with it, your distrust faded. Now, even if you don't trust it unquestioningly or follow it blindly (we are human, after all!), navigation software has won a very high level of trust from you. You didn't need to know exactly *how* the algorithm works to become confident that it does work. In fact, when you think you might disagree with a route, you will look at other routes or check to see if your preferred route is marked in red, but you don't ask about the details of the algorithm that chose this particular path.

This logic applies to most AI systems. We build trust by repeatedly observing the behavior of a system and noting that it is generally repeatable and predictable and that the results are generally good. We would argue that this is how we usually build trust in people as well.

Human in the loop: We have seen many AI deployments in which humans were initially very worried that the introduction of an algorithm could have negative consequences. The solution was often to include a human in the loop. Let's look at two examples.

In our first example, we had developed a ML algorithm to identify when an additional diagnosis code should be sent to Medicare to increase the payment for services that had already been provided, based on an automated analysis of the text in a clinical encounter note. The fear was that an erroneous code would be sent to Medicare, potentially making the customer appear to be submitting improper codes to maximize revenue. The solution was to include a human expert at the end of the processing pipeline. This expert could certify that the algorithm was correct and that the code should be submitted to Medicare. If a code was presented that the expert disagreed with, this information was passed back to the algorithm as training data to improve the algorithm. In this case, we were able to create a process that our customers trusted, and which helped us improve our algorithms.

In our second example, we were tasked with increasing the throughput of a complex human workflow in which humans reviewed text-based reports, enhanced them, and then submitted them to the proper agency. The challenge was that the number of reports per year was growing far faster than the budget for analysts could keep up with. Our innovation was to replace a very specific part of the task, the determination of *where* to send the resulting analysis, but analysts feared that the quality of the process would suffer from the introduction of an algorithm. The solution was to integrate the algorithm into the existing workflow in a way that allowed the human analysts to retain control of the process. Specifically, at the point in the process that they would normally do the very tedious work of trying to determine a location, the analysts were presented with the inputs that the algorithm used to make its decision, the recommendation of the algorithm, the confidence level of the recommendation and a pair of buttons: yes and no. Analysts had the option to accept or reject and override the findings of the algorithm, which gave them confidence that there would be no loss of quality in the process. Within a few days, analysts began to ask managers if they could have the recommendations with confidence levels above 85% just accepted automatically, because it seemed silly to hit yes over and over all day long. By clearly exposing inputs and confidence, and letting the humans make the final call, the algorithm quickly built the trust it needed to dramatically increase the throughput of the system.

Note that in both cases, no explanation was needed to build trust, and we would argue that this is by far the most applicable approach to building trust around algorithmic automation.

The Algorithm made a Mistake. What Can We Do to Fix It?

All algorithms make mistakes. In fact, all processes make mistakes. This is a fundamental mathematical truth that we must accept, but that our society struggles to understand. The reason is that the "truth" is almost always nuanced. Consider the task of classifying diabetics from their blood glucose measurements. Our plan is to measure the blood glucose of 100 patients who we have previously identified as either diabetic or not diabetic. We want to identify a blood glucose value above which we can confidently say the patient is diabetic. in other words, our classifier algorithm is blood glucose >= X implies diabetic class, < X implies non-diabetic class. The data looks like this, where dark bars are measurements for diabetic patients and light bars are for non-diabetic patients. Try picking a point along the x-axis (blood glucose) that divides the two groups cleanly. It can't be done: No matter where you put the line, some diabetics and some non-diabetics are mis-classified. It's not that our algorithm is mathematically "wrong," it's that the world is messier than we would like. This is generally true for ALL classifiers.

You might say, "Wait! What if we add another variable?" You are on the right track. Adding another variable can improve our ability to divide our patients into two groups, but as in the single-variable case, our patients will never cleanly separate into two perfect groups. It is an inescapable fact (Figure 10.9).

Accepting the reality that algorithms will mis-classify, the task of the algorithm developer is to come up with an algorithm that makes the best tradeoff between different types of errors for the specific problem we are trying to solve. We look at the mistakes our algorithm makes all the time, and we usually look deep into the code for causes that are not directly understandable by the end users of our algorithms.

When an algorithm that has been deployed in production makes a mistake, sometimes it has bigger consequences than we anticipated, and we need to be able to explain what happened. Often, it is sufficient to reconstruct the parts of the decision-making process to identify which subsystem failed, or made an error, and in this case, mundane methods like software logging and process tracking are sufficient. Occasionally we need to dig deeper into a single algorithm to understand what went wrong. This is the domain of interpretability.

Most of the techniques described above in the section on "Why did the algorithm make this decision?" apply here, so we won't repeat them. The one technique that is

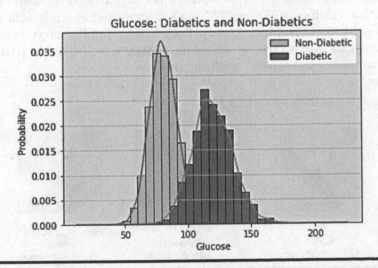

Figure 10.9 Understanding classifiers: There is no single glucose level that separates diabetics from non-diabetics.

Note: This is simulated data, not from a clinical source.

particularly useful for forensic interpretability is the method of varying input data to explore what makes the algorithm go wrong. This might be a systematic approach such as a variant of the LIME methodology, or it may be more ad-hoc experimentation with input data that is close to the data that caused the error. One approach to this is with Generative Adversarial Networks (GANs), which are networks that are trained to develop input data that can fool another algorithm.

We are bringing up the topic of GANs here for a reason: Nefarious characters have used GAN techniques to develop data tweaks that can't be seen by the human eye, but which can cause AI systems to get the wrong answer. This is a serious security issue that we need to know about in our mission to develop and deploy reliable AI in the enterprise. The images below demonstrate an example of an adversarial data attack, in which a computer vision model is shown a photo that is obviously a panda, but which has had a tiny amount of additional information added that a human cannot detect visually (Figure 10.10).

This new, tweaked image is now "recognized" by the computer vision system to be a gibbon, and with high reported algorithm confidence. It would be very difficult to work out from the tweaked image alone why the algorithm gave the wrong classification. It is essentially an AI "optical illusion." This kind of attack can be performed on almost any complex AI system, although the extent to which results can be broadly influenced depends on the details of the specific algorithm. Also, as research in this area continues, techniques to make AI systems more robust to this kind of attack are being developed.

Someone Was Harmed. Who Is Liable?

Processes in the real world can be a complex mix of different types of algorithmic and data handling steps, interspersed with human interactions. When someone is harmed as the result of such a process, there is often a need to assign liability. The two recent tragic crashes of Boeing 737 MAX aircraft and any accident involving an autonomous vehicle are in this category. Both from a public safety perspective and from the individual perspective of assessing damages to the liable party, there is a need to know "what went wrong" with the process.

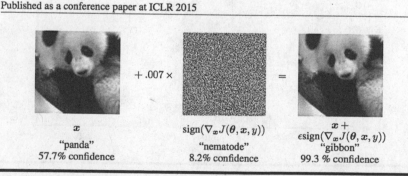

Published as a conference paper at ICLR 2015

x
"panda"
57.7% confidence

$+ .007 \times$

$\text{sign}(\nabla_x J(\theta, x, y))$
"nematode"
8.2% confidence

$=$

$x + \epsilon \text{sign}(\nabla_x J(\theta, x, y))$
"gibbon"
99.3 % confidence

Figure 10.10 **Example of an adversarial data attack: A small amount of well-engineered "noise" added to a normal image can cause an algorithm to give an incorrect result.**

Source: Explaining and Harnessing Adversarial Examples, Goodfellow et al, ICLR 2015.

In many cases, it is sufficient to track the flow of information through the process to determine where a specific failure occurred. For each block of functionality there is often a single liable entity. This tracking process does not require explainability at all. However, in many cases, the situation can be more complex. If the output of an algorithm contributes to a failure, then it may be necessary to understand exactly why the algorithm failed to prevent such occurrences in the future, as is potentially the case with the 737 MAX airline crashes. Sometimes, assignment of liability cannot be made at the functional block level because an algorithm consists of several sub-components working together. In this case interpretability is also required.

Even though the assignment of liability requires interpretability in these cases, we would argue that explainability is *not* required. The process of assigning responsibility for a failure in an algorithmic system normally works at a highly granular level and is essentially a forensic process. It is not acceptable to use heuristic estimates of algorithmic behavior, in other words typical XAI, to determine liability. This may point to regulatory and policy approaches in which source code and algorithm details must legally be discoverable for algorithms that potentially impact public safety and in other critical applications. Explainability should not be promoted as a requirement for such systems as we develop the AI regulatory frameworks of the future.

Does This Process Comply with Applicable Regulations?

This is a legal and regulatory question, which is outside the scope of this book to answer. What we can do here is identify some of the current legal frameworks that call out explainability and highlight some key topics to keep in mind during algorithm deployment and development.

General Data Protection Regulation (GDPR)—GDPR came into effect in the European Union on 25 May 2018. It is a vast and complex body of regulations and can carry stiff fines for enterprises that are not in compliance. There has been much written and said about the requirement that algorithms be explainable under GDPR. Here we simply wish to point out that the situation is not that simple. For example, it has been widely quoted that GDPR has a requirement that an automated decision about a person by an algorithm "which produces legal effects concerning him or her or similarly significantly affects him or her" would require explainability. The applicability of a requirement for explainability hinges upon whether the algorithm is entirely automated, as defined in the law. Furthermore, the exact nature of the explainability that is required, whether it be technical explainability (what we would call interpretability) at a granular level (i.e. code and model artefacts) or explainability to a lay person is a hotly debated subject at this time, and sufficient case law has not yet been established to create useful guidelines. The point here is not to provide legal advice, but rather to warn enterprise decision makers to do their own due diligence around the applicability and requirements of GDPR to different algorithmic products. Vendors who take aggressive positions on these topics can create problems for their enterprise customers or can justify less than optimal XAI development efforts that are not warranted.

California Consumer Privacy Act (CCPA)—California has enacted its own regulation that is modeled after GDPR, the California Consumer Privacy Act or CCPA (Figure 10.11).

Figure 10.11 Privacy regulations are increasingly impacting what you can and cannot do with data. Given the power of AI, this is necessary.

Equal Credit Opportunity Act—In the United States, the credit industry has had a "right to explanation" law in place since 1974. The practice in this industry is that credit decisions are accompanied by "reason codes" which come from a list of reasons why a decision would be made by the decision-making entity. As we have discussed above, the requirement for an algorithm to rigorously generate a reason code puts severe constraints on the algorithms that can be used in these decision processes. There is much interest in using more advanced algorithmic approaches in the process of approving and denying credit applications, and more broadly in assessing risk to various transactions, so it will be interesting to see how these methods evolve. Will more advanced algorithms like deep learning generate their own reason codes, or will the practices accepted by the regulators evolve to include different kinds of interpretability and explainability? We will see.

The regulatory landscape for AI is evolving rapidly. For the foreseeable future, enterprises that are developing AI-based products will do well to work closely with experts and legal counsel to ensure that their products do not run afoul of the law. Ultimately, the legal principle that will continue to hold true is that there is always an entity, and ultimately one or more humans, who are responsible for the liability generated by algorithm-based products and for the regulatory compliance of those products. The defense that "the AI made me do it" is not likely to be viable for a very long time to come.

Something That Helps Us Sleep At Night: Building Good AI

In the first half of this chapter, we invoked many of the hobgoblins of AI: The challenges that can cause AI to do harm if they aren't handled properly by the organizations that develop and deploy these powerful technologies. In this section, we talk about the many opportunities to do good with AI, and we provide a playbook for building *AI for Good* efforts within the enterprise. Such work can not only help the organization flex and grow its internal AI-development muscles, but can also create a work environment that is inspiring to employees as they see the organization creating compelling solutions with AI.

Doing Right

It's possible that your team will encounter its own version of the infamous "trolley problem," a philosophical dilemma in which an accident is about to take place and one must choose between taking no action, which will result in the deaths of several people, or to take an action which results in the death of a single person who would otherwise have been safe. Variations on this question have generated a large volume of philosophy and ethics academic literature, however, the day-to-day life of most teams building ML products is far more banal. You are much more likely to hurt users through lack of engineering competence than a lack of a sufficiently sophisticated moral calculus. As with traditional software, a diligent and well-thought-out approach to testing will help to keep you out of trouble. We still remember the first time we saw "racial bias," in a garage where a pedestrian detection system was being tested: it picked most of us visitors up just fine—but a dark-skinned colleague could walk right past without being detected. This was of course an elementary mistake that should have been caught very early, simply by testing the system using a full palette of human skin tones.

How can we make sure that our teams "do the right thing" (like speaking up when the test plan has gaps)? Doing the right thing is easy when it aligns with business goals—but what about when it means saying no to a customer, or pushing out a release date?

AI is not the first domain to struggle with ensuring high standards of behavior. Medicine is a good example of a high-stakes activity with ancient traditions valorizing a moral code (the Hippocratic Oath, in which newly trained doctors are sworn to ethical behavior, is now about 23 centuries old)[12]. Despite the length of this tradition, hospitals still struggle with the same basics familiar to parents of small children: inculcating good hand hygiene. The importance of disinfecting surfaces, tools and hands was demonstrated in 19th century Scotland by Dr (later Baron) Lister, who was able to slash the then-horrific rate of deaths due to hospital-acquired infections by the liberal application of carbolic acid. By the late 20th century rising rates of hospital acquired infection revealed that modern antibiotics had fostered a culture of complacency with respect to infection controls. As antibiotic resistance began to take hold, horrified hospital managers discovered that their staff had, quite simply, stopped worrying about handwashing. An increased attention to the placement and servicing of hand sanitizers helped, but the key innovation was social: engineering a cultural change that allowed the most junior nurse to challenge the most senior consultant. In fact, an entire research field, CRM ("crew resource management"), is dedicated to helping teams find the balance between the subordination required in their working environment (for example, on a flight deck) and the assertiveness necessary to bring serious problems to the attention of a superior.

The success of CRM in multiple domains should encourage the reader. Instead of thinking of the moral courage of your team as a fixed quantity rather like height, you should think of it as an attribute that can be developed. Of course, your example as a leader is crucial—if you are curt or dismissive when concerns are raised, your team will quickly learn not only to keep such concerns to themselves, but to squelch the qualms of their juniors with equal efficiency. Taking ethical qualms seriously—for example, publicly changing your own policy in response to your team—will set the tone for all your direct reports.

A Guide to Using AI to Effect Positive Social Change

Why AI for Corporate Social Responsibility?

Imagine you have identified a large societal issue you would like to tackle. How do you go from ideation to an actionable plan? The first thing to remember is that if you are developing a solution that can't be monetized you are creating a hobby, not a product/business. Looking for an organization that can leverage your expertise with a mission that aligns with your values is a great way to contribute without having to quit your day job or raise funds. There are numerous platforms that are crowdsourcing data science expertise to apply to societal issues, including organizations such as DataKind (www.datakind.org). If you think spearheading an initiative at your organization is the right path for you, below is a guide for how to methodically work toward your vision.

Building a Business Case

The first step in driving an AI for Good initiative is identifying the strategic alignment with your organization's mission. If you work for a large publicly traded company, your annual report is a good place to start for a better understanding of the top-line goals for the coming year. It is important to align your value proposition with the company goal for the future. One great resource to better understand your company's goals is the annual report. It is also information you can get from quarterly update meetings with the top-level executives. Focusing ways to explore technology innovation by leveraging data from non-profits can be a great place to start as public datasets are difficult to acquire. Many of the challenges facing nonprofits mirror challenges of enterprise and government customers (data privacy, cloud computing, AI, and analytics) so key learnings and case studies are transferable assets and valuable to your business group. If you are having a hard time aligning your vision with any of the company goals, you may look outside your organization to apply your skills. The second step to launching an initiative within a company is establishing an executive sponsor. This is someone who has the ability to create and allocate budgets for projects, typically at the Vice President level or higher. You need to be able to quantify the return on investment opportunity for the project, demonstrate its connections to the strategic mission of the company, be able to explain the ecosystem for the players that are addressing the issue (for profit, nonprofit, and government), and know how much funding (headcount and expense dollars) you would need to do a minimum viable product (MVP) to address the issue. This may include travel dollars to meet with potential partners, time for job shadowing at the organization, hardware/software costs, and marketing support for a pitch deck. Once you have this pitch deck in hand, it is important to map the key stakeholders across the company that could serve on your advisor board to help support the initiative. Your executive sponsor will be an invaluable resource to help you do your stakeholder mapping, and likely participate in setting up meetings with key stakeholders to gain their buy-in. It is helpful to use tools intended for entrepreneurs such as the "Lean Canvas" model and/ or a Business Plan to help you identify the financial opportunity, target market, and resources required to execute the vision. This structured process will help you to have the correct data to create stakeholder buy-in beyond your executive sponsor so if they transition on to a new role, you have others invested in your success. This will also create awareness in people who may be able to help you raise additional funds once you have taken your learnings from your MVP and would like to apply them to a more scalable solution.

There may come a time when your idea and the company's goals are no longer aligned. This is a great time to explore doing a startup. There is a wealth of information on the startup journey contained in podcasts, books, and conferences to help you explore this path. For example, the "Startup Podcast" from Gimlet Media and "Masters of Scale" from Reed Hoffman provide information on what to expect as an entrepreneur and how to grow your business. "The Lean Startup" by Eric Ries is a wealth of knowledge on how to avoid typical mistakes new founders make. We recommend finding a co-founder that is strong in the places that are different from yours. Although it is tempting to go into business with someone who thinks just like you, it is much better for innovation to have someone who complements your strengths and provides a diversity of thought. It is also important to surround yourself with mentors who are experienced in startups to guide you through the process. Many communities fund Small Business Association classes to assist founders with many aspects of running a business including incorporating, marketing, accounting, legal, IT, HR etc.

A Technical Contributor's Experience

In this section we explore the process of developing beneficial AI from the perspective of a Data Scientist whose experience in ML has been applied to help investigators as they search for the victims of sexual abuse and sex trafficking.

The Problem Domain

Around the world, hundreds of thousands of children are reported missing every year. While many will be found safe and well, others will find themselves under the control of pimps, rented out for the sexual gratification of the pimp's customers — literally enslaved. Other children, apparently safe at home, are subjected daily sexual abuse by the very people who should be their most ardent protectors.

For an investigator, the first challenge in helping the victims of such monstrous crimes is that the victim, being under the control of the perpetrator, is not in a position to seek help, and may suffer for years the most horrendous abuse. In recent years, however, these hidden crimes have become just a little bit more visible, thanks to the rise of smartphones and easily-shared digital photos:

> Online advertising has changed the sex trade more than many industries. To remain competitive, pimps need to advertise online. Extraordinary as it may seem, sex trafficking victims are photographed and offered for sale in websites easily accessed from any computer.

Sex abusers, finding like-minded people on the web, have developed a kind of dark trade, in which they exchange vast sets of images and videos. As repugnant as this is, it means that offenders are actually producing the very evidence that could let investigators rescue children who—before the age of the smartphone—might never have been found at all.

This flood of evidence is a mixed blessing for investigators:

> The first requirement for a successful prosecution is to identify the jurisdiction—this step alone can be enormously difficult.

A single case can yield not only huge numbers of photographs, but many hours of video. Reviewing so much evidence for every clue to location and identity takes a long time (and there is an emotional toll too—beneath the uniform, police officers are no more immune than the rest of us to the distress of the children in these videos).

First Find your Use Case

We sometimes hear people new to ML say "I need a dataset!." This is backwards thinking: the first step is to sit down with experts—the end-users you want to help—and let them tell you about their job. Typically, you'll find that even your questions were misconceived. Time spent listening to end-users is rarely wasted: too many Hackathons are full of well-meaning engineers building marvelous tools with no practical value whatsoever.

Thorn is a non-profit based in San Francisco that is dedicated to removing child sexual abuse from the Internet. The nature of the data they work with—images and videos—means that ML, especially deep learning, is a key tool. Part of this mission requires Thorn to help identify the children whose images are being shared in photos and videos. We were asked to focus on improved analytics for processing faces—using them to help identify (face recognition) and prioritize (age estimation).

Innovation is a Last Resort

As an engineer, innovation should always be your last resort: off-the-shelf proven components are preferred for several excellent reasons—not only must you test any alternative that you build, but also have a plan to support it throughout its useful life. Accordingly, our first steps in facial recognition were to review existing

Figure 10.12 The Labelled Faces in the Wild dataset was a starting point for training, but did not match the target population well enough to be the only data used.

work—academic, open source and commercial (many Cloud providers now offer facial recognition as a service), and to spend some time with the data we would need to process (it is our experience that time spent slogging through the samples in a dataset is rarely wasted). Should Thorn use an existing service, or build their own? How could we objectively compare the alternatives? (Figure 10.12)

A popular academic benchmark called "Labelled Faces in the Wild" (LFW) gave us one possible means of comparison. However, the faces in this dataset were a poor match for the faces we had seen in imagery related to sex trafficking: (the LFW skews male, the ladies average somewhat older than the sex trafficking victims, the ethnic mix was different, and the poses and lighting were also a bad match).

To compare different services with a metric that reflected Thorn's needs, we constructed a new benchmark, using the LFW methodology, but with imagery from Thorn. Running this benchmark on open source and commercial services, it was immediately apparent that the additional effort had been worthwhile: all the models we tested had almost perfect scores on the LFW, but the Thorn version of this metric exposed large differences between them, with even the best model showing a significant drop in performance.

Age estimation being also of interest to Thorn, we took a similar approach. Academic datasets typically under sample our target demographic so it was once again necessary to build a (slightly imperfect) custom benchmark; since Thorn's data was lacking in terms of ground truth, it became necessary to improvise, using images of actresses identified using the Internet Movie Database (their dates of birth being public knowledge). Age estimation services appear, at the time of writing to be at a comparatively early stage, relative to face recognition. When we tested them, the results fell far short of the accuracy that we obtained when we hired humans to attempt the same benchmark (human-level performance is often a good goal to set for a new ML project—we at least have the "existence proof" that this level is possible).

Building a Dataset

Having discovered a gap between the quality of commercial services and what we believed to be attainable (in the case of facial recognition) or even usable (age estimation), we proceeded to work on datasets to train (not just measure) new models.

Building training sets imposes slightly different constraints to building a benchmark dataset:

> Volume is much more important (with our benchmark datasets, we needed only enough samples to assure the statistical power necessary to distinguish between different services or models).

Quality is a little less important—neural networks tend to be somewhat tolerant of noisy data.

While matching the target domain is still a very, very good idea, it isn't quite as vital (after all, we can still use the benchmark dataset occasionally to make sure we are on the right track).

You'll probably be asked "how much data do you need"? Usually this is not knowable before you start: the best way to figure it out is to simply get just enough to train and test a very simple model (our first age estimation model was trained on just 1,000 faces). The results were just good enough to convince use that we were on the right track, and the model's failures gave us valuable clues as to what sort of data would be most valuable to improving our model.

It is often necessary to have humans label data for training algorithms. You may want to try volunteers for this, but, even for a good cause, it can be hard to get results that justify the effort of recruitment. You should really try to label a core high-quality dataset yourself (it's a great way to validate your own labelling criteria and get some domain knowledge) but after that, your best route is probably to pay crowdsourced workers (don't skip the work of building in test questions—we've had some workers just make random guesses, or select a single label for every sample in the set).

Sometimes you are lucky enough to be simply given a large high-quality dataset (this happened to us twice, and made us look rather clever—with large amounts of good data, you can hardly fail to train a decent model); even so, you should still test the quality of the labels. For example, we gave a subset of a human-labeled dataset to the same analysts that built it, and had multiple analysts relabel a sample. It turned out that the analysts agreed with the original assessment (and each other!) about 92% of the time (with the original labels hidden): this gave us confidence in the quality of the dataset and also helped us figure out a realistic performance target for our models (our customer might otherwise have expected an accuracy—say, 99%—that was simply not feasible).

First Find the Face

Working on face-based analytics means you need images specifically of people's faces. The most popular techniques—OpenCV, DBLib—turned out to perform quite poorly (again, we made our own benchmark), being easily tripped up by simple "issues" (the subject wasn't facing the camera directly, their face was partly obscured by hair/glasses/a selfie-taking phone). A deep-learning-based method (MTCNN) worked a lot better, and AWS and Azure offerings performed almost flawlessly (catching some faces humans missed). Just staying with the "default" method would have meant missing a lot of faces. As a wise old engineer once said, "If I didn't test it, it is broken").

Embeddings

The essential first step to solving any problem with a computer is finding a good way to represent the data; comparing images of two faces on a pixel-to-pixel basis doesn't work at all because tiny changes in lighting/post/expression will increase the "distance" between the two face images. We needed a way to represent a face that would be able to ignore irrelevancies like these (and cope with others too, like changes in hair, makeup and—a biggie!—Instagram filters).

Embeddings are a hot area of modern computer science because many problems get a lot easier to solve when we can transform pieces of data into something we can work with more easily. They are a way of representing an input (an image, or maybe a sound, or a piece of text) in a way that makes a solution much easier, discarding irrelevant variations (like lighting or pose). An embedding transforms a high-dimensional input into a much lower-dimensional space (the exact dimensionality is rather arbitrary) in which the axes carry information about problem-relevant aspects of the input data. For example, language embeddings typically have axes to differentiate plural and singular forms, masculine and feminine, and so on. Readers may be reminded of PCA; however, modern embeddings are created by deep neural networks which are attempting to minimize an error score related to the problem being solved, a constraint that shapes them into a problem-specific form.

Embeddings of text allow one to avoid using brittle lexical searches (to ignore details like capitalization, punctuation, spelling), instead capturing the semantics ("dog" and "Labrador" are spelt differently, but semantically very close). Similarly, we can train a deep neural network to map an image of a face to a small string of numbers—a vector—that can easily be compared to vectors of potential matches, while ignoring variations we don't care about (lighting, pose, even age). Note that embeddings have applications to a very wide number of problems (for example, Facebook makes great use of them) (Figure 10.13).

Train, Review... Train again

Reading an academic paper or a news article, you may read that "a model was trained...." This is highly misleading! You'll need to train many, many models before you reach production (should we train a model from scratch? What about transfer learning? etc.), and each experiment is going to create new results to analyze. In ML, failures are usually more informative than successes. It's important to get that 30,000 foot overview (a simple scatter plot showed us that an early age estimation model was simply guessing the median age), to be skeptical of "too good to be true" results (an actress was present in the training and the test set, photographed at about the same age, so a "sneaky" model could use her identity to guess her age), and also to get the "street level" view ("guess our face recognizer doesn't cope well with heavy fringes")—time spent poring over a model's most egregious failures is unlikely to be wasted.

Sometimes the Right Answer Is No

In the case of facial recognition, we found that we could build our own training set using data that Thorn already held, so as to shape a model to Thorn's particular

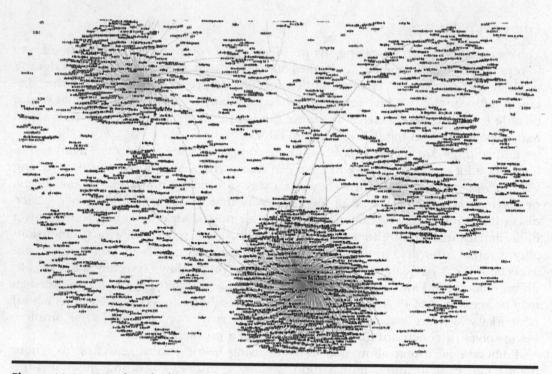

Figure 10.13 Word embeddings capture semantic relationships, place words with similar meanings "closer" to each other in a high-dimensional feature space.

needs. However, we were also able to establish that commercial offerings were a better use of limited ML resources (innovation is a last resort!): as fun as it was to train a model, we knew we should pause that work. By contrast, a build-your-own approach to age estimation easily passed a cost-benefit test: our own models matched the quality of commercial offerings when our training set reached just 1,000 images, and by 7,000 samples we were really closing the gap with human performance.

Return on Investment

Anyone considering doing similar work is bound to have a long list of other calls on their time—what an economist would call a "high opportunity cost." For us, the work has been worth it, even if we consider only entirely personal benefits: organizations in this domain are imbued with a sense of mission, and even their small size has its advantages—there is an agility and willingness to take on new challenges that some large companies would envy. The ultimate payoff comes from getting new tools into the hands of analysts and police officers and seeing them well-used: it is hard to exaggerate the satisfaction of knowing that your work has contributed to arrests for very, very serious offences.

A Note on Empathy

This work comes with obvious emotional hazards: working on a problem like child sexual exploitation, it is only too easy to wallow in the horror of these cases. Without quite aspiring to the emotional blankness of Spock or Commander Data, it is necessary to maintain a degree of clinical detachment. Try to keep your attention to the technical aspects of whatever problem you are trying to solve. This "emotional armor" has plenty of chinks, of course: the best treatment for the dark days is to get back to the keyboard and hammer out another chunk of working code.

An Entrepreneur's Experience

In this section, we describe how an enterprise can partner with a non-profit to apply AI to solve a shared technical challenge that can have impact beyond just the two organizations.

The first thing to keep in mind is that building external partnerships is part art and part science regardless of whether the work you are collaborating on is for profit or for societal good. Non-profit organizations have numerous competing priorities (many of which are tied to contractually binding grants), so it can be challenging to gain mindshare for a data science project with real-world impact. Finding the right organization to align with is key, it must be a mutually beneficial relationship and typically involves both monetary support and technical expertise. Working with another organization you want to cultivate a long-term relationship and not just do a project. It is important to do your research on the non-profit landscape that serves the societal good area you would like to affect. To learn more about a target organization, you can volunteer there, watch documentaries about the topic to educate yourself, and listen to podcasts. Check in your network (LinkedIn can be very useful) to see if you have any contacts with people at your target organization and request a networking 1:1 with them. It is important to be customer focused in this relationship and to recognize that at the end of the day you are selling your company's capabilities to them, not making a donation. Just because you don't plan to charge for your services, it costs the organization time and allocation of internal resources to absorb new technology. That may not be something they can support after you move on. If so, it is not a good fit. It is important to work with a non-profit that is mission aligned and ready to innovate from a technology standpoint to accomplish that mission. As with many public sector opportunities, expect things to move at a slow and steady pace. The collaboration will need to be reviewed at both executive and board levels to proceed.

Once you have identified a partner you would like to proceed with, it is important to get a Memorandum of Understanding in place to ensure you are both aligned on the scope of the partnership. The more explicit you can be on what is included and not included in the project the better, including timelines. This gives both organizations an opportunity to ensure a mutual understanding of scope and timing so that there are not large surprises along the way. Bad news is ok, but surprises are damaging to a relationship. Over-communication is advisable where possible and it is crucial to assign a project manager to oversee the project. Quarterly executive syncs can ensure that all key stakeholders stay engaged with the project and that the working-level team has an opportunity to share their progress and successes with leadership.

Call to Action

- Lead from where you are. You *can* affect change at your company, community, or religious organization today.

- Look around for problems that technology can help with and connect them to where they may cost money to the organization (lawsuits, time, or resources). It is always good to think about what keeps the CFO up at night.
- Build a team around you to help you ideate and prototype small MVPs so you can fail fast and learn. This will help you to home in on the great idea that is worth pitching to your leadership team or investors.

Tying It All Together: A Practical Example

An example of a very successful, impactful, and ultimately positive automation process will help clarify the value of building AI for Good. In 2016, the National Center for Missing and Exploited Children ("NCMEC") was facing a crisis. NCMEC is best known as the organization that puts age-progressed photos of missing children on milk cartons and billboards, and acts as a clearinghouse for all information and support services around missing children. NCMEC has another important role in the world of online child safety. It is the home of the CyberTipline, where all reports of online child pornography and child exploitation are processed and then forwarded to law enforcement. The challenge in 2016 was that the annual number of incoming reports to be reviewed had doubled every year for the past few years and was projected to hit 16 million by the end of the year, while the team of analysts reviewing each report to determine which law enforcement agency to forward them to was about 25. The math just didn't work out, so a 30-day backlog of cases had formed, in which reports that were not marked as "urgent" by the reporting organization could languish in a queue for up to 30 days.

NCMEC analysts, who are already performing an incredible service to the children of the world by reviewing and analyzing the most horrific cases of child abuse and exploitation imaginable, were demoralized by the exponential growth of the task before them. At Intel, we learned of NCMEC's plight, and with the financial support and executive sponsorship of the leader of the Intel Data Center Group, we formed the *Intel Inside, Safer Children Outside* program to apply AI to help NCMEC scale its process to handle the growing number of CyberTips.

Two critical tasks for the CyberTipline analysts were to determine which law enforcement agency each report should be referred to, and to connect clues from previously reported cases along with any additional available data to augment the usefulness of the information provided to law enforcement. To determine the correct jurisdiction for a referral, analysts would review clues in the report, including phone numbers, IP addresses, and any locations specifically referenced in the data. This was a tedious, and somewhat technical task that had to be completed before any additional analysis could be performed. As the caseload grew, opportunities for analysts to add value by making connections between cases and identifying additional clues in reports diminished proportionately since the augmentation of the information in each case report, and not the determination of the correct jurisdiction is where the analysts' human intellect and experience came most into play.

Our strategy at Safer Children was to build an analytics pipeline that would apply successive analytical procedures to the incoming reports, integrating automated and human steps, and featuring a ML algorithm that could automate the determination of which law enforcement agency should receive the report. We used past referral decisions by analysts as gold standard labeled data to train this ML algorithm to "predict" where the report should be sent. The result was an end-to-end report processing pipeline that could automate specific steps in the lifecycle of a CyberTip, dramatically accelerating the turnaround time for reports.

It is important to note that at this point, analysts had grave concerns about automating any part of the pipeline, not so much because they feared they would be made obsolete by this newfangled AI automation technology, but because they had concerns about the quality of the decision-making that would be done by the algorithm. Analysts are experts who are dedicating their time and experience to maximize the effect of NCMEC to reduce child exploitation and to bring perpetrators to justice. Understandably, they did not want to sacrifice quality for speed. To allay their fears, our approach was to incorporate the algorithm's recommendation, along with the information that went into the decision and the algorithm's estimate of its prediction confidence, into the existing analyst user interface. Analysts had the opportunity to review the information and approve each recommendation. To enable true automation, the algorithm was implemented so that the organization could set a threshold in the confidence level at which the recommended jurisdiction would be automatically approved without requiring the input of the analyst. Within weeks the confidence of the analysts, and thus of NCMEC, was very high in the reliability of the algorithm and a vast majority of incoming cases were shifted to automated jurisdiction recommendation, and the 30-day backlog of cases virtually disappeared. Furthermore, analysts found themselves with significantly more time to analyze cases, enabling them to supplement many cases with information that could help law enforcement to take decisive action. AI automation allowed NCMEC analysts to protect more children and prosecute more perpetrators. Analysts who started this automation journey with a mix of optimism and concern became its greatest champions.

There are a couple of key takeaways in this story. First, automation can be applied to a whole process, but is often most powerfully employed at key bottlenecks, leaving the rest of the existing process in place. This can result in an optimal mix of human and augmented human activities which gives the organization speed, agility, and control. Second, humans can feel threatened by automation, so it is important to find ways to build trust in the technology. By placing the rate of automation in the hands of the analysts, we were able to gain their confidence and get their buy-in. Finally, note that we automated a frequent and tedious task within a larger process, allowing us to leverage past human decisions as training data for a new algorithm. This is a common pattern in AI-driven automation: look for the places where you have a treasure trove of past human-generated results. You'll have lots of good training data and you'll be automating an activity that is currently costing the organization a tremendous amount of money in human time.

Summary

In this chapter we have looked at some of the risks inherent in AI, such as threats to privacy, bias in algorithms, and concerns over trust, to remind enterprise leaders that there is a role for them in leading their organizations to developing the best AI-powered technologies possible.

Rather like headline concerns about the economic effects of AI (how many months left before robots take all our jobs?), headlines relating to moral quandaries raised by AI are often only distantly related to the sorts of problems that managers and engineers are likely to face in their day-to-day lives. The most common problems—such as bias—are closely related to traditional engineering concerns like quality and safety, and should be amenable to similar management techniques.

The greatest challenges may well involve external organizations offering tempting contracts; like many other types of good, AI or ML offerings can be "dual purpose." In this area, tech companies can benefit from the example of the better firms in finance, accounting, and the defense sector, where "know your customer" is an established precept.

We have also looked at ways for large enterprises to develop technology that is explicitly intended to benefit society. This is a real opportunity: AI is powerful enough that a modest effort in cost and resources can create a substantial positive impact in the world and sometimes large enterprises can be the right environments for nurturing the development of such solutions.

Notes

1 Jonas Kaiser and Adrian Rauchfleisch, "The implications of venturing down the rabbit hole," Internet Policy Review Journal on Internet Regulation, June 27, 2019, https://policyreview.info/articles/news/implications-venturing-down-rabbit-hole/1406.

2 Zhibo Wang, Mengkai Song, Zhifei Zhang, Yang Song, Qian Wang, Hairong Qi, "Beyond Inferring Class Representatives: User-Level Privacy Leakage From Federated Learning," arXiv.org, December 5, 2018, https://arxiv.org/pdf/1812.00535.pdf.

3 Veale Michael, Binns Reuben and Edwards Lilian, "Algorithms that remember: model inversion attacks and data protection law," Phil. Trans. R. Soc. A.3762018008320180083, 2018, http://doi.org/10.1098/rsta.2018.0083.

4 Cynthia Dwork and Aaron Roth, "The Algorithmic Foundations of Differential Privacy," Foundations and Trends in Theoretical Computer Science, Vol. 9, Nos. 3–4 (2014) 211–407, https://www.cis.upenn.edu/~aaroth/Papers/privacybook.pdf.

5 Government Statistical Service, "Privacy and data confidentiality methods: a Data and Analysis Method Review (DAMR)," December 13, 2018, https://gss.civilservice.gov.uk/wp-content/uploads/2018/12/12-12-18_FINAL_Privitar_Kobbi_Nissim_article.pdf.

6 Caio Milani, "Protecting Against Linkage Attacks that Use 'Anonymous Data'," MarkLogic blog, https://www.marklogic.com/blog/protecting-linkage-attacks-use-anonymous-data/, retrieved September 26, 2021.

7 Abhishek Bhowmick, John Duchi1, Julien Freudiger, Gaurav Kapoor, and Ryan Rogers, "Protection Against Reconstruction and Its Applications in Private Federated Learning," arXiv.or, June 3, 2019, https://arxiv.org/pdf/1812.00984.pdf.

8 Fatemehsadat Mireshghallah, "Inference privacy: What is it, and why do we care?," OpenMined blog, April 11th, 2020, https://blog.openmined.org/inference-privacy-what-is-it-and-why-do-we-care/.

9 Kabir Firaque, "Explained: Why is there no mathematics Nobel? The theories, the facts, the myths,"The Indian Express, October 16, 2019, https://indianexpress.com/article/explained/why-is-there-no-mathematics-nobel-the-theories-the-facts-the-myths-6071015/.

10 Marco Tulio Ribeiro, Sameer Singh, and Carlos Guestrin, "Why Should I Trust You?" Explaining the Predictions of Any Classifier," arXiv.org, August 9, 2016, https://arxiv.org/pdf/1602.04938.pdf.

11 Wikipedia contributors, "Fundamental attribution error," Wikipedia, The Free Encyclopedia, https://en.wikipedia.org/w/index.php?title=Fundamental_attribution_error&oldid=1040464289 (accessed September 26, 2021).

12 Wikipedia contributors, "Hippocratic Oath," Wikipedia, The Free Encyclopedia, https://en.wikipedia.org/w/index.php?title=Hippocratic_Oath&oldid=1045700402 (accessed September 26, 2021).

Chapter 11

Future of Enterprise AI

Edward Dixon
Rigr AI

Contents

Introduction

> It is difficult to make predictions, especially about the future
>
> —Danish proverb

New results in artificial intelligence seem to come in a torrent. Many of the latest technical developments are in some sense complementary, feeding and accelerating each other. In this chapter, we rise above the rush of news, looking ahead to when

DOI: 10.4324/9781351032940-11

this new form of software reaches maturity. We consider the hardware, algorithms, data, applications, and economic effects, and consider the lessons of history with respect to the pace at which new technologies are commercialized and brought to their full potential. Suitably chastened, we then survey the new computing substrates that will challenge the dominance of the CPU and the GPU. What algorithms might those new processors be running? Some strong contenders are introduced. What about training data? We explore the potential for the blockchain to alleviate the data shortage. Given great new hardware, algorithms, and lots of data, what's the killer application that (almost) no-one has ever heard of? We describe a little-known application of machine learning with transformative potential. We close by considering the intra-firm economic effects of the general adoption of AI.

Suppose we try to forecast the impact—in broad economic terms—of the latest computing revolution. The *first* computer revolution might seem a reasonable starting point; born at the beginning of the 1940s, the earliest machines revolutionized *computation* and quickly dominated important application areas, such as creating tables for artillery, or code breaking. After 30 years—at the dawn of the '70s—computers were improving reporting for large companies, running our phone networks, and sitting in the nose cones of nuclear missiles. As delightful as corporate reports and weapons of mass destruction might be, they did not transform our economies. As late as 1987, with PCs flooding every office, Robert Solow, the man who won a Nobel prize for his theory of economic growth[1], observed that "you see the computer age everywhere, but in the productivity statistics!"[2].

How long does it take to adopt *and fully exploit* a new technology? The adoption of fire, stone tools, agriculture, copper, bronze, and iron are imperfectly documented, but for innovations like the electric motor, we can refer to the engineering journals of the day. Although a working electric motor was demonstrated in 1834[3], they were not commercialized till the 1870s; as late as 1908, an article in the British journal "Engineering," marveled at the use of electric motors in the yards of Harland and Wolff (then the world's leading shipbuilder[4]), remarking that *"for the greater part, each tool has its own motor"* and that this was true *"even for such small tools as sensitive drills."* How obvious were the benefits? The writer explains that:

> As the result of electric transmission of power, in preference to steam leads, which were about 1,000 ft long in some cases, the coal bill is half what it formerly totaled.

This wasn't the main advantage, however: electrical power allowed machinists very precise control over the speed of cutting heads to suit the metal they were working—which led to a more important business gain:

> Thus, it is easy to get a 10% increase on output, which is of greater value than the reduction on coal.

Even a conceptually simply device like the electric motor took 70 years to begin approaching its potential (at a leading-edge innovator like Harland & Wolff), and this progress relied on a host of other innovations: motors were invented before generators[5] (when powered by batteries, they could not compete with a 4,000-year-old source motive power—domesticated horses), and even in 1908, Harland & Wolff found it necessary to operate their own power station. There was also the need to develop an ecosystem of suppliers and maintainers: the shipyard sourced motors from different suppliers, some as far away as Zurich, and employed "only one man and a boy" to re-wind the coils of failed motors (it was well into the 20th century before progress in chemistry gave us the tough, flexible plastics that insulate our modern wires).

Seen in this light, we might wonder if—a little less than 50 years after its invention—we are still in the "exploratory" phase of the adoption of microprocessors, and whether the rest of the century will be enough time to properly explore the applications of artificial intelligence. Suitably sobered by engineering history, we turn now to recent developments—which we consider to be under-reported—that offer enormous potential.

New Computing Substrates

The Return of the... ASIC?

The current machine-learning landscape has been dominated by two types of processor—the ever-adaptable CPU, which powers inference in most machine-learning applications today and the GPU, whose architecture (throughput oriented, massively parallel, and designed for linear algebra, a mathematical topic that is key for machine learning) has won it massive market share as a platform for training deep neural networks. Although both types of processor have been adapted to improve performance on deep learning-related tasks, their primary roles place constraints on their design envelopes (rather as if "flying cars" and "flying ships" were the only aircraft categories). Enter the new contenders: processors which offer no flexibility whatever, instead concentrating on making a very small number of operations as fast and efficient as possible.

The ASIC or Application Specific Integrated Circuit, offers a relatively fast and inexpensive way of creating a custom processor (think millions of dollars, rather than billions for a full processor). As one of the first companies to apply deep learning to business problems at scale, Google was also one of the first to realize that they could reduce the marginal cost of prediction (inference) by creating their own chips—TPUs (Tensor Processing Units). The nature of deep learning inference (heavy use of matrix multiplication, in which pairs of columns and rows can be processed without waiting for the results for other parts of the matrices) allowed Google to employ a highly parallel hardware design—arrays of ASICs mounted on SSD-sized circuit boards designed to slot into repurposed storage servers, originally built to hold large arrays of SSDs. Despite the inherent limitations of ASICs, published figures show later versions of TPU "pods" outperforming GPUs on price and performance for the training of deep neural networks[6]. Now launching the 3rd generation of their own hardware (TPU v3), Google is being joined by tech giants Amazon and Facebook which are developing similar devices. Rather closer to market, Intel is complementing its traditional CPU offerings with its own ASIC-based accelerator for deep learning inference, code-named Spring Lake, and due to ship in volume in 2019. The tech giants face competition from a host of hardware startups, notably Graphcore, a UK-based firm with formidable founders and early backers and Huawei, the Chinese networking giant.

The product roadmaps of these firms suggest increasing pressure on the price point training hardware, squeezing the margins of a certain GPU-based incumbent.

Ultra-low Power Devices

Although modern research teams are using ever-larger arrays of hardware to search for new state-of-the-art results, the *efficiency* of machine learning is showing equally dramatic improvements. While the most accurate results are achieved by enormous, power-hungry deep neural networks, teams operating at the opposite end of the data and power scale are "doing more with less," focusing on moving models into production—products doing inference "at the edge" can't rely·on the lavish hardware resources of a research lab.

The training of neural networks relies heavily on gradient descent, with floating-point numbers being a prerequisite for the gradient estimates which drive model updates[7]. However, trained models are highly redundant—with the right techniques, most of the information in their weights can be discarded. Models can be compressed more than a thousand-fold—with minimal loss of accuracy[8] using a technique called model distillation and further compression is possible. Intel's OpenVINO toolkit replaces model parameters specified with 32 bits, instead using 8-bit values, in many cases *leaving model accuracy unchanged*[9]. This result will seem counterintuitive to any reader who watched the evolution of game consoles during the 1990s; the technique is complementary to model compression and recent research suggests that models may soon need even fewer bits per parameter.

However, to get to very low power levels, a combination of hardware and software changes is necessary. A good example—in terms of technique and application—was the recent development of a chip that detects the human voice while drawing just under 1 microwatt[10], using a *binarized* neural network—just 1 bit per parameter. The key here is that reducing the number of bits reduces power consumption, and this can be done *while preserving model effectiveness*.

With the main competitors in the ML hardware accelerator space all launching hardware that targets the "ML at the edge" product category, readers should expect rapid progress—models that produce more accurate results but draw less and less power.

Neural Turing Machines

Traditional software excels at data storage and retrieval—"digital" is practically a synonym for "precise." Machine-learning techniques, contrastingly, require samples to be presented to a model many times before the model's weights are changed enough to capture the new sample.

Traditional computers are all just "special cases" of a sort of Platonic Ideal devised by Alan Turing, a simple machine, capable of computing anything that can be computed. The key feature of the machine is a memory that can be read and written at will, and it is this feature that is singularly lacking in modern machine learning.

Contrary to popular belief, there are very few machine-learning models in production which learn as they work ("online learning"). Almost without exception, they are entirely "stateless," retaining nothing of the data they process—not because this is undesirable, but because the best brains in the business can't get it to work. This is of course an enormous limitation, roughly comparable to the gap between a word processor and a typewriter (both get words on the page faster than writing longhand, but I'm glad I didn't have write this chapter on a typewriter!).

Conventional software has a perfect memory with stunningly reliable data storage but suffers from the limitation that it can only perform operations simple enough for human engineers to reduce to code. Thus, traditional software excelled at calculating payroll, but not at answering the telephone. Machine-learning models can understand short utterances more accurately than human listeners, but struggle with simple arithmetic and sorting operations that would be trivial in conventional software. In effect, we can use ML to train functions—individual operations—of brilliance (have you tried machine translation recently?) but *not* to train something that even approaches a complete application.

What if we could combine the strengths of traditional computing—that elephantine memory—with the strengths of machine learning—devising functions of a complexity beyond the grasp of human engineers? Research on neural Turing machines suggest that this may indeed be possible. The key difficulties revolve not around memory *per se*, but in training a model to read or write the correct region of memory for the task at hand. If machine-learning models can learn to properly exploit the vast memory available in a modern computer, we are likely to see a very sudden step change in the complexity of tasks that they can complete—as if conventional computers had made an overnight transition from using a few CPU registers to terabytes of storage.

Bayesian Machine Learning

If machine learning has a Prophet, it would be Thomas Bayes, an 18th-century statistician and philosopher, whose formula describes how beliefs should be updated by new evidence. His modern adherents predict a second coming…

Bayesian machine learning is currently something of a backwater: it doesn't directly power the applications that are making the headlines. Its attractions stem from its mathematical underpinnings, which effectively define rational learning in a simple formula. The elegance and power of this formula have made it a (comparatively!) popular tattoo among the machine-learning community.

Bayesian techniques for ML involve a different way of thinking than more popular methods. Where a traditional model might, given some inputs (say, a headshot) predict the subject's age (MLE or "maximum likelihood estimation"—the single age that appears most probable, given the input), a Bayesian would instead output a distribution. This "distribution" would assign some probability to each possible age (0 to …?), with a peak around the "most likely estimate." If additional confirmatory evidence were to become available, the peak would rise and tighten, drawing probability mass away from other regions of the distribution. Although a gradual accumulation of evidence could eventually raise a spike around the MLE, the faintest wisp of probability will still remain over the rest of the ages: Bayesians never quite discard any outcome ("I think he's 70, but he *could* be a child suffering from progeria").

To understand the power and the limitations of the Bayesian approach, let's look at one of its most famous successes—getting humans to the moon and back! Used recursively, "Bayesian updating" is mathematically equivalent to something called the Kalman Filter. From the earliest days of the Apollo project, it was recognized that an accurate estimate of trajectory was vital to mission success. Without the possibility of in-orbit refueling, Apollo spacecraft carried only just enough fuel to make it to the moon and back: each change in orbit required burning irreplaceable fuel at precisely calculated locations relative to the Earth and the Moon. With the moon moving at about 1 kilometers per second and the closest approach of the orbiter at just over 90 kilometers from the surface, margins for error were not generous (even the return to Earth relied on hitting the atmosphere at just the right angle—too steep and you become a meteor, too shallow and you skip back into space, like a stone from a pond). It was therefore crucial to maintain an accurate estimate of the location of the spacecraft, incorporating new measurements as they became available.

Rather than a "big data" problem, the challenge of navigating the Apollo space-craft was to wring maximum value from a comparatively small set of measurements, using a comparatively tiny computer. Part of the beauty of Bayesian methods is that they are extremely economical in terms of the data required, even allowing us to explicitly incorporate knowledge ("priors") that does not come from the training set. By contrast, the most popular machine-learning techniques require the machine to learn the desired rules *only* from the supplied training data. As described previously, the other killer feature is that these techniques keep track of uncertainty (which might originate in the data, or in the training of the model) so that, when we bring a model into production usage, we know how much to trust its predictions, and when the inputs we give the model are simply too different from the material that it trained on.

So why aren't Bayesian methods everywhere already? Well, they've had a lot of success in narrow domains:

- Your smartphone probably uses an Apollo-style Kalman filter to help you find your way, integrating data from accelerometers, GPS, and Wi-Fi signal strengths.
- Google's Project Loon used a Bayesian technique called Gaussian Processes[11] to allow its engine-less balloons to remain over the same country for extended periods (exploiting the difference in wind directions at different altitudes), an unprecedented achievement for unpowered craft)

However, they have suffered from one key weakness—their computational demands quickly become overwhelming for even medium-sized data-sets (not a problem for ballooning—even Google can only launch so many broadband-in-the-sky data col-lecting trips). Nevertheless, multiple teams have scored recent successes with "low-calorie" approximations which reduce the computational demands while keeping nearly all the "flavor"; this is allowing Bayesian methods to be introduced into the convolutional neural networks that have driven the Deep Learning revolution. Expect exciting progress in the short-to-medium term to lead to more data-efficient, more trustworthy, and more transparent AI.

Quantum Mechanics and the AI Revolution

How machine learning is expanding applications of one of the greatest discoveries of 20th century physics, and how quantum mechanics will in turn transform machine learning.

Materials science! Does the phrase get your pulse racing? It should! Stone tools—with wooden shafts—were enough to elevate an ape with rather underdeveloped teeth and claws to the top of the food chain. Metallurgy gave us copper, bronze, and iron—and corresponding waves of conquest and settlement.[12] An extra pinch of carbon and a stubborn commitment to process improvement gave us high-quality steels to spark the industrial revolution. The semi-conductors inside the processor at the heart of the laptop on which I'm writing this chapter demonstrate our ability to manipulate matter at the nanometer scale… and yet, even such achievements pale beside the sophistication of the composite materials in a shrimp's claw (withstanding huge forces without the need of metals), or the efficiency (95%) of the electron-harvesting elegance concealed within the green loveliness of chlorophyll. Life excels at creating macro-scale objects with nano-scale structure—we do not.

Self-Driving Chemistry

Human mastery of matter at a certain scale is obvious—you can see our cities from orbit, and we have changed even the composition of our atmosphere. However, our ability to manipulate matter at the tiniest scales remains rather limited. As we shall see, changing what is possible in this area may well become one of AI's greatest contributions.

During the 20th century, physicists and chemists used the new understanding of the atom first to explore the structure of important molecules, and then, slowly, to learn to assemble them from simpler ingredients. Building larger molecules from simpler ones—synthesis—transformed our lives. Plastics are a great example—you have probably got some polymers in your clothes, but also insulating the wiring in your house, preventing food spoilage in your fridge and weatherproofing your exterior (even your lovely wooden furniture often relies on glues based on plastics). Chemosynthesis has been used to build more complicated molecules too, just look in your medicine cupboard—Aspirin, for example, or Salbutamol, the active ingredient in Ventolin inhalers—great medications that are now incredibly cheap to make.

It is here that we start to find some important limitations: we *can* synthesize simple molecules like these, but for more complicated ones—insulin, antibiotics—we have to "hire" some assistants. Insulin, for example, is brewed in bioreactors using genetically modified yeast or bacteria: because we can't figure out how to make it, we've copied and pasted the DNA sequence for the human version into tiny creatures who then churn it out in industrial volumes (a sort of high-end brewing process, not unlike beer-making). Although these medications have been an enormous boon, their discovery and manufacture also highlight our weaknesses:

- New antibiotics must be *found*—they are not *designed*. For example, a key step in the mass-production of penicillin was the discovery of a particularly easy-to-grow mold on a cantaloupe in Peoria, Illinois. As much as we admire the diligent search which found that cantaloupe, as a reliable, repeatable process for creating new medications, perhaps we could improve on it.

- As obliging as our tiny bioreactor-dwelling workers are, their virtuosity in crafting large molecules is limited to what can be described by a DNA sequence (which itself must be short enough for us to synthesize successfully). This rules out almost the entire periodic table.
- Even limiting ourselves to "things that yeast can make," we still need to devise a DNA sequence or set of sequences that will yield the desired result. DNA is "expressed" or "executed" by being turned into proteins that need to fold themselves into the final, functional shape. Getting the sequence just right for a reliably folding result is not a simple problem.

We have discovered laws that describe the behavior of matter at the tiniest scales with extraordinary precision—Quantum Mechanics—and so in principle, we should be able to design *and build* new structures at the tiniest scale at will. However, answering even a comparatively basic question about a new substance—"What is its boiling point?" remains extremely difficult. Instead of being designed from scratch, new materials are often found by a brute force search. Beyond finding the right material, *making it* in industrial quantities is an enormous challenge: new materials take between 5 and 15 years to commercialize[13]. Even at Intel Corporation[14], with 50 years' experience, we *do* make devices that are exquisitely nano-structured—but it takes an enormous building with a 10 to 11-digit price tag!).

One structure that illustrates both the difficulty and the potential is the carbon nanotube, a sheet of carbon atoms linked in a hexagonal pattern and rolled into a tube with walls just 1 atom thick. Tubes of this form have many interesting thermal and electrical properties—but their mechanical strength shows their potential: a cable of carbon nanotubes with a cross-sectional area of $1mm^2$ could hold a weight of 6 tons (picture a rather coarse thread suspending *two* pickup trucks!), a tensile strength more than 300 times stronger than a high-carbon steel. Why don't we see this wonder material everywhere? Two reasons:

Cost

As the 4th-most abundant element in the universe, we might naively expect carbon-based materials to be cheaper than steel (which is mostly iron, an element only about ¼ as abundant as carbon). Whilst the price of carbon nanotubes has fallen from $1600 *per gram* in 2000 (about 40 times dear than gold) to $1 in 2018 (about 1/40th price of gold), a marvelous improvement, but it still leaves us 3 orders of magnitude short of matching the price of steel (about $1 *per kilogram)*. "Cheaper than gold" isn't a very exacting cost bar!

Quality

In 2007, the longest-ever tubes were about 1.8 centimeters in length. By 2013, the longest tubes were still just 50 centimeters long.

The enormous fall in price is due to heroic efforts of experimenters to improve the synthesis of carbon nanotubes. So why can't we "simply" apply quantum mechanics to the problem of producing this material and skip all those tedious experiments?

Unfortunately, simulations using these laws are exceptionally computationally demanding (at least on classical computers). Happily, physicists have found an elegant dodge: one way to think of machine-learning models is as a *function approximator*—a way of looking at a complex piece of math and coming up with a cheaper alternative that gets us within a whisker ("within epsilon") of the right answer. Most of us think of machine learning as requiring a lot of computational power: physicists think of it as an *incredible bargain offer* that lets them simulate chemical reactions accurately for the low, low price of 1% of the cost of a "full fat" quantum simulation. We don't have to know the exact parameters of the supply-demand curve for quantum simulations to forecast a correspondingly dramatic increase in the use of these simulations, as the cheaper (but still sufficiently accurate) machine-learning-based simulations become available. Already, simulations of this type have allowed scientists working at Canada's National Research Center to predict the properties of carbon-based structures at an unprecedented scale[15], a key step to broadening the industrial use of carbon nanotubes and related structures.

Cheaper simulation is important as an enabling step, for understanding the behavior of large quantum dynamical systems at the heart of material science, pharmaceuticals, computing, and energy production. In addition, it also aids in designing or discovering useful molecules and, crucially, developing the synthesis methods needed to create them. At the time of writing, for example, designing new therapeutic molecules—new medicines—often involves working with rather hefty molecules containing thousands of atoms: amino acids and proteins are the language of molecular biology, hundreds of times larger and more complex than friendly little fellows like alcohol or caffeine.

One approach to discovering new drugs is to create a vast molecular library, then use robots to screen these molecules for therapeutic potential. Think of a drug target—a "receptor site" (perhaps serving as a gatekeeper on the surface of a cell) as being an elaborate lock, and the molecular library as a vast collection of keys—jars of old relics from yard sales, master keys already known to open many locks, and new creations fabricated in the mere hope that their creator might one day find a corresponding lock (yes, chemists create variation after variation on interesting compounds, hoping one might turn out to be useful). The screening process is one of trying key after key in that tantalizing lock, looking for something that turns smoothly and discarding those that don't fit or jam—or open too many locks we would rather not touch. Imagine trying to create *any other new product* in the same way! Experts *do* try to hand-place atoms to craft new medicines, but, the very existence of robotic drug screening processes should warn the reader that this is a difficult endeavor.

If only we could build a suitably accurate (embodying the laws of quantum mechanics) simulation, capable of running at a reasonable cost, it would be possible to work in a different way. Instead of specifying a solution in the form of a molecule, a researcher would define desirable properties (perhaps the drug needs to bind to one particular "receptor" site on a cell's exterior but *not* to a great many similar receptors, and to be susceptible to eventual breakdown into non-toxic metabolites by the liver's enzymes) and allow a form of machine learning called *reinforcement learning* to construct a custom molecule. This form of machine learning is used to train *policies* to take a series of actions in a certain environment (usually simulated to reduce costs) and development time, to make progress toward a specific goal. The learning works because the policy is adjusted by an optimization algorithm that attempts to maximize a "reward." For example, changes to a molecule that increase toxicity would result in negative rewards, while changes that enhance specificity relative to the target receptor would attract positive rewards. This form of machine learning has produced policies (models) that defeat all opponents at games like Go and chess[16], and has also had success with more frivolous tasks like using robotic hands to manipulate objects[17], or training self-driving cars.

Unfortunately, finding the right molecular structure is only the first step: we then need to design a process to create that molecule and this is *synthesis*. We've considered a kind of self-driving chemistry for molecular design, but we could also benefit hugely from automating the design of synthesis, and figuring out the steps required to produce a particular molecule is a complex business that has so far proved resistant to automation[18]. How important *is* the ability to design a synthesis process? A key component of the "green revolution" that allowed agriculture to scale up to feed modern populations, is the use of artificial fertilizers. Among these, ammonia is especially vital—plants need it as a source of nitrogen. This might seem strange—our atmosphere is mostly nitrogen, so shouldn't they just pull it out of the air? Unfortunately, the form of nitrogen we breathe (N_2) is extremely unreactive, and plants have so far not evolved the necessary chemistry. Such is the difficulty that the humans who figured out a workable series of steps—the Haber-Bosch[19] process—won a Nobel prize. The process is however extremely energy intensive, accounting for *more than 1%* of global consumption of global energy usage and contributing about half of the nitrogen in the tissues of the typical human (so great has been its contribution to agriculture).

That the synthesis of even a very small and simple molecule like ammonia can be extremely difficult (plants still can't do it, and even human chemical geniuses need to use very high temperatures and pressures) should convince you of the potential benefits of automating the synthesis design, and the impact of the Haber-Bosch process should make clear the vast social value of such innovation. The example of the humble soil bacteria—casually fixing nitrogen at ambient temperatures and pressures so very different to the high-temperature high-pressure industrial process—shows us how much better we *could* be.

To connect the potential of machine learning to one of the great problems of our day—feeding an increasing global demand for energy while *also* reducing net CO^2 emissions—better ways of generating, storing, and transmitting energy hinge on materials science. In other words, better and cheaper composites for wind turbines, more efficient and cheaper solar panels, improved battery chemistries, and high-temperature superconductors. Accelerating the discovery and production of new materials can have an enormously positive impact on how our societies develop and grow.

Returning to the topic of pharmaceuticals, it should now be clear that machine learning offers us a path to creating advanced drug design and testing in a datacenter. Given that the cost of bringing a new drug to market has reached $2.5 *billion* dollars[20] and that the steady 20th-century trend of increasing life expectancies seems to be running out of steam[21] (even in the face of unprecedented spending), the need to replace processes that hinge on luck and brute-force-search should be obvious.

In summary "self-driving chemistry" may allow machine learning to design new industrial *and* therapeutic molecules to order, and to transform the manufacturing processes which create them: it offers our most obvious path toward understanding the nanoscale world, and producing nanostructured materials in quantities and at prices that can really change our everyday lives. Since the advent of even a single new material—copper, bronze, iron, steel—can remake our society, the value of a process that makes routine the design and production of new materials can hardly be overstated.

Quantum Computing and Optimization

It has been generally known for some time that quantum computers can solve problems that are intractable on classical computers—like factoring large numbers to break public key encryption (companies like Google have already increased the key lengths they use, as a precaution against early breakthroughs). With multiple corporations demonstrating working prototype quantum computers, can we look forward using these amazing machines to accelerate machine learning? Perhaps a Quantum ML accelerator card to compete with GPUs/FPGAs/ASICs?

Quantum computers have other-worldly computational abilities (still mostly theoretical), but *also* other-worldly limitations. Take something as basic as RAM in a classical computer. We take for granted the ability to copy data to and from RAM, and to "copy and paste" data in RAM at will. Quantum computers have something called Q-RAM—Quantum RAM—in which data is stored in ever-so-delicate quantum superpositions (at temperatures very close to absolute zero, so that heat can't disrupt these states). Unfortunately, the data that is stored with such exquisite care is subject to the "no-cloning" theorem[22] which proves that quantum states *cannot* be cloned perfectly[23] (the reasons are complex and fascinating, but out of scope for this book). This complicates things quite a bit, not least error correction, which cannot be done using existing methods from classical computers.

In fact, simply *loading* classical data (bits—ones and zeros from non-quantum computers) into qubits (quantum memory) *or* extracting the results of quantum operations as classical data, can be so complex and expensive as to destroy whatever speed advantage the quantum computer enjoys in operating on the data! This problem is so pronounced that some researchers suggest *not* applying quantum computers to classical data at all, focusing instead on modeling quantum mechanical problems—the kind that we touched on when explaining how machine learning is making it possible to efficiently approximate the rules of quantum mechanics on classical hardware, enabling simulations that may well transform materials science.

> The reason most educated people today don't know simulating quantum systems is important is because classical computers are so bad at it that it's never been practical to do. We've been living too early in history to understand how incredibly important quantum simulation really is.
> Michael Nielsen, "Quantum Computing for the Very Curious"[24]

Despite the serious drawbacks in relation to operating on classical data—do *not* expect to simply substitute quantum hardware for classical-quantum computers still have strengths that suggest they can excel at machine learning due to their affinity with a branch of mathematics called "linear algebra," a key element of most modern machine-learning algorithms. Quantum algorithms have been found that offer exponential gains in performance versus their classical counterparts—for these particular tasks, work that takes 1 million hours on a classical machine might be completed in a thousand, even a hundred hours on a quantum system. Algorithms are known that could offer this kind of acceleration for machine-learning algorithms ranging from deep learning to recommender systems. However, fully-fledged commercial systems capable of applying even algorithms already devised by theoreticians on datasets sufficiently large to challenge the processing power of classical computers probably need to muster in the order of 1 million qubits—about 20,000 times larger than the prototype quantum computers that have been demonstrated at the time of writing.

It is in representing the states of quantum mechanical systems that quantum computers enjoy their most obvious edge over their classical predecessors (and avoid the difficulties associated with loading and retrieving classical bits). If modeling the quantum mechanical properties of an n atom molecule, a classical computer requires in the order of k^n bits, where k is a number that depends on the number of properties being modeled—let's take the lower bound value (2) for now. A 2-atom system will need 2^2 bits of storage—4 bits doesn't sound too bad. The trouble is that a 3 atom molecule needs 2^3 (8 bits), 4 atoms need 2^4 (16 bits), and by the time we reach 64 atoms this doubling has taken us a little past 2 exabytes (a University of Berkeley estimate is that all the data produced by humanity up to the year 1999, including all video, audio, and text was about 12 exabytes). At the time of writing, modeling a molecule with 225 atoms using classical memory would require a quantity of flash drives roughly equal to the mass of the observable universe. Even a universe-scale classical computer would be hopelessly inadequate for interesting molecules like proteins, containing thousands of atoms.

What about a quantum computer given the same tasks? It would need kn bits—so a 2-atom system would need 4 *qubits*, 3 atoms require 6 qubits, 4 atoms need 16 qubits and 64 atoms require 128 qubits. Instead of doubling our memory requirements, each new atom just adds 2 qubits to the total! Although at the time of writing existing quantum computers remain tiny (less than 100 qubits of total memory), the math tells us that it is a viable path to precise simulations of matter at the finest scale. As we described in the "self-driving chemistry" section, these simulations should ultimately allow us to mass-produce materials with nanoscale structures, transforming sectors as different as energy and medicine.

Another potential application often raised is in search—a famous (in specialized circles!) method called "Grover's Algorithm" exists that can greatly reduce the time taken to perform a search—if N items need to be checked, Grover's Algorithm can do it in $\sqrt{N}$, and so (for large N) should finish ahead of a classical computer (which needs to check all N items—so if N was 1 million, the quantum computer would need to check only 1,000). This is often described in the press as a way of speeding up database queries, but that's not quite right: databases are almost always designed to use indexing and other techniques to accelerate search (there is also the small matter of converting classical data to qubits that we already discussed). Grover's Algorithm *is* very exciting, but databases are an unlikely application: instead, we are more likely to see it being used to solve tough optimization problems, where the data to be searched are potential solutions to a problem.

Summarizing: it is already clear that machines with enough qubits would be able to take on tasks beyond the reach of conventional computers. Nevertheless, the strengths and weaknesses of the platform are so different to those of the computers we have today that it is very hard to say anything very specific about future applications. Despite great progress in terms of algorithmic development, actual hardware remains in its infancy: we've haven't yet reached the quantum equivalent of the moment we reached with the microprocessor, when "Moore's Law" kicked in. Expect Quantum Computing to be a big deal—just not for some years.

The Blockchain, Cryptography and AI

How Cryptography Can Help Solve AI's Data Problem

Blockchains are one of the more colorful flowers of the Age of Computers. Their distributed, trustless payment mechanisms have found applications among those for who find conventional payment mechanisms unsatisfactory—unfortunate citizens of certain nations whose conventional banking systems are unfit for purpose, and more notoriously among purveyors of illicit mind-altering substances and ransomware gangs. A lesser-known blockchain innovation—the smart contract—shows promise as an enabler for a remarkable variety of applications, and it is here that we first find an intersection with AI.

For the benefit of readers who've known blockchains mostly as an instrument of speculation, a brief explanation of smart contracts is in order: cryptocurrencies like Ethereum, include a *Turing-complete* scripting language, capable in principle of executing any possible computation[25]. Contracts written in these languages *own assets* and are executed on the blockchain in such a way that their execution is validated just like a more "traditional" transaction. Typically, the execution will transfer the assets entrusted to the contract to some third party (which might be another smart contract). A good analogy is the execution of a will by a lawyer, who holds the assets of the testator until they can be delivered to the beneficiaries (to complete the analogy, a blockchain contract also pays a fee to the miner who executes it). As with wills, the actual contents of such a contract (Turing-complete, remember) can be very simple, or very elaborate.

What is the connection with machine learning? A common difficulty with getting a machine-learning project under way is access to data. It frequently happens that the people who want to train a model do not control the necessary training data, and that the people who *do* hold it, while sympathetic to the goals of the would-be model trainers, are unable or unwilling to share a copy (often due to legal or policy constraints and/or the risk that further copies will be shared beyond their control).

One way around the difficulty is to leave the data *in situ* and bring the model to the data (perhaps held in onsite datacenters at several hospitals or banks), instead of vice versa. The model (carefully initialized so that changes in its weights cannot be used to infer anything about the training samples) is then trained using federated machine learning (all sites holding data train the model locally, sharing informa-tion about updates to the weights). The trust problem is now reversed—the model's owners must trust the data owners not to make illicit use of their IP, since each site providing data will also find itself holding a copy of the finished model. For joint ven-tures, this should be perfectly acceptable—but what about collaborations between more informally connected parties?

Remarkably, recent advances in mathematics offer two interesting routes to a solution. The first technique, called homomorphic encryption, allows mathematical operations to be performed on data *in its encrypted state*: "Alice" can, say, encrypt integers x and y, send Bob the ciphertexts x' and y' then ask him to add them. Upon receiving Bob's result for x' + y', Alice uses her key to decrypt this (still encrypted) result revealing the actual result of x + y—which is unknown, even to Bob and who still knows nothing of x or y. As improbable as this result might sound, it has allowed Computer Scientists using homomorphic primitives to create machine-learning soft-ware that can train a machine-learning model *while keeping both weights and data encrypted*. The goal is to allow a party who wants to train a model—and retrain full control of it—to send their encrypted model to parties holding related data, together with a public key. Data-owners then encrypt their data and use it to train the model (in an encrypted state!). The design allows contributions from many data-owning entities to contribute updates to the model weights—without revealing their data, and without giving them any opportunity to obtain a usable (decrypted) copy of the model.

A second technique, multi-party computation, splits a given unit of data into an encrypted form consisting of *n* "shards," to be distributed among multiple "worker" nodes. Somewhat similarly to homomorphic encryption, arithmetical operations can be performed on these pieces, with the result available only when the various pieces are re-combined and decrypted. Again, it has proved possible to create a federated machine-learning system using multi-party computation, with nodes able to contrib-ute to training an accurate model under strong privacy guarantees.

How are the data-owners to be compensated? "Data is the new oil," after all! Examining that metaphor more closely, oil's commodity status was arrived by defin-ing standards—"sweet, light crude," etc. on which markets could operate to match prices to demand. For data to be traded as freely, we would need a similar com-modification process (and this exists for certain specialized sorts of data). Outside of these markets, it is not so easy for buyer and seller to arrive at a price: the buyer can measure the incremental value (the beneficial effect on their model) of a given tranche of data only by using it for training—which, pre-blockchain, would neces-sitate a very trusting vendor.

An exciting open-source project called OpenMind[26] has demonstrated a possible solution: would-be model owners post a smart contract that will pay out if and only if a model reaches a particular quality threshold (protecting the data vendor), with the models being trained in a distributed fashion while in an encrypted state, with only the model owner holding the private key that can decrypt the model. The data own-ers can't steal the model (since they only have the public key), and the model owners (who could decrypt) only get their model back when the smart contract has paid out. The reward mechanism actually allows for many data-owners to make contributions, with payout shares driven by quality gains (so a small but well-curated dataset might out-earn a large but shoddy one, without either the buyer or the vendor having to bother with inspections or negotiations). Over time, the offering of rewards and the level of interest they generate among data-owners should establish prices—which, acting as a signal wrapped up in an incentive[27], ought to drive the creation of new datasets where needed, just as higher oil prices lead to innovation in oil extraction (and innovation in solar panels and wind turbines!). Since the availability of high-quality data is essential to shaping high-quality models, the development of such a market has enormous potential value as an enabler for machine learning.

All the encryption techniques discussed so far (those that underpin the block-chain, and those that allow arithmetic to be performed on ciphertexts) were designed by mathematicians and can offer privacy guarantees grounded in theorem proofs. However, they also have important limitations: at the time of writing, implementations train much more slowly than conventional equivalents, and achieve reduced levels of accuracy. Recent decades have seen rapid progress however, and so these limitations may be greatly diminished in the future.

Machine Learning has itself already led to new forms of "encryption" which offer another potential solution to the problem of allowing models to be trained on data that cannot be shared. *Neural Encryption* turns the invention of a new encryption scheme into a machine-learning problem, working along these lines:

> "Alice" creates a model to act as the encrypting function whose inputs are the plaintext and a key string, which outputs the ciphertext, while "Bob" creates decryption network whose inputs are the ciphertext received from "Alice" and the key string. Bob's training goal is simple: reproduce the plaintext as accurately as possible, given the ciphertext and the key string. A third model, "Eve" is given the ciphertext—like Bob—but is *not* given the true key string. The "Eve" model's training goal is to recover the plain-text from the ciphertext *without* needing to access a key string. What about Alice's model? The training goal for Alice is to *minimize* Bob's decryption error while *maximizing* Eve's decryption error (if we hadn't also trained Eve, Alice would probably just have learned to ignore the key string, sim-ply passing the plaintext to Bob—a high quality "adversary" is essential to a good result).

How does this help us with machine learning? Remember how homomorphic encryp-tion and multi-party computation schemes have been developed to allow arithmetic operations on the encrypted data, such that the plaintext will have also gone through the same operations? Neural encryption produces ciphertexts that (unlike the cipher-text of conventional cryptographic operations) *can* successfully be used as training inputs (but not labels) for neural networks. As exotic as this technique sounds, there is an "existence proof" in the form of Numer.ai, an algo-trading hedge fund that crowd-sources predictions from a global pool of Data Scientists. Reliant on licensed (and so unshareable) data streams, Numer.ai uses neural encryption to convert this data into an unrecognizable form that it can share publicly. Remarkably, Data Scientists are consistently able to use this "encrypted" data to make successful predictions about market movements (payouts to the best Data Scientists are—naturally!—made via smart contracts on the Ethereum blockchain and a token called Numeraire).

How does neural encryption work? To use neural encryption to enable machine learning on secret data, one first trains Alice and Bob to convergence (and Eve as well, so that Alice and Bob are forced to learn *some* form of encryption). The unshareable data is then neurally encrypted using the "Alice" model to form a ciphertext. This data—the features or data inputs—is then shared with people who want to train models, together with label data for each sample which is *not* encrypted (perhaps the samples are neurally encrypted medical records, while the labels are diagnoses?). The attractions, as compared to homomorphic or multi-party methods, are several:

■ The actual machine learning is unrestricted—any preferred library can be used.
■ The time required to train models will not be affected.
■ The actual encryption procedure need only be carried out once per sample, so imposes just a modest, non-recurring cost (at training time—later, unlabeled samples will need to be encrypted by the Alice model before we can perform inference).
■ The resulting models are more accurate.

There are several drawbacks, at least at the time of writing:

■ Neural encryption is somewhat opaque and can only offer empirical guarantees of privacy or security (Eve's failures). No theorems (yet).
■ The resulting models are *only* able to operate on encrypted data. After training is complete, possession of the "Alice" encrypting network and the encryption key are required so that samples can be encrypted prior to inference. Depending on the use case, you might see this as either a bug or a feature. Anyone in possession of both "Alice" and the key can train a new "Bob" and so decipher the training data, and so "Alice" and the key cannot readily be shared.

Again, future developments are quite likely to make neural encryption more "user-friendly." For instance, neural equivalents of public and private keys would allow inference on new samples without also allowing training data to be deciphered. Alternatively, since the *labels* are not encrypted, a set of unlabeled samples whose plaintext is available to the model *user* could be used for inference with the ciphertext trained model. The results could then be used for model distillation/student-teacher training[28] to create a new model that accepts plaintext inputs (the accuracy should be similar, but the time to process each input should be greatly reduced).

Will AI Front-runners Become Monopolists?

The ability of Google and Facebook to attract and retain top-tier machine-learning researchers has led to fears that these firms may manage to "corner the market" for machine learning. Research groups at both firms have produced spectacular results. Google used reinforcement learning to reduce the amount of power used to cool their data centers by a stunning 40%[29]. Public talks by Google's legendary Jeff Dean[30] show that machine learning is becoming deeply integrated into their applications across a broad front, displacing algorithms that had been Computer Science stalwarts. Facebook's engineers have advanced the state of the art in various aspects of natural language processing, not least machine translation[31]. There is no doubt that these firms are succeeding in converting research into new business value. Be that as it may, while the underlying innovations have broad applications, it is noticeable that the actual value realized has been within the core business areas of both firms rather than in new business areas. A look at the history of technology-based companies suggests that this will continue to be true.[32]

Consider Xerox, the copier machine giant. Understanding the need for a pipeline of innovations, it established the now-legendary Xerox PARC research unit: this is the place where the computer mouse and a windows-based GUI were first demonstrated. Notoriously, Steve Jobs, having seen their "mother of all demos," succeeded in commercializing this innovation and creating a massively successful product line... for Apple (Bill Gates and Paul Allen were also paying attention). By contrast, another Xerox PARC innovation—the laser printer—was successively commercialized by the company itself on an enormous scale. An older and even most august corporate research facility, Nokia Bell Labs has seen *nine* (!) Nobel prizes won by its staff for inventions that include optical tweezers capable of manipulating tiny objects with beams of light, the CCD sensor (the key component of many digital cameras), and the work on semiconductors that led to the creation of the transistor (and all modern computers). Other "little" projects included using fiber optic cables to transmit data.

Why didn't Bell or Xerox—with world-famous R&D departments—come to dominate the modern computing landscape? It is easy to imagine large firms—with employee numbers and budgets almost at the scale of nations rather than mere corporations, and research groups that would be the envy of almost any university—being be able to roll across the business landscape conquering all before them, rather as Genghis Khan and his sons did, riding across the steppe. Part of the answer seems to be that large firms excel *only* at operationalizing "small-i" innovation—turning incremental improvements to existing products into a repeatable, even somewhat predictable process (think of Intel, and their relentless 50-year campaign in fulfillment of Moore's Law). They can occasionally manage to introduce fundamentally new technologies—but usually only if the next technology slots neatly into an existing use-case (the telco-owned Bell Labs and their optical fibers to replace copper cables). To *get* big, companies of this type must become a kind of ultra-specialized machine for improving their sort of product, building organizational "blinkers" to avoid distractions (new products, most of which would be duds). Little upstarts aren't *smarter*—they just haven't had time to build the infrastructure that will block out new ideas, even internally invented ones.

Readers who have run software development projects will know that building a good solution requires a tightest possible loop between the software developers and the people who use the product. With each iteration, the team gets a better understanding of their user's needs—an understanding which is captured only partially in the software, the rest becoming a less tangible accumulation of "knowledge capital" and "organizational capital" in the minds of the engineers and managers. In other words, not only is the software shaped by the user's requirements, but so too is the firm, which gradually becomes ever-more adapted to delivering iterations of its particular product line. This intangible capital, so difficult to replicate, at least partly explains the high price that investors will pay to buy into a super-star firm[33] (as opposed to simply paying contractors to build a clone of a successful application) and the apparently stratospheric returns on equity of some super-start technology firms (rather than signaling the pricing power of a monopolist or a rentier, they may be more normal returns on a kind of capital that isn't apparent on a balance sheet. This product team/user cycle also helps to explain the success of upstarts like Apple—after the impetus of the Xerox demo leads to their first product, they were locked in a tight learning loop with their users, allowing them to iterate toward something much better than Xerox R&D could build.

So, while a business that relies on, say, the online retailing of mass-produced consumer goods is essentially a steppe village about to be overrun by the modern equivalent of Khan's cavalry, most businesses are protected by the complexity of the products and services they sell, much as the walls of Hungary's castles presented new difficulties to the mounted archers who had been so successful on open ground. As Adam Smith observed so presciently in 1776,[34] "the division of labor is limited by the extent of the market": our modern markets being global, firms and their offerings have reached a degree of specialization that might surprise even Smith. It is this specialization that should continue to protect many organizations: not only are the internet giants unable to bring their huge forces to bear on each business problem—they don't even have the organizational capacity to *detect* them. In fact, their sheer size means that they will not even *consider* anything other than behemoth-scaled opportunities, much as the Mongol armies could only bring their full weight to bear on lands that offered enough grazing to sustain their vast size (each warrior needed between 3 to 5 horses).

Rather than fear the giants, businesses should try to fully exploit their extraordinary openness: top-tier research teams at Facebook and Google not only publish their work in high-quality papers, but also open-source their software, even sharing models that took days or weeks to train on huge clusters tended by expert researchers and engineers. It is hard to overstate the value of the intellectual property being so freely shared—it is as if a car manufacturer were to offer free copies of all the machinery used on their lines to all-comers. Take the work these giants have paid for, and adapt it to the areas of your firm's expertise.

There is one caveat, which is that companies like Google, Amazon, Microsoft and Baidu, having experienced internally the value and breadth of applicability of machine learning, are each attempting to become *the* provider of machine-learning infrastructure—developing custom hardware and a compelling software stack. The obvious danger for customers, as with previous cloud offerings, is of a technological lock-in. This risk is lower than for conventional software however: given the existence of a prepared dataset, re-implementing machine-learning models using a new framework is surprisingly low-cost (mainly because the machine learning itself is doing the heavy lifting, so there shouldn't be much platform-specific code).

Machines of Loving Grace[35]

It has become popular to forecast a future in which machines take care of the drudgery, while we focus on roles that play to our essentially "human" traits, like empathy. *Is* empathy a defining human quality? We excel *by comparison with other species* in our ability to live and work with non-kin ("socially minded" ants, bees, naked mole rats, wolves, all limit their cooperation to close family).

Nevertheless, it isn't hard to reach the limits of our patience or compassion of the typical human—pick your saintliest, most mildest-mannered friend, ask them *the very same question* a few dozen times… and be prepared to evade airborne crockery! Where now their compassion? For most of us, empathy is a sort of shallow reservoir, easily drained by sleepless nights, postponed, or interrupted meals. Unfortunately, some of the neediest among us—small children, sufferers of certain psychiatric conditions, those afflicted by dementia—may be at their most demanding when we who care for them are at our weakest. Who among us can always claim to listen to *only* the better angels of our nature?

Anecdotally, we may already have had a preview of what interacting with an empathetic machine might look like. Judith Newman, mother to an autistic teenager, wrote in the New York Times[36] of how Apple's Siri had improved her son's use of language—partly because (back in 2014) Siri couldn't understand what he said unless his enunciation improved, partly because "she" set a high standard for good manners, and because "she" would spend hours answering her son's questions.

To the author's understanding, Siri is a combination of great voice recognition and a large database of answer templates from good writers who have carefully crafted her "personality." However, there is no reason to think that the success of machine learning in modeling our language, recognizing our faces, or imitating our movements will not soon be followed by matching or exceeding our ability to read each other's mental states. If we can then write a loss function to penalize a *lack* of grace or empathy, there is no obvious reason to suppose that our machines will not exceed us in empathy, compassion, and selflessness. A defeat for humanity, or the ultimate victory over its own nature of a flawed ape—a kind of prosthetic conscience?

Summary

We continue to see rapid progress in the development of machine learning—the hardware is evolving rapidly, the software infrastructure maturing to serve the needs of engineering teams, and the research frontier is expanding too quickly to track. There is no reason to assume that the rate of change will slacken: ever larger models will be trained on ever larger datasets—but models will also require ever less data to reach acceptable performance (hello, "Small Data").

However, early uses of artificial intelligence—every single existing product or demo!—are probably no better guide to its future economic value than early uses of electric motors (trolley cars) or microprocessors (reducing the component count in electronics which previously relied on combinations of stock logic components—Pong, the first arcade game, had 66 chips[37]!).

A better way to think about the potential of artificial intelligence is to think of it as a new way of producing software (Software 2.0?), a means of circumventing the most fundamental limiting factor for today's computers: the software engineer. Although computers might seem pervasive, they have been limited to performing only tasks which can be reduced by a human engineer to simple, stepwise instructions (non-programmers should recall their High School math teacher, and their insistence to "show your workings!").

An example: calculating sales tax is an operation which we understand explicitly, so we can easily convert our explicit understanding to software inside a point-of-sale terminal; contrast this with calculations we make when we identify a door handle, twist it with just enough force, and, with equal economy, open the door and walk through. Our understanding of the task is so thorough that we manage very well with doors and door handles we've never seen before, and even very young children (and determined pets) can manage the same trick. However, converting our implicit understanding to an engineered solution has been so challenging that a demo video of a robot managing this most mundane of tasks immediately went viral[38].

For the software engineer, machine learning offers a way around the "show your workings" obstacle: instead of trying to write instructions to identify a door handle (smarter people than the author spent about 50 years trying this approach), one can simply collect example images (even a few hundred might be enough) and use them to fine-tune an existing "model" to perform the new task. How many tasks in your business are somewhat like calculating sales tax and how many are a little more nebulous, requiring "judgement" or "experience"? For most readers, the fraction of tasks within your business that are amenable to automation with conventional hand-written software will amount to no more than a small fraction of the total. Our existing software industry, circumscribed until very recently by our human limitations, represents just a tiny subset of the possibilities offered by modern computing.

Although machine learning opens up vast new possibilities for computing, the history of engineering teaches us that finding the applications and fully developing them will not be the work of a small coterie of companies in Silicon Valley, but rather, a vast army of engineers and managers working in all sorts of industries, most well outside the "tech sector" as it is conventionally understood. It is their understanding of the problems to be solved in their market niche that will enable the potential of AI to be realized.

At the time of writing, the short-term transformative effects of AI or machine learning are perhaps overestimated, since the largest effects must await the adoption and adaptation of modern machine learning in industries where work happens in the more complex world outside the server closet. However, its longer-term potential—to transform our ability to create new materials, to design new therapeutic drugs, to advance manufacturing—is greatly underestimated (if even understood at all). It will be up to you, dear reader, and others like you, to realize this potential.

Notes

1 Four of his doctoral students have also won the prize for their own work.
2 Triplett, Jack E. 1999. "The Solow Productivity Paradox: What Do Computers Do to Productivity?" Brookings. March 1, 1999. Available at https://www.brookings.edu/articles/the-solow-productivity-paradox-what-do-computers-do-to-productivity/.
3 Edison Tech. 2014. "The Electric Motor – Edison Tech Center." Edisontechcenter.org. 2014. Available at http://edisontechcenter.org/electricmotors.html.
4 This is the shipyard that built the Titanic. A museum now stands beside the ways where her keel was laid—recommended.
5 Necessarily so! The heart of a generator is an electric motor, except that instead of using electrical current to spin, it is spun by some external force (wind? steam? cyclist?) producing electrical current.

6 Reitsma, Steven. 2019. "Cost Comparison of Deep Learning Hardware: Google TPUv2 vs Nvidia Tesla V100." Medium. January 21, 2019. Available at https://medium.com/big-datarepublic/cost-comparison-of-deep-learning-hardware-google-tpuv2-vs-nvidia-tesla-v100-3c63fe56c20f.

7 A loose analogy might help here. The gradients or slopes yield crucial information that allows the model to be made "less wrong" at each step by "walking" parameters "downhill" to an "error minimum". Quantization makes the slopes less accurate, which in turn degrades the ability to "walk" towards a region. Lower error. Imagine the difference between walking down a gentle slope in a fog, seeking a valley floor, and doing the of same thing on a terraced landscape.

8 Buciluă, Cristian, Rich Caruana, and Alexandru Niculescu-Mizil. 2006. "Model Compression." *KDD '06: Proceedings of the 12th ACM SIGKDD international conference on Knowledge discovery and data mining.* August 20, 2006. pp. 1391–139. Retrieved from https://doi.org/10.1145/1150402.1150464.

9 "Artificial Intelligence (AI) And Deep Learning Solutions." *Intel.* 2021. Available at https://www.intel.com/content/www/us/en/artificial-intelligence/overview.html#gs.09d20h.

10 Yang, Minhao et al. "A 1μW Voice Activity Detector Using Analog Feature Extraction and Digital Deep Neural Network." *2018 IEEE International Solid - State Circuits Conference – (ISSCC).* 2018. pp. 346–348. Retrieved from doi: 10.1109/ISSCC.2018.8310326.

11 Metz, Cade. 2017. "Machine Learning Invades the Real World on Project Loon's Internet Balloons." Wired. February 17, 2017. Available at https://www.wired.com/2017/02/machine-learning-drifting-real-world-internet-balloons/.

12 Studies of ancient genetic material tell us that Bronze Age settlers account for 90% of the DNA of modern-day inhabitants of the British Isles, apparently replacing the previous population of stone age farmers. Technological disruption is not a new phenomenon! See "Who We Are and How We Got Here: Ancient DNA and the New Science of the Human Past" by David Reich.

13 Maine, Elicia and Purnesh Seegopaul. 2016. "Accelerating Advanced-Materials Commercialization." ResearchGate. Nature Publishing Group. April 26, 2016. Available at https://www.researchgate.net/publication/301672209_Accelerating_advanced-materials_commercialization.

14 This author's employer, and a great supporter of this book.

15 Mills, Kyle et al. 2019. "Extensive Deep Neural Networks for Transferring Small Scale Learning to Large Scale Systems." *Chemical Science* 10, no. 15 (2019): 4129–40. April 11, 2019. Retrieved from https://doi.org/10.1039/c8sc04578j.

16 AlphaZero. n.d. Retrieved from https://deepmind.com/documents/260/alphazero_preprint.pdf.

17 OpenAI et al. 2019. "Learning Dexterous In-Hand Manipulation." ArXiv.org. January 18, 2019. Available at https://arxiv.org/abs/1808.00177.

18 Crow, James Mitchell. 2018. "AI Alchemists Spit out the Recipe for Any Molecule You Want to Make." New Scientist. Available at https://www.newscientist.com/article/mg24032000-400-ai-alchemists-spit-out-the-recipe-for-any-molecule-you-want-to-make/.

19 Wikipedia Contributors. 2021. "Haber Process." Wikipedia. October 6, 2021. Available at https://en.wikipedia.org/wiki/Haber_process.

20 Mulin, Rick. 2014. "Cost to Develop New Pharmaceutical Drug Now Exceeds $2.5B." Scientific American. November 24, 2014. Available at https://www.scientificamerican.com/article/cost-to-develop-new-pharmaceutical-drug-now-exceeds-2-5b/.

21 For example, see a report commissioned by the government of the UK, "A Review of Recent Trends in Mortality in England." Retrieved from https://assets.publishing.service.gov.uk/government/uploads/system/uploads/attachment_data/file/827518/Recent_trends_in_mortality_in_England.pdf.

22 Park, James L. 1970. "The Concept of Transition in Quantum Mechanics." *Foundations of Physics* 1, no. 1 (March 1970): 23–33. https://doi.org/10.1007/bf00708652.

23 This is a positive for some applications because an eavesdropper attempting to clone a message would cause the quantum state to collapse. However, very imperfect copying is possible.

24 Matuschak, Andy and Michael Nielsen. 2019. "Quantum Computing for the Very Curious." Quantum Country. Available at https://quantum.country/qcvc.

25 Don't expect to see your favorite database transitioning to blockchain-based execution; in order to make the contracts tamper-proof, each line of code gets executed by every node in the Ethereum network—it is as if serving a webpage required every server on the internet to all repeat the same work! This makes running code on the Ethereum blockchain about 400 million times as expensive as a more conventional implementation (Ryan, Danny. 2017. "Calculating Costs in Ethereum Contracts." Hackernoon.com. May 30, 2017. Available at https://hackernoon.com/ether-purchase-power-df40a38c5a2f.). Only code and data that really need the special properties of the blockchain have any business being there.

26 Openmined.org. 2021. "OpenMined." OpenMined. Available at https://www.openmined.org/.

27 Marginal Revolution University. 2015. "A Price Is a Signal Wrapped up in an Incentive | Microeconomics Videos." February 9, 2015. Available at https://mru.org/courses/principles-economics-microeconomics/price-system-spontaneous-order.

28 Hinton, Geoffrey, Oriol Vinyals, and Jeff Dean. 2015. "Distilling the Knowledge in a Neural Network." ArXiv.org. March 9, 2015. Available at https://arxiv.org/abs/1503.02531.

29 Deepmind.com. 2016. "DeepMind AI Reduces Google Data Centre Cooling Bill by 40%." Deepmind. Available at https://deepmind.com/blog/article/deepmind-ai-reduces-google-data-centre-cooling-bill-40.

30 His contributions have been so central to Google's success that the company added a Grade 11 to their 1–10 employee grade level scale just for him. Despite devising one of the key innovations behind modern big data processing, his most-cited work is believed to be a large statistical application that he developed for use by epidemiologists… as a teenager.

31 Ott, Myle, Marc'Aurelio Ranzato, and Guillaume Lample. 2018. "Unsupervised Machine Translation: A Novel Approach to Provide Fast, Accurate Translations for More Languages." Facebook Engineering. August 31, 2018. Available at https://engineering.fb.com/2018/08/31/ai-research/unsupervised-machine-translation-a-novel-approach-to-provide-fast-accurate-translations-for-more-languages/.

32 It is true that Amazon have created an enormous new business, in the form of AWS. Isn't this very far from their book-selling roots? No! The growth of their online retailing required them to build infrastructure on an unprecedented scale: AWS is "just" a way to monetize capabilities that they needed anyway. Baidu have gone down a similar route in China.

33 Ayyagari, Meghana, Asli Demirgüç-Kunt, and Vojislav Maksimovic. 2018. "The Role of Intangible Capital in Explaining Superstar Firms | VOX, CEPR Policy Portal." VoxEU. October 8, 2018. Available at https://voxeu.org/article/role-intangible-capital-explaining-superstar-firms.

34 Smith, Adam. 1776. *An Inquiry into the Nature and Causes of the Wealth of Nations*. Edited by Edwin Cannan. London: W. Strahan and T. Cadell.

35 Brautigan, Richard. 1967. "All Watched over by Machines of Loving Grace." AllPoetry. Available at https://allpoetry.com/All-Watched-Over-By-Machines-Of-Loving-Grace.

36 Newman, Judith. 2014. "To Siri, with Love." *The New York Times*. October 17, 2014. Available at https://www.nytimes.com/2014/10/19/fashion/how-apples-siri-became-one-autistic-boys-bff.html.

37 Szczys, Mike. 2012. "Fabricating Hardware from the Original Arcade Pong Schematics." Hackaday. December 22, 2012. Available at https://hackaday.com/2012/12/22/fabricating-hardware-from-the-original-arcade-pong-schematics/.

38 Boston Dynamics. 2018. "Hey Buddy, Can You Give Me a Hand?" YouTube Video. *YouTube*. February 12, 2018. Available at https://www.youtube.com/watch?v=fUyU3lKzoio.

APPENDIX

Case Study 1: Get More Value from Your Banking Data— How to Turn Your Analytics Team into a Profit Centre

Felipe Flores

Data Science Executive and host of the Data Futurology Podcast

Contents

Modern financial institutions collect and store vast amounts of data on their customers; however, most of it is never used to its full potential. This is as much a shame for the customer as it is for the financial institution, as this example from my former employer—a large banking conglomerate with businesses across many countries in the Asia-Pacific region—will show.

A typical approach when it comes to analytics in banking is to use the data that are available within your division. This is largely because the knowledge and approvals required to use data from other divisions are difficult to come by in large organizations such as major banks. This case study highlights the value and benefits of using data from other divisions to service your customers. In this example, we focus on institutional banking but the principles apply to other divisions as well. The key message is that the data from other divisions is valuable to your customers and a competitive advantage in the marketplace.

Institutional banking is the division of major banks that works in the business-to-business sector with the largest organizations in the world. Most large banks split their business customers by revenue. Customers will less than $10 million in annual revenue are usually classified as business banking customers. Corporate and commercial customers typically have revenues ranging between $10 million and $400 million. Customers with revenues above $400 million are usually classified as institutional customers. They are publicly traded companies, multinationals, and government organizations.

Providing banking services to the largest companies in the world is a very competitive game. Like with many other industries the competitive levers for customer acquisition are price, industry knowledge, and value add. In this example, we will see how a data science team can become a profit center by taking an entrepreneurial approach to enhancing the value-add and driving customer acquisition.

Setting Up the Team's Strategy

When deciding the work of a data science team, there are several areas to tackle, including:

- cost reduction: optimization, efficiencies, automation, etc.
- profit growth: enhance profitable products/offerings
- new products: create new offerings from existing assets

We decided to pursue *profit growth* by enhancing the most profitable financial products in the bank with data science. We had internal support as this aligned with the bank's strategic efforts. We quickly found that this definition, while useful, was too broad. Institutional banking divisions usually have about 10% of the workforce of the entire bank. This means that in most banks the workforce of the division is anywhere from 2,000 to 10,000 people. Typically, half the institutional banking staff are Relationship Managers (RMs), who are the sales component of the division. In other words, we simply had too colleagues to deal with (over 1,000!) in order to understand our market and design our offering.

To narrow the scope, we decided to focus on the new offerings to existing customers only. Having information about the customer would be helpful if we needed to narrow our scope even more. Also, having a relationship with the customer meant they would be more open to developing our new enhancement in partnership with us. Although we were now focusing only on existing customers, we still had too many Relationship Managers to deal with, so we decided to use our in-hand existing data about our customers to narrow our focus even more.

We analyzed customer profitability and found that, through a number of historical reasons (such as contract renegotiations, dropping profitable products), we had a number of customers that were unprofitable. As a result of our analysis, the bank decided to drop the customers that were very unprofitable. We (as the data science team) decided to focus on the customers that were only slightly unprofitable and that had just asked (or were about to ask) for a new product from the bank.

From this, we had a small subset of customers (and RMs) to focus on. At this point, we knew some information about the customers, but also felt the time pressure as we prepared to discuss the new offering with customers who were on the lookout for additional banking services. We ensured that we were involved when the products the customer wanted were in the top three most profitable offerings of the bank. This left us with about a dozen RMs to work with, a prioritized list of customers (by unprofitability), specific products to speak to them about, and timelines of when we were going to see them. If we could come up with a value-add offering that would convince the customer to go with us, it could be the start of something great.

Become Part of the Sales Cycle

Once we defined and prioritized the customers to target, we spent time with the RMs to deeply understand the top 6 customers, including their major business issues, recent history, business aims, and strategy. We also conducted thorough research on the customers' financials and analyzed their annual reports. This led us to the realization that most customers are looking to make decisions about the market, with limited visibility of it. Typically, businesses only have the interactions between their customers and them. We, as a bank, have a much broader view of the market as a whole. We can see how people spend their money across industries and within them.

If we anonymized and aggregated transactional and credit card data, we could provide our customers with insights about the market that they could not get on their own. We could use data from a different division (the retail division) to provide valuable insights to our institutional customers. We wanted to test this assumption as quickly as possible so we jumped into the sales cycle of the first customer on our list.

In preparation, we used our target customer's annual report to identify two main strategic goals that we could enhance with our data analytics. We worked closely with the RM to contextualize the findings and to hone in on the most impactful insights.

The two strategic goals we identified had a geographical element to them due to the nature of our customer's business. We then used unsupervised ML techniques to create clusters of customers according to their behaviors and generate heatmaps of their locations and movements at an aggregated level. This way we were able to provide valuable strategic and operational insights for two of the main pillars of our customer's business. We preserved privacy by focusing on macro insights that were unique to the customer and aligned to their goals. We offered those insights in our sales pitch.

We won that first customer and helped sign them up to one of the most profitable products the bank had. The customer said that the insights we offered helped them make the decision to choose us.

If you understand what's important for customers, you'll see the value you can provide. Becoming part of the sales cycle forces the data science team to narrow its focus and creates time pressures but also adds significant commercial value.

Create the Value and Give It Away

Find your niche and improve your offering. Aim for learning before profits.

This was our mantra. We were successful with our first customer, but as Bill Gates says, "success is a lousy teacher."

We were keen to see if we could replicate our success with other customers in different industries. Our next five customers were in the following industries: airlines, telecommunications, fashion retailing, fast food franchising, restaurant franchising.

All five customers met our selection criteria:

1. They were an existing customer
2. Customer was marginally unprofitable
3. They asked the bank to pitch one of our most profitable products
4. The sales pitch meeting had an upcoming date and time.

We followed the same formula again:

1. Worked with the RM to understand the customers' history and focus
2. Analyzed customer financials and annual reports to identify key strategic goals where we could support with our insights
3. We focused on analyzing data they wouldn't have access to
4. We offered our insights as a free value-add, bundled with a high margin financial product
5. The data science team was an integral part of the sales pitch presentation.

Offering value-add insights for free was controversial at the time. It generated many internal discussions. I'm glad we stuck to our guns and did it that way. It allowed customers to have an open mind and be much more willing to work with us to improve this valuable "freebie." These interactions allowed us to learn more and more about the customer, their needs, and the market. We were refining our product-market fit with every round of insights we provided.

We performed time series analysis for these customers. We looked at time series decompositions, forecasts of sales volumes and identified the main drivers of these through relative feature importance. We compared the behaviors of different stores/ airports in their network and compared cities and states over time. We strived to automate our work at every step so it was reproduceable and scalable.

At this stage, the insights were handcrafted and presented in a PowerPoint presentation. It took serious effort, a growing team and many, many late nights and weekends. With every customer interaction, we could feel we were getting better and better. With some of those customers, the data science team would present for 50 minutes out of the hour we had with them.

We continued this pace of doing small, focused bits of work to support the sales of our most profitable products. We kept winning new contracts. With each pitch, we learned and refined. Through every cycle we also spent a little bit of time automating our offering. Over time we found the type of insights that were most valuable to each customer and we were on the path to automating them. Through this we would send the customer a monthly report that was automatically tailored to them.

During this period, we learned to combine our internal data with external data to provide greater insights. This led us to using lots of free government data, like the census, and many other data sources to contextualize our findings. We also bought data such as company financials, company structures, and many other datasets to enhance our views and provide more value. At the time we were often the first customer to request a direct data feed from several data providers.

Build on Your Success to Become a Profit Centre

Enter the "freemium" and diversification.

At this stage, we had one offering: a free PowerPoint presentation with charts, predictions, and insights tailored for each business. Once the customer signed up they would receive this once per month. We would visit each customer once a quarter to go through the reports and get their feedback. The information presented had been refined over time through many sales pitches and customer meetings. Even though the information presented was hitting the mark, it was still a subset of what we could show.

During these ongoing meetings customers would sometimes ask for more detail, or a different cut of the data. By understanding their intent, we concluded that we could create an interactive web app to provide up-to-date information and much greater detail of the metrics we shared on a monthly basis. Customers were excited by the prospect, so we decided to test whether we could charge for this new level of access.

We built our web app in-house using cloud platforms and open-source software. We avoided licensing software, which allowed us to keep our cost low and it would enable the scale we desired. Getting our first prototype into the hands of customers was exciting. We had built industry-specific metrics (such as loyalty scores), created by understanding the Recency, Frequency, and Monetary value of their customer cohorts. We also looked at distances traveled, share of wallet, and distributions of customers versus the population in their geographies.

One of our most successful "features" during this time came from implementing proximity score matching with "random forest" ML. This technique was designed to identify subjects that are similar to one another in as many features as possible, while being different in the treatment variable.

For example, to estimate the effect going to university has on lifetime income you cannot discriminate against certain people from going to university. You can however take a dataset that includes the incomes of people who went to university along with people who did not go to university and construct artificial treatment and control groups from your observational data.

The way to do this using random forest is to run a model to predict the treatment variable, saving the proximity scores. For each treated observation, take the untreated observation with the highest proximity. Run a regression, using the saved proximities as weights. That way, we put a higher value on observations that are more like treated observations as opposed to observations that are less similar. Simulate 1:4 to get confidence intervals, especially important for small samples.

We used this technique repeatedly over time to find "similar" stores that varied in terms of customer loyalty or revenue (i.e. one store was more profitable than the other despite their similar customer demographics). Doing so allowed us to identify issues in inventories, pricing models, and locations.

All the work described above allowed us to get more deeply ingrained in our customers' businesses, increasing our understanding of them and their dependence on our platform. Often, we would analyze metrics and patterns over time at a store and even team level, providing detailed and specific insights to each manager in their network. We found that customers were happy to pay for this level of access and insights, especially if they were disseminated throughout their organization to the people who could change the business as a result of this information.

Getting the web app up and running was a huge endeavor and a great success. This gave customers much greater visibility of their operations and improvements that could be made. Once customers were comfortable with the web app, the final step in our journey was to offer them access to our APIs (which we had built as part of the web app development).

With access to our APIs customers could query our insights (instead of our data) directly. This gave them greater flexibility in using our insights. Customers also wanted to combine and analyze their internal data with ours so it could be fed back through the channels we had developed. This was an unexpected, but pleasant turn of events. We implemented this combining of data and grew our data science offerings greatly in the process.

Through this journey we were able to create a new and unlikely data science offering from a bank and increase customer value by crafting a good strategy, focusing on learning, and expanding our product offerings.

Case Study 2: AI in Financial Services: WeBank Practices—A Large Gap in China's SME Financing Landscape

Tyler Aveni
Head of International Fintech Partnerships, WeBank

Gil Guan
Project Manager, Fintech Partnerships, WeBank

Contents

Small- and medium-sized enterprises (SMEs) across the world face a large disparity between their economic contribution and relative financial support. Taking China as an example, as of the end of 2017, over 90% of enterprises were classified as SMEs, contributing to roughly 80% of employment, 60% of GDP, and 50% of tax income[1]; however, the relative proportion of loans distributed to SMEs from financial institutions accounted for a paltry 37.8% of the total volume of business loans by comparison[2]. This problem is exacerbated by the fact that SMEs often require immediate liquidity to meet their cash flow needs (e.g., many invoice orders are not fully paid until long after the final delivery of products or services).

As indicated in Figure CS2.1, the problem can be further divided into more fundamental challenges. First is the risk-adverse nature of bank lending. Traditional credit scoring methodology, which collects and analyzes information through manual processes, cannot comprehensively or effectively evaluate the financial picture of SMEs

355

Challenge: Uneven Demand and Supply of SME Lending

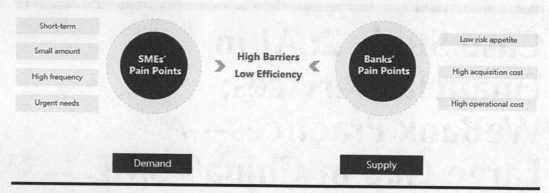

Figure CS2.1   Pain Points for SMEs and Banks in SME Financing.

in many cases. Consequently, banks rely on requiring collateral as a safeguard to offset the greater credit risk commonly associated with smaller businesses, effectively creating a high barrier to access. Second is the high cost of acquisition and operations. The potential revenue from small-sum lending to SMEs often cannot offset the costs of onboarding and servicing them. The economics of human-dependent operations at traditional financial institutions simply cannot support smaller-sum financing to SMEs, even when equipped with compelling data or collateral to do so.

For those SMEs which can gain access to credit, the entire process can still be riddled with opaque fees or terms, as well as incur heavy time costs. Collectively, these challenges account for a series of graduated pain points for SME owners looking for formal financial support.

The Conventional Approach to SME Lending Is Labor-Intensive

To understand the problem in more detail, a review of traditional SME financing is required. In simplistic terms, the SME credit loan process for banks can be divided into marketing and customer acquisition, loan underwriting, loan disbursement, post-loan management, and collection processes.

Customer acquisition typically requires client managers to identify potential SME customers and develop business through direct communication. After an SME applies for a loan, client managers conduct an in-person interview with the SME owner(s) and manually collect many supporting documents (enterprise credit information, financial statements, compliance reports, business registration, etc.) for the regulatory-mandated know-your-customer (KYC) and due diligence processes. The risk management department then manually verifies documentation and assesses creditworthiness to determine if the loan application is successful or not and the corresponding credit amount. This underwriting process collectively takes several weeks to complete typically.

The traditional approach bears high human capital costs in post-loan servicing as well. Client managers must visit SMEs regularly to monitor several aspects of the running businesses (production performance, change of acting legal person, etc.). Furthermore, a large number of call center staff is needed to support loan collection. This means that as the portfolio of SME borrowers grows, banks must hire staff in equal proportion. As a result, banks encounter high acquisition, risk, and operational costs of serving SMEs, while not benefiting from any economies of scale.

WeBank Addresses Challenges with Advanced AI Technologies

In light of these issues, WeBank began incorporating AI techniques and solutions across the entire process that could reduce the repetitive and standardized activities previously done manually in the conventional SME lending business. This reduced material and time costs, but more importantly, also freed up our resources and enabled us to invest in other areas such as big data analytics and product design—two key drivers for improved credit access and better customer experience.

The result is WeBank's unique SME loan product—Weiyedai—which first launched at the end of 2017. The product differentiated itself as being China's first-ever fully online, uncollateralized, 24/7, and paperless SME loan product offered solely through the mobile phone. Once consent for data use is authorized by the SME legal person, more than thirty data sources (enterprise credit information, personal credit data, tax bureau, national ID database, etc.) are accessed on behalf of the customer. Instantly thousands of data elements are processed by advanced models to output a robust credit score. These models are built in advance using both AI/ML and rules-based approaches to arrive at a more predictive result. After the credit score is completed, the SME credit decision is swiftly completed within minutes.

To begin this process, client acquisition is first required. WeBank leverages on big and alternative data to profile likely small business owners and then pushes suitable promotions using precision marketing techniques through third-party online platforms. Using this method, the click-through rate of such promotions at WeBank is more than twice the industry average in China, and the customer acquisition cost is reduced by 93%.

Next comes WeBank's customer onboarding process, which is largely handled using artificial intelligence. Weiyedai integrates a suite of AI technologies to perform its electronic KYC (eKYC) checks for identity verification; these eKYC AI technologies include bank card & personal ID card optical character recognition (OCR), ID verification, live body detection, facial recognition, and anti-fraud models. This critically improves security, but also reduces the time and effort required by business owners to input their key personal and business information.

The use of eKYC also effectively allows any prospective SME borrowers to apply remotely at any time of day. Use of facial verification technology is extremely mature in the China market in particular, as is typically measured by false acceptance rate (i.e., number of people who try to commit fraud who are successful in doing so) and false rejection rate (i.e., number of people who are who they say they are but are rejected). WeBank's own eKYC solution has a false acceptance rate of less than one in a million.

After receiving the SME owner's authorization as part of the loan application, WeBank collects both personal and enterprise data from authenticated sources, as

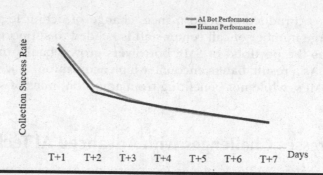

Figure CS2.2 Performance of Human Call Collection and AI Bot Collection.

previously described, to execute two-dimensional quantitative modeling. Modeling results will then be consolidated to a credit score comprising of multiple indicators (credibility, stability, growth, etc.) to arrive at a decision, including a dynamically risk-based credit line amount and interest rate if successful. On average this credit approval process takes just minutes and is fully automated.

Once a credit line is issued, loan drawdown typically takes only minutes to reach a linked bank account of the borrower's choosing. As new data is collected on an ongoing basis, models are continuously monitoring post-loan performance and the SME's business operations. The automation process then determines and handles cases that appear at higher risk, as well as issues alerts and suggested actions to post-loan management staff when human intervention is required.

AI bots play an important role in customer service and collection. A smart customer service system couples a frontline chatbot with call center staff to improve efficiency. This chatbot leverages Natural Language Processing (NLP) based on transfer learning technology, a type of ML, to understand the intent and nature of a customer's request. As a result, 98% of all inbound inquiries concerning loan products are answered successfully with WeBank's chatbot.

Finally, in the collection process, a voice-based collection bot is employed to call borrowers for repayment reminders, which improves efficiency while removing any risk of malpractice. This collection bot is able to take into account the SME customer profile to develop an intelligent collection strategy, such as the frequency or time of day of scheduled calls and communication style. Using a standard seven-day collection plan, when compared to a human-based calling scenario, the collection bot performs at similar or slightly higher levels in triggering a successful late payment, as seen in Figure CS2.2. This is achieved at an operating cost of only one-fifteenth that of a traditional collection call center[3].

Smart Technical Adoption Drives Market Impact

As of two years since the product's launch, Weiyedai has served over 900,000 SMEs, of which more than 60% reported the loan as their first ever from a bank. The credit line issued ranges in size from 50,000 yuan (USD ~7000) to 3 million yuan (USD ~424,000), with the average credit line size being roughly 400,000 yuan (USD ~57,000). WeBank also offers all borrowers the option to repay early at no penalty charge (SMEs pay off their loans in just 44 days on average, reflecting their on-demand liquidity needs). Seventy percent of SMEs are in manufacturing, high-tech, wholesale and retail industries, and the remaining 30% covers technology service providers, logistics companies, and construction firms. In total, Weiyedai has supported businesses accounting for a total employment of more than 3 million people in China.

As a result, by leveraging AI technologies, WeBank has effectively created a new cost structure for SME financing, while also helping extend financial access to a traditionally underserved segment of customers; thus, small businesses can enjoy affordable, accessible, and appropriate services for their everyday business needs.

About WeBank

WeBank was officially established on December 16, 2014. WeBank is the first privately owned bank and digital-only bank in China. Committed to strategic positioning as an inclusive finance provider, WeBank leverages fintech to provide high-quality financial services to mass retail and small and microenterprises. To date, WeBank has served more than 200 million individuals and over 900,000 SMEs.

Case Study 3: How Orchestrated Intelligence Inc. (Oii) Is Utilizing Artificial Intelligence to Model a Transformation in Supply Chain Performance

David Evans
Co-Founder Oii

Contents

Introduction

Imagine being asked to conduct the London Royal Philharmonic Orchestra because you once played piano and listed "music" as a skill on your LinkedIn profile. Or more unnervingly, being asked to compose an original piece for the Orchestra on the basis that you've written a few songs. It's possible you'd feel a little out of your depth.

Conducting an orchestra requires in-depth knowledge of the musical composition. An ability to get inside the mind of the composer and understand the patterns and nuances of the piece and then convey that to the musicians as you lead them through the performance making sure that everything comes together. Composing is

361

even harder. Putting together a score for 90 or more musicians requires the genius to blend limitless possible note combinations and musical sounds to create a transcendental experience that elevates the spirit and thrills the soul.

Were the Albert Hall to go ahead with a novice then it's likely the audience would be less than satisfied and the box office would be overwhelmed with requests for refunds. In short, the scenario is absurd and only a fool would countenance it.

Coordinating the planning of a complex supply chain is obviously not the same as conducting an orchestra or composing a symphony. But it is analogous. The goal of supply chain planning is to find an optimal balance of service to the customer at minimized cost to the network and achieving this aim requires the synchronization of a multitude of interrelated activities dispersed across complex networks. It requires an understanding of all the variables involved in the chain, their probabilistic outcomes, and costs along with an ability to compare how all these activities and the potential coordinates will interact and play out in the future.

Finding the unique equilibrium of service and cost advantage necessitates a level of mathematical modeling equivalent to Mozart arranging notes on a manuscript and the impact of getting it wrong can be as cacophonous as a novice composer plucking random notes out of the air. In fact in global organizations where $billions are at stake, the disastrous impact of failing to find the right supply chain model in monetary terms makes putting a rookie in charge of an orchestra seem insignificant by comparison.

However, this is what many organizations routinely do when they place a multimillion dollar supply chain-planning system in the hands of a planner and expect them to identify the best way to configure and plan a global network from the multitude of possible options.

If ever there was a problem for which artificial intelligence with its capability to process multiple data sources and make decisions based on evaluating patterns in data and probabilistic outcomes then this is it.

Oii™ (formerly Orchestrated Intelligence), a fast-growing startup based in London and San Francisco provides this capability. Formed in 2019, the company's mission is to utilize the power of AI to enable organizations to consistently achieve the perfect supply chain setup to meet their strategic goals. Oii's software combines multi-objective mathematical modeling techniques with Artificial Intelligence and Machine Learning to identify and maintain the optimal supply chain configuration and through that release cash, reduce costs and improve service and profitability.

Oii's USP is answering the complex supply chain conundrum of finding the optimal balance between service and cost for each specific and unique supply chain and to maintain that balance in the face of changing constraints, variables, and organizational goals. Oii's software transforms the planning paradigm by enabling the comparison of millions of potential network configuration options as it determines the best one to fit the organizations specific needs. It doesn't replace the planning system or the planner but augments their effectiveness and unlocks benefit by enabling the optimal setup.

Why Is Configuring a Planning System so Complex?

According to a recent Gartner study, over the next couple of years the annual global market for supply chain planning systems is set to exceed $19 billion. This continued growth story is in part driven by new digital capabilities and increased pressure on companies to be ever more agile and responsive in meeting customer demand. It is also reflective of the crucial role that these systems play in enabling the supply chain to function. However, unless those systems are configured correctly then that huge level of investment will not deliver the efficiencies or the savings targeted. Instead, the advancement in planning capability will simply drive faster propagation of issues just as surely as a badly written score won't sound like a Mozart concerto no matter how accomplished the musicians are.

If the balance of cost and service are not accurately built into the way plans are generated across the supply chain then the outcome can be seen in:

- Poor service and loss of sales.
- An underlying cost profile that is negatively impacting profitability.
- Stock levels that are out of alignment:
  - Too much stock on some items
  - Too little stock on other items
- Materials being written off
- Factory inefficiencies
- Reactive management as planners intervene to fix issues generated by the plans they have created.

With many businesses facing up to the biggest economic challenge since the Second World War it is no longer acceptable for supply chains to be run in this inefficient way. As we come out of the Covid-19 crisis, reducing costs, freeing up cash, and improving margin will differentiate those that survive from those that don't. Ensuring that the supply chain is set up correctly will become a key competency.

The configuration of the planning system is critical because it determines how the whole network behaves. The system performs like the supply chain's central nervous system determining what happens and when. It coordinates the interaction of multiple events involved across the network needed to ensure the product gets to the customer. This isn't just about translating demand signals into what needs to be made. It also involves determining what stock is held and where and how the supply is sequenced. Furthermore how the supply chain is configured and planned drives cost. Factors such as network design, replenishment strategy, stock holding, and delivery frequency *directly* impact underlying expenditure. Understanding these dynamics and making sure the tradeoff is transparent and the way an item is planned is in line with corporate strategy is critical to the profitability of the business.

Every item in the network will have a unique cost profile driven by factors such as:

- Demand and Supply Variability
- Production Process
- Supply Network
- Transportation Fees
- Storage Considerations

These attributes impact the way items are planned and produced and in turn the underlying costs associated with providing them to the customer. The planning configuration needs to find the optimal cost profile to meet the level of service targeted. This way the profitability of the business in maximized. However, if an item is set up wrongly then profitability is compromised due to excessive costs and suboptimal service.

The challenge with this task stems from the fact that even in simple networks there are just so many combinations for how the supply chain can be configured and this increases exponentially in complex global organizations where multi-echelon supply and multiple supply chain partners make up the network.

As the below chart shows there is a balance that needs to be stuck between higher service and greater responsiveness and the costs needed to achieve that. The specific setup will reflect corporate priorities and differing responses to service risk and margin. Moreover, the settings need to be cascaded down from the strategic level and tailored to match different priorities at business unit, brand, and item level (Figure CS3.1).

This requires transparency of costs. Clarity of what it's costing to make, transport, hold in stock, and deliver each and every item is needed to determine the most profitable planning setup to meet the service target. Often this information is not as available as you would expect despite underpinning a critical decision that affects the bottom line. Cost data are often too high level and don't link back to item configuration. Costing every possible planning setup and making these data transparent and visible is a key feature of the Oii software.

Finding the optimal configuration also requires a deep understanding of the variability inherent in the supply chain network. Greater variability in demand or supply will usually require higher costs than in networks where there is greater reliability and predictability

Oii utilizes the power of AI to find the best configuration for each item based on service target, underlying cost, and network variability. It builds scientific models of the current supply chain planning setup and simulations of all the potential configurations. It then evaluates the cost of each potential option and finds the best fit. It does this using a unique concept called SMSpace™ a multidimensional virtual hologram used to build and compare potential future supply chains for a particular network (Figure CS3.2).

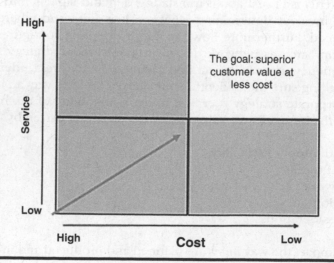

Figure CS3.1 Service versus Cost Continuum.

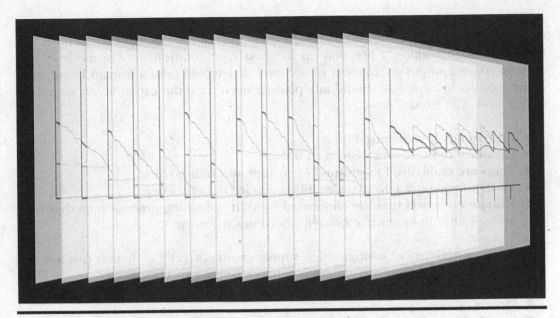

Figure CS3.2 Depiction of SMSpace—multiple plans played out over time.

In SMSpace the tool simulates what would happen in the future assessing:

- Multiple profiles of demand and supply and their probability.
- Multiple potential configuration set-ups across the full range of planning parameters

It compares different network designs, supply sequencing options, and stock-holding strategies and evaluates how each one impacts on service, cost and supply chain disruption over time. It also assesses the impact of different constraints on the outcome and the probability.

As such the Oii model could be regarded as a very powerful simulator that is playing a game; the goal of which is to find the best supply chain setup. In SMSpace the tool looks at the patterns in the data and models all the configuration options and plays these out in a virtual future, assessing both the probability of the outcomes and the cost versus service profile of each one. The model is refined by constraints that determine how costs are allocated to different scenarios. These include factors such as:

- Stock-holding cost
- Factory changeover costs
- Cost of quality testing
- Shipment and Customs
- Warehousing
- Discards

In this way the model responds to different strategic priorities and cost models such that the final recommendation is tailored to specific organizational needs. The model compares the existing configuration with all of the potential set-ups and identifies the best. The optimal is the one with the lowest overall total cost profile to meet the service goal. In making a decision on the best configuration the Oii modeler has completed an analysis in a matter of seconds that would take a human being very many months to complete should any planner even have the capability to complete such a task. The impact is:

- Profitability is maximized.
- Costs are reduced and cash freed up
- Plans are configured to respond to current and future risks.
- Variability is built into plans enabling maximized efficiency.
- Human error and bias are eliminated from the planning process such that proactive rather than reactive behavior becomes the norm

Part of the complexity of configuring a supply chain correctly is that no two are the same. A multitude of factors make each network unique such as:

- Organizational Strategy
- Supply Chain Constraints and Variability
- Product
- Network Complexity
- Costs and Margin

In the same way that no two supply chains have the same characteristics so too each item will have a unique setting. Every possible configuration option drives a different underlying cost profile, and this is impacted in turn by variability in the network, complexity of the products and supply chain constraints.

What we find is that in the absence of the capability to complete this analysis to the level of detail and accuracy required then items are set up with a one-size fits all approach. This paradoxically ensures that every item is planned and managed in a suboptimal way and drives the worst possible outcome resulting in poor service, high levels of cash tied up in inventory and unnecessary costs negatively impacting profits. Oii changes that.

Oii in Action

To illustrate in more detail how the Oii tool works it is worth looking at some recent deployments of the software to compare how their disparate supply chains, objectives and constraints were reflected in the modeling output and see in more detail how the tool transforms business performance.

Optimizing the Packaging Network of a Major Pharma Company

The first example is an American S&P 500 Biotechnology Company who engaged Oii to improve the performance of the planning systems in their Europe, Asia Pacific and Canada Division (EUAPCAN). The company had recently deployed Kinaxis Rapid

Response to plan the region but were failing to leverage the benefits of the new capability. Key issues were:

- Lack of planner capability to configure the systems
- Service issues driving a highly reactive planning and supply operation
- High levels of inventory and discards

The regional supply chain for EUAPCAN is a simple single-tier network (see Figure CS3.3). Annual sales of $6 billion are supplied from a packaging facility in the UK. Most of the items are replenished on a make-to-stock basis with inventory held in each of the 43 markets from where the primary customers are serviced. The majority of the sales go via wholesalers who supply on to hospitals and pharmacies. The company focuses primarily on antiviral drugs used in the treatment of HIV, hepatitis B, hepatitis C, and influenza. Margins are high and a high proportion of the products are deemed medically critical. Because of the life-saving nature of many of the products the key supply chain objective is to ensure product availability at all times. The portfolio has been heavily rationalized and only 701 items are supplied. Downstream supply was out of scope.

Implementation of Oii takes place in five phases, with a typical deployment lasting three months:

- Data Collection and Validation
- E2E Modeling
- Technical Integration
- Reports Development
- Handover

The process is iterative with a high level of interaction between phases in particular data collection and modeling. Data collection flexes around the information that is available. The algorithm will then flag where greater granularity is recommended. As a minimum sales, costs and current parameter data are needed along with constraints. Other data such as network performance and supply variability are taken where available. If this is not accessible it is inferred. A feature of the tool is its library of data patterns. The machine learning algorithms draw on these as needed and use this information to plus gaps, validate assumptions and refine results. E2E modeling often uncovers those areas where more data or greater levels of granular detail is recommended and this results in additional modeling iterations as we hone down to the final results. Interfaces built in the technical integration phase can be automated or run via flat-file exchange. This deployment involved the latter (Figure CS3.3).

This implementation uncovered some major shortfalls in the existing planning set-up and significant opportunity for benefit. Key issues were:

- A single service level target had been set across the portfolio regardless of item segmentation and differing impact on sales revenue
- Safety Stock levels were also set to the same figure for all 701 items.
- Factory schedules and delivery cadence were not aligned to any item segmentation strategy and were driving unnecessary factory costs and production inefficiency.

Markets
Albania
Australia
Austria
Bahrain
Belgium
Bosnia and Herzegovina
Cyprus
Czech Republic
Denmark
Estonia
Finland
France
Germany
Greece
Hungary
Iceland
Ireland
Israel
Italy
Jordan
Kuwait
Latvia
Lebanon
Lithuania
Luxembourg
Malta
Netherlands
New Zealand
Norway
Oman
Poland
Portugal
Qatar
Romania
Saudi Arabia
Slovakia
Slovenia
Spain
Sweden
Switzerland
Turkey
United Arab Emirates
United Kingdom
Total Number Markets: 43

Supply Site
UK

Figure CS3.3   Single Echelon Regional Supply Chain Structure for Global Pharma.

Each item is unique in how it needs to be planned and this needs to reflect:

■ Service targets that are aligned to commercial priorities.
■ Variability
■ Costs and constraints

Where a single setting is applied to all items then this nearly always means that every item is being planned wrongly. In this case that was reflected in an AS/ IS model that was highly suboptimal and was driving a multitude of undesirable outcomes:

- Without a segmented service level strategy, there was a disconnect between the commercial aims of the business and the operational performance of the supply chain.
- Despite high inventory levels and discards many items were configured to miss service level targets whilst others incurred unnecessary costs
- The supply chain planning operation was highly reactive and geared toward fixing issues it had created by the way the systems had been set up.

The outcome of the project was a transformation in the performance of the supply chain.

By applying segmented service targets across the range of items the tool recalibrated parameters to align to a more customer-responsive setup. Stock levels and factory replenishment plans were optimized and costs reduced. Key metrics were transformed:

- All service issues were fixed
- Stock levels were reduced by 32%, significantly freeing up cash
- Underlying costs were reduced by 37%
- Write-off risk was reduced by 43%

Early in the deployment there was some nervousness that the AI-based Oii tool was too big a step for a planning organization that was struggling with the basics. However given the simplicity of the front end of the Oii tool that concern turned out to be unfounded. The complexity of the Oii tool is "under the hood." Users found the software intuitive to use. Control of the input parameters enabled them to understand how the AI was optimizing the network and the results quickly made them see how Oii enhanced their capability to accomplish their roles. Oii delivered a transformation in the performance of the operation and provided a new paradigm to the planning function. The tool is now being rolled out across other regions with an end-to-end Pilot also being considered.

Optimizing Frozen Food Supply across a Multi-Echelon Supply Network

One of the features of the tool is that as well as calibrating the optimal supply chain setup; it also models the impact of the current settings. This provides a clear understanding of how the AS/IS configuration drives performance in terms of:

- Levels of service
- Inventory levels
- Total Supply Chain Cost

The capability to demonstrate to the business why the supply chain is performing in the way it does is highly revealing as the link between the planning setup and the outcomes is often not fully appreciated. This deployment with the number #1 supplier of several Asian food products in the US involved such a revelation. The company engaged Oii to model the supply from its California factory to customers globally. The Company's products are primarily sold in the US market through major chains, as well as through smaller "mom and pop" outlets. Their distribution is through more than 600 outlets in the US as well as multiple chains internationally. A key competency is cold chain distribution for its highly successful frozen food and ice cream products. Items are planned using SAP APO.

The principal focus for using the Oii technology was to:

- Optimize Inventory Levels across the network
- Reduce write-offs in the supply chain
- Reduce network costs

The Oii deployment delivered all of those things as well as uncovering a major disconnect in the way the network had been configured which was driving high levels of write-off, inventory, and network costs.

This implementation involved a multi-echelon network. Multi-echelon modeling involves the same basic process and steps as a single echelon network with the complexity extended across many more potential set-up options. This extension is mirrored in SMSpace, which models the multiplicity of interactions across all of the tiers in the network determining (Figure CS3.4):

- Where to hold stock and how much to hold at each point in the chain
- Variability across multiple steps of the network
- How interactions in the chain can be best managed through the configuration

In a multi-echelon network optimization the start point for the Oii tool remains the Customer node. Service level targets for the entire network are set here and

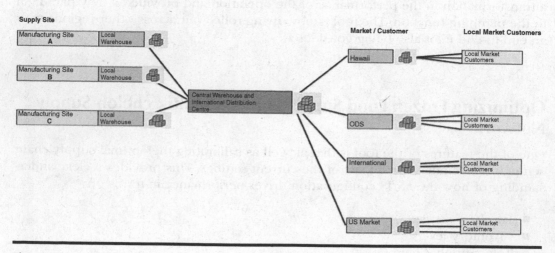

Figure CS3.4 Multi-Echelon Network US Frozen Food Supplier.

cascaded across the chain. In simulating different configuration options it considers how demand and supply explodes up and down the network and how costs and constraints impact the chain. The tool builds all the potential network configuration options and compares them as it seeks to identify the best one:

- Demand profiles are modeled and probability of different outcomes assessed
- Stock levels across the network are played out to determine the costs of each alternative setup and the impact on service
- Different throughput options of production cadence and transportation are modeled to determine the right balance between holding stock and the cost of production and transportation
- Constraints on shelf life and risk of write-off are modeled against the throughput options and different stock strategies.
- Stock levels are gamed to compare the impact of holding stock at different points in the chain on service and cost.
- Service is measured across the network such that whilst the key metric is meeting end-customer sales, internal supply ruptures are also factored in as they generate costs and upstream issues.

Even in a simple network such as this the number of potential configuration options is huge. In SMSpace the tool is able to look at all of these as it does its comparison between how the network is currently configured and performs versus the optimal.

The deployment found the following major areas of improvement:

- Inventory reduction 27%
- Total Cost Reduction 33%
- Discards Reduction 42%
- Service improvement 7%

One of the key findings was the misalignment between factory output and demand flowing through from the Customer level. To model this actual production output from the factories was used to build the AS/IS model. The data highlighted that factories were "pushing" stock into the chain that wasn't needed: a disconnect between demand and supply that was resulting in high stocks and write-offs in the network.

Realigning this and synchronizing factory output and cadence to cascaded customer demand had a huge impact on the benefits delivered and was a transformational insight. The disconnect between what was being made and actual customer demand had not been spotted prior to the tool making this visible and recalibrating the network to fix the issue.

End to End Multi-Echelon Deployment of Oii Across a Collaborative Network

In making costs transparent the Oii tool highlights areas where greater analysis of expenditure is needed to fine-tune the modeling output. This project with a regional Consumer Products Division of a Global Pharmaceuticals company facilitated major savings to the end-to-end operation and uncovered latent areas where transformational benefits could be achieved.

Oii takes what data are available and highlight areas where more information is needed. This means time isn't wasted collecting unnecessary information and ensures that where additional analysis is needed it facilitates maximum impact. A deep dive to unpack factory changeover costs and returns helped fine-tune the results of this deployment and was needed to finalize the results.

This project involved the modeling of a Multi-Echelon network comprising both internal sites and a third party logistics provider (3PL). This in turn required interacting with systems in both organizations (Manugistics and Smart IP&O). The products were primarily over-the-counter remedies for colds and flu, sold through major chains (80% sales) and smaller independent outlets (20%). The supply chain involved sites in different geographies. Active drug production takes place at a global facility in the UK based on dependent demand generated at the upstream packaging facility in Kuala Lumpur. Here the final packs are assembled and then shipped to four Regional Distribution Centres located in Kuala Lumpur, Penang, Kota Kinabalu, and Kuching. Stock is held here and at the 20 separate Local Distribution Centres (LDC) from where the end customer is supplied (Figure CS3.5).

The key aims of the project were to:

- Optimize Stock Levels across the chain to enable:
  - Improved Service
  - Reduced Inventory Holding
- Reduce overall Supply Chain Costs
- Minimize Write-Offs, and Returns

As discussed already the multi-echelon modeling process is in principle the same as a single echelon one. The objective of the Oii tool is to match the service targets of

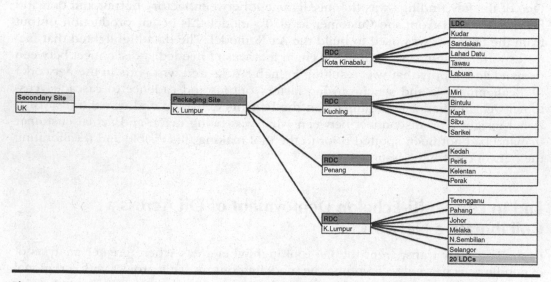

Figure CS3.5 Multi-Echelon Supply Chain Asia Pacific Region Global Pharma Company.

the customer with the minimal overall total supply chain cost across the network. However, the complexity and number of potential configurations in a multi-echelon network grow exponentially. Costs and constraints across the full supply chain are applied to the model as it looks to balance:

- What stock to hold and where
  - Active stock holding to meet packaging requirements (Asia Factory)
  - Safety Stock of Finished Packs at NDC/ LDC
- How stock is produced and moves through the network
- Order Frequencies across the network
- The right balance of costs across all the dimensions of the network

The deployment highlighted and addressed a number of issues:

- Service goals were not well defined with every item in the network having the same targets
- Stock levels were high driven by a one size fits all stock-holding policy that wasn't aligned to service goals
- Stock was distributed between locations in an inconsistent way that was not aligned to service goals and was highly suboptimal
- Write-offs were extremely high driven by the high stock holding and a misalignment between stock levels and shelf life risk.
- While service was generally good unplanned write-offs impacted onto sales when material went out of life and the chain had to react with fresh material in an unplanned way

The Oii tool addressed these issues as it recalibrated the network driving headline benefits of:

- 30% reduction in Inventory across the network
- 35% reduction in Total Supply Chain Cost
- 28% reduction in Write-Off/Returns

Providing item-level cost transparency as part of the modeling process highlighted two areas where some greater detail was needed:

- Cost of factory changeovers
- Actual Write-Off Data

Prior to the deployment of Oii the company had increased order throughput at the packaging site. What we found was a misalignment between number of orders and impact on other cost factors such as stock-holding costs. First model runs suggested an 80% reduction in the number of orders was needed based on the initial cost estimate for factory changeover costs. This seemed high and a deep dive to ascertain the true cost enabled a more accurate cost figure to be applied to fine-tune the results.

The other area where additional data were collected was write-offs. The Oii model suggested higher levels of write-off risk with the pre-modeled setup than were being recorded by the business. A deep dive uncovered that major customers were discarding stock and then billing rather than returning. These costs though genuine weren't visible to the planning team. In modeling the underlying cost and risk this activity that was negatively impacting profitability was highlighted and corrected in the optimized parameter configuration.

Summary

Each of these deployments demonstrates findings that are common in all Oii implementations:

- Supply chains are set up and planned in a suboptimal way resulting in:
  - Lost sales and poor service
  - High inventory levels tying up cash and impacting liquidity
  - Unnecessary costs impacting profitability
- There is a lack of insight on how configuration of the planning systems drives issues in network performance and supply chain costs.

The improvement in service, cost savings, and inventory reduction are common. Even where there is an organizational perception that the systems are operating effectively the Oii tool identifies major improvements.

Artificial Intelligence is a game changer in providing organizations with a method of ensuring the supply chain is set up correctly and configuration fine-tuned to ensure that as circumstances, variability and strategic goals change this is maintained. The power to access all of the potential configuration options, evaluate the cost v service implications, and find the best mix is beyond the capability of most planners for a single echelon network. For a multi-echelon network, it is nigh on impossible. Automating this crucial task is transformational.

While the tool offers a level of modeling capability beyond what a planner can achieve, it is not designed or intended to take their place. The goal of Oii is to not to replace people with Robots. Rather it is about placing this additional power in the hands of the organization to release cash and reduce costs such that company performance is strengthened and jobs made more secure. We see the tool as facilitating a more analytical approach to the planning role that in turn drives a more proactive operation. Oii will enable organizations to leverage benefit from their planning systems and provide new levels of transparency of performance.

As such a key aspect of deploying the tool is ensuring planner buy-in. That in turn involves getting them to understand:

- The link between the Planning System setup and supply chain performance
- How Oii models the optimal supply chain configuration.

A key stage of every implementation involves "lifting up the hood of the Oii engine" and demonstrating to the deployment leads how the model works. In SMSpace the system records data for every option considered. Here you can see the tradeoffs being made between factors such as:

- Holding more inventory and the cost of a missed sale
- The cost of frequent supply versus the risk of discards
- Higher service and the cost of achieving that

Walking through this helps to reveal the underlying logic. We've found it's important that planners understand how the model generates its recommendations and can trust them. This process also helps them to appreciate the interaction between the planning system configuration and underlying cost and service. This insight along with the simplicity of the front end results in high rates of adoption. Once planners see the impact the tool has on their business performance and its capability to help them get better results they embrace the tool rather than fearing that artificial intelligence will replace them.

Finally, the transparency of total cost data facilitates better decisions on what cost reduction initiatives should be advanced. A common issue with such projects is that improvements in one area are offset by negative impacts elsewhere in the network. For example, switching from air to sea reduces shipping costs but increases inventory holding due to longer transportation times. Supply chains are highly interconnected and it's critical that the way all the planning parameters combine to impact cost is understood. The tool makes the full picture transparent and ensures that unless an initiative results in total cost reduction then it's not worth deploying.

Conclusion

We began with an analogy between an orchestra and a supply chain and as we conclude we will revisit that. The two things may seem wildly different and in many ways they are. What ties them together is the need to create harmony from potential. Structure and form from random possibility. The multiplicity of notes that can be chosen by a composer and their endless combinations is not a million miles removed from the myriad ways a supply chain network can be configured by a planner. Every permutation derives a different result. With an orchestra sound, with a supply chain a different service versus cost outcome. Determining the absolute best combination is what differentiates a Mozart from a lesser practitioner.

However, the algorithm for creating the perfect piece of music for now remains elusive and the judgment of what constitutes great is a uniquely human and subjective pronouncement. The advancement of artificial intelligence has made it possible to determine in absolute terms what is the precise best supply chain setup from the myriad of possibilities available to meet a particular company's strategic goals. This is how Oii is changing the planning paradigm and enabling organizations to plan and manage their businesses with an optimal performance as standard. This advancement is coming to fruition at a moment when businesses will be under more pressure than at any time in living memory to maximize service and sales whilst minimizing costs and reducing inventory. If there was ever a time when supply chains needed to step up to the podium and play a perfect tune then this is that time. Oii is poised to be both virtual composer and conductor of that symphony.

Case Study 4: 7-Eleven and Cashierless Stores

Shahmeer Mirza
Director of R&D Technology, 7-Eleven

Contents

> Give the customers what they want, when and where they want it.
>
> Joe C. Thompson Jr. | 7-Eleven Founder

7-Eleven is a Japanese-American international chain of convenience stores. Its innovations, such as to go coffee cups, self-serve soda fountain, 24x7 operation, and SLURPEE® drink, are well known. Now 7-Eleven is on a journey to take its convenience stores cashierless through digital transformation.

7-Eleven's digital transformation began with investing in customer facing apps such as 7-Eleven Stores—a community app, 7Now—a product delivery app, and 7Rewards—a loyalty app. 7-Eleven's Digital/IT divisions made those apps possible. This case study is about the 7-Eleven cashierless store, the first major launch of the newly formed R&D group.

Business Opportunity

7-Eleven wanted to provide a frictionless experience to the customers, no matter what time of the day they were shopping. If we imagine a store powered by an AI that can handle the entire end-to-end customer experience, from entry, to transaction, to exit, this would be possible.

The Solution

In the early stages, they staffed the effort by a few 7-Eleven managers who worked with a few 7-Eleven engineers, one of whom was a new computer-vision graduate, to develop a proof of concept based on vision AI. From the beginning, the team was very sensitive to the fact that customers may not want—facial or other personally identifiable data to be tracked and instead leveraged overhead cameras to track product movement from the shelf and back and combined camera images and weight-sensors on the shelves to achieve accuracy in item assignment.

The initial proof of concept ran on a laptop and tracked four shelves using four cameras. They converted the back section of the lab to an experimental store. Scaling the prototype required moving from the single laptop to a distributed system of multiple custom-built computing systems, numerous cameras, and multiple sensors. Simultaneous to the store tracking, they developed a smartphone app to start the journey of the customer through the store. Besides the real-time tracking by the vision-server, the suite of applications for the cashierless store included the weight-server and the sensor fusion-server, which aggregated the information to track customers' virtual carts for the purpose of producing receipts. Python was very useful for rapid prototyping, but to achieve the performance of the real-time prediction of milliseconds, the implementation uses C++. The architecture leverages the stream-processing platform Kafka for reliable messaging between IoT sensors and distributed servers. Taking advantage of the modular nature of store/shelves and camera positioning, the solution achieves high availability.

Continuous review of data and labelling is helping to improve the tracking accuracy. The more quality data used for training the algorithm, the better the prediction accuracy. The item tracking accuracy is inherently high when the shopping population is low. The system is built to switch from a simple algorithm when there are fewer shoppers near a shelf to an increasingly complex ensemble of algorithms when the shopper density increases.

In the early stages of implementation, the shoppers would get a message as soon as they exited the store that they will be getting their receipts shortly. A safety-net was operating in parallel for humans to check the receipt before sending it to the shopper to validate algorithmic predictions and continuously improve the systems performance.

The side-benefits of the implementation include real-time inventory tracking, ordering, and understanding customer traffic and behavior, all of which are key to managing a retail store.

An excellent feature of this system is the fact that the final algorithmic solution does not use any personally identifiable data and that the customer is seen as a brand-new entity for every shopping session. The human labeling system may retain some customer images, but only as a means to enable accurate transaction labeling as the cashierless AI continues to be trained.

Impact and Lessons Learned

The technology developed by the R&D team was used to open an employee-only, up-scale store in November 2019. Customers love that they don't have to wait in line.

7-Eleven is well on its way with its digital transformation, and the cashierless store is seen by the executives as a viable way to automate the stores. The R&D team generated 25+ patents for the company. 7-Eleven's R&D team now has the technical capability to undertake any project that requires machine-learning expertise. The many models developed for the cashierless store could be used in several applications across the existing 7-Eleven stores to improve operations and customer experience. The team is exploring how to leverage these models to achieve that end.

It takes more than machine learning to implement an enterprise solution. The R&D team at 7-Eleven comprised machine-learning engineers, full-stack developers (half focused on run-ops/production systems, half focused on sensor-fusion/data-engineering), hardware Engineers, a C++ expert, R&D technicians (assembling shelves, computing systems, and soldering), iOS developers, Android Developers and back-end web developers. The machine-learning part of the solution was less than a quarter of the total effort.

Culture matters the most. The initial team of four or five team members worked very well together and developed the culture eagerly adopted by those who joined the team later to scale the initial implementation to a store with multiple shelves and several hundred square feet in size. If the entire team was not cohesive, the goal of going from a demo to full-blown implementation couldn't have happened so quickly.

The senior leadership encouraged the team to fail-fast. Learning from mistakes and iterating quickly took the deployment from the lab to a working cashierless store in less than a year.

Next Steps

The team is looking to have a post-mortem on the implementation, including a review of the architecture and future improvements.

The feedback captured by the smartphone app shows that the shoppers want more freshly prepared healthy foods and hot coffee. Expanding on the types of products in cashierless stores would bring challenges that the team is eager to solve.

Case Study 5: Paper Quality at Georgia-Pacific

Ranga Ramesh

Senior Director, Quality Innovation and Transformation, Georgia-Pacific LLC

Contents

Business Opportunity

In the bath tissue marketplace, softness of the tissue is one of the most critical product attributes driving consumer preference. Tissues that are softer are considered more premium. They command higher prices and enjoy a larger market share than lower softness products.

Softness is also one of the more challenging attributes to monitor and control during the manufacturing of these tissue products. For starters, even the definition of what is "soft" is a highly subjective one. Generally, the overall softness perception is considered to be made up of two subcomponents—"bulk softness" (or "cushiony softness" or "drapeability") and surface softness (or smoothness). Further complicating this is that the surface softness component could be either "velvety" or "satiny," which have distinctly different surface characteristics. Measuring and quantifying softness is also an equally challenging task. Companies employ a combination of subjective human softness panels, lab instruments, etc., to try and mirror consumer perception of softness in use.

Every manufacturer designs their product to create the right blend of bulk and surface softness based on their market research of what consumers prefer. The implementation of these designs in manufacturing typically involves a combination of:

- The paper-making technology (Through-Air Dried, Conventional Wet Press, etc.)
- The fiber raw materials (Hardwood, Softwood, Recycled paper, etc.
- Other functional additives (Softening agents, wet strength resins, etc.)

- Process conditions used during manufacturing ("knobs" on the machine)
- Converting technology (embossing, lamination, etc.)

Manufacture of bath tissue rolls involves two major steps: (1) giant rolls of the tissue are made on a paper-making machine and (2) the consumer size rolls and packages are made during the converting process. The softness of the tissue is predominantly determined during the paper-making process. However, most of the softness measurement tools used are deployed after the rolls are converted into finished product. This creates a period of uncertainty from the time the paper is made to the time softness measurements on the finished product are available. This can lead to increased quality variation, increased waste, and higher WIP costs. It would be highly desirable to have a tool that could provide feedback on softness in real time, as the paper is being produced.

The Solution

Georgia-Pacific has set out to create a transformative tool that could provide real-time feedback on softness to the operators on a paper machine. First, softness feedback on papers produced over a long period of time using traditional methods were compiled. Secondly, a vast number of process conditions and machine settings on the paper machine, while these papers were produced, were assembled. The modeling approach involved five stages:

1. Feature selection
2. Data Acquisition
3. Data cleansing and preparation
4. Model development and evaluation
5. Model deployment and maintenance

Using advanced analytical methods, deep learning predictive models for softness were developed. These models were fine-tuned and perfected to yield a best-fit model.

Impact and Lessons Learned

The model identifies a select few process conditions with the biggest impact on the paper softness and provides their operating ranges for prediction and optimization. It is embedded into the manufacturing systems for process control and monitoring. The model has been validated over several months of run time, while producing different grades of product with higher and lower softness levels (see Figure CS5.1).

This project has demonstrated that key quality measures can be modeled and can lead to a proactive approach to managing quality. This has far-reaching implications for reduced waste and rework and the role of testing and inspections in the overall quality management framework.

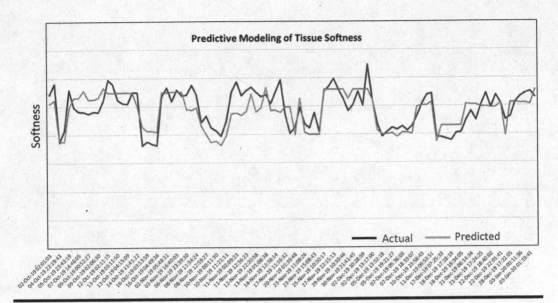

Figure CS5.1   Model Performance.

Next Steps

Customized models that are similar would be developed across the manufacturing system for the different products produced. These would be tracked and validated. The models would be reviewed and fine-tuned at least once every six months.

Case Study 6: GE Healthcare: 1st FDA Clearance for an AI-Enabled X-Ray Device

Katelyn Nye

GM, X-ray Artificial Intelligence & Mobile X-ray Systems at GE Healthcare

Karley Yoder

VP & GM, Artificial Intelligence at GE Healthcare

Contents

Background

GE Healthcare is the $16.7 billion healthcare business of General Electric (NYSE: GE). Founded by Thomas Edison's 1896 invention of the medical fluoroscope X-ray tube, it has over 100 years of healthcare industry experience and around 50,000 global employees. As a leading global medical technology and digital solutions innovator, GE Healthcare enables clinicians to make faster, more informed decisions through smart devices, data analytics, applications, and services, supported by its Edison intelligence platform.

The Edison platform and its respective horizontal team support GE Healthcare's business units that design, manufacture, and service radiology imaging equipment, patient monitoring devices, and enterprise healthcare software. Edison provides access to data, data science expertise, and developer services for the deployment of artificial intelligence algorithms into intelligent applications and smart devices.

GE Healthcare operates at the center of an ecosystem working toward precision health, digitizing healthcare, helping drive productivity for providers, health systems, and researchers, and improving outcomes for patients around the world.

Getting the "AI Product" Steps Right

Delivering an AI-enabled product to market follows a clear playbook with defined phases. Each phase has its own distinct keys to success and associated pitfalls.

1. **Verifying Product Definition and Design**: AI is not a silver bullet. If the advantages of a strong data science solution are not packaged in a design that delights your customer, then you have created a science project, not a market-leading product. The best AI is invisible; a clinician does not even know they are benefiting from AI, they just know they are more effective, more efficient at the task they have always done.
2. **Data Volume**: Effective AI requires large amounts of data to become "intelligent." The "training sets" for an AI model in healthcare are no exception. In order to stand a chance to perform on par—or better—than industry standards, large volumes of data are required as inputs. These data must also have clear lineage and rights to be leveraged in a commercial product.
3. **Data Variety**: Although high volumes of data are imperative to make effective AI, volume alone is not sufficient. The variety of data matters if you intend to make an AI product that will generalize across many different types of people, geographical locations, and healthcare situations. Additionally, if you are not intentional about the variety of data in training a model, it becomes all too easy to introduce unintended bias into AI solutions. This is why GE Healthcare established AI Principles[4] to leverage the benefits of AI in all of its products while establishing guardrails to prevent bias and engender trust.
4. **Data Fidelity**: The adage of "garbage in, garbage out" applies to the development of AI models, meaning AI models will only perform as well as the curation, or ground truth, that they contain. In the realm of healthcare, this means that in developing AI-enabled products, you need to work closely with clinicians who can annotate the true healthcare insight of the data you are working with. You need to ensure this clinical fidelity both when data are being annotated for training sets and when a completed model is being tested and validated on brand new data.

Verifying Product Definition and Design

The first business unit within GE Healthcare to develop and productize AI leveraging the Edison platform was in fact the oldest business within the company—X-ray. X-ray exams alone contribute to 60% of imaging procedures[5], making it the most common imaging procedure compared to the more advanced radiology techniques introduced over the past five decades, such as CT and MRI. It is estimated that billions of X-rays are taken globally on an annual basis[6]—as it is the most accessible imaging technology, in price, portability, and operator training. X-rays are commonly the patient's entry point into their healthcare journey. Whether it is a suspected broken bone or re-occurring cough, an X-ray image will help physicians triage, diagnose, and monitor health conditions. As such, GE Healthcare's X-ray slogan is "Helping you make the first image count."

To verify what kind of AI algorithms X-ray customers may benefit from the most, as well as the best method for how they should consume the results, a small team was formed to conduct discovery research. Many interviews with radiologist key opinion leaders in the field were conducted, revealing themes of interest for AI to triage findings, detect subtle and uncommon abnormalities, and to conduct consistent measurements—reducing intrareader variability. Additionally, the team spent a week immersed within a clinical environment, courtesy of the Florida Hospital Innovation Lab (now known as the AdventHealth Innovation Lab), observing and interacting with not just radiology stakeholders, but also X-ray technologists, nurses, IT, administrators, and surgeons. A new concept of automating quality control on the X-ray device emerged, in addition to validating the desire to leverage AI for triaging and detecting critical findings. Lastly, but arguably the most impactful, was a formal, long term clinical partnership established between GE Healthcare and the University of California San Francisco Center for Digital Health Innovation (CDHI)[7]. This collaboration provided the GE product development team access to radiology and surgeon thought leaders, who proposed and later co-developed a suite of AI algorithms to detect critical findings in a chest x-ray, such as a collapsed lung (pneumothorax) or misplaced medical tube—branded as "Critical Care Suite." Dr. Rachael Callcut who is the Director of Data Science & Advanced Analytics at CDHI, as well as a General Surgeon and Associate Professor of Surgery at UC Davis Medical Center, said the following "There is an extraordinary amount of interest in healthcare to realize the hope of artificial intelligence. The reality is that few solutions have been impactful to clinical care despite tremendous investments. Some of the most promising applications in my mind are those like the Critical Care Suite that offer augmented decision support to make care more timely, effective, and safe. Following on the success of the Critical Care Suite, the partnership between industry and academic medical centers will be key in shortening the development cycle for healthcare AI applications."

A strategy was formed stemming from the insights gained through all the collaborations, in which embedding AI algorithms within the X-ray devices to improve clinical decision support, quality, and efficiency, would be beneficial upstream at the patient beside and downstream in the PACS, a picture archiving and communication system where radiologists review and diagnose medical images. This is what GE Healthcare would later refer to as a "Smart Device."

GEHC X-ray, Vision for AI

Efficiency
AI can be leveraged to **automate workflow steps**, leading to faster exams and more efficient resource allocation

Quality
Embedding AI into the imaging device can **flag and help reduce quality errors**

Clinical Decision Support
Embedding AI onto the device can help **flag critical information** at the point of care and in PACS

Data Volume

Early in initial AI prototype development, the GE X-ray and Edison teams ran an experiment demonstrating that an AI algorithm trained on the same data source, with the same ground truth (i.e., clinical annotations), and tested on the same test set, had an accuracy improvement of 6% when the volume of the training data was increased from 572 images to 1500 images (2.6X increase). This is a simple demonstration of the importance of training data volume.

In order to drive this necessary volume, GE Healthcare entered into data collection partnerships to bring in-house large datasets for AI training & development. One of the standard challenges during this data collection phase is aggregating data that will have the condition of interest—in this case x-ray critical conditions (pneumothorax, a missed placed tube, etc.)—especially when you are looking to build an AI model around low probability occurrence. Therefore, it is necessary to develop a plan to not simply collect a large volume of data, but to collect a large volume of the *right kind* of data.

One of the most successful partnerships was with Humber River Hospital in Ontario, Canada, which provided more than 150,000 privacy-compliant chest X-rays and associated radiologist reports for AI training.[8] At this institution, a commercial application, Primordial, was already integrated with the radiology reporting tool and provided the option to search for keywords within the text reports using Boolean logic and to export the findings into a .csv file. The text output was processed by a GE internally developed natural language processing (NLP) tool to increase confidence in which exams had the inclusion or exclusion criteria of interest. The output of this process led to a list of target exam or accession numbers, which were then used to conduct a PACS query to retrieve the corresponding DICOM X-ray images and anonymize them. At the time of creating this dataset, GE considered the future roadmap of AI algorithms desired for the next 5 years—and hence the data can now be reused by GE for multiple AI model training, reducing future data collection activities.

Collecting images and radiologist reports from PACS was necessary for the development of clinical decision support AI algorithms, with clinical findings at the core. PACS, however, is not by itself a enough data source to develop AI algorithms for quality or efficiency improvements on the X-ray device. X-ray technologists manually conduct a quality control procedure where they review the image on the X-ray device, determine which images meet diagnostic quality standards to be pushed to PACS, and which fail, for what reasons, and should be manipulated or "rejected" and "repeated." To access such data and subject to data rights agreements, GE Healthcare leveraged a business intelligence analytics application to automatically mine anonymized image data from an install base of X-ray devices spread across multiple geographically located campuses, and pair them with the annotations labels. The idea was inspired by reCAPTCHA[9], which utilizes the manual tasks of labeling data within a daily activity from a large population of people, to produce a secondary benefit.

Data Variety

Complementing the earlier mentioned experiment that demonstrated AI accuracy improvement with increased data volume, a second experiment demonstrated that with data volume increase in combination with data variety (i.e., data sources being increased from 1 to 3), GE Healthcare observed an improvement in the accuracy of the AI algorithm by 13%. This outcome reinforced the conclusion that addressing data volume alone is not enough to reach an algorithms accuracy entitlement. The core underlying tenet at work is that an AI model trained on data from one source will remain "brittle," meaning it won't perform well on a new data set for testing; however, as you add in new data sources and variety, the model moves toward the ability to "generalize" and associated performance metrics increase.

Data scientists commonly introduce "data augmentation," in which the training images are resized, rotated and sometimes combined with synthetically generated images (generative adversarial networks -GANs) created to add more variation into the training process. Expert understanding of clinical workflows needs to be gathered to understand what type of image variation could be introduced on global data. Therefore, the GE Healthcare X-ray and Edison teams conducted manual data collection from global X-ray users, which revealed the following differences in image variety per regions:

■ *Patient size*: patients may be generally smaller or more obese per a region
■ *Patient health condition*: general lack of access to healthcare causing "sicker" more severe cases of disease and deformities
■ *Quality of images*: varying rates in operator errors, likely coinciding with operator training/skillsets, such as labeling the body part laterality inconsistently with a left or right lead marker, or under/overexposing an image
■ *Patient positioning*: variation seen in the distance at which a patient is imaged, causing abdomen anatomy to be in the field of view of a chest X-ray, as well as how the patient's arms are positioned
■ *X-ray equipment used*: range of older technology, from computed radiography (CR) detectors to the latest digital X-ray systems with bone suppression or tube/line enhancement image processing looks

The importance of these variations was made apparent when an early prototype of a pneumothorax detection algorithm was trained on North American data where the patient's arms were either placed along their side or wrapped around a wall stand. When an image from Asia with the patient's hands on their hips (an akimbo position) was tested with the algorithm, a false positive was detected—mistaking the air pocket between the thorax and arm, for an air pocket within the chest cavity.

For these reasons, many medical device regulatory bodies require validation of an AI algorithm from data source within their respective countries.

Data Fidelity

All data curation approaches are not created equally. The more detailed the annotation, the more quickly an AI model is able to "learn." For a simple example of this concept, if you were training an AI model to recognize dogs your annotation approach would move from crude to sophisticated in the following manner:

a. Image level labels: Simply labeling an image "dog" or "no dog"
b. Bounding box labels: Applying a box around the general area where the dog could be found
c. Pixel-Level Region-of-Interest (ROI): Tracing the exact outline of the dog within the picture

Beyond the method of annotation, sophistication around data fidelity can also be found in how many annotators review an image and what is the process setup to ensure a high level of quality.

Initially, the GE Healthcare X-ray and Edison team contracted with various global institutions of radiologists, such as CARING Mahajan Imaging, India and St. Luke's University Hospital, USA and provided training on the desired annotation methodology and tools using an internally developed annotation platform called the Edison AI Workbench. This platform also allowed GE Healthcare data scientists to take these carefully annotated images and then leverage SageMaker—an Amazon Web Services (AWS) machine-learning platform—to build the final AI models all in one platform where the data could be traced from origin to annotation to final usage for AI model development.

What worked well with this annotation approach:

■ The X-ray images and their corresponding annotations applied were securely stored in the cloud, with traceability to data rights agreements, ensuring data security for GE Healthcare—allowing only GE access to exporting
■ Secure logins and activity data allowed GE project managers to track the annotation progress from each site remotely per the program plan
■ A GE in-house physician could oversee quality control of the annotations in real time and catch annotation mistakes early for correction and retraining

What didn't work:

■ Contracting and payment overhead working with multiple institutions
■ Many contracted radiologists were busy with full-time clinical practice and were slow to complete their assigned annotation tasks
■ Variation in annotation methods between readers, e.g., if a clinical finding was suspicious, but not certain—one reader may select a binary label of "positive," while another may choose "negative"; or the drawing of an ROI using the interior vs. the exterior border of the anatomical finding
■ The hourly cost of USA radiologists to perform annotation work would have been better spent in an overseer position, enabling lower cost resources (by skillset or region) to perform the more time-consuming annotation tasks

Per the learnings, subsequent algorithms leveraged an annotation firm (e.g., CapeStart) instead of individual institutions, which have dedicated, scalable, full-time resources to conduct annotation work—resulting in faster and more cost-efficient results. To ensure top quality, a dedicated GE internal physician oversaw the work and consulted with expert radiologists from University of California San Francisco, USA and the University Hospital of Szeged, Hungary.

Conclusion

By 2020, the GE Healthcare X-ray business commercialized six AI algorithms, branded under offerings called the "Critical Care Suite," "Quality Care Suite," and "Helix 2.0." GE Healthcare has embedded the six AI models within the X-ray device to provide benefits across clinical decision support, efficiency and quality (Table CS6.1).

Table CS6.1

#	GE Embedded X-ray Device AI Algorithms (2020)	Clinical Decision Support	Efficiency	Quality
		Flag critical information	Automate workflow steps	Help reduce quality errors
1	Pneumothorax Detection	X		
2	ET Tube Measurement	X	X	
3	AI Brightness and Contrast		X	
4	Intelligent Auto Rotate		X	X
5	Intelligent Protocol Check			X
6	Intelligent Field of View		X	

The "Critical Care Suite" was the first medical device cleared by the U.S. Food and Drug Administration (FDA), for AI within an imaging device for triage and quality control[10]. In 2019, the first three clinical evaluations were conducted globally in India, United Kingdom, and in the USA. The clinicians had the following to say about their experience using the AI embedded X-ray device:

> We clearly saw advantages of the system in the sensitivity of detecting small pneumothorax in some patients, enhancing the speed of alerting the treating teams regarding development of PTX in their patients.
>
> Dr. Bharat Aggarwal, Director of Radiology,
> Max Super Specialty Hospital, Saket, New Delhi, India

> The Critical Care Suite provided a useful adjunct to the identification of pneumothorax in the setting of Cardiothoracic Surgery. Pneumothorax in the setting of Cardiothoracic Surgery is common and despite the requirement for intensive monitoring in the peri-operative setting, the Critical Care Suite was able to identify pneumothoraces with a high level of accuracy.
>
> Dr. Elizabeth Belcher, Consultant Cardiothoracic Surgeon, Oxford
> University Hospitals NHS Foundation Trust

> We are overall very happy with the performance of the algorithm and currently using it for routine patient care. Critical Care Suite represents the easiest implementation of novel radiology software, specifically AI-integration, that I have encountered in my career.
>
> Dr. Amit Gupta, Cardiothoracic Radiologist and Modality Director of
> Diagnostic Radiography, University Hospitals Cleveland Medical Center

The first time through any process is always challenging; you simply don't know what you don't know. However, as outlined in this "Critical Care Suite" example, there is a clear playbook for creating AI products. This playbook isn't simple to execute, but the steps are known and well documented.

In order to move with speed, the following key learnings are essential for scaling enterprise AI-product development:

1. **Verifying Product Definition and Design**: seek direct user feedback from multiple stakeholders and immerse yourself within the user environment for first-degree perspective.
2. **Data Volume**: optimize manual data collection efforts to apply for a multi-year roadmap strategy, select data partners with sophisticated IT tools for data filtering or invest upfront to create these tools yourself, and whenever possible—create an automated flow of pre-annotated data.
3. **Data Variety**: intimate workflow understanding is key to ensure variation from various data sources is being accounted for during algorithm training, whether it is regionally applicable or with respect to steps within a process—as in the case of pre vs. post X-ray technologist quality control practices on an X-ray device vs within a PACS.
4. **Data Fidelity**: leveraging the right tools, methodology, and resources for timely execution of annotation, with appropriate oversight is key.

Artificial intelligence is a powerful technology with the potential to make transformational impacts in healthcare. However, just like hardware manufacturing or software development, developing AI-enabled products requires a precise product development lifecycle to harness the potential and deliver products that are adopted, impactful, and lasting. Through the journey to bring the X-ray "Critical Care Suite" to a global market, GE Healthcare developed an AI playbook that will continue to be leveraged to bring many future products to life and continue to positively impact patients around the world.

Case Study 7: UCSF Health and H2O.ai—Applying Document AI to Automate Workflows in Healthcare

Ramakrishna Yerramsetty and Lu Chen
UCSF Health

Mark Landry
H2O.ai

Contents

Problem Overview

The University of California, San Francisco, health system ("UCSF Health") receives over 1.4 million faxed documents per year. In the absence of artificial intelligence (AI), each of these documents must be handled multiple times by humans to determine what kind of document it is, which patient it pertains to, and what specifically must be done to further process or respond to the document's contents. These faxes include a variety of document types including patient referrals, prescription refill requests, durable medical equipment requests, lab results, and school forms. They are received from thousands of providers and vary in structure, quality, and content. They are received as electronic faxes ("e-fax") and stored in a PDF format on a fax server.

Each type of e-fax has a specific workflow associated with it. In the case of patient referrals, a referral coordinator at UCSF has to review the incoming document, identify if required information is missing, and request this missing information from the referring provider. The referral coordinator has to extract patient demographics, referral information, insurance information, etc., from the fax and enter this information into multiple screens in the Electronic Health Record (EHR). This manual work is cumbersome and inefficient and results in delays in patients' access to care, negative patient experience, and high operational costs. Across the UCSF Health System, this human effort adds up to more than the work of a hundred full-time employees.

The team at UCSF Center for Digital Health Innovation ("UCSF CDHI") envisioned a day when the processing of the majority of these e-faxes would be automated. To accomplish this, an application would have to: automatically recognize the type of request [referral, medical refill, Durable Medical Equipment (DME) request, etc.], parse the information in the fax document, simplify the human review of parsed information, input the data into the EHR, and enable the workflow specific to the type of referral fax document.

In 2018, as the first step toward that vision, UCSF decided to focus on the most important of those e-faxes—"Referrals." These e-faxes are sent to UCSF by providers in the community when patients need a higher level of care from the doctors at UCSF. UCSF CDHI built an e-fax referrals automation application ("Referrals Automation") to process them.

Referrals Automation leveraged a commercial OCR software engine from Kofax to build templates for frequently received forms. When an e-fax matches one of the templates, the OCR engine extracted the demographics and referral information and Referrals Automation helped create a digital referral object in the EHR after a manual review of the extracted information. This solution saved a few minutes per referral processed.

The Referrals Automation application was deployed in a few patient access centers at UCSF. Between January and June 2021, the average time to process a referral decreased by 40% and the average number of referrals processed per full-time equivalent per day has increased by around 50%.

However, Referrals Automation had significant limitations because the information extraction was based on labor-intensive, manually created templates. The team learned a lot from building and deploying the OCR templates-based solution and could now see the possibilities for a more effective, scalable solution for e-fax processing with AI.

UCSF Medical Center | UCSF Benioff Children's Hospital

REFERRAL FORM

Thank you for choosing to refer your patient to us. To start the referral process, please fax this form to the UCSF service to which you are referring your patient.

▶ Fax numbers can be found online at www.ucsfhealth.org/prd2010
▶ Include brief pertinent medical records, including test results that support the consultation

If you require additional assistance, please call (800) 444-2559 and ask for either the UCSF practice or the Referral Liaison Service.

Date: 7/7/2017	From: DocTor, Doctor
No. of pages: 1	Title:
To UCSF practice: Pediatrics	Phone: 415-111-1111
Fax: 415-222-2222	Fax:

PATIENT INFORMATION

Name of patient: Monkey, Doll

DOB: 01/01/2005   Interpreter needed: ☒ Yes ☐ No   Language: Spanish

Home phone: 415-333-3333   ☒ Work or ☐ cell phone: 415-444-4444

If child, name of parent: Monkey, Big Doll

Address: 11 donkey road, apt11

City: Zoo City, ZO   Zip: 88888

Insurance: Include patient's insurance card (both sides) and HMO authorization if required

CONSULTATION REQUEST INFORMATION

Diagnosis/ICD10 E13- diabetes

Name of UCSF MD (if known): Doctor Right   Specialty: endocrinologist

Reason for consultation: High A1c and FBS

By providing the information requested and signing below, you agree that we may initiate treatment following consultation or perform medically necessary diagnostics, in association with this consultation. We look forward to collaborating with you on your patient's treatment plan.

REFERRING PHYSICIAN INFORMATION

Referring MD: Doctor, New   Specialty: Pediatric

Phone: 415-555-5555   Fax: 415-666-6666

PCP name: Doctor, ABC   Phone:

Signature:

Figure CS7.1   Sample format of a referral form.

What worked well:

■ The application was able to extract *some* patient information from 62% of referrals
■ Saved ~2 minutes/referral and processed > 50K referrals/year

- Referral coordinators who use the application love it. The application has become the standard tool for processing referrals

What did not work well:

- **Scalability**: Building and verifying templates is manually intensive. Multiple referring providers use similar forms with minor variations that make building templates tricky. New providers are onboarded frequently who may use very different formats for their e-faxes. The implementation costs for onboarding a new health system onto Referrals Automation are prohibitive.
- **Maintainability**: The formats of the forms change over time. The template library has to be regularly reviewed and updated.
- **Amount of information extracted**: Template-based approach can extract information only from one or two pages per fax. Faxes have a lot of useful information on other pages such as patient's medications, progress notes, lab results, and imaging.

Given the successes of Referrals Automation and the fact that artificial intelligence (AI) has evolved significantly in the last few years making it possible to extract detailed information with confidence from semi-structured and unstructured documents, the UCSF CDHI team resolved to build a next-generation e-fax processing application ("Intake Automation") based on AI.

Intake Automation would process not just referrals, but any e-fax document types that come through and would leverage AI to create a self-learning system that would go beyond canned templates while delivering deliver on better outcomes and user experiences.

By powering all the e-fax processing workflows with AI-powered Intake Automation, UCSF is expected to save more than 25,000 hours (~12 FTEs equivalent) of access center staff time and 5000 hours (~2.5 FTEs equivalent) of clinician time. The time saved will be used to

1. Provide a more personal experience for patients navigating the health system for their complex conditions
2. Help patients navigate their care after their visit for follow-up visits, procedures, external referrals, etc.
3. Handle the year-over-year increase in the volume of referrals without adding more administrative overhead

UCSF: –H2O.ai Partnership

Objectives

To identify a partner to provide AI models for Intake Automation, UCSF CDHI conducted a thorough market survey and evaluated several companies. The search narrowed down to two candidates—H2O.ai and another company. The CDHI team designed evaluation criteria to prove that the technology works and to ultimately select a partner.

UCSF CDHI provided detailed annotated data and set performance goals for two machine learning tasks:

- Identify the content type on each page of a faxed document ("Page Types")
- Extract up to 116 key-value pairs of information ("Referral Fields") from each referral document whenever they are present

The performance standard was set as average 85% accuracy for identifying page types, and the extraction of entities to meet the same number of key-value pairs that were extracted by the template-based OCR approach.

Within four weeks, H2O.ai was able to use H2O's document.ai to build high-performing AI models required to make Intake Automation more powerful and generalizable. These models were deployed in the UCSF AWS Cloud environment, tested with actual e-faxes that were received by UCSF in the past, and their performance was recorded and evaluated.

H2O.ai's Document AI

For the evaluation and solution, H2O.ai deployed the Document AI cloud service that is a part of the H2O AI Hybrid Cloud product suite. Document AI product features are designed to address the opportunities and challenges associated with understanding, process, and managing the large amounts of unstructured text data in the enterprise. The information and knowledge contained in unstructured text and documents have historically been difficult to extract and reuse. As a result, there is a vast reservoir of untapped insights in electronic documents, document images (faxes), emails, forms, invoices, etc.

As described earlier, using Optical Character Recognition (OCR) that is rules-driven, template-based, and based on a database of known fonts is limiting. The variety of document templates, version changes, and the need to process new and unseen documents require Intelligent Character Recognition (ICR). Compared to OCR, ICR leverages learning algorithms for generalizable character and word recognition, document layout understanding, and Natural Language Processing (NLP).

With the advances in AI algorithms, it is now possible to use text, linguistic choices, data entry preferences, and document structure to understand documents and process them with efficiencies and flexibility that were not possible with traditional OCR. We can now classify documents, classify pages/sections within a document, extract entities, group entities together, and refine the extracted information through appropriate post-processing. As a result, we are now able to achieve higher accuracy, ICR performance, and easier integration with downstream human and system uses. The types of documents that benefit from AI-enabled ICR and NLP can be diverse and address enterprise needs around

- Documents with regular text "left to right/top to bottom" (CSVs, emails, editable forms)
- Documents with embedded text which have text and layout metadata (PDF docs, Word docs, HTML pages)

■ Image scans (faxes in PDF or other formats, pictures with text, and non-editable forms)

What are the advantages of using Document AI ICR and NLP compared to traditional approaches?

■ Frees up employees to do higher value work activities
■ Provides relief to users/analysts/managers by increasing efficiencies and reducing process redundancies
■ Enables solutions and ecosystems that emphasize continuous learning to optimize document understanding, scalable processing, and timely management
■ Allows the enterprise to go beyond OCR-based template methods and RPA-based memorization efforts which are not scalable as variety and volumes change
■ Organizations can focus on quicker time to value for primary users and secondary consumers by focusing on developing applications and quicker integrations using highly accurate extracted information and knowledge (as opposed to updating rules, re-automating template management, and moving documents)

Product Features

The Document AI component service in the H2O AI Hybrid Cloud addresses the end-to-end needs of the enterprise with the following product features:

■ Labeling and annotation
  – Connectors to third-party labeling tools
■ Pre-processing pipeline of documents and document images
  – PDF to image conversion
  – Custom token recognizer
  – Text transformation
  – Image recognition (for example, recognizing logos)
■ H2O.ai's Argus ICR and NLP frameworks, algorithms, and libraries
■ Interoperability between input and output formats
■ AI-ML engine that uses multiple algorithms for diverse AI tasks
  – Entity recognition
  – Grouping (set identification)
  – Form understanding
  – Document and page classification
■ Language understanding and layout recognition using learning based on deep learning, Transformer architectures, and machine learning
■ Post-processing
  – Organizing prediction sets
  – Customized post processing
  – Datatype standardization
■ Integrations
  – APIs
  – JSON
  – Use case-specific microservices

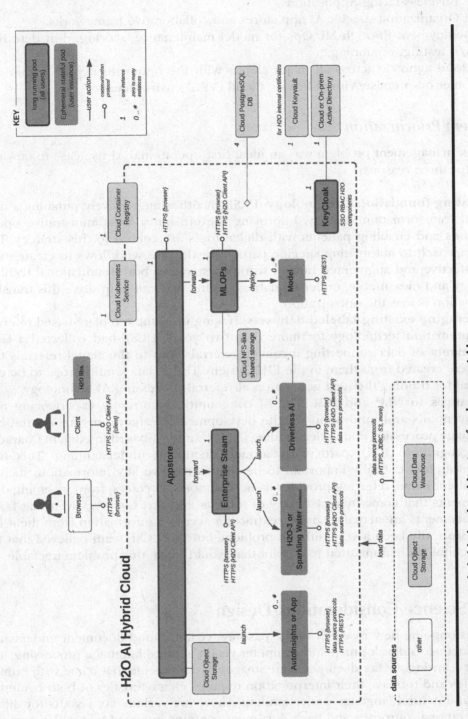

Figure CS7.2   H2O AI hybrid cloud architecture for document AI.

- ■ AI Applications
  - – Business-facing Applications
  - – Organization-specific AI app stores and collaborative frameworks
- ■ Deployment through ML Ops for model maintenance, scoring, drift detection, A/B testing, versioning,
- ■ Cloud agnostic across all major clouds with the option to deploy within customer on-premise/Virtual Private Cloud (VPC) environments

Problem Prioritization

The fax management problem was an ideal first operational AI use case to tackle at UCSF for three reasons:

Creating foundational technology: UCSF Health is aggressively pursuing a digital transformation strategy. Improving the efficiency of administrative operations and enabling patients with digital tools are central to this strategy. This approach to automating specific parts of healthcare workflows to create more effective and augmented human workflows creates both foundational technology and measurable, understandable benefits that can help drive this transformation across the organization.

Leveraging existing labeled data sets: Having used the template-based referrals automation technology for more than two years, UCSF had collected a large amount of data connecting incoming referral faxes to the actual referrals that were created from them in the EHR system. These data would prove to be crucial for training the next generation of referral-processing AI technology.

Advances in NLP and ICR: The AI community is currently experiencing new inventions and innovations in the development of algorithms for natural language processing and understanding (NLP/U) and AI-based Intelligent Character Recognition (ICR), particularly around document understanding. This new research is critically important to be able to retrieve key information, such as patient name, referring provider name, diagnosis, et cetera, from incoming documents that come in a vast array of formats and text quality. Given that faxed documents are actually images, extracting accurate information from them has historically been a very difficult problem, but the UCSF team believed that the technology had matured to a point that would make this problem tractable.

Data Science Considerations/Design

There is ongoing new research in the past few years around document understanding tasks due to developments in computer vision, natural language processing, and transfer learning. As fax documents are images of documents that come with numerous styles and formats, their interpretation requires characteristics of both computer vision and natural language understanding. There are various fax layouts for different operational purposes and each document contains nuanced text which requires sophisticated processing and understanding.

When we think about processing fax documents at UCSF, there are two general objectives:

- Recognizing what is the document
- What to do with the document

These two objectives can be then mapped to two machine learning tasks:

- Page classification that can define the next operation
- Information extraction

Nine of the most common Page Types across multiple UCSF departments and *116* Referral Fields were selected as the target outputs for the algorithms in the POC and the production-grade solution. The performance of the algorithms on each of these machine learning tasks was evaluated separately. Both problems involved understanding both the context and layout of the page content. The best solution used two instances of the same algorithm, one with nine Page Types as the goal, the other with the *116* Referral Fields as the goal.

One choice in problem formulation for extracting the details within the referrals is whether to frame it as form understanding or entity extraction. The goal of a form understanding task is to identify every set of keys and values throughout the entirety of a form. The entity extraction task is framed as a standard classification task where the algorithm will learn features specific to each desired value. For example, if a phone number were detected in the referral form, then a classifier that could take the context of the phone number into account was used to predict the type of phone number that had been found—for example, was it the patient's mobile number, the patient's home number, the referring provider's phone number, or something else?)

Entity extraction aims directly at the problem we need solved, whereas form understanding would still leave us needing to group keys from common synonyms since there is not a universal standard for referral form language. Thus, we experimented with entity extraction from the start and achieved high accuracies to confirm that choice.

Modern NLP algorithms utilize the neighboring words to perform their tasks. A classic example is using context to determine whether "bank" applies to a financial institution or a river. Form documents convey additional meaning through the layout, so we have chosen an algorithm that also considers the location of the text when it is trained. Within a referral form, a simple example is whether a date is the patient's date of birth or date of service. The neighboring context is required to differentiate between these two types. The value alone is a date in both cases, so it is not sufficient to determine one from the other. To differentiate between the two an algorithm must understand additional context, and we chose an algorithm that uses the context in all directions. Through transfer learning, we have used an algorithm pre-trained on *11 million* scanned business document pages as a starting point and fine-tuned it with our data and targets to perform our specific referral tasks.

A key to achieving high accuracy from all AI tasks is the consistency of the target fields. We focused on ensuring the targets were consistent across templates because we discovered variability in the granularity of certain keys within some templates. So we consolidated keys that already existed but were not consistently used. This step significantly increased accuracy scores throughout the range of referral keys. The model did not attempt to learn templates from each other to distinguish otherwise identical information labeled with different keys. This is a common experience in unstructured and semi-structured content, and highlights the importance of analysis within the AI workflow, and not just model execution.

The entity extraction algorithm requires the text and location on the page. Optical character recognition (OCR), which is the process of converting an image of printed words into an actual electronic document, has continually improved through the use of deep learning algorithms for computer vision and natural language processing. With our referral faxes, OCR results varied with the input fax quality, but the OCR accuracy exceeded our expectations. Another key to ensuring success with AI workflows is to ensure that the data used to train the algorithm is consistent with the data it is expected to process in production. Fortunately, the large volume of data stored from Referrals Automation provided excellent coverage of a variety of forms, fields, and fax qualities.

Putting these together, our full AI workflow converts the fax from a PDF document to an image for each page. The image is sent to the OCR algorithm, which produces the text tokens and their locations on the page. These data are sent into the page classification algorithm and if parts of the document are predicted to be a referral, then the same input data are sent to the information extraction algorithm as well. The Referral Field extraction algorithm output includes the text, pixel locations for display in the UI, predicted class/key (What type of phone number is it?), and the algorithm's confidence in that class assignment.

Key results from This Successful AI Program

Page classification: Ability to classify a fax page into referral form/insurance/authorization/Lab results/Imaging, etc.

- 85% accuracy on a balanced distribution of classes
- 91% accuracy on a production distribution of classes
- 0.869 F_1 score[11] for identifying referral pages, which is of high importance to us, since it automatically feeds these documents into the Intake Automation system
- Two-page classes are very similar, and we observed that when the model struggled to separate these, it chose the more prevalent class. Further work will focus on increasing the recall of the less prevalent class.

Referral Field extraction: Ability to extract patient demographics and referral information as key-value pairs such as address, phone number, email, and diagnosis

- Token classification: which of the 116 keys each word belonged to
  – 0.821 F_1 score, weighted average across all values
- For documents that the template-based OCR engine was able to extract information

Figure CS7.3   Screenshot of Intake Automation.

Note: All the information in it has been mocked up and does not pertain to real patients.

- – 33% more key-value pairs were extracted by the AI than the template-based technology
- – The information was also of higher quality since templates do not have intelligence to adjust for exceptions
- For documents that the template-based OCR engine was unable to extract any information
- – The AI was able to extract 80% of the critical key-value pairs.
- – This is an exciting result because it demonstrates that the AI approach is able to generalize beyond the training examples it was provided.

Last Mile: How Do You Enable Workflows with AI?

As the exciting AI-driven results described above began to emerge, we asked ourselves the following questions: "We've built the AI models to classify the faxes and extract the patient information. Now, how do we enable the workflows with these models? The answer is to build a document processing pipeline to put all the necessary steps together, including a user interface that allows referral intake coordinators to review, validate and correct the output from the AI algorithms. The following describes the current setup for the new AI-driven Intake Automation application.

Incoming faxes are converted to PDF documents using a digitization service (RightFax) and stored in a fax file server. Intake Automation's backend service picks up the file from the fax file server, stores it in the application database, and calls the H2O.ai product API with a request to classify the pages, the fax document, and extract all relevant information. The response from the AI service is stored in the application database.

Intake Automation was built using Substitutable Medical Applications and Reusable Technologies (SMART) and Fast Healthcare Interoperability Resource (FHIR) platforms to allow for adaptability into other healthcare organizations and software applications.

A user can access the application by launching it from within the EHR. When the user clicks on a launch icon in the EHR, Intake Automation uses SMART-on-FHIR for authenticating the user and passing user context information from the EHR to the application.

When the application is launched, the user is presented with a list of files along with the meta data that has been extracted by the AI service. This is how the extracted information is used to automate the workflows:

AI Service Output	Workflow Automation
Document classification, e.g., Referral, Rx refill, DME request	Initiate appropriate workflow by fax type Sort and assign faxes to different team members. Prioritize processing by fax type. Upload file into the patient record in the EHR by file type
Page classification	Segment large referrals into their components (e.g., Referral form, Insurance, Labs, Progress notes) so the provider can easily get to the rele.vant patient history
Extracted key-value pairs	Referral Priority: Order of processing the files Referral specialty: Route referrals to the right team Patient demographics and referral information: Review and updated the patient record in EHR

Even the best technologies can only realize their potential when they are delivered to users with a great user experience, and integrated into existing workflows. This is particularly true in healthcare where the staff members are extremely busy and all the workflows are centered around the EHR. The design team at UCSF CDHI takes an agile approach to design. Every design improvement is tested with actual users. Product team gathers data from application logs and verifies if new enhancements are working as designed. Product and design teams collaborate to improve the design based on the user feedback and application log data collected.

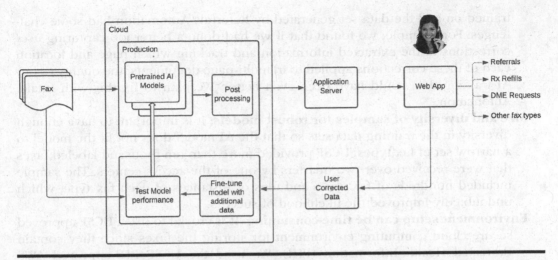

Figure CS7.4 Data flow diagram for Intake Automation representing how user feedback on information extracted by AI is used to re-train the AI models.

Feedback Loop: Retraining Models with User Input

The power of an AI-driven approach is that algorithms can continue to improve as they are used. The key to this is to measure output performance and fine-tune the models regularly by incorporating user input as new training data in a feedback loop. Intake Automation presents the information extracted by the AI models to the user and captures all the user updates to the information. The user may:

- Accept the file types and extracted values
- Modify file types and extracted values
- Identify key-value pairs not extracted by the model

New incoming faxes and the corrections made by users of the software become the new training data set for the next round of re-training. After an AI model is re-trained with this data set, it is important to back-test the model to ensure that performance has improved.

What Did We Learn?

This has been an incredible journey from launching an application with simple template-based information extraction to working on this iteration to integrate generic AI-based extraction. Here are some learnings along our journey.

The need for high-quality labeled data sets: The information captured by Referrals Automation and the corresponding faxes became the labeled data set to train the AI models. However, AI cannot perform better than the data it is trained on and the data set generated by Referrals Automation had some challenges. For example, we found that if we had done a better job capturing user corrections to the extracted information and tracking which page and location each of these corrections applied to in multi-page documents, the quality of our AI training data could have been even better. We plan to fix this with Intake Automation.

Size and diversity of samples for robust models: It is important to have enough diversity in the training data sets so that the AI model does not fit the model to a narrow set of fax types. UCSF provided more than ten thousand labeled faxes that were received over two quarters by one of the access centers. The sample included hundreds of fax types and tens of instances of each fax type, which undoubtedly improved the likelihood of success.

Environment setup can be time-consuming: It is crucial to use a UCSF-approved secure cloud computing environment for storing the faxes since they contain Protected Health Information (PHI). We used the UCSF PHI-approved AWS cloud for this work. UCSF IT performed a security review of the H2O.ai software stack that was installed in the UCSF infrastructure.

While the setup process worked fairly well, it took multiple weeks of effort that impacted the project cost and limited the number of solutions that could be evaluated simultaneously. Recognizing this need for a secure environment for evaluating AI models using PHI, UCSF has been working on a platform called "BeeKeeperAI" that allows secure computation on the PHI data within the health system's own cloud environment, while ensuring that any algorithm IP is not visible to any party, including UCSF.

Precise problem definition leads to better outcomes: Since UCSF CDHI worked on Referrals Automation, we clearly understood the user problems to be solved, the technical problems to be solved and the accuracy levels to be achieved to make AI models viable. Clearly defining the page types to be recognized, fax types to be recognized, the key-value pairs to be extracted, and having the labeled data sets ready for the AI team streamlined the POC process and the teams were able to build and validate the models in less than four weeks.

What Do We Go Next?

Now comes the exciting part—of deploying the models, learning, and improving them.

UCSF CDHI and H2O.ai are defining the APIs for Intake Automation to interface with the new AI services created. We are planning to use FHIR object models to represent the extracted information.

We are also designing the data models and toolchains to capture user feedback loops as described above, to re-train the AI models, and to test the resulting updated models. The teams are planning to support two AI model re-training workflows: 1. Re-training based on original extracted information and user corrections to the information 2. Re-training based on new annotations of high-value use cases which will include bounding boxes around key-value pairs in the fax images.

To streamline the workflow of re-training models, testing, and deployment, the team is developing a toolchain (Dev Ops) so the models can be easily upgraded on a regular basis.

About 30% of the referral forms received by UCSF have handwritten information. As OCR matures, the advent of Intelligent Character Recognition (ICR) has emerged. This is most commonly associated with the ability to read handwriting, and looked at as alternative choices: OCR if one expects most documents to contain printed text and ICR if one expects most documents to contain handwritten text. H2O is integrating OCR and ICR into its Document AI product to handle more difficult documents, including the handwriting content in UCSF referral forms.

There are several opportunities to further improve the access center workflows using AI. For example, today patients receive a text message with a link to a web page to self-schedule their appointments. However, that mechanism may not be appropriate for patients who are older, who have to be scheduled for complex surgeries, or for patients who have not responded to such requests in the past. It may be better to just call and schedule these patients. AI can be applied to improve such decisions to improve staff productivity and improve the patient experience.

The EHR also contains millions of historical fax documents which contain critical patient history. Using AI, this information can be extracted, organized, and presented to providers at the point of care. For using information extraction to improve care, the sky's the limit because (for better or for worse) faxes still dominate in health systems and they are not going away anytime soon.

It is also time to start thinking of other opportunities to support complex decision-making and enable AI-powered chatbots and other technologies to improve care delivery.

Conclusions

UCSF

When we started this journey, we were hopeful that information extraction from semi-structured documents was possible, but we weren't sure. Some in the industry told us it couldn't be done. Now that the UCSF-H2O.ai collaboration team has delivered, it opens up many possibilities.

Inspired by the success of this program, UCSF is moving rapidly toward optimizing additional workflows with AI. New use cases surface weekly as other groups in the UCSF Health organization begin to recognize the characteristics of a problem that AI can solve. Many of these use cases are already backed up by years of manual work captured in the EHR and other information systems, making them imminently ready for algorithm training. For others, this work has helped identify where more, or better, data needs to be captured to enable future AI automation efforts. As this more mature and nuanced understanding of what data to store, how to store it, and how it might be used in future AI algorithm training spreads across UCSF, it will continue to move UCSF into the highest echelons of digital-first healthcare organizations.

This collaboration between UCSF and H2O.ai to create cutting-edge information extraction and workflow automation technology for faxed documents has energized both teams and we expect it to be the template for the future of healthcare AI at UCSF and beyond.

H2O.ai

For H2O.ai, this experience demonstrates the applicability of the Document AI product in a new domain. Built from experience with financial documents, this program with UCSF has been equally successful in the medical domain, and with an aggressively comprehensive scope of the referral document. The power of the product enables us to continue pursuing additional document types, solving as wide or narrow a scope as needed for each individual business problem. H2O.ai has seen the large potential in untapped semi-structured documents, and that state-of-the-art AI can solve business problems where the technical barriers were previously thought to be too high and failure as the assumed outcome.

The H2O.ai team sees the Document AI product as bringing value to financial services, healthcare, insurance, life sciences, e-commerce, retail, manufacturing, transportation, government services, and every other vertical. The product solves the challenges that bedevil the processing and management of large numbers of unstructured data and documents and uses AI to solve difficult problems: diverse formats, data entry styles, linguistic choices, amount of text detail, and varying templates.

H2O.ai's Document AI provides scalable and repeatable solutions for receipts, bills, invoices, medical referrals, insurance claims forms, contracts, bank statements, banking confirmations, emails, grant applications, RFPs/RFIs, and policies—among others.

About UCSF Health

UCSF Health is recognized worldwide for its innovative patient care, reflecting the latest medical knowledge, advanced technologies, and pioneering research. It includes the flagship UCSF Medical Center, which is ranked among the top 10 hospitals nationwide, as well as UCSF Benioff Children's Hospitals (Oakland and San Francisco), Langley Porter Psychiatric Hospital and Clinics, UCSF Benioff Children's Physicians, and the UCSF Faculty Practice. These hospitals serve as the academic medical center of the University of California, San Francisco, which is world-renowned for its graduate-level health sciences education and biomedical research. UCSF Health has affiliations with hospitals and health organizations throughout the Bay Area.

About UCSF CDHI

Founded in 2012, the Center for Digital Health Innovation (CDHI) at UCSF enables, creates, and accelerates digital technology necessary to transform care delivery bringing the right treatment to the right patient at the right time. CDHI collaborates with industry and UCSF scientific innovators to envision and realize new solutions to improve the lives of patients and providers. We bridge emerging technologies and the healthcare ecosystem to enable real change and drive health innovation by bringing bold ideas to life.

About H2O.ai

H2O.ai is the leading AI cloud company, on a mission to democratize AI for everyone. H2O.ai is the trusted AI partner to more than 20,000 global organizations, including AT&T, Aegon/ Transamerica, Allergan, Bon Secours Mercy Health, Capital One, Commonwealth Bank of Australia, GlaxoSmithKline, Hitachi, Kaiser Permanente, PayPal, PWC, and Walgreens in addition to over half of the Fortune 500 companies and hundreds of thousands of data scientists. Goldman Sachs, NVIDIA, and Wells Fargo are not only customers and partners but strategic investors in the company.

H2O.ai's customers have honored the company with a Net Promoter Score (NPS) of 78— the highest in the industry due to our customer focus, state-of-the-art technology, and deep employee expertise. Many of the world's top Kaggle Grandmasters (the community of best-in-the-world machine learning practitioners and data scientists) are employees of H2O.ai.

In addition to our expertise and products, we are passionate about our mission. A strong *AI for Good* ethos to make the world a better place and Responsible AI drive the company's purpose.

About the H2O AI Hybrid Cloud

The H2O AI Hybrid Cloud is a state-of-the-art artificial intelligence (AI) cloud platform that enables organizations to easily use AI to rapidly make, operate and innovate in order to solve complex business problems and accelerate the discovery of new ideas. The H2O AI Hybrid Cloud contains capabilities and automation across the data science lifecycle, including feature engineering, a variety of AI disciplines (automated machine learning, time series forecasting, natural language processing, and computer vision), machine learning interpretability, machine learning operations, and the ability to provision and manage end-user AI applications. The platform is deployed on the open-source Kubernetes container management platform, so customers can run on any cloud, multi-cloud, or on-premises infrastructure. AT&T, Bon Secours Mercy Health, Aegon/ Transamerica, and UCSF are among the organizations that rely on the H2O AI Hybrid Cloud to accelerate their strategic transformation and achieve business outcomes.

Notes

1 Yi Gang, President of People's Bank of China, The 10th Lujiazui Forum
2 iResearch
3 Tencent Research

4 https://www.gehealthcare.com/article/ethics-in-healthcare-arent-new-but-their-application-has-never-been-more-important

5 World Health Organization Report -Communicating Radiation Risks in Pediatric Imaging

6 https://www.paho.org/hq/index.php?option=com_content&view=article&id=7410:2012-dia-radiografia-dos-tercios-poblacion-mundial-no-tiene-acceso-diagnostico-imagen&Itemid=1926&lang=en#:~:text=It%20is%20estimated%20that%20some,every%20year%20in%20the%20world.

7 https://www.hcinnovationgroup.com/analytics-ai/news/13027792/ucsf-partners-with-ge-on-algorithm-development-for-clinical-support

8 https://www.canhealth.com/2020/03/30/ai-improves-diagnostic-imaging-at-canadian-hospitals/

9 https://en.wikipedia.org/wiki/ReCAPTCHA

10 https://www.cnbc.com/2019/09/12/ges-health-unit-wins-first-fda-clearance-for-ai-powered-x-ray-system.html

11 *F_1 score—the F-score is a measure of classification accuracy that combines recall (sensitivity) and precision (positive predictive value); F_1 balances both measures via the harmonic mean of recall and precision.*

Index

Page numbers in **bold** indicate tables and page numbers in *italics* indicate figures.

Printed in the United States
by Baker & Taylor Publisher Services

Printed in the United States
by Baker & Taylor Publisher Services